# NIGHT FIGHTERS

## A DEVELOPMENT AND COMBAT HISTORY

BILL GUNSTON, OBE, FRAeS

Foreword by John Cunningham

SUTTON PUBLISHING

First published in 1976 by Patrick Stephens Ltd.

This revised edition published in 2003 by
Sutton Publishing Limited · Phoenix Mill
Thrupp · Stroud · Gloucestershire · GL5 2BU

British Library Cataloguing in Publication Data
A catalogue record for this book is available from the British Library.

ISBN 0-7509-3410-7

Typeset in 10/13 pt Sabon.
Typesetting and origination by
Sutton Publishing Limited.
Printed and bound in England by
J.H. Haynes & Co. Ltd, Sparkford.

# CONTENTS

# FOREWORD

## GROUP CAPTAIN JOHN CUNNINGHAM CBE, DSO**, DFC*, DL, FRAeS

Bill Gunston, who has a well deserved reputation as an aviation historian, has an exciting story to tell of the development of night fighting from its earliest gropings in the dark to the highly sophisticated electronic art that it now is. His account of First World War pilots searching the night sky for Zeppelins in stick and string aeroplanes of frightening lack of performance, and totally unequipped for venturing aloft in the darkness, fills one with admiration for those bold spirits, while the contrast he draws with the modern Mach 3 all-weather fighter with its armoury of guided weapons and automated systems of unimaginable sophistication makes one realise how far the 'trade' has developed in sixty intervening years.

There could be few better guides to this painstaking evolution than Bill Gunston, who combines the personal experience of a pilot of wartime night fighters with the detailed background knowledge of a one-time technical editor of *Flight* magazine.

I commend this well documented and outstanding piece of research which, for me and others who may have been involved in the business, recaptures the spirit of the times and reawakens vivid memories of exciting days.

*John Cunningham wrote the above for the original, 1976 edition of this book. Sadly, he died in 2002.*

** And two Bars. * And Bar.

# AUTHOR'S INTRODUCTION

to the First Edition

I am grateful to the publisher for asking me to write this book. My immediate reaction was the neutral one that, if a publisher believes he can see a successful book, who am I to argue? But as I got down to the task I increasingly recognized what a splendid story they had chosen for me to tell.

All flying is uplifting and exciting, even when you have book-ends for your log-books. Flying to fight other fliers is more exciting still. But flying to fight by night reaches pinnacles of human experience that are touched but rarely.

Do not be deceived into thinking that I am one to glorify war, or revel in armaments; I doubt if any one alive would do this. There are many who are even antipathetic towards technology, but they would probably accept that, out of aerial night fighting, man has hastened his ascendancy over cloud and darkness.

The whole subject is shot through with contrasting threads. Night fighting was not all excitement. Much of it was little more than danger, discomfort and frustration. From 1915 until about 1942 night fighters killed far more of their own pilots than they did of the enemy. And the fact that the ratio thereafter gradually changed had little to do with increasing skill or courage but a great deal to do with a new species of airborne equipment called AI radar.

I have added a glossary, because most readers will consider one is necessary. One of the problems in writing a book of this kind is that – unlike a book about the Crimea or Jutland – it is impossible to tell the story without delving into a lot of fairly modern technology. It is simply not possible to produce a book about a technical subject that will be all things to all readers. I would be less than human if I did not occasionally try to take the reader aloft, sometimes in aircraft I flew myself, and sometimes by borrowing the words of others who flew and fought by night. The publisher would certainly take it amiss if I omitted to discuss sub-types of night fighters, their colour schemes and even the occasional serial number. But to produce a history of any value one has to explain what the problems were and how they were solved.

This was simple when the technology did not go beyond a Lewis gun, a searchlight and a flare made of petrol-soaked asbestos. But how many readers are conversant with multiple-time-around echoes, or even such basic things as the difference between clutter and glint? I heartily concur with the publisher's belief that the bulk of the book should deal with the two World Wars. The story here still needed a lot of tying together, whereas the development of combat aircraft during the past fifty years is very fully documented and can be consulted in a thousand places. That does not mean I have not covered the modern scene, but I have skimmed much faster over the surface of a subject that has become awesome in scope and complexity.

Indeed, perhaps the very notion of a 'night fighter' is no longer a valid one. Until the 1950s it had a very clear meaning, but today all fighters are quite big, all are exceedingly costly, and all are designed to do their job equally well by day or night. Even in those fortunate countries where the weather is always clear, I doubt if any defence staff would be rash enough to buy a fighter which was not also a night and all-weather fighter. Indeed, today the pressures of inflation have speeded the increasing versatility of combat aircraft, so that a 'platform' that is a night fighter by night may take off next morning as a long-range reconnaissance aircraft with multiple sensors, and then fly again in the afternoon as a bomber with a load as heavy as that of three B-17 Fortresses. So the main part of this book is concerned with aircraft that were night fighters and night intruders and did nothing else.

To give an idea of shapes, sizes and the operational equipment fitted, line drawings of 32 night fighters have been included in the text. I am grateful to my former colleague Arthur Bowbeer for preparing most of these drawings. My thanks are also due to the following: British Aircraft Corporation Ltd; Air Commodore Roderick Chisholm CBE, DSO, DFC (and Messrs Chatto & Windus, publishers of *Cover of Darkness*); Group Captain John Cunningham DSO**, DFC*; Ferranti Ltd (in particular Tim Notley, former night-fighter pilot); Hawker Siddeley Aviation (Hatfield); Edward H. Heinemann, of Rancho Santa Fe (who designed more successful night fighters than anyone else); Squadron Leader Jeremy Howard-Williams DFC (author of *Night Intruder*); Hughes Aircraft (Culver City and Tucson); Imperial War Museum (J.S. Lucas, Deputy Head of Department of Photographs); Luftwaffenamt, Porz-Wahn, Federal Republic of Germany; McDonnell Douglas Corporation (Harry Gann, Douglas Aircraft, and Herman Barkey, former MCAIR chief engineer of the Phantom); Marconi (Mrs Hance, company historian) and engineers of today's GEC Marconi Electronics Ltd; MIT Research Laboratory for Electronics (John H. Hewitt, librarian); Ministry of Defence RAF (Group Captain E.B. Haslam, Air Historical Branch); Alfred Price, who has now left the RAF and devotes himself to the books for which he is famous; Royal Radar Establishment, Malvern; AEG-Telefunken; US Air Force (Lieutenant-Colonel King, Pictorial/Broadcast Branch); and Westinghouse Electronic Corporation.

Throughout, I have used the British word 'aerial' instead of the US 'antenna'. The fact that the opinions expressed are my own is self-evident. I would welcome critical comment, especially if it throws new light on a dark subject.

## Introduction to the New Edition

In the 27 years since the original edition the trend outlined above has proceeded to the point where the very term 'night fighter' has become meaningless: all today's fighters have to be night-capable. Indeed, some of today's battlefield helicopters merited a careful look before I decided not to include any. Another fairly obvious point is that, whereas in 1976 we knew little about many aircraft of the Soviet Union apart from an invented NATO reporting name, today we know all about them, and may even be pressed to buy one, to help out with the bank balance.

Another change is that this time my thanks are due to Sutton Publishing, who have taken over the PSL aviation list. Thanks are again due to Philip Jarrett, whose unrivalled photographic library has produced most of the many new images required for this considerably upgraded new edition. Another source, completely unrivalled for aircraft of the USSR and its successor republics, is Nigel Eastaway's Russian Aviation Research Trust, to whom further thanks are due.

Haslemere, 2003

Bill Gunston OBE, FRAeS

# Riddles of the Night Sky

The history of aerial night fighting contains a curious number of unsolved puzzles. Referred to in greater detail in the text, they are summarized below.

1    During the First World War the RFC and RNAS (from April 1918 the RAF) were forced by the enemy's attacks to try to construct a scheme for defending south-east England against night bombing by airships and aeroplanes. By 1918 this had become quite effective, but it was then allowed to fall into disuse, and by the 1930s Britain had no operative night defence system and no plans to build one.

2    RAF bomber squadrons enjoyed an unbroken history from the First World War to the Second World War. Many were explicitly night bomber units, yet, once the First World War was over, little attempt was made even to discover the problems of navigating and finding targets by night, far less solve them.

3    Despite the fact that the Air Ministry, Air Council and RAF bore the collective responsibility for the defence of Britain against enemy air attack, no attempt was made in the inter-war period to discover how this should best be done. When in 1934 a civil servant decided to focus attention on the problem he did so purely by chance (because he had decided to see how many files there were on how to stop enemy bombers, and was horrified to find so few).

4    When, as the result of this chance attention being paid to the problem, an expert on radio was called in, the latter proposed in great detail the system we now know as radar. But this again was purely by chance; nobody had asked him for such a suggestion, and his advice had been sought purely to pronounce on the feasibility of a 'death ray'. He had no reason to do more than state his opinion that such a ray was not at that time practical, and leave it at that.

5    By 1936 the concept of a radar carried by a fighter, to allow it to find its prey at night or in bad weather, was fully understood by the British Air Staff. In 1937 the first such equipment began flight trials, in a converted bomber. Yet in the remaining years of peace no attempt was made to plan for a radar-equipped night fighter of any kind. Throughout the Second World War Britain's night fighters equipped with radar comprised an inadequate converted light bomber, a large and capable fighter developed purely by chance (because top designers at Bristol thought it would be useful), an even better aircraft converted from a fast unarmed bomber developed in the teeth of official lack of interest (indeed outright opposition) and a converted American attack bomber. The first aircraft for the RAF planned as a night fighter did not enter service until 1956.

6    Radar enabled British fighters to defeat the *Luftwaffe* (German air force) in the daylight Battle of Britain. This was known to the Germans, and on two occasions bombers attacked the CH station at Ventnor, Isle of Wight. But the *Luftwaffe* never attempted in any concerted way to knock out the whole CH system, which would have been entirely within its capability, nor to approach the British Isles at low level, where the system was useless and the defending fighters would get no advance warning. On many occasions strong *Luftwaffe* forces approached at above 15,000 feet, where they were visible on radar over their own airfields in Europe, and then dived to bomb and strafe at low level.

7    In November 1939 British Intelligence was given a large hand-written report (by a 'well-wishing German scientist') which described in some detail a wealth of unknown German defence systems. So impressive was the list that it was *dismissed as a hoax*. Many of the systems described were of an electronic nature, emitting signals that could be detected by any suitable receiver. The British could have tested the validity of the report by detecting the German radars and blind-bombing beams with receivers over Britain or in the hundreds of Bomber Command aircraft sent on leaflet raids over Germany. No attempt was made to do this, even though this would have yielded vital information in the first weeks of the war. As it was, the existence of such enemy achievements was not acknowledged until more than a year later, when they had done great damage to both British cities and British bombers.

8    The first mass-produced German radar for point defence on land was *Würzburg*, designed for gunlaying. Pressed into service as a night-fighter control radar, its information output remained totally unsuitable. The ideal kind of presentation, the pictorial PPI (plan-position indicator) had been invented in Germany, but rejected by Goering as unnecessary. When a completely new *Gigant Würzburg* was developed, the output was kept in the same useless form of bearings and ranges, which had to be converted by cumbersome plotting devices into a form of crude synthetic PPI.

9    British scientists developed several electronic navigation aids specifically for bombers during the Second World War. One, Oboe, proved unacceptable to non-technical but powerful members of the government and air staff, because it claimed to allow people in Britain to know the position of an RAF bomber far over Germany more accurately than its own crew; many high-level calls were made for 'this preposterous scheme' to be stopped. Yet Oboe was the bedrock on which the entire attack method of the RAF against difficult Ruhr targets and elsewhere in Germany rested. It was the sole primary means for accurate target marking by the Pathfinder Force.

10    In contrast, another aid, H$_2$S, immediately gained the massive support of the technically unqualified VIPs, who urged its large-scale introduction no matter how this disrupted Bomber Command. It helped the navigator by giving him a crude picture of the terrain beneath, though its accuracy was poor and it could be hoodwinked by the enemy. Worse, its emissions gave away the presence and exact position of the bomber using it. Yet the RAF crews were never told how lethal this device was, and in consequence it was switched on throughout the mission. German night-fighter crews and ground controllers could watch the H$_2$S emissions from bombers that were still over Yorkshire. And the development of accurate route marking and target marking removed any need for it.

11    The greatest weakness of the German night fighters was their need to rely on AI (airborne interception) radar, emitting powerful signals betraying the fighter's presence and position. RAF

bombers needed a passive detector to give warning of such signals, without giving away the bomber's own position. Yet the bombers were actually fitted with Monica, an active radar that itself emitted signals. At one stroke this rendered the device both useless and dangerous. Useless because nearly all its 'warnings' were caused by the presence of other bombers in the dense stream proceeding to the target. Dangerous because the German night fighters were soon equipped with their own passive detector, *Flensburg*, which could home on to a working Monica set from up to 130 miles away. This supposed guardian of the bombers was probably responsible for more bomber losses than any other single device, Allied or enemy, until in August 1944 (nearly two years later) crews were told not to use it.

**12**    The obvious way for a night fighter to attack a bomber in the Second World War was from below and slightly behind, giving the best view of the biggest target. RAF bombers were designed with three gun turrets giving perfect coverage of the whole area around the bomber except below. This vital area was not only completely undefended but also totally blind to every member of the crew. Even after it was obvious that *Luftwaffe* night fighters were closing with their quarry from below, no attempt was made to give any of the crew a downward view.

**13**    The *Luftwaffe* night fighters were large and powerful aircraft, and they closed to within 100 or even within 50 feet before opening fire. Almost any detection system looking obliquely downards – visual, radar, infra-red or sound – could not have failed to give warning, but no attempt was made to do anything.

**14**    Nearly all the *Luftwaffe* night fighters were old designs that were overloaded with extra equipment, fuel and weapons. Their performance margin over the bombers was usually small, and if the RAF heavies had had their useless front and mid-upper gun turrets removed, and they had been instructed to cruise at maximum weak-mixture power when over enemy territory, losses would probably have been dramatically reduced. There was no attempt to do so (except for removal of the front turret from Halifaxes, the fastest of the British heavies).

**15**    Likewise, the *Luftwaffe* night fighters were cramped and overloaded, yet nearly all carried a rear gunner with a hand-aimed machine-gun. Such armament served no useful purpose, and was no deterrent to Mosquito night fighters, yet it added significantly to weight and drag.

**16**    From mid-1943 *Luftwaffe* night fighters used oblique upward-firing cannon. This extremely effective armament had been the subject of prolonged experiments by the RAF and other air forces since 1916, yet in 1943–4 its use by the *Luftwaffe* caused disbelief, shock, and morale-sapping tales of 'secret weapons' among the surviving crews of Bomber Command. Still nothing was done to give bomber crews downward vision or armament.

**17**    Despite its proved superiority, the upward-firing gun was ignored by the post-war Allied air forces. When the RAF at last got round to buying jet night fighters, it not only stuck to forward-firing guns but put them in the outer wings!

**18**    Night after night the RAF's heavies over Germany behaved as powerful flying radar beacons continuously advertising their exact position. With a total of 94 lb of *Naxos-Z* and *Flensburg* passive homing receivers, all the German single-seat fighters could unerringly have tracked down the RAF bombers at night, but only a few were ever fitted with *Naxos-Z* and none with *Flensburg*.

**19**    The RAF never had a proper single-seat night fighter until the Lightning entered service in 1960. But from 1940 it had used Hurricanes (with and without radar), the *Luftwaffe* had used Bf 109s and Fw 190s (without radar), and the US Navy, Marine Corps and Air Force, and the

Fleet Air Arm, had used 29 different types of radar-equipped single-seat fighter with complete success. No explanation of the British policy has ever been given.

**20**   From 1917 onwards it has been obvious that, given a choice, bombers would prefer to penetrate defended airspace by night rather than by day. Yet, until the advent of the Lightning, the RAF equipped most of its defensive squadrons with 'fighters' which were incapable of intercepting at night or in bad weather; the 'night and all-weather fighter' was regarded as a specialized type and bought only in much smaller numbers.

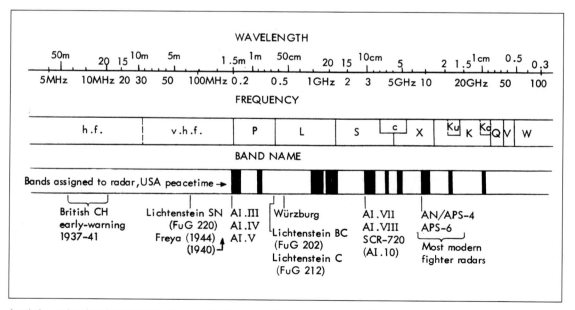

*A radar's wavelength is the reciprocal of the operating frequency. One megaherz is one million cycles per second; one gigaherz is 1,000 million. The portion of the electromagnetic spectrum used for radio and radar is subdivided into 'bands', each identified by a letter; thus, most modern AI radars operate in the X or K band. In the United States a new letter system is coming into use.*

# ONE

# STICK AND STRING

History has not recorded the name of the first pilot to fly at night. He was probably a Frenchman, and the year was almost certainly 1909. Several aeroplane flights had been made more or less in the dark by the time both competitors in the race from London to Manchester, Claude Grahame-White and the winner Louis Paulhan, kept going into the night of 27/28 April 1910. Grahame-White boldly made a take-off in the pitch blackness at 2.50 a.m., but this race took place along the main line of the London & North Western Railway, with its succession of red or green signals. The event was well publicized and had attracted thousands of lighted houses, lighted cars and even bonfires. It did not by any means signify that pilots could henceforth fly from one place to another in darkness.

Probably the most fundamental of all the things a pilot needs to know is which way is up. It is dangerous, and potentially lethal, to rely on 'seat of the pants' sensations. An aeroplane can move in any direction, and in doing so can impart every conceivable kind of push, pull or rotary motion to the strapped-in pilot. This is no problem in what is called VMC (visual meteorological conditions), because the pilot can see the ground. But the modern VMC pilot is forbidden to fly near clouds or at night. Put him in the centre of a large cloud, or in the sky on a cloudy, moonless night, and he may soon cease to know which way is up. He can fatally easily enter a gentle diving turn, which can become ever tighter and steeper, while feeling through his 'seat of the pants' as if he was maintaining straight and level flight. Of course, if he was in a modern aircraft and had been trained in instrument flying he would know better. But in the earliest days of flying there were no instruments. Everything had to be learned the hard way.

Several of the pioneer aviators did learn, and the fact that the way was often not hard masked the true peril of the learning. Even more lethal than a clear night to the early pilot was dense fog. Sensible aviators stayed on the ground in a thin mist, but young Geoffrey de Havilland once made a complete flight in quite thick fog – saying long afterwards, 'In those days we didn't realise how dangerous it was'. Several of the early aviators at Brooklands and Hendon often flew by night when the weather was fine, and the same was true at Issy, Pau and other fields in France. It was recognized, however, that the landing was made more difficult, because there was no airfield lighting, and little to give the approaching pilot accurate information on his position and height above the field. Some pioneers remarked on the fact that the clear horizon, visible all round on a fine night, tended to vanish as altitude was lost. Only very few killed themselves; far more died because of loss of control in broad daylight.

In parallel with the select band of sporting pilots there grew up a new species of pilot who served his country in military uniform. Some flew for fun at their own expense, but from the mid-nineteenth century there had been officially appointed military balloonists, and from 1908 military aeroplane pilots. In 1910 the first aeroplanes appeared with guns. A French Voisin biplane – the sort of flying machine immediately pictured by the expressive phrase 'stick and string' – was burdened by a monstrous 37 mm (1.46 in) cannon; fortunately nobody dared to fire it. In August 1910 a Springfield rifle was fired, many times, from an American Curtiss pusher; but when young Major Robert Brooke-Popham, of the Air Battalion, Royal Engineers, fitted a Lee-Enfield to his Blériot in 1911 he was promptly ordered to remove it. In 1912 Colonel Isaac N. Lewis fitted one of his promising new air-cooled, drum-fed machine-guns to a Wright biplane of the US Army; his demonstrations were received with such complete lack of interest that he packed up and went to Belgium, there to set up a gun factory at Liège that not only kept the Allies supplied with Lewis guns in the coming war but also established Belgium as a leader in the international arms business. In British service the Lewis was standard rifle calibre, of 0.303 in (7.7 mm).

British pilots were discouraged from showing any interest in either aerial armament or flying after dark. Indeed, night flying as such was expressly forbidden in the Standing Orders of the Royal Flying Corps when it was formed in April 1912. The whole purpose of the flying machine – if it had any purpose at all – was obviously that it could provide a useful elevated position for battlefield reconnaissance, as had already been proved with balloons and kites. The first RFC pilots spent their first year, mostly on Salisbury Plain, learning not only how to reconnoitre, and to 'spot' for artillery, but also how to communicate with ground forces. A few, including Brooke-Popham, flouted authority and practised firing rifles in the air, a task which for several seconds at a time meant that the pilot had no free hand to hold the control column. Others daringly persisted in flying at night. This was especially the case with the bold spirits of No. 3 Squadron, which Brooke-Popham now commanded.

In April 1913 Lieutenant Cholmondeley of 3 Squadron flew on a moonlit night from Larkhill to Upavon and back, making a good landing. He and other pilots later flew 'circuits and bumps' by the light from the open hangar doors, until in June 1913 Lieutenant Carmichael asked Brooke-Popham whether he might experiment with a row of petrol flares laid across the landing ground. Carmichael thereupon supervised the first airfield lighting, pioneering the flare-path that was to serve military flyers until after the Second World War. He also got his B.E.2 fitted with a battery-fed lamp that shone upon his cockpit instruments. Though rudimentary, and accomplished without any considered discussion or design process, these advances were real enough. With proper direction they could have resulted in the RFC becoming the nucleus of a trained fighting force, able to give battle by day or night, by the time the First World War began on 4 August 1914. Unfortunately the direction from above was totally negative. The very notion of aerial combat was regarded as a pipedream. No combat aircraft were ordered or even considered in Britain, and when war came the RFC was still a puny force equipped with a few entirely unsuitable aircraft. Its sole mission was day reconnaissance for the land armies, and until many tragic mistakes had been made no RFC pilot's report was even believed if it conflicted with what the Army had expected.

Hardly anybody in any of the warring nations gave much thought to war in the air, except for the growing airship services of the Imperial German Army and Navy. The Army airships

*Avro 504K E4356 was made at Eastbourne, and converted into a single-seat night fighter.*

were a mixture of Zeppelins, designated LZ, and wood-framed Schütte-Lanz ships, designated SL. Unfortunately for their crews the Army was obsessed with the belief that its airships would prove formidable tactical bombers over the land battlefields. The Navy, which concentrated entirely upon light-alloy-framed Zeppelins, designated L, thought in more strategic terms and intended to use its airships for ocean scouting and for bombing attacks on Britain. The British government did not have its head totally buried in the sand; it recognized that German airships might be sent to bomb Britain, and wondered what it could do about it. Only the Royal Naval Air Service had any immediate answer. On 8 October 1914 an RNAS Farman flew from Antwerp to Düsseldorf to bomb and destroy LZ 25 in its hangar (on 25 August 1914 this same ship had caused great alarm and 26 civilian casualties in Antwerp). On 21 November 1914 came an even more daring raid when three RNAS Avros flew 250 miles from Belfort to bomb the Zeppelin works at Friedrichshafen. Then the advancing German armies put the Zeppelin bases out of reach of Allied aircraft.

On the other hand, the German advance made it easier to raid Britain. Such raids seemed to begin very quickly. On 21 December 1914 a lone German seaplane droned over Dover soon after midday and dropped two bombs, which both fell in the sea. Three days later, on Christmas Eve, it came again and dropped a single bomb which fell on British soil, breaking windows near

Dover Castle. On Christmas Day another seaplane slowly made its way high over the Thames estuary. A Vickers FB. 5 Gunbus tried desperately to reach it, and despite suffering a spluttering engine and jammed Lewis gun, succeeded in making the intruder drop his two bombs at Cliffe, Kent, rather than London. Perhaps the Germans were foolish thus to alert Britain to its state of complete nakedness to aerial attack. With unbelievable slowness the sluggish and reactionary politicians and staff officers set about thinking of a wholly new subject: air defence.

To be fair, the problem had been at least thought about in British government circles since 1912, but nothing tangible was done until the end of 1914. Then the first rudimentary steps were taken to defend London against possible aerial attack by setting up a system of lookout posts, three small guns (not, of course, designed for use in the previously unheard-of anti-aircraft role) and twelve searchlights. The idea of a blackout, by extinguishing or screening the lights of London, was discussed but considered to be too drastic. There seemed to be a lack of people who combined authority, leadership and the ability to think clearly. The possibility of aerial attack by both airships and aeroplanes had been self-evident for years. The fact that such attack did not begin at the very outset of the First World War should, perhaps, have been regarded as a blessing, giving the nation time in which to set up defences. The weeks stretched into months, but still nothing was done. Then came the unexpected seaplane visitations at Christmas, and the talking acquired a note of urgency. And then, on the night of 19 January 1915, northern East Anglia echoed to a distant throbbing of engines.

It was a dirty winter's night, with snow squalls and rain. Those on the ground soon knew that above them were two Zeppelins, and there was absolutely nothing anyone could do to interfere with them. Inside the Zeppelins – L3 and L4 of the Imperial German Navy – it had been a long and tiring flight from their base at Fühlsbuttel. They had set out twelve hours earlier, in company with L6 from Nordholz. L6 had set course for London but been forced to turn back with engine trouble. In fact, all three ships, plus L5, had set out for England six days earlier, and all had been driven back by severe weather. On this occasion, however, L3 and L4 did succeed in reaching the British coast, and saw the occasional lights of towns and villages. Their target was Humberside, the great city of Kingston upon Hull; but neither airship could identify the ground beneath. Eventually each let go its bomb load on the best collection of lights it could see. Bomb aiming was still in its infancy, though the crews of naval Zeppelins had trained for several years and from 10,000 feet the best crews could usually get most bombs within about 650 feet (200 metres) of the aiming point. But on this occasion they could only see the ground at intervals and did not know for sure which country it was! L3's nine bombs went down on Yarmouth, killing two people, injuring three and damaging sixty houses. L4's load went down on King's Lynn, though one bomb nearly hit the wireless station at Hunstanton, the casualties being two killed and thirteen injured. Bombing ordinary towns was then something totally new, and the Germans mollified their lingering feeling of guilt by claiming that King's Lynn's anti-aircraft (AA) guns had 'opened hostilities'. In fact, no such guns existed.

As virtually the entire RFC was in France, the only aircraft available to defend Britain in January 1915 were those assigned to the task by the RNAS. Three such naval 'fighters' were in a condition of readiness at Great Yarmouth on 19 January, but it would have been futile to take off. There was no hope of reaching 10,000 feet within three-quarters of an hour, by which time the airships might be impossible to catch. And they would have been extremely lucky to get back on the ground again in one piece.

While the British public angrily argued over what those in authority ought to be doing, the Zeppelins came two or three times a week. Today it seems almost beyond belief that this could have happened. Early Zeppelins were 490 feet long, and they grew bigger as the months went by. They had a ceiling with full load of about 10,000 feet, though this also increased and eventually reached higher than 20,000 feet late in the war. At full throttle they could make about 50 mph, a speed that was later slightly improved upon; but in a stiff gale the speed over the ground might be barely walking pace. Each ship was a spidery network filled with inflammable hydrogen gas. One might be forgiven for thinking that, with a combination of such existing technology as the telephone, the searchlight and the gun, it might be possible to destroy every airship that dared poke its nose over the British coast. What actually happened was that nothing worried the raiding airships in the slightest, apart from the weather. (Admittedly it was a different story with the Army ships over the Western Front, which generally had very short lives indeed.)

With the RFC quite unable even to build up the required forces for the land battle, the entire burden of trying to shoot down Zeppelins fell on the RNAS. Urgent experiments were made with Lewis guns firing different kinds of ammunition, with darts, grenades and, in particular, with a crude but promising anti-Zeppelin bomb. This comprised a tube filled with petrol and fitted with a series of hooks and a fuse. The aeroplane pilot carried several clipped to the sides of the cockpit, and released them through a hole in the floor. As each fell, a lanyard triggered a mechanism in the fuse which both lit the petrol and released the spring-loaded hooks. The bomb was intended to hook on to the fabric of an airship, burn through and set fire to the gasbag inside.

During the spring of 1915 the bigger and more powerful P-class Zeppelins made their presence felt from Kent to Scotland. One of these, LZ38, was held in searchlight beams as she came in over Essex on the night of 17/18 May. RNAS Flight Sub-Lieutenant Mulock saw her – the first pilot of a night fighter ever to experience the sudden thrill of seeing his enemy – and urged his Avro 504 towards the illuminated monster, its willing Gnome engine at full throttle. He would have had no chance if he had had to take out much difference in altitude, but he was already at about the same height. Unbelievably, he realised he was going to get within firing range. Closing to about 2,000 feet distance he opened up with his Lewis. He could hardly miss. Then the gun jammed! LZ38 got away, and so did her sister LZ39, despite the latter being intercepted by no fewer than three RNAS pilots as she crossed the Belgian coast on her way back to her shed at Evère, Brussels.

One of the three unsuccessful fighters over Belgium was a Morane-Saulnier Type L, flown by Flight Sub-Lieutenant R.A.J. Warneford, which had simply been unable to climb fast enough. Warneford had been hoping, against all odds, to be able to encounter an airship when he was already at its altitude and carrying the flaming anti-Zepp bombs. On the night of 7/8 June 1915 he was detailed to bomb the sheds at Evère, and his Morane was carrying instead six 20 lb Hales-type high-explosive bombs. At about 3 a.m. on the 8th, as he was setting course for Brussels, he suddenly saw LZ37 homeward bound over Ostend. Climbing as hard as he could he managed to get above the monster and, taking careful aim, began to release his bombs. The last bomb caused the whole airship to explode. As the Zeppelin vanished inside a vast fireball, Warneford's Morane was tossed upside down and went into a spin with the engine stopped. As the red-hot skeleton of LZ37 fell into the grounds of a convent near Ghent, Warneford was forced to land with a broken petrol pipe. He was able to effect a temporary repair before the

*The Morane–Saulnier Type L in which Lt Warneford won his VC. Note the can marked 'Gnome' and the funnel, probably for castor-oil lubricant.*

arrival of German troops, and he took off again in the dark and reached his base. The first wholly successful night interception in history won Warneford the VC. Ten days later he crashed on take-off and was killed.

This victory, though over Belgium, did much to improve public morale in Britain, and improve the image of the frustrated night-fighter pilots. But literally hundreds of subsequent sorties resulted merely in extreme fatigue, sometimes in a distant sighting of a Zeppelin and, approximately as often, a crash either at the home airfield or in a totally unsuitable place for landing as a result of engine failure. Dozens of new airfields were hastily set up – not difficult, because all that was needed was a windsock, Besonneau canvas hangar and a few tents – and freshly trained pilots arrived to fly newly built aircraft. The trouble was, the sky seemed to be a very big place, and for a pilot of a defending fighter to intercept even as huge an enemy as an airship was pure luck. There was absolutely no *system* of interception whatever. Pilots took off with only the vaguest idea whether airships were about at all. There was no means of communicating with them once they were airborne, and they had to rely on what they could glean from searchlights or gunfire. Unlike the airship captains, they could not safely shut down their engines and listen for enemies.

On the other hand, the Kaiser's Imperial Navy did enlist the new sceince of wireless communication, and went one vital step further. On 15 June 1915 L10 made the long trip from Nordholz to the Tyne. She bombed very accurately on an ideal target: blast furnaces and coke ovens all going flat out and visible for more than twenty miles, with surrounding factories and houses also brightly lit. The Zeppelin hardly needed the new radio navigation system that was used that night for the first time. Special receiver aerials and instruments in the airship picked up coded signals from Nordholz and from Borkum, the most westerly of the German offshore islands, so that when each signal strength was at a maximum the crew could work out their position by a rudimentary triangulation. Certainly one of the first, if not the first, airborne radio navaids in history, this simple form of the later DF (direction-finding) loop system at least ensured that never again would an airship intending to bomb Hull cruise aimlessly and finally bomb Yarmouth, 120 miles away.

At the same time, the German radio DF system was nothing like accurate enough for blind bombing. It could ensure that an airship arrived over a particular large city, but its accuracy was measured in kilometres rather than metres. On several subsequent raids, especially that on 9 August 1915, clouds and rain so interfered with visibility that the Zeppelins just let go their bombs at random. No airship dared penetrate hostile airspace by day, and in the short summer nights the timing had to be right if the lumbering ships were to retain cover of darkness throughout the dangerous part of the mission. It was at this time that the Naval Zeppelins introduced a bold observation technique. An observer was lowered in a streamlined car on a 2,700-ft cable carrying a telephone line. The intention was that the height difference should allow the observation car to dangle below the cloud base while the airship remained hidden; the isolated officer could also listen for the sound of night-fighter aircraft. He relied totally upon the cable; he had no parachute.

In the second half of 1915 the RFC gradually began making a positive contribution to British aerial defence. When it took over from the RNAS officially in December it had ten permanent night-fighter airfields, each with two aircraft at readiness, with many more being prepared. Virtually all the RFC combat aircraft were by now of the B.E.2c type, the mass-produced general-purpose machine designed as standard RFC equipment by the Royal Aircraft Factory at Farnborough. Its dominant feature was strong inherent stability, and while this was an often fatal handicap on the Western Front in daylight, in one-sided combat against the agile Fokker monoplane, it was a major advantage in night missions against airships. On the other hand, the B.E. had only a slight performance advantage over the 1915 Zeppelins. The quoted maximum speed on the level was 72 mph and the ceiling 10,000 feet, but a B.E. significantly lower than an airship was unable to make an interception; it could overhaul the airship or climb to the same level, but could not do both simultaneously. Indeed on the night of 13 October 1915 Lieutenant J.C. Slessor – who much later was to become Chief of the Air Staff – found the greatest difficulty in maintaining control of his B.E. as it staggered along at full throttle at its ceiling in a vain attempt to reach L15, clearly visible high over a brightly lit London. Eventually he had to give up the chase, and with tanks almost dry, he glided back to Sutton's Farm, near Hornchurch, easily found because of its distinctive coloured petrol flares. As he neared it, the airfield was swiftly becoming covered in a thin layer of dense white mist. Left alone he might have pulled off a good landing, but as he descended into the mist the searchlight crew at the side of the airfield decided to help. Aiming their beam at him he was blinded, and the mist suddenly became brilliantly white. Slessor was lucky to finish with a B.E. that was, after some discussion, judged repairable.

As the first night fighter in history, the B.E.2c might deserve careful study, but in fact it was merely a lash-up – as were most combat aircraft of the early part of the First World War. The B.E. had been designed when the War Office was adamant that the only possible use for aeroplanes was reconnaissance. Later many hundreds of all kinds of B.E. were used as bombers, being flown solo from the rear cockpit. They were hacked down in droves by the deadly Fokkers, being low, slow, incapable of rapid manoeuvre and, usually, unarmed (because they could not carry bombs and also a gun). As a night fighter, however, they were at least less likely to be shot down. In this role they were again flown solo, and a drum-fed Lewis was mounted on the centre of the upper wing, firing at an angle that cleared the propeller disc. Instruments were marked in luminous paint, and some had an internal lamp. Their stability made them steady gun platforms, and probably safer than any other aircraft in the still extremely chancy business of night flying; but their performance was marginal in the extreme.

One wonders why nothing was done to build up a strong force of faster, higher-climbing night fighters. One of the best aircraft would have been the little Bristol Scout, which as early as February 1914 reached the then excellent speed of 95 mph. Even when carrying a machine-gun the Scout C of 1915 could comfortably exceed 90 mph, and climb to 15,500 feet. Though used by many RFC and RNAS units, the Scout was issued in ones and twos, and total production

*This B.E.2e night fighter had launchers for Le Prieur rockets on the interplane struts.*

was trivial (for example, 87 C models for the RFC and 74 for the RNAS). Very easy to fly, highly manoeuvrable, and capable of climbing to 10,000 feet in twenty minutes to intercept a Zeppelin, the little Scout seemed in 1915 to be the ideal night fighter, but the number in use at any time could be counted on the fingers. Indeed, it seemed to be a perverse law of the British procurement machine that, while the excellent Bristol Scout and M.1C monoplane were almost ignored, along with several other potentially outstanding fighters, the almost unmanoeuvrable B.E.2 family were built in ever-greater quantities by more and more factories.

One of the weapons carried by the Bristol Scout was the Ranken dart, a development of the hooked petrol bomb. Devised by RN Engineer Lieutenant Francis Ranken, it comprised a slim dart with an explosive head and four sprung vanes at the rear. Carried in metal boxes of 24, the darts were released three at a time. The idea was that the head would pierce the fabric of the airship, the fuse would be detonated and the charge would explode before the tail vanes had torn through. Even if no fire was caused, the rent was thought certain to cause gross loss of gas. The little Scout often carried two boxes of 24. Another weapon was the Le Prieur rocket, originally designed for destroying observation balloons. This was the simplest possible rocket, with a hard pointed nose, launched from a tube carried on the interplane struts, giving an upward inclination at launch. Many fighters carried up to eight or even twelve rockets, which were usually salvoed all at once. Incendiary ammunition, and later explosive Pomeroy bullets, were predominant in the 97-round drums made up for the Lewis guns of fighters on night Zeppelin patrol. In the experimental shops of Royal Ordnance Factories, Vickers, and other works were to be found several purpose-designed guns for destroying the raiding monsters. Certainly the few pilots who did succeed in reaching a Zeppelin were greatly disheartened to pump drum after drum of 0.303in ammunition (incendiary included) right through the vast silvery envelope and see no evident effect. In two cases there was an effect, the airship later making a forced landing; but this was not known to the fighter pilot.

During 1915 a spate of more or less bizarre aircraft were designed expressly to beat the Zeppelin raiders. One of the first was the A.D. Scout, designed by Haris Booth at the Admiralty Air Department. This lofty but quite unsuitable aeroplane had a nacelle about ten feet off the ground attached to the upper pair of wings, and carrying the Davis recoilless gun. The Davis came in several versions, the most common firing a ½ or 2-pounder shell, and had its development been carried to completion it would probably have been a formidable weapon. The Davis was also specified for the Blackburn Triplane, which resembled a slightly less grotesque form of the A.D. Scout, and also for the P.V.2 designed at the RNAS Experimental Depot at Port Victoria, on the Isle of Grain, in the Thames estuary. The P.V.2 was a fine-looking seaplane which actually flew (in June 1916). So did the Robey-Peters three-seat gun carrier, a pugnacious biplane carrying Davis gunners in streamlined nacelles on both the left and right upper wings.

Two of the aircraft featured in the author's small sketches (overleaf) are the Royal Aircraft Factory N.E.1 and Vickers F.B.25. These undistinguished aircraft were both fitted with a powerful searchlight in the nose. There seems to be no evidence that either aircraft was used for any serious experiments to see whether or not a searchlight might be of value in finding hostile aircraft at night, but it is at once obvious that switching on an airborne searchlight instantly betrays the presence and location of one's own aircraft. Like so many weapons and counter-weapons, an airborne searchlight might increase a night fighter's vulnerability, rather than its

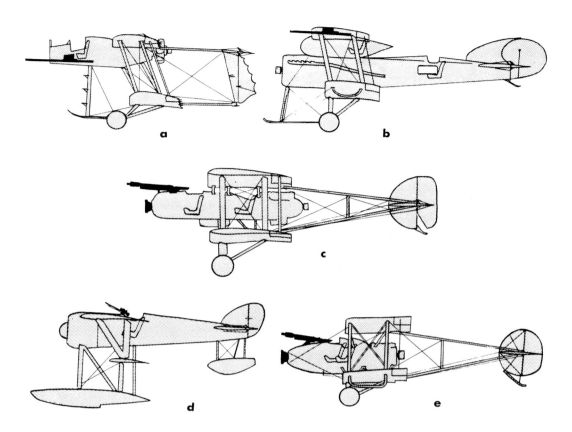

*First World War night fighters. Most of the effort devoted to night air defence in the First World War was British, for the most obvious reasons. In practice the types of aircraft used as night fighters were all modifications of aircraft designed for other purposes (as was again to be the case with British night fighters in the Second World War), but a number of interesting machines were built explicitly as night fighters. Here, shown to a common scale, with combat equipment in solid black, are a A.D. Scout (2pdr Davis recoilless gun); b Robey-Peters RRF 25 Mk II (two upper-wing nacelles with Davis guns, or possibly one Davis and one Lewis .303-inch); c Royal Aircraft Factory NE1 (Vickers Crayford rocket gun and searchlight); d Port Victoria PV2, as originally built before the upper wing was raised above the fuselage (.303-inch Lewis); and e Vickers FB25, as built without nosewheel (Vickers Crayford rocket gun and searchlight).*

lethality. At the same time, when one considers that visible light is merely electromagnetic radiation, just like the emissions from radar, one is left wondering why all the later effort was put into radar, and almost none into airborne searchlights. The only serious trials with later airborne searchlights were, in the author's opinion, ridiculous; for some reason the device was called a Turbinlite, as described later.

Returning to the First World War, all these supposed anti-Zeppelin night fighters pale into insignificance beside the weird creations of Noel Pemberton-Billing. 'PB' was a colourful character, to put it mildly. When the First World War broke out he asked the Admiralty what sort of aircraft it wanted, went back to his factory, drew outlines on the walls, and did not let anybody go home until the prototype was completed seven days later. (It was a surprisingly good machine.) By 1916 PB had gained a commission in the RNAS, resigned to become MP for East Hertfordshire, and designed several further combat machines. The latest, completed in the first four weeks of 1916, was the P.B. 29E, a vast but fragile-looking quadruplane. In PB's book *Air War: how to wage it* appeared an explanation: 'A fleet of defending aeroplanes is necessary. Each must be so armed as to be capable of destroying an airship at a range equal to the range of its own searchlight, which must be not less than one mile. It must have at least a speed of 80 mph in order to overtake airships. It must be able to fly as slowly as 35 mph to economise fuel and to render accurate gunfire and night landing possible . . .' Other requirements were 12 hours' endurance, silenced engines, dual pilots (because of the long missions) and ability to reach 10,000 feet in 20 minutes. Fast climb was not expected to be needed, because, to quote PB, the idea was 'to stand still in the air in a 28 mph breeze and lie in wait for Zeppelins'. Commander Seddon flew the 29E at Chingford in February 1916 but it later crashed. This did not discourage PB from later building the even more extraordinary P.B.31E. Planned in mid-March 1916, this was again built for the Admiralty, and was a veritable sky battleship. The main armament was a 1½-pdr Davis on the upper floor of the crew compartment, level with the uppermost of the four wings. In the bow cockpit was a pair of Lewis guns, and on the extreme nose was mounted a powerful searchlight carried on gimbals and trained by the bow gunner. The generating plant 'sounded like a T-T race'. Clifford Prodger got the contraption into the air

*Probably the best photo of a Bristol Scout, showing Type D, Serial No. 5553.*

*On 25 March 1917 this F.E.2b (A781) was photographed at Farnborough during trials with twin Lewis guns fixed to a searchlight fed from the windmill-driven generator. Aiming them, Capt. W.S. Farren became Sir William Farren, an eminent 'boffin' and captain of industry.*

in February 1917, but it was doomed by the feeble 100 hp of its Salmson engines. By this time PB had sold the works to his co-directors and it was renamed Supermarine Aviation; so the 31E was an early ancestor of the Spitfire!

Another specialized anti-Zeppelin weapon was the Crayford rocket gun, developed by the Vickers works at that Kentish town. This fearsome weapon was tested on the range but may never have flown. The first designated carrier was the Zeppelin Scout built by Parnall Aircraft in 1916. A large single-seat biplane, the ZS had the monster gun fixed on the right side at an elevation of 45°. In contrast, Vickers' own F.B. 25, flown in the first weeks of 1917, entrusted the rocket gun to a gunner in a separate cockpit just ahead of the pilot and on the right side, with a manually aimed mounting. The corresponding machine from the Royal Aircraft Factory was the N.E.1 (Night Experimental), a slender biplane with a central pusher nacelle. In the bow was the pilot, with his own Lewis and a searchlight. Behind was the gunner, with the Vickers rocket gun and a second searchlight.

While these and other strange anti-Zeppelin night fighters swiftly took shape in British factories, established machines were used in new ways. RNAS fighters, in particular, were used in experiments aimed at increasing the proportion of each Zeppelin's mission in which it could be attacked. Sopwith 1½-Strutters and Pups, and later Camels, with wheel or skid landing gear, were towed far out across the North Sea on lighters, some of them to alight again after their patrol on rubber-fabric inflatable bags. A few Sopwith Babies, Camel 2F.1s and Pups were equipped as night fighters operating from the world's first aircraft carriers, HMS *Furious* and seaplane carriers *Engadine* and *Vindex*, with the usual fixed Vickers gun replaced by a tripod-mounted Lewis and with floats or flotation bags. Perhaps most remarkable of all, one of *Vindex*'s Bristol Scouts was successfully borne aloft and released from above the upper wing of a Porte Baby flying boat, on 17 May 1916. The aim was to carry the little fighter to about 6,000 feet altitude some one hundred miles beyond the furthest point it could reach in unaided anti-Zeppelin patrol; but, like all schemes which relied on a chance meeting with an airship, it was of little practical use.

Moreover, whereas the earliest German military and naval airships had had no defensive armament, their larger and more powerful successors bristled with many guns. On 30 May 1916 the first of the so-called 'Super Zeppelin' R-class, ship L30, entered service with the Naval Airship Division. Powered by six 360hp Maybach engines, she had a displacement of no less than 1,949,600 ft³, and was fractionally under 650 feet long. Her lifting power was such that, while the 1914 ships could barely climb above 10,000 feet with a tonne (2,205 lb) of bombs, the R-class could load five tonnes of bombs (over 11,000 lb), plus all-round defensive armament, and still climb to 20,000 feet. L30 entered service, commanded by Oberleutnant Baron von Buttlar, with a total of ten Parabellum machine-guns; soon at least one of these was replaced by a Becker 20 mm cannon. As an interesting aside, whereas the boundary layer of sluggish air at the bows of an airship might be only an inch thick, 500 feet further aft it would have grown to at least three feet. A man could crouch on top of the ship and not be swept overboard; only his hair would be ruffled by the slipstream. For this reason, defensive gunners were usually placed near the stern, where they could man their gun(s) partly outside the envelope in a gentle breeze and with a clear field of fire.

Thus, in the middle war years the advantage tended to swing in favour of the attacking airships. It was increasingly evident that the only answer to these attacks lay in improved early

*Pemberton-Billing hoped the P.B.31E would cruise the night sky waiting for Zeppelins.*

warning, improved tracking of the raiders, improved communications, and more and better fighters. By the end of 1916 there were thirty night-fighter airfields at instant readiness from Kent to Scotland, housing 2,000 RFC or RNAS Home Defence personnel, backed up by a further 15,000 manning searchlights or anti-aircraft gun posts. Though the airships seemed to lead a charmed life, almost every one of them encountered close AA fire over Britain and, on an increasing number of occasions, a successful interception by a night fighter. On one occasion, in April 1916, a veteran Zeppelin and crew – L15, the one that got away from Slessor – was hit by AA fire at Purfleet and finally succumbed to darts dropped by a B.E.2c; but she went down gently, and finally broke up more than two hours later off the Essex coast. What the British public wished to see was a raider going down in flames.

When it came, it came in textbook manner, seen by millions of Londoners (including the author's mother, watching from Harrow). It was the night of 2 September 1916, when there were no fewer than fourteen German naval and military airships over England (sixteen had set out). Many of them were over the London area, and so were many fighters. One of the latter was a B.E.2c flown by Lieutenant W. Leefe Robinson, of 39 Squadron. He had taken off from Sutton's Farm just after 11 p.m. For two hours he had droned higher and higher on his patrol line between Hornchurch and Joyce Green on the other side of the Thames. Suddenly, at 1.10 on 3 September, he saw an airship held in searchlights near Woolwich. He was higher than the airship and overtaking it, until it disappeared into cloud. Frustrated, he cruised about for 43 minutes looking for it, but eventually returned to his patrol area. Seeing a glow far to the north he headed in that direction, thinking it was a fire on the ground. It was the airship! As he neared her, nose slightly down in a full-throttle chase, Leefe Robinson saw AA shellbursts filling the sky above, behind and below the airship, but none within one airship-length (about 600 feet). Flying right through the bursting shells, he pulled round in a turn about 800 feet below the monster, got it in his gunsight and emptied a drum of Lewis ammunition along the whole length. Tossed about by the AA fire, he changed drums and fired the second from bow to stern along the other side. He reported 'I then got very close behind at about 500 feet range and concentrated the third drum on the underneath rear part. The drum was hardly finished when I saw the part I had

been firing at begin to glow. In a few seconds the whole rear part was ablaze. I quickly got out of the way of the falling Zeppelin, and, having very little oil or petrol left, landed at Sutton's Farm at 2.45 a.m.'

Leefe Robinson happened to be in the right place at the right time. His achievement was far greater than the mere destruction of an airship (which was not a Zeppelin but the almost new Army Schütte-Lanz S.L.11); it showed that it could be done, to a public wearied of the apparently complete lack of success of the defending fighters. It had a greatly encouraging effect on the other night-fighter pilots. To an even greater degree, it struck fear into the other airship crews, many of whom saw the huge fireball and knew exactly what it meant. On that night 486 bombs were dropped on England, killing a mere forty people. It was the airships' biggest disaster yet, and while Leefe Robinson collected the Victoria Cross, the crew of S.L.11 were buried with full military honours at Cuffley, Hertfordshire.

For days the surviving airship crews were singularly thoughtful, and discussed openly whether they would rather fry or jump to their deaths. Then, on 23 September, eleven ships set out for Britain. One, L33 of the huge new R-type of almost two million cubic feet

*On the reverse of this photo is written in German 'Schütte-Lanz 11 over England'.*

displacement, heavily bombed east London but was caught near Chelmsford by 2nd Lieutenant Brandon, also of 39 Squadron, who had been the one to fill L15 with fatal dart perforations. This time he braved the fire of possibly ten machine-guns to fire drum after drum of Lewis ammunition into the monster. Every round hit, but there was no fire. Unknown to Brandon, L33 was losing gas fast, and she hit the ground very hard near West Mersea, her crew being made prisoner. Worse (for the Germans) was to come. As he returned to Sutton's Farm, out of ammunition, Brandon saw another of the monster R-class ships caught in searchlights. Suddenly he saw what looked like 'liquid fire' being injected into it. It was his brother officer from 39 Squadron, Lieutenant F. Sowrey. After a chase lasting more than 25 minutes he had finally come up with the monster, looking almost transparent against the blackness of the sky. He fired drum after drum into her, to no apparent effect. Then Sowrey saw a tongue of flame amidships, followed by a huge gout of flame at the bows. Within seconds L32 was going down like a catherine wheel near Billericay.

No longer could the airship crews claim that the loss of S.L.11 was mere bad luck. Britain's night defences had at last, after two years of testing, got the measure of the Zeppelin. Henceforth airships would point their nose over the British coast at their peril, and for a week the only raids were on the Midlands and northern areas. On 1 October eleven ships set forth, and one of them, L31, headed for London. Only one commander dared to take on the British capital: Kapitänleutnant Heinrich Mathy, the most experienced and skilled of all Zeppelin captains. Even he was shocked at the intensity of the opposing searchlights and AA fire, and after releasing his bombs he turned and twisted in an effort to escape or find cloud. From fifteen miles away he was seen by yet another member of 39 Squadron, 2nd Lieutenant W.J. Tempest, who had managed to stagger up to 14,500 feet on his patrol line between Joyce Green and Hainault. The airship was held at the peak of a great white mountain of searchlight beams. Eventually Tempest reached her and, disregarding a storm of AA fire, opened up with his Lewis. Again it took drum after drum. Suddenly L31 became a mass of flames. The great ship slowed violently and plunged to the ground. Tempest, who had been below and astern, had a desperate struggle getting out of the way. He could feel the intense heat beat across through the cold night air, and heard the roaring of the flames above the sound of his own engine. What was left of L31 fell near Potters Bar. Mathy deliberately leaped out on the way down.

This knocked the stuffing out of the Zeppelin crews. They now knew that their great hope of beating England to its knees through airship attack would never succeed. Never again did airships come to London; they concentrated their efforts on northern and coastal targets. Many times they came, but seldom without loss. On 17 June 1917 four set out for Harwich, two turned back and L48 was shot down, the sole hideously injured survivor afterwards describing what it was like to fall for five minutes while being burned alive. On 19 October 1917 five huge new Zeppelins were lost out of a raiding force of eleven, and this was especially significant because all operated at their maximum altitude of just over 20,000 feet. Indeed, this major attack was known as 'the silent raid' because neither the airships nor the night fighters could be heard from the ground. After this catastrophe there were never again more than five Zeppelins over Britain, except for 12 March 1918 when there were six.

The 3½ years of struggle against the night airships had taught Britain a fantastic amount. The campaign could not teach so much to the airship crews except that courage of the highest order cannot compensate for an inherently vulnerable weapon. From a long period of inertia and fumbling, the British defences had grown to be formidable. Altogether the German airships made fifty-one raids on Britain, all by night, dropping 196 tons of bombs and killing 557 people. It sums up the campaign to record that most of the damage and casualties were caused in 1915 and nearly all the airships destroyed were shot down after mid-1916.

During these middle war years the towns of Kent had often been bombed by aircraft, sometimes with serious results. By day and by night a variety of small two-seaters had made brief attacks, against which the defences were almost powerless. On two occasions single aircraft had even ventured to central London. Then on 25 May 1917 no fewer than twenty-three twin-engined Gotha G II bombers took off from Belgian airfields bound for London. From then on, the big bomber presented a far worse threat than ever the Zeppelins had done. On their third major raid, in broad daylight on 13 June, one group of fourteen Gothas caused 597 casualties in central London – all in the space of a few minutes. Time after time defending fighters received more punishment than they meted out, or their guns jammed or, as in the frustrating attacks on airships, they pumped drum after drum of ammunition into the bombers without evident effect. The RFC realised it needed more speedy fighting scouts, and took squadrons from the front line in France. On 7 July 84 Home Defence aircraft of twenty-two different types searched aimlessly for twenty-two Gothas, and 2nd Lieutenant F.A.D. Grace and his observer G. Murray, flying an Armstrong Whitworth of 50 Squadron, did manage to shoot down a straggler. In a panic, the government at last took positive action, recalling Brigadier-General E.B. Ashmore from the RFC in France to form a properly organized London Defence Area covering south-east England. It was the chaotic and haphazard air defence against this major attack that, backed up by a leader in *The Times* and a stormy debate in Parliament, was eventually to lead to the formation of the Royal Air Force as an independent service on 1 April 1918.

Before then, however, both the Home Defence squadrons and the Imperial German Army *Bombengeschwader* were due to be at each other's throats – and by night. The first night attack came on 4 September 1917, when four G IV bombers crossed the coast and one killed 130 people with two bombs that hit the RN barracks at Chatham. This kind of thing could not go on for long without public indignation spilling over. Until this time the authorities in Whitehall had been extremely restrictive in allowing aircraft to fly at night. Apart from the officially favoured B.E.2 series, and its offshoots such as the B.E.12, almost the only aircraft permitted to fly in darkness were those still in manufacturers' hands, and thus not subject to the same rules. The caution was born of ignorance rather than stupidity. Though the RFC was a huge organisation, it had grown up with explosive rapidity. There had been no time for anyone to set up an experimental or operational research unit, other than Farnborough, the Royal Aircraft Factory, which was concerned solely with developing better aircraft. Such basic questions as how best to fly at night, and in what kinds of aircraft, had to be answered unofficially by enquiring spirits in the operational squadrons.

One of the first such pioneers had been Carmichael, back in what seemed the prehistoric era of 1912–13. Now there suddenly arose another. While the Gothas were overhead on 3 September 1917 the CO of 44 Squadron sought permission of his GOC, General Higgins, to try to intercept the enemy using his Sopwith Camel. With almost any other pilot the answer would have been a curt 'Certainly not', and perhaps a rebuke at the suggestion. But Major W.G. Murlis-Green was a very experienced pilot (and so, at that time, was any officer who had survived with a front-line squadron longer than about ten days!) who had emerged as the undoubted 'Ace' on the Allied side in distant Macedonia. He was the kind of man able to bear responsibility for his own actions, and permission was given. Immediately No. 44 was electrified. The Camel was a superb fighter, but it was also the trickiest thing in the sky. Small, powerful, and able to turn on the proverbial sixpence – especially when turning right, helped by the gyroscopic effect of the spinning rotary engine – it also needed delicate judgement borne of experience. Many pupils died soon after take-off because they did not know just when, and how far, to lean off the mixture (rather like taking the choke off a car) and prevent the engine spluttering to a stop. Many stalled and spun through hamfisted turns at below 1,000 feet. Those who survived likened the Camel to a thoroughbred racehorse, with almost frightening sensitivity to the controls. They might have added it was a lopsided racehorse, always, except in a glide, under powerful torque and gyroscopic effects from the engine. Nothing less like a B.E. could be imagined, and if the Camel could be flown in the dark, so could any other aircraft.

Instantly, Murlis-Green was surrounded by all the other pilots on night duty, asking to come too. He picked Captain Brand and Lieutenant Banks, and the three quickly grabbed helmets, gloves and hand torches. Within minutes the field at Hainault Farm, in those days in open country to the north-east of the capital, was echoing to the sound of three Camels speeding out of the flickering light of the flares and into the blackness. Among the other pilots there was intense excitement, but the ground staff were – so legend has it – morose. Many were the predictions that the trio would never return; or, if any did, that they would be bound to crash on landing. But return they did, and all taxied back safely to their parking places. They had seen nothing of the enemy, but that was largely because there was no way of guessing whereabouts to look. What was more significant was that even the Camel could be a night fighter, and the news went through the Home Defence gravevine like wildfire.

Over the next few weeks the whole system of British air defence – such as it was – underwent drastic revision, as the Gothas came again and again, seemingly without hindrance. Scratching around for some way of stopping the bombers, British inventors came up with more than eighty suggestions, many of them the subject of patents. One that was actually tried was simply to site standard kite balloons east of London and around the Thames estuary. Each balloon was a gastight fabric envelope resembling a short but fat airship with (usually three) tail surfaces like the flights of a dart. The standard pattern was designed to carry an artillery observer aloft; without him the balloon could take its steel cable to 20,000 feet, but there is no record of any pre-1918 German bomber being brought down by one. (In contrast, in the Second World War the British barrage balloon [as it was called] destroyed many aircraft, a major proportion being British.) In fact possibly two of the big bombers had been shot down over the sea, and over Belgium. Several more had been lost through running out of petrol, adverse winds and landing accidents; but the British public knew nothing of this. It wanted to *see* aircraft being shot down, as had ultimately been achieved with the airships. But bombers were more difficult, for obvious reasons. Though London and the south-east became ringed with hundreds of searchlights, none seemed able to hold a bomber in its beam. Though there were hundreds of guns, which fired 14,000 shells on 29 September 1917 alone, often from barrels practically glowing red-hot in the darkness, and another 12,000 on the 30th, no shell hit a bomber. What was desperately lacking was any precise system of finding and tracking the raiders and quickly passing the information to gunners and night fighters. In the absence of this, thousands of shells, and

*Like most Sopwith Camel night fighters, B2402 had the usual fuselage-mounted twin Vickers guns replaced by two Lewis above the upper wing.*

thousands of hazardous night-flying hours, achieved nothing beyond causing concern to the Gotha crews. With so much hardware flying about in the night sky, someone might get hit by sheer bad luck.

It seemed obvious that searchlights must play a central role. They were the only way easily to point out the enemy to both AA guns and night fighters. Small fighting scouts could not carry the clumsy radio sets of 1917, and even if one was told 'Enemy over Harrow' by a radio message no night fighter could find that particular suburb by night, nor would he know the enemy's altitude or heading. Morse messages by ground beacons were studied, but were even less useful. But if bombers could be tracked by several searchlights the confluence of their beams would give geographical position and altitude. By the third week in September a London Defence Area operations room had been set up, overlooking Horse Guards Parade, with a huge table covered with a map showing south-east England from Portsmouth to Harwich. On it were placed large counters, representing hostile aircraft, pushed along by girls with croupier-style rakes, to positions determined by messages passed to the centre by telephone from a network of ground observers. The whole area was marked out into a grid, with numbered and lettered squares. It was a fine system, wholly Ashmore's creation, and one that was destined to play the central role in a more crucial battle over the same territory twenty-three years later. But in 1917 it lacked the essential input of quantified data.

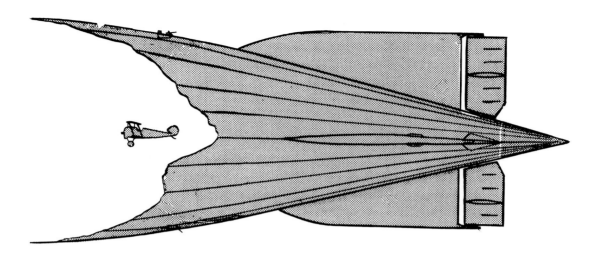

*Zeppelin airship: tail of a late-model Zeppelin (R, V, W, or X class), showing typical rear-dorsal cannon and ventral machine-gun positions, with Sopwith F1 Camel to same scale.*

Many people in various uniforms could telephone in reports of where bombers seemed to be. The only input that made any pretence at accuracy was a succession of bearings passed by listening posts. Sound seemed to be the only way of establishing the direction of night bombers. Humans have two ears, and binaural listening was once (and still is, among primitive peoples) vital to the accurate hunting of game. Today the most accurate binaural hearing is possessed by people who have lost their other distantly stimulated sense, sight. Blind people had top priority in south-east England in September 1917, and soon they were able to give a fairly accurate bearing on a Gotha at a range of up to five miles. Several such bearings from different sites gave a very helpful fix. At the same time, there was basic inaccuracy in the system. Fixes could be passed only by giving the designation of the lettered and numbered square. Searchlights and guns concentrated all their attention upon this square; but this was by no means the same as concentrating upon the bomber. Gradually, as the listening-post bearing changed, the controller eventually switched to an adjacent square. The problem of a bomber at the junction of four squares can be left to the imagination!

Then came a new bomber. On 28 September 1917 two of the nocturnal visitors were not Gothas but the first of the R-class (*Riesenflugzeug*, or Giant aircraft) to visit England. There were several makes of Giant, but the chief family came from the Zeppelin Werke at Staaken, and these first two were Zeppelin R IVs. Though not as big as later R-types the IV was formidable enough. Powered by four 220 hp Benz engines, it carried almost 2,000 kg (4,410 lb) of bombs, several times the load of a Gotha; and it was protected by seven machine-guns. Moreover, the noise of a Giant was quite unlike that of a Gotha, and the new intruder threw the listening posts into confusion. September was not a good month for the British night fighters. Indeed, the only way to hit the German bombers seemed to be to attack them at their airfields, and this was done to good effect in October, until the surviving Gothas and Giants were dispersed. (In modern jargon this would be called a 'counter-air strike', and in most scenarios it is still widely held to be the best way of blunting the edge of enemy offensive air power.)

But bombing German airfields in Belgium did not provide much of an answer to the long-suffering Britons who were being bombed almost nightly. In frustration they cried out for reprisals against German cities, and burned an effigy of the outspoken Lord Montagu of Beaulieu (father of the present peer), who urged the government to 'come clean' and tell the public that no effective defence against night bombers existed. Then, suddenly, there was a glimmer of light in the darkness. In fact, for the man who did it, the light was altogether too much. It was none other than Murlis-Green, and on 18 December 1917, by sheer luck, he found himself virtually in formation with a Gotha. Instinctively pulling in behind it, he opened up with his two Vickers guns. Their sudden bright flash completely blinded him for several seconds. During the next few minutes he tried, in effect, to sight on the Gotha and then fire while looking the other way. He saw his quarry drop a bomb, and he was able to follow its attempts to escape; but as soon as he fired he completely lost his 'night adaptation', the enlargement of the pupils that occurs gradually in subdued light, and which is vital to a night-fighter pilot. Suddenly the Gotha had gone, and Murlis-Green never found it again. Not until

*Powered by five 245-hp Maybach Mb.IVa engines, R48/17 was one of the last Staaken 'giants'. Defensive gunners were in the upper wing (2), nose, dorsal and ventral positions.*

next day did he learn it had force-landed in the sea off Folkestone, trying to regain the British coast with both engines dead, and that the crew had been made prisoner. The night fighters had begun to score against bombers at last!

Immediately the Home Defence Camels were hastily modified to fit them better for night flying. The twin Vickers were replaced by two Lewis guns on a Foster adjustable mounting above the upper wing. Unfortunately this demanded a rearwards shift of the cockpit, which not only greatly lengthened the delay in getting the Camel NF into service (it retained its original designation of F.1) but also worsened the forward view, which in night landings was a matter of the greatest importance. Eventually, by the end of the year, NF Camels were ready for combat. Able to climb at over 1,000 feet per minute, they could easily outrun any German bomber and fire long bursts without significantly affecting the pilot's vision.

Nor were these the only really effective night fighters. The equally good S.E.5a, faster than the Camel and much more relaxing to fly, was overcoming the unreliability of its original French engine and serving in several Home Defence squadrons. So too was the superb Bristol F.2B Fighter, as fast and manoeuvrable as any other combat aircraft despite having a crew of two. In night-fighter use aircraft began to appear in a new livery of dark olive green, and bearing a new night-flying roundel of plain red and blue, with no intermediate white ring. Guns were fitted with flash eliminators on their muzzles. As Murlis-Green discovered the hard way, on a dark night muzzle flash could cause temporary near-blindness. The incandescent source could be rapidly cooled by adding an expanding cone to the gun's muzzle. Attention was paid to damping the flames from exhausts, and a new night gunsight was introduced with an illuminated ring just filled by a Gotha's wings at a range of 100 feet. Dim cockpit lighting was introduced, and such unheard-of luxuries as a parachute, oxygen and a compact radio set were soon to be added.

London enjoyed a respite from bombing during the first weeks of 1918, but simply because it was blanketed under dense fog! Then on 28 January there were big headlines, in both Britain and Germany. The Germans read stirring accounts of the mission of a single Giant, which emphasized how difficult it was, with the existing defences, to bring one of these aircraft down. Though to modern eyes they looked huge, ungainly and frail – and indeed they could not safely be left on the airfield in a strong wind – the Giants were in fact reliable and strong. Their crews, numbering up to thirteen men, wore electrically heated suits and sometimes parachutes; some had enclosed cabins and an oxygen supply, and they communicated via a pneumatic message-tube system. Radio provided communications with the home base and with special navigation centres, while the number of cockpit instruments was not the four to seven then usual in combat aircraft but an unprecedented thirty-one, including a gyro-horizon to provide an attitude reference at night or in cloud. They were also prickly customers, with single or twin Parabellum machine-guns in the nose and above and below at the rear; some versions had gunners in wing nacelles or above the upper wing. In all respects they were worthy foes, and when manned by a brave and experienced crew could prove seemingly invincible – though of course, as in all air combat, a lot depended on luck.

On 28/29 January 1918 luck certainly favoured the most experienced crew of all, that of Hauptmann von Bentivegni, CO of *Riesenflugzeugabteilung* 501 (Giant Aircraft Unit 501). Flying an R VI, number R39, they thundered across Essex carrying a bomb load of 2,420 lb, included in which were two 660-pounders. Suddenly a night fighter appeared, and opened fire;

von Bentivegni flung his vast machine into a tight diving turn and they never saw the fighter again. A little later they were attacked by a Bristol Fighter of 141 Squadron. By rights the fighter ought to have shot them down; instead the withering fire from the Giant was so accurate that the Bristol soon had to break off and glide down to a forced landing, with a wounded observer and bullets through the fuel tank and engine. R39 thundered on, skilfully breaking free from one searchlight beam after another until it was over central London. After making its bombing run it was again intercepted, but this time the fighter's guns jammed. Over Chingford the Giant ran right into the cable of one of London's many barrage balloons, yet contrived to slide clear without major structural damage. From there on its flight home was uneventful. And one of its 660-lb bombs did more damage than any other dropped in the First World War. Falling on the great Odhams printing works in Long Acre, it exploded inside the building. The huge presses crashed down to the basement, where over 500 were sheltering. The blast, the presses and fire killed thirty-eight, and seriously injured eighty-five.

And what was the good news for the patient British? Simply that, at long last, the defending fighters had managed to shoot down a bomber in flames over England. It was an unfortunate Gotha that got in the way of Lieutenant Banks – one of the bold trio who had proved that a Camel could be flown at night – and a fellow member of 44 Squadron, Captain Hackwill. With their Foster-mounted Lewises they could aim and fire without being blinded, and in a very short time the crippled raider was spiralling down, burning fiercely, to crash near Wickford.

Carefully directed, the German bomber arms, *Kagohl* 3 with its strong force of Gothas and Rfa 501 with its handful of Giants, might have held the initiative until near the end of the war. But it was not to be. Impetuous von Bentivegni, openly seeking the coveted *Pour le Mérite* (the 'Blue Max'), ignored his weather officer's dire Forecast on 9 May 1918 and sent four Giants against England. R39 got back in one piece, through either the sixth sense of pilot von Lenz or else pure luck, because the airfield was completely covered by fog. The other three did not make it, and crew casualties were severe. There was only one further major raid on England, and it was the biggest of all. On 19/20 May 1918 no fewer than forty Gothas and three surviving Giants were readied, and all but two of the Gothas set out. It was a mistake, spurred on by the great German offensive on the Western Front, and a wish to mount a 'maximum effort' attack on England. In the half-light of near-summer the unprecedented number of bombers provided clear targets; three were shot down by the guns and three more by night fighters, one of the successful pilots being the third of the pioneer night Camel-drivers, Captain Brand.

Had such heavy attacks continued there is little doubt the German losses would soon have become unacceptable. Though thirty-eight Gothas had taken off on 19 May, only nineteen penetrated near London and only thirteen to the city itself, and yet six were shot down. After so many months of frustration the Home Defence squadrons of what had, on 1 April, become the Royal Air Force (largely because of public outcry over the divided managment of British air defence) were at last confident of destroying at least some of the enemy. Though there was still no proper system, and the whole creaking edifice rested on chance encounters or the lucky aiming of the searchlight crews, the whole added up to significant deterrence. It was especially noteworthy how great was the contribution, on both sides of the bomber-vs.-fighter battle, of a handful of individuals of skill and experience. Men such as Murlis-Green, Banks and Brand appeared in dispatches again and again. They had begun to learn a new and challenging trade, while others lost their lives merely trying to survive in the night air. In the hardest of all schools,

*Night-fighter Sopwith Dolphins appeared in February 1918. They had steel half-hoops above the upper wings to protect the pilot's head, should the aircraft overturn.*

the Home Defence squadrons had become the world's first defence against aerial attack by night. No other country created such a force; nor did Britain after 20 May 1918, because the German bombers were tied down in the great land battle until, in August, the High Command in Berlin decided 'on military and political grounds' to abandon attacks on London and Paris. Had they not done so there is little doubt the RAF night fighters would soon have stopped such attacks by making them demonstrably not worth while.

Immediately before this decision was announced, the Zeppelins of the Imperial Navy had one last fling. On 5/6 August, possibly having come to the conclusion that sudden death might be no worse than prolonged inactivity in a defeated Germany, Peter Strasser, the great pioneer who had formed and commanded the Navy Airship Division, climbed aboard one of his biggest and newest 'super-Zeppelins' (the great L70), boasting that it would be immune to Britain's guns and fighters. He set course with four other monsters, his head filled with plans for a proposed three-ship bombing raid on New York – which in theory would have been within his force's capabilities. Intending to cross the English coast at 21,000 feet, L70 instead made landfall at not much above 16,000 feet, and this proved fatal. By 1918 some RAF aircraft could climb much higher than this, and none more easily than the D.H.4, which – like its descendant, the Mosquito of the Second World War – had been designed as a bomber faster than contemporary single-seat fighters. A D.H.4 from RAF Great Yarmouth – the very town that had been attacked in the first airship raid on Britain – droned lustily towards L70 in the sure hands of Major Egbert Cadbury, with Captain R. Leckie manning the rear Lewis with Pomeroy ammunition. They closed with L70 and shot her into the sea in flames. Indeed, they almost shot down L65 as well, but Cadbury's Vickers jammed at the crucial moment and Leckie was out of ammunition, and the frightened crew of L65 were able to put out the fire the D.H.4 had started.

Five days later, on 11 August, Lieutenant D.S. Culley climbed into his naval Camel 2F.1 as it stood lashed to a lighter towed at full speed behind the destroyer HMS *Redoubt*. Released, he climbed towards L53 far out in the North Sea and shot it down from 19,000 feet. It was the last of twenty-nine German airships to be destroyed in the First World War, along with sixty-two Gothas shot down, crashed or missing. It brought to a fiery close the first aerial bombardment campaign in history, in which men had courageously gone out night after night and faced exhaustion, anoxia, tortured eardrums, nose-bleeds, frostbite and death by bullet, fire or impact with the ground. The night fighter could hardly have been born in a tougher environment.

# TWO

# PIERCING THE DARKNESS

After a major war it appears to be a natural reaction on the part of a democracy to dismantle its war machine. Predictably, after 1918 the proved and effective British Home Defence forces were swiftly run down and disorganized, and the infant Royal Air Force even had to fight for its very existence in the teeth of bitter opposition from the longer-established services. Against a background of extreme financial parsimony, which literally counted the shillings and pence, and worked on the basic assumption that aeroplanes had become little more than expensive toys, the Air Staff spent most of its time engaged in internal squabbles and external politics. The RAF survived, though as a mere token force which from April 1920 until September 1922 had but a single fighter squadron with which to defend the United Kingdom!

This squadron was No. 25, based at Hawkinge, in Kent. It was equipped with the Sopwith Snipe, a natural development of the Camel, which in 1919 had been selected in preference to several other aircraft as the standard RAF day and night fighter. It marked a great advance over the Camel in that, as well as having superior speed and climb, it was not so tricky to fly. The pilot had a more comprehensive range of instruments, a better view, oxygen, an electrically heated suit and (from 1923) a parachute as standard equipment, while the new electrical system also served navigation lights on the wing tips and tail, and cockpit lighting with a rheostat dimmer. Increasingly, radio became a standard fit, the first experimental one-way link having been set up with a transmitter at Biggin Hill in 1918, enabling the London Area Controller to talk to any radio-equipped fighter in south-east England. Night-fighter Snipes were also equipped with brackets for small parachute flares, chiefly to facilitate landing on unlighted fields. The permanent RAF airfields invariably had a landing area crossed by an L-shaped array of Money flares, each comprising a basket of steel mesh containing a roll of asbestos soaked in paraffin and lit when night flying was in progress.

With the Snipe the armament reverted to a pair of 0.303 in Vickers fixed immediately ahead of the pilot. Improved flash eliminators, in the form of simple divergent cones that both cooled the flame aerodynamically and shielded it, were made effective in partnership with the development by the Royal Ordnance Factories of special ammunition with propellant giving a less-brilliant flame. Buckingham tracer ammunition, inserted at intervals into each belt to give a visible trail and thus facilitate aiming, had been used on a restricted basis during the war, and by day had proved extremely effective. At night it had been almost too bright, but again small changes in formulation provided the answer. Further ammunition improvements, coupled with almost perfect reliability in the Constantinesco CC synchronizing gear, made it no longer hazardous to use 'special ammunition' (explosive or incendiary) in guns firing through the propeller disc. Not least, the original wartime night-fighter sights, the Neame and Hutton models, were replaced by the improved 1.8in Aldis optical sight backed up by an ordinary ring-and-bead sight for day use.

As in practically all so-called 'developed' countries – other than the 'emergent nations' of the day, which included China, Japan and the major countries of South America – Britain begrudged every penny spent on arms, even in self-defence. Wherever possible wartime equipment had to soldier on, though as the concept of cost/effectiveness had not then been recognized there was no knowledge of whether money was actually being saved or whether nations were getting the best value. In the RAF, and in the peacetime fighter squadrons of the French *Aviation Militaire* and US Army Air Service, wartime engines, guns, bombs and racks, and much other hardware had to be retained in use, despite the high costs of trying to maintain it, because of refusal by the government to buy anything new. In Britain it was 1924 before the first small batch of post-war fighters was bought, and even then they used much existing equipment. Though not particularly distinguished, the design selected, the Hawker Woodcock, deserves mention as the first aircraft in history explicitly ordered as a night fighter that actually went into service. Its chief advantage lay in its Bristol Jupiter engine, which offered reliability, economy and service life all of a standard totally unattainable with wartime engines such as the Bentley rotary of the Snipe.

To avoid flash-blindness, which was obviously still a problem, the Woodcock's two Vickers guns were mounted well down on each side of the fuselage, hung exposed in the airstream along with their large boxes for collecting the empties. In subsequent fighters the guns were tucked inside, firing through troughs in the fuselage skin. Several later fighters, such as the Hawker Fury, restored the guns to the top of the fuselage, ahead of the windscreen. This did not indicate that the flash problem had been solved, but that night fighting had been virtually forgotten. Moreover, despite many detail improvements in aircraft structures, engines and equipment, the fighter – and especially the night fighter – of the early 1930s differed from that of 1918 only in degree. Though the Hispano-Suiza firm, mainly in France, was successfully promoting its vee-12 water-cooled engines with a 20mm (0.79in) cannon firing through the hub of the propeller, most nations agreed with Britain that the 1918 armament of two rifle-calibre machine-guns was good enough. Such guns were exciting to fire, and as squadron pilots were able to practise for years they were eventually able to make very good scores in firing at sleeve and banner targets towed by their friends. It was at this time that the author, as an enthusiastic small boy, became familiar with RAF operational squadrons, making his third flight as an unauthorized passenger in a Fairey Hendon heavy bomber. The Hendon was avowedly a night bomber, painted dark olive green and with plain red/blue roundels like the night fighters of First World War. Yet only rarely was it actually flown at night, and the briefest acquaintance with its crews unearthed the fact that virtually all their training missions, and all their operational planning, were based upon flying in the daytime. Even more was this the case with the fighter squadrons. Though the pilots of such aircraft as the Bulldog and Gauntlet were occasionally detailed for night flying, they regarded this as an end in itself. All the fighters in the RAF were doped bright silver, and were very much day birds. Night flying was dangerous, and the last thing the RAF wanted was bad publicity, injured airmen, damaged civilian property or a lost aircraft. The idea of night cross-country flying, or night air-to-air firing at a towed target, filled senior staff with horror (one is tempted to add 'unless they were doing it themselves'; it was apparently all right to make night cross-countries if you were an air marshal).

It was pretty much the same in other countries. Irrespective of the political circumstances, armed forces tended to become less and less finely honed weapons of war and more and more instruments of pageantry and show. After First World War there were many officers, not all of them doddering old fools, who called for the tank to be outlawed; they wanted a return to 'real soldiering' with the horse. It was only natural that governments, wishing to impress others, should have preferred to see armies goose-stepping in bright uniforms rather than merged into the background with mud-smeared faces. In the same way, though the air force of every country nominally had some kind of responsibility for that nation's defence, most fighters (or, as they were called in the United States, pursuit ships) spent most of their time practising impeccable formation flying while painted in brilliant colours. The only exception I can think of was the Curtiss PN-1 (Pursuit, Night) of 1921, which came painted black. Three were ordered, one cancelled, and the two that were delivered were never used. The lessons of First World War were forgotten, as combat pilots settled into a routine that revolved around public display, showing the flag and, sometimes, acting as overseas ambassadors for their country. Their real purpose, superiority in deadly combat, was seldom manifest in anything other than 'manoeuvres' of the most genteel kind. One of my grown-up friends in 1938, who had been a fighter pilot nine years, had flown a total of under three hours at night, never fired his guns by night, and never fired his guns at anything save targets on the ground or towed sleeves travelling in a predictable straight line.

This is not to suggest that the pilots of the air forces between the wars were in themselves lacking in initiative or guts. They were, in most countries, career professionals. Competition between units was intense, and within certain limits operational squadrons were extremely capable. Pilots were complete masters of their machines, provided they flew in VFR. Inside a cloud it was still all too easy to lose control, especially as clouds are often violently turbulent. During the 1930s aircraft instruments were dramatically improved in design and precision, and extended in type, until the average fighter after 1935 could be relied upon to have a sensitive altimeter (often with two or three pointers geared to read in powers of ten), climb/descent indicator (today called a VSI, vertical speed indicator), artificial horizon, turn/slip (in Britain then called turn/bank) indicator and a directional gyro. Instrument flying began to be taught as a basic accomplishment of every military pilot, the first courageous steps having been taken in 1929–31 by such exceptional men as Jimmy Doolittle in the United States and Pat Johnson in Britain, who dared to fly 'circuits and bumps' completely blind while their cockpits were covered by an opaque hood. Blind flying had an obvious immediate relevance to civil transport, where the objective was straight and level flight from A to B in all kinds of weather, night or day. Man's inability to do this had been tragically manifest in February 1934 when the US Army Air Corps (created in 1926) had temporarily taken over responsibility for flying the US Mail over some of the toughest routes in the world, to the Pacific coast at Seattle and San Francisco. Though huge bonfires were lit as beacons, experienced pilots lost their way in the dark, lost control with vertigo, and suffered from freeze-ups and engine failure while trying to do what the technology did not yet allow. Mailplanes suffered fifty-seven crashes, approximately one every other day, twelve of them being fatal.

*The idea of formating below an enemy aircraft and destroying it with a no-deflection shot probably originated in 1917 with Capt. Lanoe G. Hawker VC. In 1927 it was resurrected with Specification F. 29/27, calling for a Coventry Ordnance Works 37 mm gun firing obliquely upward. The Vickers F.29/27 had the gun in the nose, and must have pitched nose-down with each shot. The specification was soon forgotten, because of 'changing requirements'.*

Five years later aircraft were far more reliable, and flying from A to B was no longer much of a hazard even at night (though there was, as yet, no complete answer to fog). The fighter pilot with his new range of instruments could strap himself in, dim his array of cockpit lighting to his choice and fly by night from one flare-lit airfield to another while simultaneously communicating with ground stations via two-way R/T (radio-telephone), with earphones built into his leather helmet and a microphone incorporated in his oxygen mask. But there was still much he could not do. The new gyro instruments 'toppled' if tilted beyond a specified limit, such as 55° climb or dive or 60° angle of bank. Such constraints are nonsense in aerial combat, yet for a fighter to perform a roll or loop meant that the vital blind-flying instruments would instantly become useless. Their needles, horizon bars or other presentation would sink dismally into one corner or up against one of the limit stops. Gradually, if the aircraft kept flying, they would over the next ten minutes re-erect themselves and once more become usable. So flying by night or in cloud meant that aerobatics were prohibited, and turbulence could cause dire trouble. On top of this, the overriding wish not to run into trouble exerted a powerful constraint on air staffs and caused them to husband their precious, and essentially irreplaceable, pilots and aircraft. Mock combat by night, or gun firing by night, would have been pushing their luck.

This inability of fighter squadrons to operate effectively at night, or in any save clear weather, was to some degree countered by the fact that bomber squadrons – even those called night-bomber squadrons – could not do much better. In only one country, the United States, had the scarcely understood world of electronics been enlisted on a nationwide scale to ease the terrifying problems of long-distance navigation without seeing the ground. Here the old bonfires were swiftly replaced by a rapidly growing network of designated air routes which at first were marked out by powerful (two million candle-power) revolving beacons every ten miles or so, then by radio beacons, and then, in the early 1930s, by 'radio range' stations which transmitted directional beams (typically with an A in morse on one side and an N on the other, with a continuous note along the centreline), so that an aircraft equipped with the appropriate receiver could hardly get lost. Airfields, too, were dramatically improved, with tarmac or concrete runways equipped with electric lighting and other visual or radio aids. But in other countries progress was slower, partly through less-urgent need but chiefly through a lack of incentive to find the money. Military airfields in most countries were not much better in 1938 than they had been in 1918; virtually all had grass landing areas, with no lighting save derivatives of the Money or the later Gooseneck flare. There was a vicious circle at work, with the incentive to improve the operating environment curtailed by the fact that hardly any aircraft flew at night – because the inadequate environment made it dangerous.

This wish to fly only in the daytime was understandable in peacetime 'playing at war' and colonial policing, but it even extended to warfare itself. The chief conflicts between the two world wars were those between Japan and the Soviet Union, Japan and China, Republican and Fascist Spain, Italy and Abyssinia, and the Soviet Union and Finland. Air power played a major role in all of them, and in Spain the air participation was multiplied far beyond what the Spaniards themselves could have sustained because the Republican air force was backed up by large air fleets sent from the Soviet Union and the Fascist side by equally large air forces sent by Mussolini's Italy and Hitler's Germany. All were eager to try out new warplanes, new equipment and new tactics, and the struggle was long and bitter. Yet each side was content to slog it out in the daytime sky; neither found its bombers in such peril by day that they were forced to bomb by night. Indeed perhaps the main lesson of the wars of the 1930s is that many of the supposed 'lessons' learned by the co-belligerents were later shown to have been grossly misleading. The Soviet Union was left with a belief in rigid political control extending right down to details of how a mission should be flown. The Japanese continued to believe that nothing mattered to a fighter except supreme power of manoeuvre and good pilot view; speed, rate of climb, armour and firepower could all be sacrificed. Italy's fighter pilots thought along exactly the same lines and even disliked monoplanes of any kind (especially those having an enclosed cockpit). The fast-growing *Luftwaffe* was based on the use of tactical air power to serve the needs of the land battle; its bombers were planned to be the He 111, Do 17 and Ju 88, each armed with three machine-guns aimed by hand, and the Ju 87 dive-bomber.

Curiously enough, the supposed reactionary and decadent British, who did not take part in any war at all (except that many left-wing Britons individually joined Spain's International

The Westland F.29/27 was a more workmanlike design, and the massive gun was more sensibly aligned with the aircraft transverse axis. It is almost certain that, when this armament was being assessed, nobody thought how deadly it could be to bombers that were defenceless against attack from below, as were the RAF 'heavies' of the Second World War. Astonishingly, the idea that German night fighters might have upward-firing cannon was ridiculed, until a few bombers managed to get back and be examined.

Brigade), came to totally different conclusions. Unlike other nations, it established in 1925 an Observer Corps (later the Royal Observer Corps, ROC) which in the Second World War was to prove valuable beyond anyone's wildest dreams, by day and night. The RAF rightly judged that the highly loaded monoplane fighter with enclosed cockpit was the right answer, and bought two types carrying the unprecedented armament of eight machine-guns to be sure of getting enough hits in the brief periods enemy machines were thought likely to be in the fighter's sights. Bombers were planned not for mere close support in a land battle, but as strategic weapons to strike at enemy heartlands, with four engines and power-driven multi-gun turrets. Compared with their predecessors they were to be extremely bold and advanced aircraft. For example, while each square foot of wing of the Vickers Virginia, the standard RAF night bomber in the first half of the 1930s, supported a load of 8 lb, each square foot of wing of the Short Stirling, the first of the four-engined 'heavies' planned in 1936, had to support 48 lb. This meant that the new bombers would have to take off and land at much greater speeds. Instead of being gentle lightweights covered with fabric, warplanes were becoming heavy monsters with thick skins of metal. Operating such heavily loaded, high-speed aircraft at night was obviously going to pose major problems. Beyond doubt, airfields were going to change from being short boggy fields to huge tracts of land with 2,000yd (1.83 km) paved runways.

While these changes were coming about, with quite surprising suddenness in the late 1930s, small groups of research workers, scattered in little-known laboratories in different countries, were playing with scientific toys that were to revolutionize the whole of warfare and, later, man's ability to navigate by air and sea at night or in bad weather. These pioneers, whom a later generation would call 'boffins', were a mixed lot. Some were government employees. Some were postgraduate students at universities. Many worked for large industrial companies. A few were so eccentric or eminent that they worked completely alone, enveloped in a cocoon of their own deep thoughts. Some openly discussed their work, were eager to publish and to correspond with kindred spirits elsewhere. Others were aware that their work might have military importance, while many had to work under conditions of strict secrecy. But they were not by any means all doing similar things.

Anyone looking for ways to pierce a veil of darkness or bad weather naturally finds himself considering the human senses: touch, sight, hearing, smell and taste. He has to be equally fundamental in studying the classical branches of physics: heat, light, sound, magnetism and electricity. This was about the state of play in the years following the First World War, and it is interesting that none of the research was funded by any air force, or even – in most cases – by governments at all. Though with foresight they would have realized that they would be the greatest and most immediate beneficiaries, the world's armed forces showed virtually no interest in trying to see through darkness and bad weather until much later. Most of the basic groundwork was done by individuals or small groups primarily concerned with finding out for its own sake.

Some of them really did consider the human sensory inputs and wonder whether, in the absence of distant vision, any of the others might fill the gap. A great deal of effort was put into the use of sound, at first by building ever-better sound locators and, in some cases, by conducting experiments with reflection of sounds from distant objects. Until 1938 the sound locator was the chief non-visual directional tool of the world's anti-aircraft gunners. Most were merely slightly better versions of the locators used in the First World War by one or two fortunate units, with a planar array of exponential or conical horns to concentrate the incoming sound at microphones at their centres. In essence the converse of a loudspeaker, each horn might vary in size from a dustbin to the size of a delivery van. The most common arrangement was a vertical row of three plus a fourth displaced horizontally beside the middle horn, but some countries used locators with as many as sixteen receiver horns. The whole array could be rotated in azimuth (trained about a vertical axis) and elevated to the desired angle, until the received sound was at its most intense. The azimuth and elevation were then read, and telephoned and shouted to the accompanying searchlight. During the 1930s sound location was refined to the extent of coupling the locator pivots electrically with the searchlight, in what we now call a 'synchro', so that the light followed the locator automatically. By about 1936 the technically leading nations were going one step further and adding a 'predictor', a clumsy and very complicated mechanical computer to work out where the enemy aircraft would be by the time the AA shells reached it. In turn, the output from the predictor had to be translated into the correct azimuth and elevation of the AA gun barrel. Of course, because of the time of flight of the shell, which might be from 10 to 30 seconds, nothing could be done if the bomber pilot made unpredictable changes of course (as became standard practice over Germany in the Second World War). Sound location swiftly faded from the scene with the coming of radar, but not before some huge and novel schemes had been carried into effect.

Next to sound, heat was originally thought the most likely solution. Today we have a wealth of IR (infra-red) detectors of amazing fidelity, and nobody any longer bothers to put into a press release that a particular missile can home onto a cigarette-end ten miles away. In the early 1920s this was very far from being the case, and thermal detection systems were an uphill struggle. The idea is obvious. In a totally dark room we could still find our way to a hot object, even if it was not hot enough for any of its radiation to be visible. A night fighter carrying a modern directional IR detector could easily intercept anything emitting heat, such as an engine in another aircraft. Of course the detector has to be very sensitive. The received radiation falls away as the square of the distance, so at air-to-air ranges measured in miles or kilometres only a few parts in a billion of the heat emitted by the target ever reaches the detector. But this is due to fundamental mathematics that apply to all detection systems. They certainly apply to the system that swiftly came into ascendancy, the one now called radar.

Radio waves were discovered by Heinrich Hertz in 1886. Few people appeared to be very interested when he pointed out that they have many properties similar to those of visible light (which we now know to be an identical form of electromagnetic wave but having very much shorter wavelengths). In particular, Hertz showed that radio waves are reflected by metallic objects, and to a lesser degree by other solid surfaces. Another pioneer of electricity and radio, Nicola Tesla, wrote in 1900 that with radio waves 'we may determine the relative position or course of a moving object, such as a vessel at sea, the distance travelled by the same, or its speed'. Three years later young Christian Hülsemeyer of Düsseldorf suffered the sad fate of trying to push a brilliant invention long before the world was ready for it. He experimented with radar, tried to produce a compact workable system, gave it a name (Telemobiloscope) and took out patents. The British patent, filed on 10 June 1904, described the Telemobiloscope as 'Hertzian-wave projecting and receiving apparatus adapted to indicate or give warning of the presence of a metallic object such as a ship or a train . . .' His patents and ardent missionary work were met by a deafening silence. Nobody showed the slightest interest.

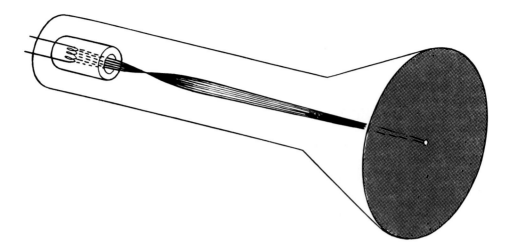

*Except in the latest radars, the basic device used to provide the display is the cathode-ray tube (CRT). A hot filament sends out a stream of electrons (cathode rays) which are focused by a magnetic field and made to impinge on a glass screen which is coated with a phosphor so that, when bombarded by the electrons, a glowing spot can be seen.*

In 1906 the Italian Artom and his pupils Bellini and Tosi devised a series of improved radio direction-finding (DF) systems, a relative of which was the one used by the German Navy Zeppelins in 1916. By the First World War a completely new and vital device was in production: the cathode-ray tube (CRT). This was essentially an almost evacuated glass flask containing a heated cathode at one end and a screen at the other. Electrons emitted from the cathode (so-called cathode rays) are focused by the magnetic field of anode coils into a fine beam which falls on the screen, causing the coating of the screen to fluoresce (see diagram above). Such a simple CRT would produce a bright spot at the centre of the screen, but adding two pairs of deflector plates to cause left/right and up/down deflection of the beam transforms the tube into a device at the heart of most radar systems. By feeding in signals to the deflector plates the beam can be made to paint successions of dots, dashes, lines or even (as in a TV set) pictures (see further diagrams opposite). In 1921 Dr Albert W. Hull, of the American colossus the General Electric Company, described a new kind of oscillator, basically a novel diode valve, which he called a magnetron. It could generate power at wavelengths measured in centimetres, whereas other radio devices could not operate at wavelengths shorter than metres. Hull and the magnetron will appear in a later chapter. In 1925 two more Americans, Drs Gregory Breit and Merle A. Tuve of the Carnegie Institute in Washington, took the idea of their compatriots Swan and Frayne and used it to measure the height of the ionosphere. This idea was pulse-ranging, in which the radio energy is sent out in very brief pulses separated by silent periods long enough for the reflected pulses to return and have their flight times measured.

Thus by 1925 there existed all the basic ingredients of modern radar. Indeed, workable systems could have been used in the First World War if anyone had given the matter any

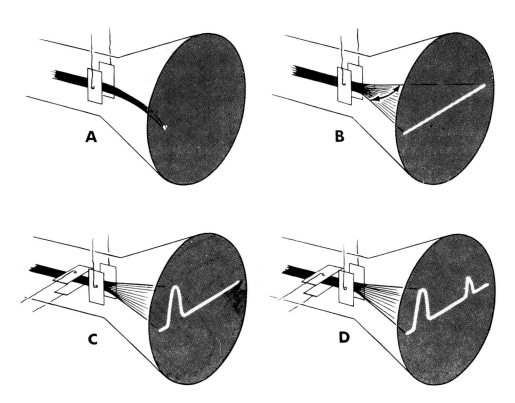

To make a simple radar the CRT is provided with two deflector plates (A) which, when an electrical voltage is applied, bend the beam. If a high-frequency signal is applied to these plates the beam is made to oscillate along a 'timebase', causing a bright line (B). If two further deflector plates are added, the beam can be deflected in the vertical plane. If these latter plates are connected to a receiver aerial then a large 'blip' will appear as each pulse of radar energy is sent out (C). If there is another aircraft in the sky ahead, a small portion of the pulse will be reflected back to the receiver aerial, causing a second blip at a point on the timebase corresponding to a known target range (D).

thought. Hülsemeyer had pestered the British Admiralty six years before the war broke out. His invention cannot have come to the ears of the great Sir Henry Jackson, who was probably the world's first user of radio when he introduced it to the Royal Navy (antedating Marconi) in 1895–6, and who as First Sea Lord in the First World War was eagerly on the lookout for new ideas in what today we call electronics. He knew Marconi, yet Marconi apparently never told him that radio can do more than just carry messages. Before the First World War the famous radio pioneer had noticed reflections from metallic objects, and yet he did not follow the matter up until, in 1922, he at last unburdened himself in a speech, saying, 'It seems to me it should be possible to design apparatus by means of which a ship could radiate or project a divergent beam . . . . reflected back to a receiver screened from the local transmitter on the sending ship and thereby immediately reveal the presence and bearing of the other ship in fog or thick weather . . .' Had Marconi, Tesla, Hülsemeyer or any other expert who understood the reflective properties of radio waves been consulted in the First World War there is no doubt that, before the end of that conflict, the Zeppelins, Gothas and Giants would have been utterly defeated. In the subsequent years of peace the incentive was lacking, and it was left to a few scattered workers to discover the same things all over again.

Possibly the first group positively to start research into radio detection was that under Dr A. Hoyt Taylor at the US Navy Radio Division at Anacostia (predecessor of the Naval Research Laboratory, founded in 1923). In September 1922, probably triggered by Marconi's recent speech, Taylor and Leo C. Young did experiments with 5 m (200 in) wavelength 'radar' and obtained startling results from a small wooden steamship. They wrote the Navy Bureau of Engineering an historic memo which, among other things, mentioned detection of aircraft. The report was filed and forgotten. But Taylor and Young kept picking away at the problem and in 1930, in the course of radio DF experiments, noticed reflections from aircraft and measured the range. The result was a second memo, *Radio Echo Signals from Moving Objects*, dated November 1930. This time it was not ignored. The US Army was brought in, and Colonel William R. Blair, who had for years been prodding a team trying to replace the sound locator by either a heat detector or radio waves, attacked the problem of aircraft detection with renewed vigour on the basis of the Navy report. His Signal Corps laboratories at Fort Monmouth, New Jersey, began working round the clock trying to build a radar not only using metre waves but also the much shorter (centimetric) waves now known as microwaves. These experiments, the first in the world on microwave radar, produced clear echoes from nearby targets (see diagram below). However, at that time there was no known way of generating microwaves except at extremely small powers, quite useless for practical purposes. Such waves could be generated by

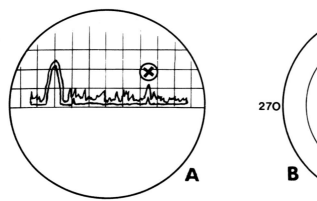
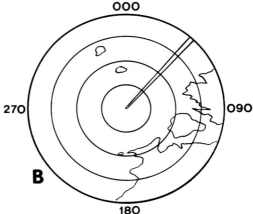

*The earliest radar displays had horizontal or vertical timebases giving target range or elevation (A). Instead of being a thin bright line, the timebase was invariably filled with 'clutter' reflected from many kinds of objects or caused by 'static' or other unwanted interference (it was called 'grass', because that is what it looked like). It was the operator's task to pick out real target blips, such as that at X. Later, in 1940, the British introduced a new display called a PPI (plan-position indicator). This had a circular or semi-circular display with the timebase visible as a rotating radial line of light (B). Each time it passed a target, a coastline, or any other reflective object, it left an illuminated area. The scene illustrated might be two islands or two aircraft as seen by one flying a mile or two offshore.*

various means, including Hull's magnetron, but it took until well into the Second World War before British workers achieved the vital breakthrough and generated high-power microwaves.

In 1933, while a team that could be counted on the fingers was toiling at Fort Monmouth, another team got into the act in the communications research department of the German Navy. This had nothing to do with the coming to power of the Nazis under Hitler, and the opening of the financial floodgates for new German armaments. It was simply the gradual belief, fostered in the mind of Dr Rudolph Kühnold, department head, that if sonar worked with acoustic waves under water, radio waves ought to do the same in the atmosphere. (Exactly the same idea occurred to King George V; after listening to an Admiralty lecture on Asdic and echo-sounding, he asked the speaker if the same thing could be done with radio waves against aircraft, receiving the reply that, so far as was known in 1931, it could not). Kühnold, knowing little of the wealth of prior work in the field, boldly plunged into the challenging field of microwaves. Late in 1933 he obtained a marvellous new magnetron valve from the Dutch Philips works at Eindhoven. It could generate 70 watts at 600 MHz, equivalent to a wavelength of about 0.5 metre, thousands of times more powerful than had previously been possible. A good radar was quickly made as a 'breadboard' (an untidy, non-portable laboratory lash-up), and in January 1934 the GEMA company was formed to accelerate this now highly secret work. By March 1934 a complete set was operating in a room overlooking Kiel harbour, with dish aerials on the balcony aimed at the old battleship *Hessen*. With a few changes to prevent the receiver from being flooded with radiation from the adjacent transmitter, the GEMA team got an excellent picture.

Work now went ahead fast, the GEMA team was moved to a bigger research establishment at Pelzerhaken, near Lübeck, and soon pulsed radars were giving good results against both ships and aircraft. By 1936 the GEMA team, now expanded to many hundreds, had the prototypes of two of the most important German radars of the Second World War. One was the big *Seetakt* gunnery radar for major surface vessels. So poor was British intelligence in 1938 that it did not notice the huge bedstead aerial of *Seetakt* on the three 'pocket battleships' and then on the battle-cruisers *Scharnhorst* and *Gneisenau*. The Royal Navy fondly believed itself the only navy to have heard of radar, even though it was not due to get the first British equivalent of *Seetakt* until 1941. The other GEMA set was even more important: it was a mobile land-based early-warning set for use against aircraft, with 360° cover and range up to an unprecedented 120 km (75 miles). Named *Freya*, after the Norse goddess, it went into large-scale production for the *Luftwaffe* and German Navy and was by far the most important German early-warning radar until the end of 1942.

Nor was this all. By 1936 the concept of radar had moved right out of the laboratory in Germany and become a weapon that could be specified and put into production. The *Luftwaffe*'s rapidly growing *Flak* (AA artillery) wanted an extremely accurate radar for blind gunfire at night or through cloud, to complement the superb guns it was receiving of 88, 105 and 128 mm calibre. The answer was a first-class set developed by Lorenz and Telefunken, the *Würzburg*, operating at about 0.5 metre on 560 or 570 MHz. Nowhere else in the world in 1937 was there a radar giving such good discrimination and precision, because nowhere else could one be made to operate with such power (8 kW) at such a high frequency and short wavelength. Indeed, special versions tested in 1938 generated a power of 50 kW. These were the best general-purpose mass-produced radars in the world before the Second World War. British intelligence never noticed the rotating dish aerials, nor did it detect the transmissions or get into helpful talk with the crews. In November 1939 a well-wisher gave a fat parcel to the British naval attaché in Oslo. Among masses of highly secret information it contained on German developments were details of the *Freya*, *Würzburg* and other radars, and of guidance beams used by the *Luftwaffe* to aid night bombers. The British authorities dismissed the report as a trick. True, the facts already known to them tallied; but that was to make Britain fall for the rest. Everyone knew the Germans had no radar!

This unbelievably smug attitude did not extend to the outstanding team working on radar in Britain. This team had many beginnings in many places, but it was drawn together in a sensible way by the not untimely belief, in 1934, that perhaps all was not well with Britain's air defences. There was no way of detecting hostile bombers at a distance; defending fighters had to fly exhausting 'standing patrols' where it was thought that the enemy might appear. The sole attempt to find a new method had been the construction on Romney Marshes, on the southern shore of Kent, of a 220-foot concrete 'sound intensifier' intended to pick up the sound of distant bombers (there was another, not far away, which was never finished). The Romney Mirror could just about do its job if the bombers were expected, and there was no background noise of birds or motor-boats. It could not, of course, say anything about the raiding force's height or range, numbers or direction; and the effective range varied from short to useless. The bombers also had to cooperate by approaching from the right direction. As in the early 1930s the only large bomber force on the local part of the Continent was French, the structure's axis was directed towards Paris. As the eventual 'father of radar' Sir Robert Watson-Watt put it, 'Reinforced concrete is rudely uncompliant to the winds of diplomacy.'

Nobody was really satisfied with the giant Romney Mirror, even in the days of slow bombers. One who appreciated the gravity of the situation was Harry Wimperis, the first Director of Scientific Research (DSR) at the Air Ministry in London. In June 1934 his Personal Scientific Assistant, A.P. Rowe, sought solace in researching the whole subject of science as applied to air defence. He was merely interested; he had not been asked to do this. He ultimately unearthed fifty-three files on the matter. Lest this should sound encouraging, there were at that time several times 53 *thousand* files in the Air Ministry on other topics; and many of the fifty-three contained mere brief letters or one-page memoranda. Rowe was deeply concerned. 'Clearly,' he concluded, 'little or no effort had been made to call on science to find a way out. I therefore wrote a memorandum summarizing the unhappy position, and proposing that the DSR should tell the Secretary of State for Air of the dangers ahead. The memorandum said that unless science evolved some new method of air defence, we were likely to lose the next war if it started within ten years. Unfortunately, I was not clever enough to think of a new method.'

When one reflects on the situation the mind boggles at how it could have come about. The need for a method of unfailingly detecting, locating, and tracking enemy aircraft had been clear and obvious from 1915 onwards. There surely appeared to be only a very limited range of possible methods, each derived from heat, light, sound, magnetism or electricity (accepting further that heat, light, magnetism and electricity are all manifestations of one of the most fundamental phenomena in the universe, the electromagnetic wave). Any bright schoolboy asked to think about the matter would have gone to see eminent physicists, radio and acoustics engineers, and the matter would have snowballed as each worker named others prominent in the same field. Within twenty-four hours our schoolboy would have heard of Hertz, and of the shoal of subsequent workers who had demonstrated the reflective properties of radio waves and patented Telemobiloscopes. He would hardly have been able to avoid discovering that as lately as 1932 four engineers researching VHF (very high frequency) radio for the Post Office had included in their large published report how cross they had been at interference from aircraft, describing the measured aircraft ranges and the way the beat-interference varied with the aircraft's speed. In 1933 Bell Telephone Laboratories in the United States published even more extensive observations. Yet here was Rowe, in June 1934, armed with the sum total of knowledge of the British Air Ministry still unaware of any of these things, yet feeling there must be a better way than a 220-foot 'sound mirror' made of concrete.

Wimperis read his report and in November 1934, after an unexplained wait of half a year, suggested to the Secretary of State that there should be a Committee for the Scientific Survey of Air Defence. The CSSAD was duly formed, but before its first meeting Wimperis telephoned a man who knew a lot about radio waves, Robert Watson-Watt, Superintendent of the Radio Department at the National Physical Laboratory at Teddington. Virtually the only new kind of air defence anybody could think of in 1934 was the 'death ray'. Since the First World War inventors had come to the British government at frequent intervals with paper proposals and even with secret black boxes promising wondrous things. Eventually the Air Ministry offered £1,000 cash (a fortune then) to anyone who could kill a sheep with such a box at 100 yards (91 m), the secret to remain with the owner. No sheep was so much as singed. But, not knowing what else to do, Wimperis asked Watson-Watt whether such a ray was possible. Again one is amazed that the Air Ministry had never asked before.

'Wattie' could merely have answered 'no'. But, having devoted a minute's thought to the problem, he could see that the first thing one had to do with a death ray was to ascertain the exact direction of the hostile aircraft. As the radio energy sent out would otherwise have to be millions to billions of times the energy hitting the target, knowing the latter's position was all-important. So the radio expert – while pointing out that in January 1935 there was no known way of generating sufficient radio energy at sufficiently short wavelength even 'to make the pilot's blood boil', let alone destroy a bomber – added that he had also considered the 'still difficult but less-unpromising problem of radio-detection as opposed to radio-destruction, and numerical considerations on the method of detection by reflected radio waves will be submitted if desired'. This unsolicited offer was the start of what is probably the biggest and most widespread revolution in the history of warfare.

Things moved fast. On 10 February Wimperis asked for the 'numerical considerations', and Watson-Watt and his colleague Arnold Wilkins worked them all out and submitted them in an historic memorandum dated 12 February 1935. The answer came out unexpectedly favourable – so much so that W-W wrote 'I am still nervous as to whether we have not got a power of ten wrong, but even that would not be fatal.'

In this document W-W described much of radar as it has existed up to the present day. He showed how the airframe of an aircraft (not just a metal-skinned one) would behave when flooded with short-wave radio energy as a conducting receiver aerial, and thus also as a transmitter. The observers on the ground would scan the skies with short-wave energy until they found a target; then, using techniques that the Radio Department had already devised, they would track it automatically and measure its range, bearing and height. W-W himself had many years previously invented an instantaneous-reading cathode-ray direction finder (CRDF), showing on a CRT the direction of a distant thunderstorm. There seemed to be no barrier to refining the technique to give immediate, and more accurate, 'radio location' of an aircraft, with two CRTs showing range, bearing and elevation (and thus height). Use of radio pulses would allow the transmitter valves to pump out enormously greater bursts of power, and could also assist range measurement. On the other hand, there was a technique of using continuous-wave (CW) radiation that would enable moving objects alone to be detected (so-called moving-target indication, MTI, which was eventually put to use long after the Second World War). By no means least, there was a need for an identification friend-or-foe (IFF) method, so that defenders would know when to shoot; this too, wrote Watson-Watt, could be provided.

In this document – as important to British history as Magna Carta – he described not just the basic underlying principles of radar, which had never before been set forth so comprehensively, but also the way a complete British defence system should be constructed, approximately how it would perform, and how the complete system – with communications to plotting centres and to fighter pilots, IFF and even enemy anti-radar countermeasures – would eventually function. Not the least thing about it was its air of total authority. Watson-Watt, in precise and official language, was describing techniques and often even existing hardware that he and his colleagues had devised, built and used. This was no 'mad inventor' with a harebrained and unexplainable secret, but a mature engineer with a proposal that was wholly valid, wholly explainable and capable of swift verification. By no means least, it was enormously encouraging; Watson-Watt promised, 'The amount of reflected energy you will get back is amazingly big.' How the whole thing seemed to an Air Staff previously barren and desolate of ideas can be imagined.

Within days Watson-Watt had seen the Air Member for Research and Development, Air Marshal Hugh (later Sir Hugh) Dowding. On 26 February a Handley Page Heyford bomber, with light-alloy structure covered by fabric, shuttled up and down a twenty-mile path, passing each time approximately over a very ordinary field in Northamptonshire. Unknown to the pilot, the Heyford was in the centre of the powerful short-wave Empire radio beam from the BBC radio station at Daventry. In the field was a huddle of figures. Watson-Watt, Wilkins and A.P. Rowe quietly watched a tiny stub of green light on a CRT grow longer and then shorter, as the bomber reflected back the radiation. With crude and hastily thrown-together equipment they were detecting the Heyford at a range of up to eight miles. As Watson-Watt drove Rowe back to London they discussed a future that seemed open-ended – if their country was granted enough time. From the fairly short-term possibility of early-warning over ranges of at least sixty miles, and possibly 200, could be derived short-range precision guidance for searchlights and guns, and possibly, one day, a radar that could be carried aloft in a fighter. But Watson-Watt, a frequent visitor to a Germany now ruled by the Nazis, did not think he could be sure of having more than two years to turn talk into reality.

It is commonly thought that British government circles, especially in 1935, either tended to take negative decisions or to put off taking any at all. This was emphatically not the case with radar. Though the first RAF exercise using the new invention, in September 1936, tended to throw up problems rather than successes, Britain was by this time officially 'sold' on a completely new defence system, had voted money for the start of an operational chain of five stations and was already building them. Basic construction was, in fact, the one thing that held the programme back and prevented good results. On the technical side there was a mixture of sheer brilliance and sheer luck. One of the lucky things was Watson-Watt himself: he was possessed of fantastic energy, drive and infectious enthusiasm that until 1945 sustained a pace of research that continually astonished his political masters. Another was that he did not think of his future hostile aircraft as small spheres (as many experts did) but as horizontal pieces of wire. His original calculation determined the current that would be induced in this wire from wing tip to wing tip, which not only gave an encouraging result but set the team working on a wavelength of 50 metres, twice a typical bomber wing span. Had he regarded aeroplanes as spheres he would have chosen a much shorter wavelength, and no good results would have been attained for years – by which time the Air Staff and government would have gone back to the fruitless chase after sound or heat detection, losing the Second World War before the end of 1940.

Another mix of luck and brilliance concerned the design of the hardware. There were an almost infinite number of ways of arranging a radar station, and the team that was eventually set up as Air Ministry Research Establishment (AMRE) at Bawdsey Research Station, on the remote Suffolk coast, hardly put a foot wrong. Sticking at first to the long 50 m wavelength, they designed each station to be monostatic, serving as a self-contained transmitter and receiver. Watson-Watt hit on a brilliant method of using multiple crossed dipole aerials so that each station could determine the exact direction of each target, with a PPI (plan-position indicator) giving its immediate bearing. The team's already existing CRDF was a godsend in giving the necessary background of experience. Each station did not send out a directional beam, which would have had to rotate like a lighthouse, but behaved like a floodlight, pumping out pulses in all directions; eventually 90 per cent went outwards, out over the sea. Special circuits indicated whether a target was in front or behind. With some difficulty, bothered at first by the Earth's surface and some unexpected reflections from the lower parts of the ionosphere, it became possible very accurately to measure elevation angle and thus target height. By mid-1936 all the elements could be said to work, when properly set up and calibrated by experts – though not when used by anyone else, a feature that was long characteristic of this new, secret and often amazing invention, the first and greatest creation of the select race soon to be called 'boffins'.

At first all the emphasis went into the emergency building of this single chain, like a modern castle wall round the British south and east coast. Its original name was RDF (radio direction finding, a plausible cover), later changed to radiolocation (which revealed what it did) and in January 1944 standardized with the United States as the name by which the world knows it today, radar. This initial chain used 240- and 320-foot towers serving fantastically powerful transmitters, made mainly by Metropolitan-Vickers and containing huge valves devised by HM Signals School at Portsmouth. To the latter's horror, Bawdsey ran the filaments far too hot, pumped in more than double the voltage, and instead of the rated power of 10 kW pushed the output by stages to almost 200 kW! Combined with the equally rapid progress with the receiver, made chiefly by Cossor, the 1936 RDF station could detect aircraft at well over one hundred miles, at any attainable altitude, and indicate whether the 'blip' (the small spike of light denoting the target) was a single aircraft, two, three, or more than three. (By 1940 girls of the WAAF had become so expert they could even give a reliable approximation of the strength of a large formation.) The only obvious shortcoming was that the system could be jammed. In early 1938 Bawdsey's E.C. Williams flew offshore in the prototype Sunderland flying boat, then on trials at Felixstowe, sending out powerful waves of interference from a modified hospital diathermy apparatus. Within days his colleagues were making the first operational radar in the world resistant to jamming – the start of the mighty science of ECM, electronic countermeasures. By this time the 50 m waves had been halved in length, and four separate frequencies could be chosen by each station to defeat hostile ECM.

While this 'RDF 1' went from strength to strength, Watson-Watt – many said Sir Henry Tizard thought of it – lost little time in beginning 'RDF 2'. His reasoning, immediately backed up by Tizard, was so obvious it might have been overlooked. He had no doubt RDF 1 would do its job. By giving early warning and location of every enemy raid it would, when combined with a proper reporting and control organization, eliminate the need for standing patrols and enable every available fighter to make a sure interception – something that had never before been possible. It would enable the day raider to be defeated, which was just what the Air Staff had been trying to do for twenty years. So what would happen next? Why, the enemy would come only in foul weather or by night. Day fighters could not even fly safely under such conditions. Even if they could, they could no longer make a sure interception and get the enemy in their sights. So RDF 2 was a project to put a radar set in a fighter. Compared with RDF 1 it was several times more difficult.

RDF 1 sent out giant pulses from an aerial system about as big as a football field, supported by huge towers. To provide the energy, a transmitter about as big as a house took as much current as a small town, and the reflected pulses were picked up by an equally large receiver manned by a team of experts. All this was a bit much to put inside a fighter. It obviously meant starting again on a shorter wavelength and, somehow, slashing the weight to turn tons into pounds. It was indeed a formidable undertaking.

# THREE

# YEARS OF CRISIS

Fortunately for Britain, Watson-Watt's 1935 guess of two more years of peace proved to be pessimistic by 100 per cent. But from the Prime Minister – who in 1932 had publicly proclaimed, 'The bomber will always get through; the only defence is in offence' – down to the general public, they were years of ever-heightening fear and tension. Instead of France, the nation's likely enemies emerged with increasing clarity as Germany and Italy, both of them totalitarian régimes bent on building up armed forces, and especially aerial forces, of unchallengeable might. Both openly scorned the democracies of Britain and France. 'I saw them at Munich,' said Hitler, 'they are little worms.' They were encouraged by the prevailing wish in those countries to appease the two dictators, not to stir up trouble, and in particular to hold back expenditure on armaments. In contrast, a desperately worried minority urged that time was precious.

In fifty aircraft plants across France a chaotic attempt was being made to re-equip the *Armée de l'Air*, with a massive effort being made in the newly nationalized factories at the expense of the remaining private sector. Dozens of different types of warplane were under development, backed up by panic buying from other countries (especially the United States) on a scale never dreamed of since 1918. Most of these aircraft suffered from major deficiencies in design, equipment or timing, and even by May 1940 the *Armée de l'Air* could offer little inconvenience to the *Luftwaffe*. In Britain there were fewer programmes, better planning and, by no means least, two really formidable types of day fighter had been put into production just early enough for them to be available in large numbers when they were desperately needed. At least as important was the sure growth of the first RDF chain from the south-east of England up to the tip of Scotland and westward to the Isle of Wight, a task which was complete by the outbreak of war in September 1939. This 'Chain Home' (abbreviated to CH) was complete with filter centres to sort out possibly hundreds of good or misleading blips, and pass the ground controllers nothing but reliable information on attacking forces. Invaluable exercises, on an increasingly large scale, sorted out a myriad of problems, and made the world's first modern electronically based defence system actually work in practice. It required the training of uniformed crews and staff, adding gap-filler radars where (for various technical reasons) the CH 'floodlighting' was incomplete, tightening and refining the control and reporting procedures, and showing the day-fighter pilot that he could rely on the guidance of the ground controller.

Creating this air-defence system was far and away the biggest advance ever made in defeating the day raider. But even this impressive system was practically useless at night – though this was a matter of the detail, not the technology. The basic concept of Watson-Watt, called successively RDF, radio-location and radar, worked equally well by day or night. But the CH system actually built had rather coarse limitations in discrimination and plotting accuracy. It was ideal for giving early warning of hostile aircraft, and for giving their present and likely future position accurately enough for defending fighters to be vectored by ground controllers to within five miles, and with luck to within two or three miles, and within about a mile (say, 5,000 feet) of the same height. By day this was good enough; there was never to be a single occasion in the Battle of Britain when RAF fighters were to be vectored on to the enemy and fail to make contact. But at night a miss was as good as a mile. Knowing the enemy – not a formation at night, but a single bomber – was within five miles, and possibly within two, was merely frustrating. The night fighter had no means of knowing in which direction to search, and experience was to show that a skilled and experienced pilot could spend an hour within five miles of a known E/A (enemy aircraft), and even accompany it on its bombing run across the target and see its bombs explode, and still have no idea whether it was one mile ahead or five, or to left or right, or above or below. Moreover, CH blips were insufficiently accurate to be much help to searchlights or AA guns.

This again was because of the nature of the CH surveillance fence. From the start, in 1935, Watson-Watt had pointed out how useful a radar of shorter wavelength would be to tell searchlights, AA guns and many other kinds of artillery exactly where to point, and in a relatively slow and uphill struggle the Army and Royal Navy were eventually persuaded to get into the radar business. But the abiding problem of effective night air defence was just as insoluble as it had been before 1935, except for the vital fact that a method of solving it completely had been sketched in broad outline. The answer might be to cover the nation with some form of radar working on the shortest possible wavelength – only a small fraction of 50 m – to provide precise angular data on individual aircraft for night fighters, searchlights and AA guns. Alternatively, and possibly not capable of early attainment, radar might be developed that could be installed in fighter aircraft, so that they could themselves hunt down enemy bombers in the night sky. In the event, both schemes were proceeded with; but it was the second, called RDF.2 and later AI (airborne interception) radar, that led to the modern night fighter.

Before describing how the first night fighters were developed, it is worth recalling what types of fighter the RAF bought during these critical years. Even the briefest study suggests that perhaps something was amiss with the Air Ministry's procurement machine. No fewer than sixty fighter designs were submitted, and eighteen types of fighter actually built, yet nowhere could one find any attention being paid to the problem of defence by night. The traditional 'night fighter' continued to mean a fighter that carried cockpit lighting and flares. Some advances were made in aircraft armament, the standard for a single-seat fighter being improved from two machine-guns to four, and finally, in 1936, to eight. Much attention was also given to the development of two-seat fighters with trainable guns in a turret. This stemmed from the open-cockpit Demon (Turret), a 175 mph biplane, deliveries of which began in 1936(!). This led in 1935 to the development of two-seat turret-equipped monoplanes, the Boulton Paul Defiant being selected for use. In the same year of 1935 plans were laid to buy a twin-engined fighter (specification F.37/35), which ultimately entered limited service in early 1941 as the Westland Whirlwind. Its one good feature was that in the nose were four 20 mm Hispano cannon. In 1937 another twin appeared, the Gloster F.9/37, with either one or two seats and radial or liquid-

*In 1937 the RAF's latest night fighter was the Hawker Demon, modified to provide the gunner with a Lewis gun mounted on a Frazer-Nash 'lobsterback' turret – and with a flame-damping exhaust pipe!*

cooled engines. Yet none of these fighters had any relevance to night fighting. Though it was too early to try to anticipate the size, weight and electric power consumption of the eventual RDF.2, it would have seemed prudent to procure an aircraft having the power and performance to become a good radar-carrying night fighter in the course of time. No such aircraft was ordered. By sheer luck, two aircraft companies chose to build such machines in the absence of any official interest, not appreciating quite how useful their products would turn out.

Of course, it is possible that the Air Staff and the experts who drafted fighter specifications had never heard of RDF.2, though as this was being discussed with senior officers by October 1936 this is unreasonable. It is more likely that, in the vital years 1937–9, airborne radar was regarded almost as pie in the sky, and unlikely to be achieved in the foreseeable future – though a chat with Ted Bowen would soon have put that right. Dr E.G. Bowen, now in Australia, had been one of the original team working with Watson-Watt even before setting up shop at

Bawdsey. RDF.2 landed in his capable lap. He knew at a glance he could not use CH stations as a starting point. These took their power from the National Grid, had aerials hundreds of feet across, sent out gigantic pulses of energy and received the return signals at aerials some hundreds of feet distant. Fighters come smaller, with more limited power supplies. For a start, Bowen decided to repeat the historic first experiment of Watson-Watt and illuminate a target with a ground source; he thought he could at least fly a receiver.

Again the aircraft involved was an ungainly Heyford. It was made even more incongruous by a large dipole aerial between the spatted wheels. In early March 1937 its Kestrel engines were droning off the Essex coast, near a powerful ground transmitter emitting pulses on a wavelength of 7 metres. Inside was intense concentration. Bowen and a colleague were getting blips which occasionally could be assigned to targets visible below. But a useful RDF.2 seemed as far away as the four-minute mile at that time. Only with painful slowness did the tiny handful of brilliant workers find a way to make a self-modulating transmitter, working at about 1 metre with pulses peaking at over 95 watts. On 16 August 1937 the complete installation, the world's first airborne radar, flew in one of the earliest Ansons, K6260. Results were exciting, especially against ships. For some months the effort was directed mainly at ASV (air-to-surface vessel) radar, at least partly because in this field it seemed easier to get useful hardware.

Not until early 1938 did RDF.2 make much progress, and by this time it was known as AI (airborne interception) radar, to distinguish the air-to-air equipment from ASV. Bowen's team still could be counted on the fingers: king of the receiver was Dr A.G. Touch, while the aerial installation was the task of Robert Hanbury Brown. Their problems were enormous, but at least they now had a clear idea of what they were trying to do. The attractive idea of a lighthouse-type rotating aerial, serving alternately as transmitter and receiver, could not unfortunately be made small enough (though during the war it was, with the new technology of microwaves). Instead the pulses were emitted from a dipole array projecting ahead, whence they departed as spherical waves that illuminated the whole sky ahead and the ground below. If a single receiver aerial had been fitted, accurately switched off just as each pulse was being emitted, a good CRT display would give target range. But Bowen put a receiver aerial well out on each wing, with a high-speed commutating switch that connected first one and then the other to the receiver. By reversing the voltage from one aerial it was possible to generate a blip on each side of the central timebase. If the two blips were of equal length, the signal strength was the same at each aerial; if not, the target was nearer to the aerial giving the stronger blip, giving a rough idea of whether to steer left or right. A further pair of aerials, above and below the wing, were likewise made to give an idea of whether the target was at a greater or lesser altitude than the airborne radar.

It was actually a lot more complicated than this. Perhaps the most basic problem was plain lack of transmitter power, and AMRE staff appear not to have visited US General Electric, Philips at Eindhoven or any other laboratory where relatively high powers were being achieved. But British industry now came increasingly into the AI picture, and in late 1938 GEC's (the British General Electric Company, no relation to US General Electric) Hirst Laboratories at Wembley came up with a robust thermionic valve that gave adequate power on the usefully short wavelength of 1.5 metres. By this time several rudimentary AI radars had flown in the Anson and Heyford, both aircraft also carrying auxiliary petrol-driven generator sets supplying at least 1 kW on a relatively stable frequency. Probably the best set was that in the Anson, and this had from the start given accurate ranges and directions on ships at distances of several miles. But aircraft targets were much more difficult, and to see an aircraft blip at all was an achievement. The lower the carrying aircraft flew, the closer came the all-swamping signal of the direct pulse reflected from the ground beneath. Neither the Heyford nor the Anson often climbed above 10,000 feet, so in the AI role nothing could be seen beyond this distance; 5,000 feet was a more common maximum. Because of the need to isolate the receiver from its aerials as each pulse was emitted, nothing could be seen at ranges nearer than about 1,000 feet. Bowen had an impossible dream of a much shorter wavelength and much greater power, giving pin-sharp pulses and the ability to focus the emissions ahead, avoiding the ground reflection.

As 1939 began, and the international scene tottered from bad to worse, construction proceeded apace on a radar good enough to be given an official designation: AI Mk I. It was still very far from an optimized design, but it was expected to prove a useful research tool. Had 'the balloon gone up' it would even have gone to war – though it would probably have done more harm than good by suggesting to influential people that AI was quite useless. At this time the first of many arguments began about who would work the AI set, and who would look into the CRT scope (which had now grown a long rubber viewing hood to exclude outside light). Watson-Watt, who had worked among pilots ever since he had been at Farnborough in 1915, could see no reason why the man to work the set and study its picture should not be the pilot. Pilots were the people who steered the aircraft, so why interpose additional links in what was likely to be a tenuous and difficult chain of guidance? The argument grew, and when AI Mk I was ready for flight no decision had been taken. The carrier was a Fairey Battle light bomber, proving that there was no difficulty in fitting AI into a single-engined aircraft. So that a boffin or VIP visitor could see what was being displayed, the CRT scopes were installed in the rear cockpit. There was ample room for the transmitter, receiver, power pack and other items in the wing bomb cells and bomb-aimer's prone position in the fuselage.

This installation flew on 21 May 1939 – by when the sands of time had all but run out. Here for the first time was a really useful AI radar, able to detect aircraft at ranges as great as the height (which reached 17,000 feet) and down to about 900 feet. Though nobody yet realized that this kind of installation could lie convincingly, the two CRT viewing scopes gave what seemed to be clear left/right and up/down indications, or in more proper terms azimuth and elevation. In July Dowding, who had been appointed AOC-in-C Fighter Command, gave the set a good air test and landed feeling that this equipment could be as important as the CH chain. So too did many other 'top brass' who flew in the draughty Battle, as well as Sir Henry Tizard and Professor Lindemann (later Viscount Cherwell, Churchill's top defence scientist throughout the coming war). But on the matter of who did what, Dowding had no doubt. AI radar should be carried in a big twin-engined machine and managed by an *ad hoc* member of the crew. This was a decision of profound importance. In the context of the time, it was unquestionably right. A Spitfire could not have carried early AI equipment, and its busy pilot would merely have found the scope frustrating. There were many other snags, including the need for a night-fighter pilot never to look at anything bright if he could avoid it (the Air Ministry were even worried about luminous watches). But in the long term I believe the policy was continued long after good single-seat AI installations had been not merely developed but amply proved in combat, by the US Navy.

There was thus only one sensible carrier. In October 1938 the Air Ministry belatedly recognized that there might be a need for a long-range escort fighter with two engines. Lord

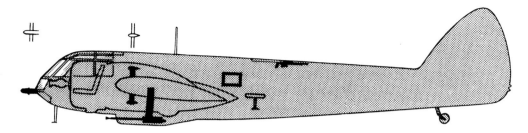

*Bristol Blenheim IF with AI III; four fixed .303-inch Browning and one stowed Vickers K (Turret shown replaced by gunner's hatch). Insets show aerial plan views.*

Dowding told me this was principally because of the existence of the Messerschmitt Bf 110, which required a response. It ordered an emergency 'crash programme' to convert Bristol Blenheim light bombers as the only suitable aircraft available. Even this, be it noted, had nothing at all to do with night fighting. In 1938 the Blenheim was still regarded as a modern machine of outstanding performance; it could, for example, easily overtake the Gladiator single-seat biplane fighter, which had entered service only the previous year and was fast becoming the RAF's main day (and night) fighter. Contracts were placed with the Southern Railway's Ashford (Kent) works for an eventual total of over 1,300 gun packs, each containing four of the reliable Browning machine-guns which had been designed in the United States as a 0.300 in calibre weapon in 1916, used in the First World War, adopted by the Air Ministry in 1934 (in the absence of any modern British gun) and put into production by the BSA company following a licence agreement of July 1935. The four-gun pack for the Blenheim was bolted on under the bomb bay, in which were stored the four belts of ammunition each containing 500 rounds, amply meeting the requirement for twenty seconds' continuous firing (see drawing above). The railway workers met every tight schedule imposed upon them, and also delivered several other items making up each aircraft kit. Other companies supplied the reflector sights and extra armour to give some frontal protection. The first contract was for kits to convert 200 Mk I Blenheims into the Mk IF fighter, and these began to enter service in December 1938 with No. 25 Squadron. Later contracts covered the conversion of the long-nosed Mk IV into the IVF. These makeshift long-range fighters were among the busiest aircraft in the RAF during the first two years of war.

Had the conversion not been ordered it is difficult to see what aircraft might have been used to carry the first operational AI radar installations. By 1939 the AI Mk I, with its heterogenous assortment of hand-fitted parts and wiring, which made no attempt to comply with any airworthiness standard, had been replaced by AI Mk II, which was broadly similar but was a properly designed installation which had been 'productionized' and improved by industrial firms. Main contractor for the transmitter was Metropolitan-Vickers, while the receiver was made by Pye (the chassis was based on a commercial TV set). A main subcontractor was A.C. Cossor. The installation weighed about 600 lb, and exerted only a slight detrimental effect on the Blenheim's performance. At high power settings an AI-fitted Blenheim could usually reach 250 mph without trouble, which was ample to overhaul a lumbering Heinkel. On the other hand, it was much too slow to catch a Ju 88 that had become jittery and 'poured on the coals';

even a cruising Ju 88 or Do 17 was hard to overtake. One felt that lack of a properly designed long-range or night fighter was something that might have been avoided.

The Blenheim was before the author's time, though as a cadet he twice sampled them as a passenger. Inside there was a distinct absence of room, which must have been worse with radar fitted. The pilot sat on the left of the nose, his seat, instrument panel and controls filling exactly half the width of the fuselage. If a dual instructor station was added on the right, the two pilots rubbed elbows. Most of the nose structure comprised twenty flat Perspex panes, which reflected illuminated items in the cockpit and interfered with external night vision. The highly rated Mercury engines were reliable, and seldom put the pilot in the rather marginal position of having to go round again on one, with landing gear and flaps down. Behind the pilot, facing aft, the AI operator fiddled with his box of tricks and tried to get intelligible blips so that he could tell the pilot which way to steer (he had to remember which way he was looking and not muddle left and right). In an AI chase he had no time to clear stoppages with the guns or do anything but look into his viewing hood, which was retained even though it was dark in the middle of a Blenheim at night. Usually a third man, the observer, was also carried; he manned the turret, with a Vickers K gun, and tried to live up to his name.

The world's first radar-equipped night fighters resulted from a secret minute from the Air Staff dated 17 July 1939, calling for the fitting of radar to twenty-one Blenheim IF long-range day fighters 'as quickly as possible'. The document continued, 'A requisition is enclosed incurring an expenditure of approximately £4,650 to cover AI transmitters, receivers and associated equipment.' (Though the comparison could hardly be more meaningless, twenty-one AI radars in the year 2000 would be likely to cost something over £10 million, provided they were already in full production.) The AI II sets were delivered quickly by Pye and Metrovick, and much of the material needed for installation was bought by local purchase by the RAE at Farnborough, which did the installation with the help of engineers from Bawdsey. AMRE itself was being torn apart ready for emergency evacuation, in a badly planned way, to Dundee and other locations.

Despite this upheaval, AI staff were able to help at Farnborough, and deliveries of improved Blenheims began to 25 Squadron on 31 July 1939. When the Second World War began on

*The world's first radar-equipped night fighters to become operational were Blenheim IFs, fitted with AI Mk II. This example, Bristol-built K7159, was photographed on 8 September 1941 while serving as a trainer with 54 OTU.*

3 September a total of fifteen aircraft had been delivered, and the last of the twenty-one was in service by the end of September. All these aircraft had a much more sensible interior arrangement. The useless dorsal turret was removed and replaced by a hatch. In theory a Vickers K machine-gun could be fired from this for rear defence, but I cannot imagine this ever being done. The important thing is that removal of the turret enabled the bulky and heavy radar to be moved aft to preserve the aircraft's centre of gravity in the correct place. Its viewing scopes could now face aft, so the operator no longer had to think in terms of mirror images before giving directions to the pilot. There was no longer a need for a third crew-member.

In November 1939 three of these Blenheims were delivered to a special flight of 600 (County of London) Squadron, Auxiliary Air Force, at Manston. Here they did special trials, in addition to crew training, and in early 1940 formed the nucleus of the Fighter Interception Unit (FIU), which grew rapidly and built up a collection of many kinds of fighter in its task of solving every sort of interception problem. Other early Blenheim night fighters were issued in ones and twos to existing Blenheim IF squadrons, beginning with 25, 29, 141, 601 and 604. The RAF grapevine buzzed with talk of 'Magic Mirrors' – talk which, as is traditionally the case with new RAF equipment, became slightly soured. The Magic Mirrors were difficult to use, and results in training flights varied from poor to non-existent. A basic snag was that the target was seen, if it was detected at all, in a position relative to the aerials on the fighter. If the fighter banked, the apparent target position moved in response, and it was eventually judged that ordinary Blenheim crews would have little success unless their aircraft was flying straight and level. Another of the many problems was that, unless the target was within a 20° cone ahead of the fighter, the aerials gave ambiguous indications; for example, the target could be to the upper left, or at the same angle to lower right. It was also impossible to get clear indication unless target range was between 5,500 and 1,200 feet, and the equipment was almost useless at heights below 8,000 feet because of the ground return. From the start of the war low-flying aircraft, mainly He 115 seaplanes, had laid mines by night in the Thames estuary and elsewhere round the coast. Early AI radar was completely useless in trying to intercept them, though some crews tried to spiral down from directly above. Bearing in mind that most crews were not very experienced, and still found it hard to add two and two correctly while trying to navigate on a pitch-black night, it is easy to see that successful radar interceptions even at high altitude proved consistently elusive.

By October 1939 some of the difficulties had been at least partly rectified with AI Mk III, which had first flown in August. This had similar circuitry but a new aerial system which gave fewer ambiguity problems. The transmitter sent its pulses from a pair of swept-back dipole aerials, looking like a harpoon, on the Blenheim's nose. Two similarly inclined dipole aerials well aft on one wing picked up reflections from the target and sent them to the elevation circuitry to show whether the target was above or below. Two pairs of plain vertical dipoles on the outboard wing leading edges did the same to indicate azimuth, left or right. The different signal strengths received in the various aerials made the bright blips grow longer or shorter, and displaced above or below, or to left or right, of the time-base centrelines on the observer's display scopes. It still took a long time to get repeatable and reliable operation, or to interpret the indications correctly.

On 14 February 1940 an Air Ministry appreciation tried to look on the bright side: 'In the general disappointment over the behaviour of AI Mk II and III it is possible that the limited but very real advantages of this equipment have been overlooked.' The implication is clear: there were influential people incapable of seeing beyond the existing situation who were calling for AI radar to be abandoned as useless. Had they won the day it would have been serious for Britain, and later for the United States.

After the original crash programme to equip twenty-one Blenheims with AI Mk II, all AI installation was done by 32 Maintenance Unit at RAF St Athan, Glamorgan (South Wales). St Athan was a large base, and the arrangement was at first ideal because, after a disastrous few weeks in Dundee, AMRE was again moved, to St Athan. Here more than sixty Blenheims were fitted with AI Mk III during the first six months of 1940. All stripping out, rewiring and preparation with brackets and aerials was done at St Athan, but many of the aircraft were actually fitted with the transmitter and receiver at FIU, which moved from Manston to Tangmere. FIU organized training courses for aircrew, and the handful of crews that could claim to be proficient began the practice of continually visiting the operational squadrons. Night fighting was a new technique, which made the most severe demands on crews. More than

*A 'second-generation' night fighter, in that it was fitted with AI Mk VI, the Boulton Paul Defiant was too much equipment for the airframe. This example, DZ-V of 151 Sqn, is seen with the turret fairings (and, unusually, the rear ventral radio mast) retracted.*

in any previous type of warfare, the problems, the techniques and the equipment never stayed the same but were constantly changing. Later, from 1941 onwards, experienced night-fighter crews were often taken aback by visiting FIU teams who treated them like raw pupils (which is what they soon discovered they really were). One of the RAF's abiding deficiencies was a three-seat night fighter for proper training in radar interception techniques. With the Beaufighter an FIU man would have to squat behind the pilot or observer, though there was at least plenty of room. With the Mosquito only two could get on board, so half the crew had to stay behind.

Throughout the Phoney War and the campaigns in Norway and France there was only sporadic night activity over Britain. There was thus no desperate pressure to get the night interception business really sorted out, but in between the frantic efforts in other fields a lot of good work was done. One of the obvious fundamental questions was, 'Can AI radar be carried by a single-seater?' I have always believed that the RAF committed an error of considerable magnitude in giving a generally negative answer to this question until well into the 1950s, but I am just being wise after the event. At the time, the possibilities were far from obvious. AI was bulky and heavy, and the aerials increased drag, all degrading aircraft performance. The extra electric load on the engine-driven generator degraded performance still further. One of the first aircraft studied, after the Blenheim, was the Defiant two-seater, powered by a Merlin and carrying as its sole armament four Brownings in a power-driven turret. The turret could be slewed so that the guns pointed dead ahead, when they were fired as fixed armament by the pilot. This automatically coupled in synchronizing gear, and the muzzle flash blinded the pilot at night (nobody thought much about night fighting when the Defiant was planned in 1935–6). Compared with a Hurricane, the Defiant was heavier and had a smaller wing, so it was a poor performer in combat. Its one asset was that the gunner could drive his guns quickly on target with a control stick, with a firing button on top, and once or twice Defiants flying in formation did achieve successes, due mainly to the fact that the *Luftwaffe* thought they were Hurricanes. In the day-time Battle of Britain they were recognized for what they were, and hacked down; survivors were relegated to night fighting – with radar or without. In fact it was without, because, after spending fourteen weeks on the problem, the RAE at Farnborough issued a report on 2 May 1940 confirming that it was impossible to fit the Defiant with radar.

This deeply considered conclusion was unfortunately accepted at face value, and it strongly influenced Air Staff policy. Discussions on the subject with Sydney Camm at Hawker Aircraft and Joe Smith at Supermarine were brief and not enthusiastic. It was mainly because of pressure from Pye and Metrovick that, during the first ten days of July 1940 (when night raiding over Britain had become more than sporadic), a standardized AI installation was schemed for single-seat fighters, with the transmitter dipoles on the outer right wing, elevation receiver aerials on the left, and azimuth aerials on each side of the forward fuselage. The pilot would have had a single az-el (azimuth-elevation) scope. Total installed weight was estimated at 202 lb (100 kg), and the extra electrical load and aerial drag were calculated to reduce top speed by 10 mph. With hindsight I think this should have been pressed ahead with all speed, if only to see what problems emerged, but at that time nothing was done. On 17 July Dowding, by now AOC-in-C Fighter Command, wrote, '. . . a pilot cannot look into a brightly illuminated tube and retain the night-adapted vision . . . I suggest that GEC or EMI be asked to develop an AI set for use in single-seater fighters on a very short wavelength so that the aerials may be as small as possible.' Reasonable enough, but I cannot find any record of any action being taken. Part of the trouble was that single-seat fighters tended to have very short endurance; indeed, the British concept of an interceptor was that it climbed steeply up to an enemy bomber, shot it down and returned. Another problem was that fighter pilots were not used to flying in bad weather or at night, and this influenced the thinking of almost everyone involved, especially at FIU.

During that long, hot summer of 1940 hundreds of night missions were flown over southern England with AI radar, many of them in the face of the enemy. Success was conspicuously absent, and combat reports tended to revolve around all the usual snags: 'low oil pressure . . . ASI u/s . . . had to switch off right engine . . .', plus 'hopeless intercom' (now of vital importance to get near the enemy at all) and new ones peculiar to night fighters: 'severe shock as I touched the firing button', and 'interception abandoned when the AI set started to burn'. In the first of five interceptions on the moonlit night of 18 June the pilot of a Blenheim who had seen an enemy bomber visually was shot dead by a short burst from the Heinkel's dorsal gunner. Five He 111s were downed on that night, but all by day fighters; nearly all the *Luftwaffe* losses on those summer nights were caused by Spitfires, and a few Hurricanes, which went up hoping to catch someone held in a searchlight beam. Then at last, on 22/23 July, a Do 17 was shot down after a true AI-directed interception. The Blenheim was flown by F/O Ashfield, with P/O Morris as observer and Sergeant Leyland as AI operator. Ashfield's combat report was tantalizingly brief, commenting in one sentence on how they were hit by debris from their victim and then discovered that they were at a low altitude in an inverted attitude.

Could a crew of three really get upside down without being aware of it? The answer is, emphatically yes; an AI chase took every atom of one's conscious attention. Irrespective of whether the AI operator had clear unambiguous blips or a maddening flickering fuzz, trying to decipher the true position of the target and pass steering commands to the pilot was more than a full-time job. There was no chance of attending to anything else. It was the simplest thing in the world to make one's gyro instruments topple, and in the cold, clinical concentration of closing for the kill I almost believe a wing could come off and not be noticed.

In the midst of all the excitement the few really great brains involved were always able to spare a moment to take a broad look at the problem. It was Tizard who made sure that one point of fundamental importance was not overlooked. In May 1940, in writing an appraisal of the use of AI radar, he commented, 'We have insufficiently considered its use by day, especially in cloudy weather.' Tizard never ceased to prod the Air Ministry into giving the most careful consideration of every new idea that was not openly ridiculous. By 1940 sound location was fortunately dead, but infra-red (heat) methods were very much alive, and an IR detector was flight-tested. The brightest IR team was led by young Dr R.V. Jones at the Clarendon Laboratory, Oxford. Director of the famed Clarendon was none other than Lindemann, whose antipathy for Tizard was equalled only by Tizard's for him; as Tizard had for over twenty years been the only rival to Lindemann's claim to be most senior defence scientist, the problem may be self-evident. Watson-Watt managed to sidestep political feuding, to his own and radar's benefit. It was Tizard who suggested that Jones might leave the Clarendon, though in 1937 his IR detector had sensed other aircraft at a range of just over 1,500 feet, and was easier to package and use than AI radar. Maybe Tizard was gifted with foresight to see that IR would for many years to come be thrown off the scent by fires on the ground, by the Sun and even by sunlight reflected from lakes and rivers. It was almost certainly a correct decision in 1937 to drop IR detection, though the technique returned in the 1950s, as will later be related.

Other techniques included searchlights and aerial mines, as well as an increasingly long list of impractical suggestions helpfully sent in by the public. As noted earlier, use of as obvious an idea as the airborne searchlight simmered during the First World War (but was never actually used) and emerged again with the sudden mushrooming of air defence in the late 1930s. Most of the airborne-searchlight effort prior to the outbreak of the Second World War comprised paper studies and argument, whereas reason suggests that it would have been more sensible to do a few cheap experiments and see if the idea worked. Instead, little or nothing was done until the night blitz was actually hitting the country in the closing months of 1940, as will be recorded in the next chapter. The same is true of almost all the other ideas, including mines. It was even true with the fundamental fact of how far a night-fighter pilot might be expected to see at night. This highly variable factor was self-evidently one that demanded the most carefully designed scientific research in an attempt to get meaningful numerical results. Instead the Air Staff, Air Ministry, the scientific committees and even night-fighter pilots did nothing but argue – quite literally a case of heat overcoming light. The CH system's limit of accuracy of between three and five miles was much too far to be of any use at night; Dowding said, 'It might as well be fifty miles.' Hence the urgent and crucial need for an additional sensor – Churchill always called it a 'smeller' – carried in the fighter. Despite Jones' neat IR installation, it was clear that it would be AI radar or nothing.

In the closing months of 1939, while the AMRE research team was uprooted yet again and set up shop at Worth Matravers, near Swanage on the Dorset coast, their masters in the Air Ministry became increasingly concerned about the basic AI radar problem of minimum range. AI Mk III had a maximum range of two miles (say, 10,500 feet) and a minimum range of 1,000 feet, though in those days AI was temperamental and actual results were less predictable. Frankly, even AI Mk III was pretty useless except for the vital task of training crews. For the stern test that could come at any time there was an overwhelming need for an improved AI radar with minimum range as near as possible to 300 feet, and with clearer and more positive left/right up/down indication than the 'squint-eyed' Mk III. With the coming of war, the whole British defence scene had changed dramatically. Radar, previously the secret preserve of a tiny team of 'back-room' workers, suddenly gathered into its fold fresh manpower by the hundred and soon by the thousand. Watson-Watt personally scoured the universities to scoop up bright talent and open their eyes to the scarcely believable facts that in a government defence laboratory it was possible to find academic freedom, a most enjoyable atmosphere, and technical problems as gripping as any posed inside ivory towers. Industry, too, was harnessed in the biggest possible way to provide brainpower and manufacturing capacity.

It was mainly the newcomers that were to make the dramatic breakthroughs in AI radar. Everything – minimum range, inability to focus into a narrow beam, and inability to intercept the low-flier because of the ground echo – kept emphasizing the need for much shorter wavelengths. Nobody knew how to generate enough power at short wavelengths, but in fact one major hurdle had been crossed back in 1921 in Schenectady, when Dr Albert W. Hull, of the US General Electric Company, had described a novel valve he had devised and named the magnetron. Many workers improved it during the inter-war years, but in essence it remained a resonant-cavity device like an organ pipe or other wind instrument. Unlike almost every other oscillator the magnetron could generate energy at fantastically high frequencies, with wavelength down to a few centimetres; but power was still very small. Much later a quite different valve called a klystron was invented, mainly by W.W. Hansen at Stanford (who devised the crucial part, the rhumbatron) and the Varian brothers. In the klystron the main structure is a special CRT, whose steady pencil-beam of electrons is turned into a succession of intense bunches by one rhumbatron and then caught within another. Both the klystron and the magnetron could generate waves so short they were called microwaves. By the end of the 1930s brilliant workers at MIT and Bell Labs had developed the basic theory of waveguides – essentially just very accurate metal pipes – for carrying microwaves and, by physically adjusting their dimensions, for tuning the waves to exact wavelengths. It was a new and exciting field, pioneered in the United States but, like normal scientific research in peacetime, freely published.

Shortly after the start of the Second World War Watson-Watt gathered some of his best captures from the universities and – after assuring them that, though they had arrived on 'the Shanghai express' they had return tickets – asked them to think about microwave radar. Some of them knew enough about the subject to know that it could not be done, except with uselessly feeble power. A few others thought it worth chasing, but doubted that anyone could build a receiver. By the end of September 1939 two groups had used their return tickets, but only so that they could go back to work on the problem in their own laboratories. One group under Professor Mark Oliphant returned to the University of Birmingham to study transmitters. Another under J.H.E. Griffiths went back to the Clarendon Laboratory to work, in partnership with the Admiralty (under C.S., later Sir Charles, Wright, Director of Scientific Research), on the receiver. It was a mighty task. Every previous attempt to generate powerful microwaves had merely dissipated the energy into the atmosphere, or into heating the hardware (at least once it actually melted). No way was known of building any kind of practical radar on a centimetric wavelength. Indeed, almost a year later a VIP in the scientific world, leading a party of visitors to see the first demonstration ever given of what can fairly be called 'modern radar', summed up rather loudly by saying, 'Centimetric radar is for the *next* war.'

In the first month of war such a comment could not have been disputed, because nobody then knew how well the shanghaied men from Birmingham would do. In the meanwhile conventional 1.5-metre AI had to go ahead with all speed. There were quite suddenly a succession of minor breakthroughs, the greatest of which was the development of a new modulator by A.D. Blumlein of the His Master's Voice gramophone company (the electronics giant EMI). This dramatically cut the time duration of each pulse, and overcame the problem of overlay at the receiver by the direct pulse from the transmitter. The General Electric Co. (no relation to the US giant) began its radar career by producing a smaller yet far more powerful main transmitter valve, the Micropup, giving 10 kW on 1.5 m (190–195 MHz). It was hardly bigger than a household filament light bulb. W.B. Lewis, an AMRE newcomer, achieved a breakthrough with minimum range. The resulting radar grew to have little left of AI.III save the aerials; receiver gain and time-base deflection were increased, and the boxes were so arranged that a single technician could adjust settings with a screwdriver and simultaneously watch the tube-faces (previously he could not do both). The result was AI.IV, the first AI radar that could give real results in Service hands, and the only one in quantity service until late 1943. Provided that a target was within a 40° cone ahead of the fighter, its direction could be indicated unambiguously within 10°. Straight off, in September 1940, Pye was given a contract for 600 sets, with major assistance from EMI.

Thus, during the crucial summer of 1940, there were already in Britain three generations of AI radar, discounting AI.I and II. They were separated in timing by weeks rather than years, yet such was the pace of development they were utterly dissimilar. Mk III was primitive, the minimum that could reasonably be supplied to the RAF. Mk IV was better, yet still a 1.5 m set with all that wavelength's inherent shortcomings. Still in the laboratory was the new generation using centimetric microwaves. (Incidentally, the FIU was very proud of the fact that, despite not being an operational unit of the RAF, its crews shot down the first enemy aircraft to be destroyed by every type of AI from Mk III to Mk X.) But despite all this work by the 'boffins', the night-fighter strength of the RAF was woefully small. Almost the whole establishment of Fighter Command comprised Hurricanes (about thirty squadrons in mid-August 1940, despite terrible losses in France) and Spitfires (about nineteen squadrons), few of whose pilots had even tried flying at night, and which could find night raiders only by chance. There were a few squadrons of Gladiators, some of which had done a little night flying, and an embryonic night force of Blenheims and Defiants. In September 1940, when the night blitz started in earnest, Fighter Command had, for all practical purposes, six squadrons of Blenheims and three of Defiants for night fighting. About one-third of the Blenheims had AI.III, and there were still a few AI.II installations.

This modest night-fighter force would still have been of little use without four further technical developments which formed vital links in the chain of aerial defence. One was a grand design called GCI (ground control of interception) which owed much to W.S. Butement, who had proposed a 50 cm naval radar at the Signals Experimental Establishment as early as 1931. GCI included CHL (chain home, low) and gap-filler radars to cover the lower airspace, but the main item was a radar giving a picture showing the positions of fighter and bomber. The second essential was IFF, already mentioned, the earliest example of so-called secondary radar. Fitted to all friendly aircraft, it was triggered by the defending radar pulses to send back an enhanced and specially coded reply. Thus, when 'interrogated' by either a ground station or a night fighter, the 'friendly' would automatically show up on the display screens in a characteristic way, without its aircrew even being aware of what was going on. A 'hostile', on the other hand, would not know the IFF code, which was constantly being changed, and thus its radar 'blip' would be suspicious. However, it could not just be shot down without visual identification, because it might be a 'friendly' with its IFF unserviceable, or even just switched off. Over the years IFF, like ECM, was to grow fantastically in complexity and cleverness, and to give rise to the modern field of secondary surveillance radars (SSR) and transponder beacons. The third new development was a related system of Racons (radar beacons) placed in a chessboard pattern over southern England to give an equally distinctive blip on night-fighter radars (AI.IV onwards) and thus help the fighter to return safely to base.

One could overlook the fourth link in the chain, unless one had been a pilot at the time. Aircraft had previously used HF radio, which suffered from 'static' and speech distortion so badly that to a layman any received message sounded like unintelligible gibberish. Even professional aircrew often had to request, 'Say again'. In 1940 VHF (very high frequency) radio arrived with marvellously clear speech just in time to play its vital part in the night battle. The fact that it had shorter range was of no consequence. With it came a standardized GCI language. Today one is amused, but in 1940 the GCI command, 'Flash your weapon', caused not a trace of a smile: it came at a time of mounting tension in the chase, and meant 'switch on your AI radar'. 'Increase speed' was partnered by 'Throttle back', and at the end of the interception the crew would be told 'Darken your weapon'.

It needed all these new inventions and techniques to construct an effective scheme of night defence. It is unfair to describe it as sheer luck that it all came together in the autumn of 1940; it was planned with great care and forethought, and had it not been for the fact that the Air Ministry Works Department – responsible for civil engineering and buildings – stubbornly resisted every attempt to substitute speed in place of perfection, almost the entire scheme could have been operational by the beginning of the war. For the first time in history it enabled a country to wait until hostile aircraft were approaching, and then send fighters where they were most needed. The only shortcoming was that the GCI system alone could not put fighters in visual contact with the enemy at night. Modern air traffic controllers will see the problem only too well. Their job today is to keep aircraft apart; in 1940 the task was to bring aircraft together, and to do it with primitive radars giving very ill-defined blips that flickered and jumped and sometimes just disappeared for no obvious reason. Visual contact at night meant a few hundred feet, whereas the best accuracy a really good GCI controller could hope for in 1940 was more than three miles. Even then, the fighter had to be going in the same direction at the same height. There were countless other snags, not least of which was the fact that the 1940 controller himself had little experience. Until many months had been spent sifting unsuitable people, he often lacked an understanding of the fighter pilot's problems, and often also lacked the right kind of confident patience and encouragement that was vital to proper teamwork. Controlling was an art.

Few indeed were the people in night fighting who in 1940 had any artistry, experience or even confidence. Come aboard the Blenheim night fighter of F/O (later Air Commodore) Roderick Chisholm, as he tried to learn basic steps in the new trade at Middle Wallop that summer:

I was kept waiting, signalling for permission to land but ignored, for about half an hour. I was anything but composed, and when a turn proved too much for the directional gyro, which spun, I also lost my sense of direction. At last I was given a 'green', but the dim pattern of aerodrome lights made little sense by this time, and my approach to land was not aligned with the flare-path, whose direction I understood too late. I had to go round again. The wheels and flaps on a Blenheim came up rather slowly, and by the time I was ready to start a circuit I knew that I was several miles from the aerodrome; but I could not picture my position, and the lights which I could see did nothing but confuse me. I was flustered, and the situation suddenly got out of hand. I did not know where I was; therefore I was lost. A feeling of panic came over me, and I could not think of anything except getting down somehow on to terra firma. It must be this paralysis that causes the inexplicable night-flying accidents. It took a great effort for common sense to overcome this one instinct, which seemed still to work, to return to earth as soon as possible; but slowly this happened and item by item things were checked. What height? What speed? Climbing or diving? Where was I likely to be? Each of these checks, usually done instinctively and instantaneously, now needed a special effort . . .

There's a beacon – what's it flashing? – dot something, missed it – climbing too steeply, must level out – now, where's that beacon again? – get the beacon paper (it's too flimsy) – where's the torch? – mustn't get flustered again – there's plenty of time – climbing again, must level out – Andover VL, Wallop DA – now, where's the beacon? – there it is, think clearly, read it slowly – looks like a V then L – read it again, there it goes again: it's Andover – about 240° for Wallop – settle down, align the gyro – steady – lights ahead – a beacon – flashing DA, that's Wallop – this is simple – I could go on, I'd like to go on now – this will be a joke tomorrow.

I doubt that there is a single pilot who does not have similar memories from his early days when it all seemed to be just too much. Flying by night could bring the feeling flooding back – often fatally – to pilots who, like Chisholm, had long experience in daylight. For almost a year such men tried to master the Blenheim by night, while an experienced few operated AI-equipped aircraft at FIU and, increasingly, in the squadrons. Not many German aircraft came over at night to begin with, but FIU mounted night patrols to see if they could intercept any, and from 5 June 1940 AI was used in real chases of real targets. Time after time the enemy got away, usually because the harassed AI operator could make no sense of the erratic blips of the shaky Mk III and was incapable of giving his pilot clear steering commands. The only exception was Ashfield. His was the first of a handful of victories gained by the NF Blenheims. Courageously flown for long, cold and exhausting patrols night after night, they simply lacked a good enough AI set to complete the chain of defence. Unlike most other fighters, including the Defiant, their guns could be fired on the darkest night with no flash problem. Performance, however, was marginal, even after the Blenheims had had their turrets removed in September 1940.

By sheer chance an aircraft existed that was so much better than the Blenheim that comparisons were pointless. Like many of the greatest RAF aircraft, it owed its existence purely to private enterprise, and not to any official specification. It was in June 1938 that the leaders of the Bristol aircraft and engine teams, respectively Leslie Frise and Roy Fedden, had come to recognize that there was a more obvious solution to the nagging long-range and night-fighter problem than clever projects with flat sleeve-valve engines buried in the wings. By fitting powerful Hercules engines in a Beaufort torpedo-bomber with a new fuselage something might be done quickly. Something was done quickly, and the first Beaufighter flew in July 1939. It was exactly what was needed. It ended the crisis by night.

# FOUR

# THE BLITZ

On the evening of 7 September 1940 my school friend, Roy, appeared at the front door saying, 'Heck of a big fire down Rayners Lane way.' Later that night we had plenty to do in our own little locality, but next morning we learned that the frighteningly large glow to the south-east had, in fact, been London's dockland more than twenty miles away. It was the beginning of what Londoners called the blitz. Coming while the daytime Battle of Britain was still in progress, it went on right through the winter until the early summer of 1941. In a way, it was encouraging: Britons knew they were not going to be defeated in the daytime sky, and invaded and conquered. But, unlike the Battle of Britain, the Blitz seemed one-sided. Though the AA guns made a spirited noise, and the barrage balloons rode aloft, and the night fighters patrolled for hour after hour in the darkness and cold, enemy bombers were scarcely ever brought down.

At this time the AA guns had no radar, and they suffered from several other deficiencies, so that it took an average of about 32,000 rounds to bring down each night raider. (Soon, with radar, the average was to fall to 7,000.) Results of the fighters were even worse. On a few fortuitous occasions, when there was bright moonlight, or when relatively low-flying (under 15,000 feet) bombers were illuminated and held by searchlights, *Luftwaffe* raiders were shot down by radarless Blenheims, Spitfires, Hurricanes and Defiants. These aircraft were usually painted black, and had 'flame-damped' exhausts; the single-seaters merely had strips of aluminium to shield the flames from the pilot's eyes, but not from the enemy. They had to operate on a freelance basis. They were in VHF contact with a controller, but the latter could do little more than tell them which city was the target and the approximate positions of 'customers'. The special GCI radars were still being built, and trying to guide a fighter onto a particular 'bandit' was next to impossible, especially over Britain behind the CH chain. The solitary encouraging part of the picture was the Beaufighter.

The Beaufighter entered service, at first without the AI.IV radar being fitted, in late August 1940 at FIU, and the following month with 25, 29, 219 and 604 Squadrons. Until very recent times, most new RAF aircraft have had to surmount a hurdle of derogatory rumour which preceded them into service and denigrated the performance, handling, serviceability and other real or imagined shortcomings. But the 'Beau' was so potent and capable that the rumours were reduced to: 'Well, the bloody Magic Mirrors are nothing but a dead loss in the Blenheim, so how are they going to work any better in this?' Such feelings were at least leavened by one's trying the Beau in the air, and a few times I was fortunate enough to do this myself (but long after the Blitz).

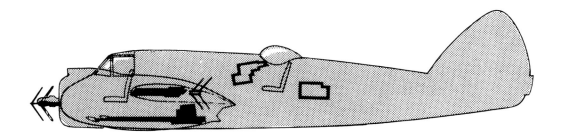

*Bristol Beaufighter IC with AI IV; four fixed 20 mm Hispano and six fixed .303-inch Browning. The observer's seat could swivel fore, as here, or aft.*

Though comparable with the Blenheim in span and length, the Beaufighter stood higher off the ground, because the mighty Hercules sleeve-valve engines needed larger propellers. It exuded an aura of unbreakable strength, and in fact the empty weight exceeded 14,000 lb compared with 8,100 lb for a Blenheim. One got in by pulling down a belly hatch with integral ladder, and climbing up inside. The observer had a similar hatch, and sat under a transparent bubble facing aft, his AI.IV displays in front of him. The pilot climbed up the sloping floor to the cockpit. It was quite a job to clamber over the wing and across the hinged-down back of the seat, and next to impossible to do it wearing a seat-type pack. The proper drill was to put the parachute on the seat, clamber over, and then strap everything together. To get out was not too bad if the aircraft was parked or flying straight and level: the pilot folded the spring-loaded seat, reached up and back to grab parallel bars in the roof and swung down to the floor behind, leaving via the belly hatch, which was so pivoted that, in emergency escape in flight, air load kept it open.

View from the rather cluttered 'office' was exciting. In front was a superb non-distorting bullet-proof windscreen about two inches thick that, especially in later aircraft which had larger windows, filled one's forward field of view and never caused any Blenheim-type reflections on the darkest night. On each side was a whopping Hercules, projecting ahead of the extremely short nose and with flame-damped exhausts on the right of each cowling. The tear-jerking sound of Merlins is world-famous, but I would be just as moved by the lusty booming song of two Hercs – and it was far more soothing! On take-off the Beau would swing if you let it, and early versions had mild stability problems on climbing away (mine were later, with a big dorsal fin and dihedral tailplane that eased this characteristic). As for landing, that was straight-forward if you had brake pressure; but hearken to what happened to *Flight* colleague Tony Taylor whose brakes failed: 'The Beau, after a comfortingly accurate three-pointer, ran absolutely straight for a few hundred yards. Then, in spite of full rudder and instinctive jabs with the thumb on the useless brake lever, it began to swing to starboard. Full power from the starboard Hercules failed to check it, and the thing left the runway in a rapidly tightening turn, during which it slid bodily sideways on the muddy grass and ended up travelling backwards at quite a smart clip . . .'* Of course, nothing broke; the Beau was built like a battleship.

*From *Test Pilot at War* (Ian Allan).

Almost all the first batches of Mk I Beaufighters were night fighters. The earliest deliveries had no radar, but in September 1940 one of them was flown to the FIU for trials with one of the first AI.IV installations. By November 1940 AI.IV was standard on production Mk IF aircraft. The installation was good, and a skilled operator could obtain a clear and unambiguous target blip over a range of at least three miles (provided that the aircraft was about three miles above the ground) down to a minimum range of something like 100 feet. This minimum range was closer than with AI Mk III, but it was still too far for certain visual contact in adverse conditions. One of the most important and most difficult skills an AI operator had to acquire was to judge the rate of closure on the target simply by watching the blips. With the Beaufighter there was ample in-flight performance for overtaking any *Luftwaffe* bomber of 1940, even if the bomber had become frightened and tried to get away. But it was far from simple to guide the pilot with absolute precision, so that he came up astern to visual contact without overshooting or colliding with the bomber from behind. At that time, sudden closing of the throttles on British engines generally resulted in severe backfiring and large gouts of flame from the exhausts. The Hercules was better than most engines in this respect, but still could not equal the German engines, whose direct-injection fuel systems did not suffer from this failing,

*In the author's opinion, the Beaufighter was the world's first really capable night fighter. T4638, one of a batch of 500 built by Fairey at Stockport, is seen serving with 604 Sqn. Matt black overall, this aircraft still has Type A.1 national markings, whereas another 604 pilot, John Cunningham, had new C.1 markings (narrow white and yellow) on T4625!*

which at night could mean life or death. The fact that a night fighter needed powerful airbrakes was not then realized, and much later many Beau pilots learned that the best procedure was to keep on plenty of power and drop the landing gear. The Beau's great strength is reflected in the fact that the gear-down limit was 240 mph IAS, well above any likely indicated speed at around 15,000 feet (the later Mosquito was red-lined at only 180).

It was thus fairly safe for the pilot to go on closing on the target after the AI blip had vanished off the bottom end of the range scale. With practice one could judge just when the range ought to be dropping close to zero, and visual contact by this time ought to be certain. Should the enemy suddenly appear dead in front, a cool pilot could then slow down by lowering his wheels briefly (though this was not realized during the night Blitz). Once in a firing position the pilot, having made certain that his firing-button outer ring was set from 'Safe' to 'Fire', could open up with devastating armament. The first fifty Beaufighters had four 20 mm Hispano cannon under the nose, ahead of the hatch. Subsequent deliveries added six Brownings in the wings, four on the right and two on the left.

This armament was the heaviest of any RAF fighter in the Second World War, and still sounds impressive today. In the RAF's hour of desperate need in 1940 it was manna from Heaven to a service that had nothing more powerful than rifle-calibre machine-guns, which were swiftly becoming ineffective as the Germans bolted armour on to their bombers. What amazed the author, even at the time, was that there was no modern British shell-firing cannon. The 20 mm Hispano-Suiza had been designed at the end of First World War. Installed singly between the cylinder blocks of the same company's fighter engines, it did not matter that it was eight feet long and weighed 109 lb. Also fitting neatly between the cylinder blocks was the 60-round drum of ammunition. Lacking any obvious alternative, a licence for this was obtained at the proverbial 'eleventh hour' in 1937, and by 1939 it was coming into production by British MARC Ltd at Grantham. By 1945 a group of British factories had delivered just under 100,000, later versions having a shorter barrel. Fortunately, the British armament experts showed little interest in the mounting on an engine (and to bolt it on a Merlin would have meant major redesign of the reduction gear). Instead, its first British application was to mount four in the nose of the Westland Whirlwind, though this odd fighter was never of any importance. More to the point, one was – with difficulty, turning the gun on its side – mounted in each wing of the Spitfire IB. The first trial installation took place soon after the outbreak of war, and in March 1940 one of the experimental Mk IBs shot down a Do 17 with sixteen rounds. In the Battle of Britain the Mk IB equipped 19 Squadron, though maddening stoppages and other faults persisted. These were gradually cured, and by 1941 the standard Spitfire fighters were of the B type, with two Hispanos and four Brownings (though in the week the prototype Spitfire first flew, in March 1936, designer Mitchell had schemed a version with four Hispanos!).

Wisely, Bristol could see the futility of the four Brownings of the Blenheim fighters, and replaced them in the Beaufighter by four Hispanos. In this aircraft there was no need for the clumsy drum feed, and the Bristol design team devised a superb installation with continuous belt feed from four 240-round magazines. Air Ministry armament experts rejected the scheme, claiming that it would either jam the guns or be wrecked. Bristol then proposed an air-driven servo feed, tested on the fourth Beau in competition with the established French feed using 60-round drums. In French single-seat fighters only one such drum could be fitted, but in the Beau the observer could leave his radar, clamber forward and exchange used drums for fresh ones. As each drum weighed about 100 lb, and the fighter might be pulling *g* in a tight turn, changing drums was not popular with the observer (the drum racks had sharp edges, too). More time was wasted comparing two further servo-feeds, by Avro and Hydran. Then suddenly, as France fell, two *Armée de l'Air* officers arrived with drawings of their own newly developed Chatellerault belt feed. It was at once adopted, though it took until September 1941 to get it into production and in service (on the 401st aircraft). So all the Beaufighters in the long winter Blitz had hand-changed 60-round drums. It was only when Bristol studied the French feed that it was realized it was just like their own, original, rejected feed, except that it extracted rounds from the belt by pushing the nose instead of pulling the case. This proved to be a disadvantage, and it was changed to case-pulling, making it identical to the British scheme that could have been on the very first production aircraft!

Beaufighters became operational during September 1940, and during the winter their numbers increased rapidly, reaching 100 that year and 200 in May 1941. Production of AI Mk IV more than kept pace, and the improved radar was retrofitted to most of the early Mk I aircraft that had been delivered without it. A few Mk IV sets were also installed in Blenheims of FIU, and it was one of these, piloted by none other than Ashfield, that scored the second AI night victory on 7 November 1940. Was Ashfield – who was later killed in action – a superman? At first glance, for the whole RAF night-fighter force to have no success at all using AI, while one crew engaged in research scored two victories, does seem to require explanation. There is always an element of luck in being in the right place at the right time, but I think it is fair to describe night fighting as something uniquely difficult. Until it was mastered, neither a GCI controller nor an aircrew could ever say it was in control of the situation. Then, once one or two exceptional crews had begun to work with gifted controllers, the whole thing snowballed.

In November 1940 the *Luftwaffe* switched its assault from London to Midlands cities. At that time the RAF was just beginning to discover that its night-bomber crews – thanks to failure to practise before the war – were hardly ever able to find their targets. In contrast, the *Luftwaffe* had foolproof and easily used radio navaids that had been developed during the late 1930s, based on technology related to the Lorenz radio landing aid. Using *X-Gerät* and *Knickebein*, a jumpy and unskilled crew could fly direct to any British city and automatically release their ordnance at the correct point in space for a near-direct hit. These precision radio beams had been reported in the notorious 'Oslo parcel'. British experts foolishly scorned the notion of the *Luftwaffe* having in service an advanced aid that had not even been thought of by the RAF, but, fortunately, Tizard sent for young Dr R.V. Jones, the infra-red researcher from the Clarendon mentioned previously, and his methodical sleuthing uncovered the unpalatable truth. Not only did this prove that the German radio technology had been seriously under-rated – *X-Gerät* manufacturers' date-stamps mostly went back to 1938 – but it enabled Britain urgently to set up jammers and even spoof beacons, which caused more than one Heinkel to come to grief. Unfortunately there was one occasion, on 4 November 1940, when for various reasons no jammers were operating. On that night the city of Coventry was devastated.

Riding their fine Beaufighters, the handful of RAF night-fighter crews who had been converted to the type watched the burning cities, and helplessly chased one 'contact' after another (they all just seemed to disappear). Even if they had known that the first waves of bombers were following invisible lines in the sky, like transport aircraft flying the American radio range, they could not have accomplished the vital final step of drawing in close enough

*R2274 was one of two Merlin-engined Beaufighter IIs, with AI Mk IV, which in April 1941 were converted to Mk V standard by adding a Boulton Paul Type A turret. Two of the four cannon, and the six wing machine guns, were removed. Not only was the turret pointless, but it meant that the pilot could not bail out! This official photo had the caption altered to Mk VB.*

behind to see the enemy, identify it and shoot it down. Then, on 19 November, one crew did it. It was 604's John Cunningham and his observer Sergeant J. Phillipson: during a raid on Birmingham they shot down a Ju 88. Chisholm, also of 604 Squadron, wrote, 'The news was electrifying. For me it meant that the bombers we were sent to chase were really there . . .' In the minds of the NF crews, the Magic Mirrors, with their overtones of useless trickery, had become AI Mk IV, a system which, placed in the right position by increasingly adept ground control, could – with a modicum of luck – take a good crew to a visual contact. Cunningham quickly gained other successes, became a national hero, and for the rest of his life suffered being called 'Cat's Eyes'. Bombers were being shot down at last. With radar unmentionable, a common Ministry of Information cover story at the time was that night-fighter pilots not only wore dark glasses before take-off, to become night adapted (which they certainly did), but also derived abnormal night vision by eating copious quantities of carrots (which most of them did not). Even today there are thousands of the British public who have a lingering image of cat-eyed pilots munching this vegetable.

A vital role in closing the last links in the world's first night defence system worthy of the name was provided by the GCI stations previously mentioned. It was essential for the ground controller to have an up-to-date (real time) picture of the local situation; a lag of thirty seconds could well make interception impossible. What had been AMRE at Bawdsey, and was now renamed TRE (Telecommunications Research Establishment, a pure 'cover') at Worth Matravers, played the chief role in creating the GCI radar, with its PPI (plan-position indicator) picture painted by successive sweeps of a rotating radar beam, just as in so many radars today. Some of the GCI team were in the wooden huts on the Dorset coast, and others at the airfield at Christchurch – rather an inconvenient distance on the other side of Bournemouth – where TFU (Telecommunications Flying Unit) kept its growing fleet of night fighters and other trials aircraft. The PPI was swiftly improved until each sweep took sixty-five seconds, instead of the original eight minutes, and reached out to a distance of ninety miles. It could not indicate height, which had to be telephoned in by a CH station.

TRE undertook a crash programme to make the first dozen GCI sets, often using any suitable hardware that was handy, and delivered the first on 16 October 1940, at Durrington, Sussex, where it was operational two days later. The last of this batch was operational by 6 January 1941. Percival Rowe, by then Superintendent of TRE, recalled:

> In theory, it looked simple enough to us. All that was needed was for a night fighter to patrol up and down the English Channel until told by R/T from the Worth Matravers GCI station that there was an enemy bomber in a suitable position for interception. Bomber and fighter would then be tracked and their heights assessed. When the fighter had been put on the tail of the bomber by directions from the GCI station, the latter would give the signal 'Flash weapon', which would tell the fighter crew that the AI set should be switched on and used to complete the interception. The time was to come when it really was almost as simple as this, but not at Worth Matravers.

The civilian boffins at that establishment were the very first controllers to direct night fighters using the original prototype GCI, but there seemed to be too many problems for a kill to be achieved. Not least of the problems was that, like Chisholm near his home airfield, the night fighters continually got lost. There were three important answers. The first was a regular pattern of bonfires across southern England maintained by the ROC (often at peril to their lives from people who thought the blackout was being sabotaged). The second was the building of the Racons – passive ground radar beacons – which showed up strongly on the fighter's own AI scopes. The beacons were arranged in a regular checkerboard pattern across southern England, and the fighter observer could always see the blip from at least one and usually from two. By measuring the distances it was possible to get a fair idea of position, refined if necessary by actually plotting with a compass and pencil on a topographic map (not a plotting chart). The third way of solving the navigation problem was to learn to trust the GCI controller who, once the PPI sets were in use, always knew where the fighter was; he could identify it by its IFF signal. If required – and when lost on a dark night one is less concerned about loss of face – the controller could talk the fighter pilot home to his own airfield. To quote Rowe, 'Once this had been demonstrated, the fighter pilots poured over from Middle Wallop to see the new brand of magic, after which they came to believe that, though *they* might not know where they were, there was an "eye" on the ground that could watch them and lead them home.' This again was a fundamental advance in the technology of aviation that today is taken for granted.

This ability to be guided home was especially helpful to the pilots of single-seaters and Defiants, which had nobody on board to help the pilot navigate. With Racons and GCI radar the concept of the AI-equipped single-engined fighter was looked at again, and it was soon realized that AI could be put in the Defiant and the Hurricane after all. Boulton Paul Aircraft were given drawings of the pilot-indication AI Mk V, which had a novel CRT scope with a U-marker around the blip, and the company completed installation drawings for the Defiant on 19 November 1940. The aerials were as in the single-seat scheme of the previous July, with the transmitter on the right wing. The transmitter itself was behind the turret, the receiver, control box and power pack behind the pilot's seat, the display on the pilot's left, and the control panel on his right. This pioneer single-engine installation suffered from moisture and bad electrical screening, and for some reason was not cleared for service until August 1941. By this time the radar had become AI.VI, with a wider bandwidth of 188–198 MHz and an added beacon facility. The radar-equipped Defiant IA served with 264 Squadron and later with 96, 125, 256 and 410. The more powerful Defiant Mk II served additionally with 141, which had destroyed an He 111 the previous December without AI, and with 151 and 153 Squadrons.

Having discovered that there was no law of nature forbidding radar in a single-engined aircraft, the Air Staff also fitted AI.VI to twelve Hurricane Is in late 1941. In November 1942 a report on their first year of operational service simply glowed with enthusiasm, especially commenting on their high serviceability and rapid accumulation of flight time, leaving the impartial observer mystified at why it was not done before and not done again.

Of course, as soon as the night Blitz started, the number of people – not by any means all of them in Britain – who tried to invent an effective way of destroying night bombers underwent a fantastic increase. The public knew nothing of radar, but did know about night fighters (carrots and all), AA guns and barrage balloons. The additional concepts were many and varied. The British Air Ministry recorded the proposals under twenty-eight headings, recommended that several be studied in depth, and actually took two (at least) to the stage of operational trials. One was the LAM and the other the Turbinlite. The night Blitz was a time when Britain would clutch at any straw, but the authorities persisted with both schemes long after their impracticalities had been proved.

LAM stood for Long Aerial Mine, and was accurately described in a memo of 11 September 1940 as 'a makeshift weapon'. It was the outcome of dozens of enthusiastic proposals for using balloons, slow aircraft or fighters to project, drop or trail canisters of explosive in the path of enemy bombers. In fact, if only the authorities who persisted with LAM had not been so disbelieving about *X-Gerät* and *Knickebein* the scheme might have been very effective, because once an LAM aircraft had detected that night's guidance beam, all it needed to do was accurately stay in it, but higher than the Heinkels. What the RAF actually did was to fly endless trials that were completely aimless, and the night sky is a very big place. Readers can work out why these trials were code-named 'Mutton'.

The LAM explosive device was an unpropelled version of the mass-produced Type K surface-to-air rocket. In some trials it was released on a parachute, while in most it was trailed on a 2,000-foot cable. Some of the first trials were flown by Handley Page Harrows, heavy bombers of the mid-1930s, but by 1941 the usual carrier was the Havoc. This excellent night fighter was

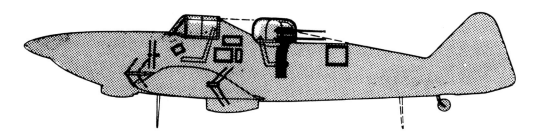

Boulton Paul Defiant with AI VI; four .303-inch Browning in power-driven turret.

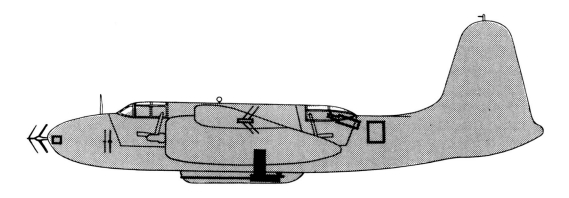

Douglas P-70 Havoc with AI IV; four 20 mm M-2.

produced on a production-line basis at RAF Burtonwood, near Warrington, by converting Douglas DB-7 (Boston) bombers diverted from the *Armée de l'Air* after the French collapse. Both the Havoc I, with Twin Wasp engines, and the Havoc II, with Cyclone 14s and a broader vertical tail, were used for Mutton missions. The idea was that enemy aircraft hitting the cable would draw the charge violently up to explode on contact. Trials with dummy mines were inconclusive against towed targets. Then 93 Squadron at Middle Wallop trailed live charges; on 1 May 1942 they were foolish enough to bring down a *Luftwaffe* bomber, which kept the scheme going until November. By this time it had been agreed that LAM was dangerous mainly to its carriers.

Havocs were also the main carrier of the Turbinlite, though this was also fitted to individual aircraft of other types. It was a 2,700-million candlepower searchlight, fitted in the nose, drawing current from a large generator set in the fuselage. Its name was originally the Helmore light, after its chief proposer, Wing Commander (later Air Commodore) W. Helmore, pilot, engineer and wartime broadcaster. The idea was that the Havoc should take off, in pitch darkness, in close formation with two Hurricanes, which could see special rear-facing lights on the Havoc. The formation would be vectored on to the enemy by GCI, until the Havoc could

*Turbinlite Douglas Havocs had several types of searchlight installation. This one seemed designed to impose the greatest possible drag. Note the AI.IV transmitter aerial.*

use its AI Mk IV, which had a transmitter aerial on each side of its flat glass nose. Eventually the formation might be lucky enough to come within 1,000 feet of the target, directly astern of it. Then, instead of shooting down the enemy, the Havoc would switch on its searchlight – which might or might not score a bull. At this, the Hurricanes had to overtake the Havoc and shoot the enemy down. What happened in practice was that the target instantly jinked out of the bright beam faster than the Havoc could follow, usually by turning one way and then, when the Havoc had set up the 'wrong' bank, by reversing the turn. The Hurricanes got in each other's way, and in the Havoc's way; or they obstructed the beam, or (on several occasions) got the Havoc in their sights instead. What almost always happened was that the target got away, while a Havoc and two rather helpless Hurricanes floundered about completely lost, and with their pilots' night-adapted vision destroyed. Only once, in 1942, was the system credited with a kill; unfortunately the victim belonged to the RAF.

It is perhaps hardly surprising that the Turbinlite was not a success. If one had to illuminate the target, the wavelength chosen should not have been a visible one at all. There are plenty of other parts of the electromagnetic spectrum where it is possible to pump out energy and detect any coming back, and today probably the leading technology is IR (infra-red), which (as recorded earlier) had been dropped in this role before the Blitz started. Bearing in mind the appalling difficulties that were encountered with the Turbinlite and its generator, it should not have been more difficult to install a very powerful IR illuminator and fit the Havoc and its minions with a detector. This would not have alarmed the hostile crew (at least until the enemy latched on to what was happening and devised a countermeasure), and the closure and aiming could have been carried out almost at leisure. Fundamentally, the weakness of the basic idea was that if a night fighter can be got into a position where it can project a beam of light at its target, it is obviously more sensible to project cannon shells instead. The one advantage of illumination is that it can be made to work even if the target is not quite in the line of fire, whereas with the Turbinlite everything possible was done to project a narrow pencil beam.

Studying the records, it is hard to find any Havocs that managed to avoid being Turbinlite-converted. Ten RAF squadrons operated thirty-one Mk I and thirty-nine Mk II aircraft from 1941 until the third quarter of 1943, and the total number of conversions, by Alan Muntz & Co., was considerably greater. One is left nonplussed that so little was done to use the Havoc conventionally. It was a fine performer with Cyclone 14s, its nosewheel-type landing gear had no tendency to swing or ground-loop, its exhaust stacks were extremely well flame-damped, and it could have done a superior job with AI and heavy armament. A few had a nose designed and made by Martin-Baker containing twelve Brownings, and later (as described in the next chapter) the US Army used versions armed with four 20 mm; but the RAF never used the Havoc as a proper night fighter, except briefly with 85 Squadron.

Though it was impossible for anyone dogmatically to say so until they had been tried, both the Turbinlite and the LAM proved to be the useless aberrations that they had always appeared to be. Late in the war I talked with several people involved in the trials in a fruitless endeavour to find out why so much time and money was spent persisting with them, and the only answer I ever got is that it was correct policy to investigate any method that offered some hope of beating the night raider. This was certainly true in 1940, but to go on messing about with demonstrably impractical schemes until late 1943 takes some explanation. This is because in early 1941 the classic night-interception system, using GCI and AI to allow an otherwise conventional fighter to bring its guns to bear, at last began to achieve success.

One of the first to prove that the system really could work was Chisholm, who had tried without success all winter and then suddenly destroyed two bombers in one night. It was the moonlit night of 13 March 1941, and he got a good vector – as now was increasingly the case, with experienced controllers – behind a bomber that was unfortunately going home empty. Over Bournemouth,

> Ripley, my observer, got a close radar contact over to the left. I turned a little to the left, and I could hardly believe my eyes, for there was another aircraft about a hundred yards away and on the same level. It was black and its fish-like fuselage glistened dully in the moonlight; it was unmistakeably a Heinkel . . . I was able to creep up unmolested . . . the wings seemed to blot out the sky above me . . . I saw the four rows of exhausts, each with six stubs, and now and again one of them would belch out a bigger flame than usual. The moment had come to shoot. It was now or never. Holding my breath I eased the stick back a little and the Heinkel came down the windscreen and into the sight. It went too far and I

found myself aiming above. Stick forward a bit and the sight came on it again. How ham-fisted this was! I pressed the firing button. There was a terrific shaking and banging, and to my surprise I saw flashes appearing, as it seemed miraculously, on the shape in front of me. Pieces broke away and came back at me . . .

After emptying his four drums containing 240 cannon shells Chisholm could see nothing much more happen:

Suddenly I thought that it was going to get away. I had had a chance, a sitter, and I had not hit it hard enough . . . And then I saw a lick of flame coming from the starboard engine. It grew rapidly and enveloped the whole engine and most of the wing. The machine turned east and started to go down slowly; it looked by now like a ball of flame. We followed it down from 11,000 feet until, minutes later, it hit the sea, where it continued to burn.

Later the same night, after rearming, Chisholm destroyed a second Heinkel flying home *with its navigation lights on*. A little later he again destroyed two Heinkels in one night. Two nights later came his fifth. Then followed a succession of failures, and the doubts and fears flooded back: 'It was testing to be close to an opponent, unseen though known to be within visual range, sometimes flying through his slipstream with a sickening bump, and to persevere, waiting for the hail of bullets from an alert gunner (which, in fact, seldom came), with the suspicion growing all the time that the radar was at fault – for this early type could lie most perfectly.' It was at this time that, as RAF night-fighter pilots began to suspect, an increasing number of *Luftwaffe* pilots began taking routine evasive action when over Britain. Once during a heavy raid on Plymouth, Chisholm found himself flinging the Beaufighter into tight turns, first left and then right, to try and keep the blip on the radar scope. He tried everything, including simply looking for aircraft illuminated by the glare of the burning city, but had no luck. It needed only the mildest of enemy manoeuvres to throw off pursuit.

Yet despite this, the growing number and skill of Beaufighter crews could not fail to make their presence felt. In the first two months of the night Blitz RAF fighters shot down a total of eight aircraft, most of them without proper use of AI, out of 12,000 hostile sorties (a *Luftwaffe* loss rate hardly worth calculating). In the next three months the figures were even worse. But in March 1941 the *Luftwaffe* tapered off its efforts; the great Blitz finally ended late in that month, and the remnants of the KG (bomber) wings flew away to the east. Hitler was committed to Operation *Barbarossa*, the invasion of the Soviet Union in June 1941. He had intended by this time to have finished the job against the obstinate islanders. He failed, partly because of poor German policy and partly because they had eventually learned to jam his bomber guidance beams, confuse his navigators with spurious beacons and, above all, shoot down his bombers on the darkest nights. The fact that sheer chance had frequently played a major part in assembling the night defence system of CH, CHL, GCI, radar beacons, AI.IV, VHF, IFF and, above all, the Beaufighter, was no comfort to the *Luftwaffe*. From this time on, Britain was to be a perilous place for night raiders.

# FIVE

# CENTIMETRIC AI

During and for some years after the Second World War the British indulged in the belief that they were the world's greatest researchers. While others put huge teams onto every conceivable alternative, bulldozing the problems out of the way and never having to choose a single solution, the tiny British team would (it was thought) pick exactly the right answer at an early stage, simply because there was insufficient manpower to do anything else. This cosy (and nonsensical) belief was given credence by some remarkable achievements in the Second World War. In trying to unlock the riddles of centimetric radar Britain sought, and gained, the best of both worlds. The number of actual researchers could almost be counted on the fingers. The money spent was trivial, and facilities were modest. Yet the tiny team was split up to explore all the known ways of generating high power on wavelengths of a few centimetres. (By 'high power' was meant not the megawatt pulses of CH but something at least measured in watts rather than milliwatts.)

The need for centimetric radar for night fighters had been obvious since AI was thought of in 1936. Such radar could be miniaturized, and could send out a beam like a searchlight that could be directed by a reflector. It would overcome the problems of minimum range, ground reflection and many other difficulties, besides giving a sharper blip and, in theory, even being able to picture the target's shape. It would also be more difficult to jam. But in 1939 it was simply incapable of being built. One who knew this was a nuclear physicist, P.I. Dee, one of those who was dragged from an ivory tower by Watson-Watt, discovered a challenge in centimetric AI and eventually headed the relevant TRE team. Percival Rowe knew how vital a breakthrough in this field would be, but wisely played it down in talking to visiting VIPs; nobody knew if it could ever be made to work. And for a while all the results were negative. One of the least-successful teams was J.T. Randall and A.H. Boot, at the University of Birmingham, who were seeing what could be done with modified Barkhausen tubes, and with plasma oscillations in mercury vapour. Plasma was almost a non-starter, and the Barkhausen would not even work as an oscillator to test other tubes of the same kind. So Randall and Boot decided to make a little magnetron to use as a test oscillator. They talked far into the night about the magnetron as a possible high-power generator in its own right, conscious of the fact that dozens or hundreds had been made since the First World War without high-power success.

As outlined on p. 36, a magnetron is a resonant cavity, like a penny whistle. It has an anode in the middle, a surrounding cathode, a high-voltage electric field and a powerful magnetic field. The two fields result in a cloud of electrons being 'blown' round and round like a small whirlwind of fierce intensity. Just as in a whistle – a better analogy here is a siren – the 'whirlwind' can be made to give a steady 'note'; instead of sound, out comes electromagnetic energy in the form of microwaves. But nobody had been able to get any power. Randall and Boot looked at the way resonant cavities were used in earlier magnetrons, and in the rival klystron that had always been one of the apparent best bets. They happened to have the right blend of theoretical, practical and industrial experience to know what needed to be done and how it could be done. One afternoon in November 1939 Randall and Boot sat down and wrote out the whole story, ending with a detailed specification for a radically new kind of magnetron. There followed three frantic months of turning those vital sheets of paper into hardware. The work was different from any seen before in radar: it involved the accurate machining of a massive block of copper, coupling up water pipes to keep it cool, and arranging round it a very powerful electromagnet.

It was all put together and switched on on 21 February 1940. The result surpassed Randall's and Boot's wildest dreams. The fact that it worked was obvious. Indeed, if one brought one's hand anywhere near the output lead, that hand soon became uncomfortably hot! As power was increased, the output began to be seen and heard as a sizzling violet arc dissipated into the air of the lab. A nearby garage supplied a succession of 6-volt bulbs as each in turn was burned out, and soon the output was blazing forth from large neon floodlights. This was obviously not milliwatts but hundreds of watts. On the second day a crude measuring device, hastily rigged up for a totally new task, measured about 450 watts at a wavelength of 9.8 cm; three months later a properly designed pre-production magnetron, engineered largely under C.C. Paterson at the GEC Hirst Research Laboratories at Wembley, was delivering 50 kW at 9.1 cm! It was a breakthrough that ranks alongside man's greatest technical accomplishments. It had a profound effect on the war, and on man's subsequent ability to navigate the skies and oceans.

TRE received the first supposed centimetric AI hardware on 8 June 1940. Supplied by a klystron, it merely confirmed everyone's belief that it couldn't be done, and it even had to have its own vacuum pumping plant. But the following month the establishment set up the first radar fed by one of Birmingham's new magnetrons. This was wholly practical, the magnetron was evacuated and sealed, and thus needed no pumping, and from the start of operation – the target was a boy on a bicycle – it was clear that centimetric AI was 'on' at last.

By May 1941 TRE, GEC and the Clarendon Laboratory had virtually finished the engineering of the receiver, and in particular had devised a clever high-frequency switch which enabled a single small aerial an inch or so in length to serve alternately as transmitter and receiver. Thus with centimetric radar there did not have to be any remote aerials near the tips of the wings. To focus the pulses of 10 cm waves into a pencil beam a paraboloidal metal dish was placed behind the aerial. Then the combined unit, called a scanner, was mounted on pivots so that it could point anywhere in a large cone ahead of the fighter carrying it. The complete unit, comprising pivoted scanner, a mechanical drive system and associated circuitry at the rear, was then mounted in the fighter's nose. The main boxes containing the transmitter, receiver, power supplies and other parts might be anywhere, while the control and display units naturally were in the cockpit. To smooth off the nose contours the scanner was then enclosed by a 'radome' of thin non-conductive (dielectric) plastics. All this was breaking completely new ground, and one of the most difficult mechanical engineering tasks was achieving sufficient precision, speed and angular movement to point the beam everywhere it had to go.

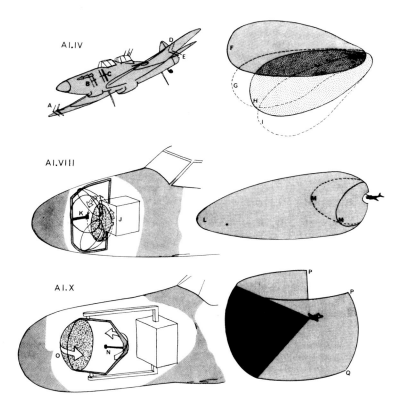

The first effective night-fighter radar in the world was the British AI IV. Its installation differed according to aircraft type. In the Defiant the transmitter aerial was mounted well outboard on the right wing (A). The right azimuth receiver aerials (B) and left azimuth aerials (C) were on the fuselage, while the upper elevation aerials (D) and lower elevation aerials (E) were on the left wing. Radiation was emitted in all directions, but the receiver aerials were rapidly sequenced by a rotary switch. The diagram at right shows the volume of sky that could be searched (provided the fighter was at well over 8,000 feet). Useful limit of range was about four miles, to point F with receiver aerials B and D, G with aerials B and E, H with aerials C and D, and I with aerials C and E. Direction-finding was accomplished by comparing the strengths (blip lengths) from the four signals.

The British designers of the world's first centimetric fighter radar did not attempt the tricky task of piping microwaves from the modulator (J) to a pivoted, scanning aerial. Instead AI VIII had a fixed aerial (K) around which a parabolic reflector was driven in successively increasing and decreasing spirals. The reflector dish is shown in four positions at maximum deflection of 30°, one position being shaded. Every 1.2 seconds the dish returned to an instantaneous rest position reflecting the beam dead ahead. Then the aerial was exactly at the focus, giving a range of 6½ miles (to point L), even at quite low altitudes. Unfortunately, as the mirror spiralled out to maximum deflection its focus moved away from the aerial, degrading the beam until at 30° offset (giving a beam angle of 45°) the maximum range was barely two miles (points M). A further shortcoming was the single radial-type presentation, but the set was still a vast improvement over Mk IV.

AI Mk X (SCR-720) was the best night-fighter radar used by any air force in the Second World War. It was designed for the P-61 Black Widow, but was also widely used in Mosquitos. The purely schematic sketch shows how the microwave energy was piped to a transmitter/receiver aerial (N) which was mounted in a frame facing a parabolic reflector (O). An electric motor spun the frame in azimuth at six revolutions per second, while a second motor tilted the whole assembly between selected elevation limits, such as 50° up and 20° down. The sky coverage was outstanding. Points (P) were 50° up and between 80° and 100° from dead ahead, while (Q) was from 15° to 30° below. Maximum range was almost ten miles, in all directions within the region covered.

The first airborne centimetric installation was made in a TRE Blenheim at Christchurch in March 1941. The scanner was driven in spiral fashion, starting at the centre dead ahead of the aircraft and rapidly spinning round an ever-increasing cone to a maximum of 45°; then it would spirally scan inwards until, for a brief moment at the centre, it would again be motionless. Other scanners followed different patterns, one obvious one being a sequence of horizontal (or slightly sloping) left/right right/left sweeps working their way up and down between maximum elevation and maximum depression. The first scanner was produced mainly by Nash and Thompson, who also made RAF gun turrets. But when RAF 'erks' (ground staff) at Christchurch saw it in action, recorded Rowe, 'doubts were cast on the sanity of the scientists. Before the system reached a speed of rotation greater than the eye could follow, it could be watched rotating in a curiously irregular fashion with the one apparent desire of escaping from the aircraft altogether.'

To get the 10-cm technology into service as quickly as possible GEC was awarded a 'crash programme' for 150 more or less hand-built radars designated AI.VII, all to be delivered by December 1941. These were rather compromised by the need for haste. The aerial was fixed to the nose of the aircraft, at the focus of the spirally driven scanner, to avoid the need for solving the difficult problem of feeding microwaves from a fixed transmitter to a rapidly oscillating aerial. This had the drawback of making the transmitted beam become broader and thus less intense as it departed from the central axis, so that whereas maximum range dead ahead was seldom less than four miles over land (even at quite low altitudes), and six miles over the sea, the range at about 30° from the axis was a mere two miles. Moreover unless a target was fairly close to the axis its angle-off could not be measured accurately. It was thought that, as the objective was to reduce angle-off to zero, with the night fighter pointing at its quarry, that this was not serious, but in practice the shortcoming made it more difficult for the radar operator (called variously the operator, navigator or observer) to interpret the situation. Angle-off was often assessed by p.r.f. interval: two quick blips and a gap showed a large angle, and a regular blip a medium angle. The first AI.VII flew in November 1941 in Beaufighter IF X7579. This was the first fighter to have centimetric radar and the first to have a radome, the latter's shape resulting in its being called a 'thimble nose'. Before the end of the year thimble-nosed Beaufighters had been cleared for operations, just a year after the eminent expert said that such short wavelengths were for the *next* war.

A few months behind came the refined and productionized AI Mk VIII, with a better transmitter and aerial giving rather greater maximum range and closer minimum range. Provision was made for IFF interception and for Racon facilities in the initial AI.VIIIA (ARI.15093A, ARI meaning aircraft radio installation). In AI.VIIIB the Lucero facility was added for position-fixing from 1.5 m ground beacons. No fewer than 1,500 sets were ordered from E.K. Cole (Ekco), mainly at the Western Development Unit at Malmesbury, and 1,000 from GEC at Coventry. These were to be the standard British AI radars during the rest of the war, though for security reasons it was June 1944 before they were allowed to fly over enemy territory. To speed production, radical short cuts were taken, the most remarkable being delivery of over 1,000 of the first AI magnetrons not from industry but from a production line in the laboratory at the University of Birmingham, with an average age of worker of under 19. Another huge job that was completed swiftly was to train the RAF. Unlike the now old-fashioned CH, and even the original AI sets, centimetric radar was new technology. It was highly secret. Nothing was in any textbook, and if one or two key boffins had suddenly been killed much of the knowledge would have died with them. So, at a remarkable pace, thousands of the growing class of RAF tradesmen skilled in radar were told how microwaves behaved, how they were generated, and what they did – and how AI Mks VII and VIII should be looked after. Night-fighter observers learned how to use them, helped by one of the first training simulators (devised by TRE's G.A. Dummer, later a pioneer of solid-state devices) and by the excellent films for which TRE was becoming famous.

What the microwaves could do was plenty. When the new Beaufighter VIF entered service at the beginning of 1942, initially with 604 and 68 Squadrons, crews were enthusiastic. By this time TRE had learned to teach the user all about each of their many new devices beforehand, so that instead of crews saying, 'What the hell's this useless new gadget?', they had seen the captivating training films, handled the actual hardware, understood what the production device would do, and eagerly awaited its appearance in the squadron. The biggest advance with the new radar was that it could be used at low level; previously AI was almost useless against any target flying lower than about 5,000 feet. The new fine beam scanned the whole sky ahead of the fighter, had excellent angular resolution, and close to the axis could pinpoint target position within 1°, as accurate as the crew could wish. Maximum range varied with target aspect and target size, but it was never less than six miles, even against a small aircraft from dead astern. Minimum range with a top-notch AI.VIII and a good operator could be a mere 100 yards, by which time the pilot would have had to be half-blind not to acquire the target visually. TRE's J.A. Ratcliffe formed a special PDS (Post-Design Service) group which actually fitted the first thirty-six AI.VII sets into fighters and lived with the first squadrons, sharing in the jubilation at the first victory over the now very scarce *Luftwaffe* raiders in April 1942.

April 1942 was notable on a second count: it saw the first 'op' by a night-fighter version of the de Havilland Mosquito. The prototype 'Mozzie' had flown on 25 November 1940. At that time the whole project – which was entirely the idea of the de Havilland Aircraft Company – was fighting for its very survival. To most experts, especially air marshals, the idea of an unarmed bomber seemed ridiculous, and to cap it all, this one was to be made of wood! The all-powerful Beaverbrook, Minister of Aircraft Production, wanted to concentrate on established types, made by the thousand. When he saw 'D.H.98 Mosquito, 50' he struck it off the agreed programme. He did this with assurance, because a month after the prototype had flown the Chief of the Air Staff, Sir Charles Portal, had dismissed the Mosquito as 'useless'. A few visionaries, including Air Chief Marshal Sir Wilfrid Freeman, quietly put the order back. It was still regarded mainly as a possible reconnaissance aircraft, but the initial order was actually for twenty bombers and thirty fighters.

It was soon realised that here was the most versatile aircraft the RAF had ever had. It even rivalled the Ju 88 for versatility, and fought in almost every role in every theatre of the Second World War. Later I was lucky enough to fly Mosquitos, but not fighter versions. The latter were powered by the same Rolls-Royce Merlin engines, with coolant radiators in the inner wings, but the pilot and observer had to enter through a side door, via a rickety ladder, because in the lower part of the nose were four 20 mm Hispano cannon. The original fighter, the Mk II, also had four 0.303 in Brownings in the nose, because instead of having a radome its AI radar was the old Mk IV. The cosy cockpit seated the observer on the right of the pilot, and an inch or two further back. The observer could thus look into the viewing scope, or help the pilot peer ahead through

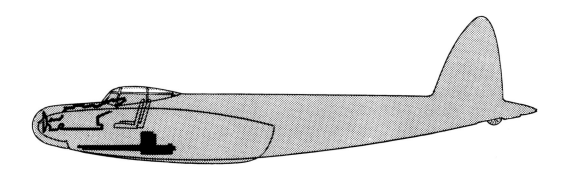

*De Havilland Mosquito XIX with universal nose (AI VIIIA shown installed); four 20 mm Hispano.*

the large flat windscreen of bullet-proof glass, while the pilot flew with a control column instead of a 'spectacles' handwheel – all quite different from non-fighter Mozzies. Much faster than the Beau, though not quite so good in initial climb, the Mosquito gradually replaced the old Bristol battleship as the standard RAF home-defence night fighter. Eventually, in March 1943, it appeared in Mk XII form with a thimble nose housing AI.VIII. Later, this and subsequent marks were to take the offensive and search for trouble far across Germany, as will be described.

From the summer of 1940 it had been obvious that centimetric radar was one of the truly great breakthroughs in technology, with importance far transcending mere air combat or even warfare. It was, of course, highly secret; but far across the grey Atlantic was another great member of the British Commonwealth, and further south another English-speaking nation that was industrially so powerful it was being called 'the arsenal of democracy'. In the spring of 1940 Professor A.V. Hill had visited the United States as a roving 'British ambassador for science'. In May Hill was appointed Scientific Attaché at the British Embassy in Washington, where the Ambassador, Lord Lothian, had proposed a unilateral disclosure to the US government of recent British advances in military technology. Why should Britain, fighting for its life and saved from extermination only by a narrow strip of sea and a few fighter aircraft, tell its preciously guarded secrets to a neutral country that might pass them on to others? Simply because the benefits seemed to outweigh the hazards. The United States was, on the whole, friendly to Britain and did not want to see the island democracy conquered by Nazi Germany. American scientists and engineers knew that Britain had been making big technical advances, though the details were extremely well guarded. Irrespective of when, or whether, the United States might have to enter the war, it seemed good sense to share information and compare notes.

In July 1940 President Roosevelt approved an agreement for a British military mission to visit the United States, be accredited to the US armed services, and exchange information. They would also meet the National Defense Research Committee (NDRC), which had been formed in Washington the previous month. Accordingly the Tizard Mission arrived in August. It goes without saying that many Americans viewed the whole thing with deep suspicion. It was a long-established American belief that, while John Doe is a transparently honest and simple kinda guy, John Bull is the most subtly scheming creature on Earth. Many were the urgent talks that began, 'What are the Limeys up to?' It is also worth noting that the British and Americans each thought that they were way out in front, and that their opposite numbers would be able to reveal little of interest.

It took two weeks to get the US Army to give formal agreement to free disclosure, and another four days for the US Navy to agree to show rather less. The British, however, had immediate authority from Churchill to deal all their cards face-up. When the talks began, the British were surprised at the breadth of radar work in the United States, though none of it had anything to do with fighter aircraft. But the Americans were staggered at what had been done in Britain. The Whittle turbojet was mentioned, but took the US by storm only after General 'Hap' Arnold's visit to see it for himself in April 1941. Several other new concepts were equally unexpected, but it was the cavity magnetron that was rated No. 1. This swept away all talk about 'cunning Limeys'. The official history of the US Office of Scientific Research and Development states, 'There is no question . . . that in the early days of the scientific interchange the British gave more than they received' and describes the magnetron as 'the most valuable cargo ever brought to our shores'.

It was on 28 September 1940 that the magnetron was revealed to members of the Microwave Committee of the NDRC. The revealers were Ted Bowen, the original pioneer of AI, and J.D. (later Professor Sir John) Cockcroft. The Microwave team comprised Professor Ernest O. Lawrence (University of California), Dr Ralph Brown (Bell Laboratories), Hugh H. Willis (Sperry), George F. Metcalf (GE), J.A. Hutcheson (Westinghouse) and Professor E.L. Bowles (Secretary, MIT). The historic meeting took place at the private laboratory at Tuxedo Park of lawyer Alfred Loomis, an amateur pioneer of microwaves. For the US team the high-power magnetron had come at exactly the right time; they were stymied by lack of just such a microwave oscillator. Loomis proposed that, his own facility being small, a huge new laboratory should be set up for microwave research and development. This was precisely what the Tizard Mission recommended; one of the prime reasons for the mission was to get the US started on microwave radar, and on centimetric AI in particular. The decision to develop an advanced 10-cm AI radar was taken on 18 October 1940; it was the first of many projects managed by the NDRC Division 14.

After the OSRD's Director, Dr Vannevar Bush, had considered setting up the proposed new Radiation Laboratory at its own Department of Terrestrial Magnetism, or at the Air Corps' Bolling Field, or leasing facilities from Bell Laboratories, the final choice was MIT, the giant university of technology at Cambridge, Mass. MIT began work at the Radiation Laboratory on 10 November 1940, under Director Dr Lee DuBridge (from the University of Rochester) and with Ted Bowen assigned to tell the lab what to develop and how. From then until the end of the Second World War radar was a joint effort.

At this time the British AI.VII and VIII were scarcely gleams in their designers' eyes, and to some degree it was fortuitous that the Americans aimed their AI sights even higher. Work went ahead at the Radiation Laboratory, at the Aircraft Radio Laboratory at the Army Air Corps technical headquarters at Wright Field, and in an increasing number of firms in industry. This was a time of remarkable progress and enthusiasm, and the first of the many occasions when the whole spectrum of government and industrial effort on both sides of the Atlantic was to be harnessed in a common cause. One has to remember that the United States was not an ally of

Britain, but a neutral country. Emotionally, most of the Americans involved did openly favour Britain's fight against aggression, but the main motivation for the work was that it made sense. The new microwave technology was obviously a world-beater, and the British had brought it with no strings attached.

There was at this time a lack of understanding of Americans by Britons, and vice versa. Until they learned better, the British thought the Americans boastful talkers, with the implied corollary that their actual performance was somewhat less. This was never a problem with the early development of American AI radar; both nationalities worked together day and night, and at a fantastic pace. Learning all about the magnetron, how multi-kilowatt microwave power was controlled and measured, how a complete pulsed radar should be designed and engineered, and how an industrial task force should be organized for the hardware, took the Americans just one month. Getting the pilot plant tooled, the laboratory in full operation, and the prototype radar designed, built, delivered, assembled and erected took a further month. Two days ahead of schedule, on 4 January 1941, the first microwave radar in the United States was showing a picture of the Boston skyline across the Charles River. It had a British magnetron, Westinghouse pulser, Sperry power-driven dish aerial, fixed receiver aerial, Bell Telephone Laboratories receiver (with IF unit by RCA) and a GE oscilloscope display. On 7 February it was tracking aircraft, while construction was then almost complete on the first airborne set with a Sperry klystron T/R box so that the same dish could be used for both transmission and receiving. On 10 March this second radar made its first flight in a Douglas B-18A of the Army Air Corps. It started by detecting aircraft at a range of five miles, and gradually improved the performance to eight miles. On 27 March the same set put up an outstanding performance in ASV and anti-submarine tests, spinning off a fresh family with PPI display which became the famed Raytheon SG and SCR-582.

The basic design of the American radar was strongly influenced by Bowen, and it took shape as an advanced equipment utterly unlike AI.VIII. The most startling difference lay in the scanner. The aerial was fixed inside the dish and the whole assembly was counterbalanced and mounted on ball and roller bearings so that it could spin continuously about a vertical axis. In operation its rotational speed was 350 rpm, or 5.5 turns per second, so that to the eye it was a mere blur. A typical production set had a 30-inch scanner and put out a peak power of 100 kW. The scanner transmitted as it swept through the arc ahead of the aircraft from about 75° left to 75° right. Throughout this large angular coverage the beam remained constant, so D/F accuracy and range stayed constant at about 5° and ten miles. To search, the gimbal frame carrying the scanner could nod up and down. The operator could choose the vertical arc. A typical coarse search mode might be between 50° above the horizon to 20° below, but this could be reset on the ground to different limits. Once a blip had been seen, the arc could be changed to narrower limits, so that by repainting the blip more often it could be seen better, even in the presence of jamming. Some sets could be switched to +20°/-5°, and then, for the final attack, to +10°/0° or any other narrow band. The presentation was equally new. There were two displays. In some, the left scope was a PPI of the sky ahead of the fighter, while the right scope was azimuth/range. An alternative presentation was for the left to be azimuth/range and the right azimuth/ elevation. By the end of the war many sets had a PPI scope and a second scope switchable to give azimuth and either elevation or range.

In February 1941 the Army Air Corps ordered fifteen production sets, designated AI-10 (ambiguous later, in view of the British numbering system), for the prototypes of a completely new purpose-designed night fighter, the Northrop XP-61 described later. In April two pre-production AI-10 radars were completed for installation in Douglas A-20 attack bombers, the US Army version of the DB-7 which was used by the RAF as the Boston and Havoc. One of these sets did eventually fly in an A-20, as related shortly. The other was lent to Bell Telephone Laboratories and used as the starting point for the SCR-520A made by that firm's production company, Western Electric. The next installation was an AI-10 in a Boeing 247 transport for the RCAF; this was installed in June 1941 and was then flown to England for demonstrations and tests, which were completed in September 1941. One immediate result was that the British government placed an order with the US government for the production AI-10, an initial ten sets being purchased for installation in Beaufighters. Amazingly – because I think the decision showed a certain lack of boldness – it was then decided that the American radar would not fit into the nose of the Beaufighter, and the aircraft were cancelled in December 1941. The ten radars were rebuilt as the ASV-10 for overwater search. A single AI-10 was installed in an RCAF Bolingbroke in February 1942 for Atlantic patrol tests.

While the Boeing 247 had been flying in England its radar had been evaluated against AI.VIII. It was decided that the British set had a more sensitive receiver, but the American set had higher pulse rate and greater peak RF power. A marriage of the two seemed fruitful, and eventually some AI.VIII circuits were built into the American receiver, which was further developed with advanced features to resist possible enemy jamming. The SCR-520 was terminated at the 108th set, and replaced by this more advanced anti-jam radar designated SCR-720. In 1943, this was at last to go into production, for the P–61 and for the RAF. Meanwhile, the remaining radar of original SCR-520/AI-10 type earmarked for use in an A-20 did get into one of these aircraft, in August 1941. All Radiation Laboratory experimental aircraft installation was done in special hangar facilities under military guard at East Boston Municipal Airport (today Boston Logan International). In September 1941 the Douglas A-20 began a successful flight development programme. On 1 October it was delivered to the Army, and after Pearl Harbor (7 December) its home base was moved to California.

This was not by any means the first DB-7 type aircraft to have AI radar. The DB-7 had been designed by Ed Heinemann at Santa Monica in 1938. Production three-seat bombers had served with the *Armée de l'Air* before the French collapse, and it was part of a French order that was converted into the first Havoc night fighters at RAF Burtonwood, Lancashire, in 1940. Later Havocs were, as previously described, rigged up with Turbinlites and LAMs. All this deeply impressed the US Army Air Corps, and in 1940 that service began its own conversion programme. It had sixty semi-finished A-20 three-seat attack bombers; prolonged trials had shown that their R-2600-7 engines, with turbocharger, could not be satisfactorily cooled in the A-20, and nobody knew what to do next. Eventually the Army bought 147 A-20A bombers with non-turbo engines, and decided to turn the sixty A-20s into night fighters designated P-70. It took about a year, from November 1940, to convert the batch into one XP-70 and fifty-nine production fighters. The bomb bay, bomb sight, nose cockpit, exhaust turbos, radio and rear guns were removed, and the aircraft were completed with R-2600-23 engines with flame-damped exhaust stacks, unglazed nose, 24-volt electrics, N-3A pilot gunsight and a belly pack containing four 20 mm M-2 cannon fed by boxes of 60 or 120 rounds. Most surprising of all, AI.IV radars were obtained from Britain and fitted with British help. The result was a fine night fighter. Thousands of hours were logged in NF training, then a

*The Black Widow was a real battlewagon, even though this P-61A-5 was one of those with no dorsal turret. The leading-edge inlets served the superchargers and intercoolers.*

completely new activity to the Army Air Corps, first at Orlando, Florida, and then at Salinas and Fresno, California.

Later many more A-20 conversions were made, to train crews for the P-61. The latter was the first aircraft in history designed from the start as a radar-equipped night fighter. So far the RAF, the only force that had really had much need for night fighters, had managed with lash-up conversions of day fighters, long-range fighters, two-seat day bombers and American three-seat attack bombers. When a nation has its back to the wall in wartime there is strong motivation to go on making do with whatever is proved and available; conversely there is a powerful disincentive to design new things that will have no effect on the war until years later. Though this feeling eased as 1940 receded – in Britain, but not in Germany – the existence of the Beaufighter and Mosquito, both produced by the initiative of the manufacturer and with no thought of night fighting, resulted in the RAF never receiving a single purpose-designed night fighter until long after the Second World War was over! Yet this is what the Army Air Corps, in the neutral United States, sought to acquire in the autumn of 1940, when Britain's radar was a closely guarded secret unknown to the public, and AI-equipped night fighters consisted of a handful of primitive converted Blenheims.

It is a matter of historical fact that in October 1940 the US Army Air Corps drafted a specification for a night fighter, designed from the proverbial 'clean sheet of paper', within a week of first hearing of AI radar from the Tizard Mission. After reviewing the entire British experience with the Blenheim, Defiant, Beaufighter (hardly operational) and the planned Havoc and other proposals – but not the Mosquito, which had not even flown – the US Air Technical Service Command and other agencies decided that what was needed was a night fighter designed for the job. The British lash-ups were obviously too severely compromised; in any case the night fighter was suddenly recognized as a type of combat aircraft fully equal in importance to any other, and it was only common sense to design one properly. A laudable objective, but the design finally accepted tottered on the brink of going too far. It is easy, especially when trying to meet an official specification, to end up with an aircraft that is big, complicated, expensive, ponderous and difficult to maintain. The world's first purpose-designed night fighter went a long way in this direction, took a long time to become combat-ready, and emerged into a world that was about to regard all propeller-driven fighters as obsolete.

This was a pity, because the Army wanted a good night fighter urgently. It studied the proposals submitted on 31 December 1940, picked that from Northrop Aircraft, ordered two XP-61 prototypes on 11 January 1941, and followed with thirteen service-test YP-61s in March, a run of 150 P-61As for the inventory in September, and a further 410 in February 1942. It was named Black Widow after the venomous spider. Northrop had no choice in making the P-61 big, and one of the unquestionably good features of the design was that the engines chosen were two Pratt & Whitney R-2800 Double Wasps, the most powerful engines available, which gave even the P-61 an adequate all-round performance. A small engine would have been a failure, and to choose any of the wealth of seemingly more attractive new engines then on the drawing boards and test beds at Pratt & Whitney, Wright, Lycoming, Chrysler and Allison would have caused delay and, eventually, redesign (because most of those engines were cancelled). Northrop left the entire nose free for the AI radar. Behind was the pilot, with a good view ahead, but not to the rear. The theory was that this did not matter much, because on board there were two other pairs of eyes, which between them could cover almost the entire sky except for directly down and ahead. Above and behind sat the observer (radar operator), in a superbly equipped cockpit with his own even better view of the forward hemisphere, including ahead and down over the pilot's roof and nose. In the bulged belly were four 20 mm M-2 cannon, each fed by a belt of 150 rounds. On top, behind the radar operator's cockpit, was a General Electric turret mounting four 0.50 in Brownings, each with 500 rounds.

This turret was a questionable asset, but technically it was a remarkable achievement. Not only had no turret ever before delivered such firepower, but it was also sighted and fired remotely. It could be driven electrically to cover the entire upper hemisphere. (Like so many American aircraft of this era, the P-61 was all-electric, and its instructional manuals were of unprecedented size and complexity. When the guns were locked directly ahead they were part of the fixed armament fired by the pilot, giving firepower unequalled by any contemporary fighter in service (because four 0.5 in guns far surpassed the effect of the six 0.303 in of the Beaufighter). As an ATC cadet, I visited a P-61 squadron which was getting operational ready for D-Day. I was told that the powerful turret was principally to defend against any hostile aircraft attacking from the rear. They told me this explained why the tail was carried on two booms. Thus, the turret came primarily under the control of the third crew member, who sat in the rear of the nacelle facing aft. He had the option of transferring control to the R/O (radar operator), who could swivel the turret to fire directly ahead (which is where it was when the aircraft were parked), or to cover the forward and upper airspace, with electric cut-outs to prevent the projectiles from hitting the 146 in Curtiss Electric four-blade propellers. Firing ahead could temporarily blind the pilot and R/O.

Altogether, the Widow was an impressive battlewagon. I was even given a short flight, in the course of which I crawled from the 'rear gunner's' seat into the very tip of the nacelle, which was an enormous moulding in Plexiglas. I was impressed by the view it offered, even ahead over the wings. It was a bumpy day, and when I crawled back I saw for the first time that the joint between the transparency and the nacelle was marked by a not very obvious red line, with the warning, 'No weight to be placed aft of this line'. I had been wearing only the harness of my clip-on chest-type parachute, so would like to thank Rohm & Haas, makers of Plexiglas. Whether or not a fighter needs rear guns, for either defence or offence, is open to argument.

Northrop flew the first XP-61 on 26 May 1942. It had a vast wing with outstanding high-lift flaps of a kind seldom seen until the 1950s, and in most respects was a potential winner. But it was so complex it took a further year to get production models out of the door – by which time the distinctive and highly secret black-painted aircraft had been anonymously featured in a coast-to-coast newspaper cartoon strip, whose artist afterwards explained he had often seen it and thought it looked great! During 1942 and 1943 the restyled Army Air Force waited for the P-61 and, as months became years, tried to make do with the P-70. In fact the P-70 was eventually judged inadequate for the European theatre, mainly on account of its poor rate of climb and modest ceiling of about 27,000 feet – all on account of the inability to use turbocharged engines. During 1942 the AAF took aircraft in small batches from the A-20G line and existing machines at field modification centres and turned them into the P-70A, with the AI.IV relocated in the bomb bay and rear cockpit and with six 0.50 in guns in the nose. There followed a further batch with the new American AI radar, as described later.

With the P-61 taking a long time and the P-70 inadequate, the AAF swallowed its pride and equipped European night-fighter squadrons with the Beaufighter. By 1942 night activity over

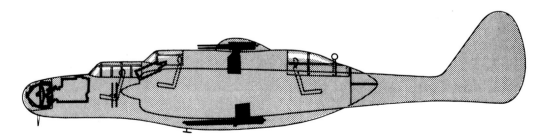

*Northrop P-61A Black Widow with SCR-720; four 20 mm M-2 in belly and four .50-inch Browning in power-driven turret.*

Britain was trivial and sporadic. Indeed, from early 1941 the intruder version of the Havoc, with nose navigator and carrying a bomb load, had been looking for trouble over *Luftwaffe* airfields; one, manned by three sergeants, shot down three enemy bombers in three consecutive visits to Belgium. The only place where there was much activity was North Africa. In the early campaign in Cyrenaica the *Regia Aeronautica* and *Luftwaffe* did not do much at night, but after Operation Torch (the Anglo-American invasion of North Africa in November 1942) things hotted up. Matters came to a head when, after increasingly severe night raids by *Luftwaffe* units hastily transferred to Italy and Sardinia, Maison Blanche airfield at Algiers was damagingly attacked on the night of 20 November. A few Beaufighters, of 252 and then 108 Squadrons, had been based in Malta since 1941, together with a vital GCI set, but the night situation over Algiers was stupidly one-sided until Beaufighters were transferred from the Western Desert and from Britain. Then the boot was on the other foot; No. 600 Squadron in particular rang up a big score by night, and in early 1943 wrought havoc among Ju 52/3m and giant Me 323 transports. In July 1943 RAF Beaufighters destroyed fifty enemy aircraft by night in the first week of the invasion of Sicily, against the loss of three of their own number, with GCI control provided by a radar and control room in an LST landing craft. By this time the US 12th Air Force (1st Tactical Air Command) had several squadrons of Beaufighters in action, the first being Nos 414 to 417 inclusive. All had the Beaufighter VIF, with AI.IV, VII or VIII, until replaced in late 1943 by the Mosquito 30. They operated with these aircraft very successfully right through the Italian campaign, until the P-61 at last reached the Mediterranean in July 1944.

By this time SCR-720 was a very different equipment from the rather primitive one that had operated at MIT back in January 1941. It was powerful, precise and reliable, and had one feature never seen before. From the earliest days of radar, experts in Britain and Germany had been worried at the possibility of the vital blip being smothered by a cunning enemy surrounding himself with what is today called passive jamming. Small pieces of wire or tinfoil scattered into the sky would each behave as a dipole aerial, so that if scores of thousands were released, they would form a reflective cloud through which the real target could not be seen. At first there seemed to be no answer to this, other than to change to a completely different radar frequency, but SCR-720 did offer some help in having anti-jamming circuits, two forms of display, and the ability to close down the field of view once the target had been acquired. This was the beginning of the process that has gone on ever since to try to defeat countermeasures and make the fighter's task easier by working on the 'raw' radar picture to make it clearer and more informative.

Western Electric delivered the first SCR-720 in November 1942. Some of the first sets were installed in the final Douglas P-70s. The 65 P-70B-1s were A-20G-10s modified as night fighters on the production line, and the 105 P-70B-2s were A-20G and J bombers converted at AAF bases. All these aircraft were used only for training in the United States. Whereas in 1940–1 the RAF had to learn the hard way, by actually trying to do the job, the AAF in 1941–3 was able to study the theory of night fighting in great detail, coming to the conclusion that there was no point in trying to organize a night-fighter force in elements larger than a squadron. It was decided that the whole thing rested on close teamwork, and a shortcoming of the P-70 was that with radar fitted it was not possible to train a P-61 crew of three.

Indeed it may have been partly owing to the lack of training that only the first 37 P-61s had the turret fitted. It was said at one time that the turret was left off because it caused 'severe

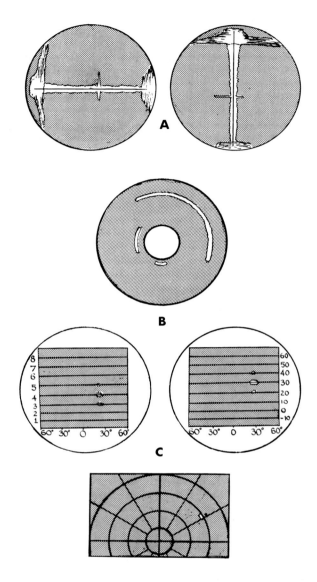

These were the displays used in the most important Allied AI radars in the Second World War. In AI IV there were invariably two scopes, each with a linear timebase running across a diameter (A). The left display showed range and elevation; if the fighter was at 15,000 feet (the whole distance across the timebase to the ground echo at left) the target shown might be 7,000 feet ahead. There is more blip above the timebase than below, so the target is at a higher altitude. The right display shows azimuth; there is much more blip on the left than on the right, so, as well as climbing, the fighter must turn to the left. In the centimetric AI VIII there was usually a completely different radial presentation, with extreme range at the edge and a blank centre due to the direct pulse (B). In the scope illustrated the operator can see a very close target (short arc at 6 o'clock) only half a mile away, but as it is such a short line it can be described as at 45° off, below and slightly left. On the left is a target 1½ miles away, 18° to the left and slightly above. The long blip is a target at four miles, only 7° off to the right and above. A target dead ahead would give rise to a complete circle. At (C) are three displays used with SCR-720 (AI. 10), an azimuth/range scope (60° left to right and range to eight miles), an azimuth/elevation scope (-10/+60°), and a C-scope radial display like a PPI in the vertical plane with circles at 20°, 40° and 60° aim-off from dead ahead. In each display a target is visible at four miles, 30° right and 30° above. Most SCR-720 installations had two of these three possible displays.

buffeting', but this is hard to believe because eventually the turret was put back. Northrop delivered the last of the service-test YP models in October 1942, each incorporating significant additional features and modifications. Delivery of the production P-61A began at last in January 1944. The 18th Fighter Group in the SW Pacific Area became operational in May 1944, and units of the 9th Air Force in England began to operate just before D-Day (6 June 1944), with the black exterior painted with white/black 'invasion stripes', the clearly visible markings applied hastily to all Allied aircraft to render them safe against trigger-happy Allied AA-gun crews. In the event, the only aircraft those ground gunners saw were Allied, and in Europe the P-61 did not have a great deal to do, though it destroyed several *Luftwaffe* aircraft from 7 July 1944.

Altogether, the P-61 was a unique mix of superb and near-miss. Though a huge aircraft for a fighter, the rate of roll was augmented by unique surfaces called plug ailerons, which were normally retracted into the wings ahead of the flaps. Northrop had gone to great lengths to provide powerful landing flaps over almost the entire span, with just miniature conventional ailerons at the tips. After the war, when I understood how the P-61's lateral control worked, I was astonished to discover that the plug ailerons could not be used in unison, but only for roll. The one thing a night fighter really needs is some way of slowing down extremely rapidly, so that it does not ram its quarry from behind, and if used together the plug ailerons could have served as powerful airbrakes. (I explained earlier how Beaufighter and Mosquito pilots sometimes had to extend the landing gear in order to avoid overtaking the target.) I first visited Northrop in 1955, and to start a discussion going I suggested that Northrop had tried too hard with the Widow. My hosts wanted to discuss the F-89 (see later), but were interested to hear that most RAF night-fighter pilots to whom I had talked sincerely rated the Mosquito and even the old Beaufighter as better night fighters than the complex P-61. In their opinion the British practice of permitting manufacturers to bypass official specifications enabled them to create superior aircraft, which could then be tailored to particular missions. All said they would rather go hunting in a Mosquito than in a Black Widow, though they did admit that, in the intruder role over enemy territory, they would have liked to have someone keeping a watch on the rear, which the P-61 did have. One of the Northrop men, 'Woody' Woolwine, also told me that Northrop had indeed given much thought to the problem of overshooting the target, and that that was the chief reason for the turret. He also reminded me that Northrop had had to fit the 650 P-61A and B models with ordinary engines, giving a speed of about 376 mph at 20,000 feet. At the end of the war they were replaced on the production line by the P-61C, with turbocharged engines giving a speed of 430 mph at almost 30,000 feet, but these were too late to see action.

For the best AI radar to have had but one US combat application was rather remarkable, and it gave Western Electric spare capacity. Britain had spent 1941 busy with a considerably redesigned development of AI.VIII, which in 1942 matured as AI Mk IX. Its main design team had been led by TRE's Dr Downing, who for the first time had had to assume that the enemy might use passive jamming of the kind already described. By 1941 these proposed clouds of half-wave dipoles had been named 'Window' in Britain; the Germans, who were testing the same idea, called it 'Düppel' after the country estate near Berlin where they held the first trials; the Americans just called it 'chaff'. As in most things, and especially with 'radar', it was the American name that survived. All tests suggested that the idea was dynamite; nobody dared to

*MM748 was a Mosquito XXX (postwar NF.30) built at Leavesden. These were superb, with two-stage Merlins (note intercooler intake behind the propeller) and AI. Mk X.*

use it, for fear of being severely attacked when it was adopted by the enemy. (Some, perhaps unjustly, said thousands of RAF bomber crew-members died unnecessarily, as we shall examine in the next chapter.) In Britain the most senior practical expert on Window was Dr Derek Jackson. He was one of those rare men who can bridge several dissimilar fields. He was an Oxford don, who had worked under Lindemann at the Clarendon. He had ridden his own horse in the Grand National. He had become the RAF's No. 1 experimental radar observer, as a wing commander. By December 1942 he was ready to bring his Window knowledge to bear on Downing's AI.IX, to see if he could defeat it.

By this time Mk IX had been taken 'a long way down the road', mostly by Metropolitan-Vickers, and it was a sophisticated and clever set. Its chief new feature was completely radical, but one ultimately destined to be found in almost all air-interception radars. To overcome Window clouds, and any other jamming, the aerial dish could be physically driven by electro-hydraulic servos under the command of the operator. It could be made to point exactly at the target (the operator did this by slewing and elevating the scanner until a small ring encircled the blip.) Triggering a thumb-switch made the set 'lock-on'. In this new mode the target was tracked automatically, the scanner driver receiving azimuth and elevation commands to keep the received signal at a maximum. To put such a lock-follow radar off the scent, Window or later forms of jamming have to make the two-way link 'break lock' and look at them instead of at the target. Another challenging feature was that the AI.IX display could be projected on to the fighter's windscreen. This was not a new idea; it had been discussed at AMRE in August 1940, and trials with AI.VII projected on to the windscreen together with an artificial-horizon indication began in September 1942. This was the first 'head-up display' (HUD), which is a feature of every modern fighter. Back in the Second World War the projected display was too dim by day, too bright by night, and not focused at infinity, though by spring 1943 these problems had been rectified.

AI.IX first flew in a Beaufighter at Defford on 6 November 1942. About a month later it was at Coltishall for Window trials. The resident Beaufighters of Max Aitken's 68 Squadron were always glad to help, and Jackson flew as observer in one, heading out over the North Sea until he was sure that none of the secret Window would be washed ashore; he then carefully released packet after packet to scatter in the slipstream. Downing, aboard the TFU (Telecommunications Flying Unit) aircraft, tried to get a good lock on Jackson's aircraft, but to his dismay found the new radar preferred the Window. After several totally negative interceptions the sortie was abandoned. Downing flew back to Defford, and the AI.IX was modified to improve discrimination (its ability to pick the right target). On 23 December the special Beau was back at Coltishall. As before, Jackson flew as a guest of 68 Squadron and headed out to sea. Just as he was picking up the first packet of foil, the Beau was hit by a burst of cannon shells. They were being attacked by a Spitfire (flown, it was later discovered, by an eager Canadian on his first op). While Jackson's Beaufighter limped for home a shattered wreck, the other Beau was shot into the sea, killing Downing and his pilot and destroying the precious AI.IX.

There had been so many tragic occurrences like this that people were sad and angry but not especially surprised. The subject of aircraft recognition, while continuing to be taught (to night-fighter crews as much as to anyone else), was eventually judged to be incapable of being mastered by the mass of brutal and licentious soldiery – and to an even greater degree by the sailors, who had long had a reputation for firing first and asking questions afterwards – hence the need for invasion stripes in June 1944. It was, however, rare to have such errors in air combat, even with inexperienced fighter pilots who should nevertheless have learned how to use IFF and who, in December 1942, should immediately have asked a ground controller to advise on any hostile activity. Long after the war I was shocked to be told that RAF day-fighter pilots often did not know how to use their IFF!

Just a month before this happened, the first SCR-720 had arrived from the United States. Its fame had travelled before, and TRE – which had moved from Worth Matravers to Malvern in late May 1942 – was eager to try the actual hardware. Not far from Malvern, the TFU had been relocated from Christchurch to Defford, later using the airfield at Pershore as well. It was in a Wellington VIII at Defford that the new US radar first flew in Europe in the same week that the British Mk IX was shot down. The results exceeded expectations, and were particularly good in the presence of Window jamming. In early 1943 the significant decision was taken to suspend AI.IX, and adopt the American radar as AI Mk X (later written AI.10, though it was not the same set as the American AI-10 of 1941). During discussions in London and Washington in January 1943 it was agreed that the bulk of early production from Western Electric would go to Britain. The US government stated that 2,000 sets could be supplied very quickly, and later that month the British ordered 1,000, not as Lend-Lease but as a direct commercial purchase. A further 1,900 were similarly ordered in January 1944. This was possible largely because of the delay with the P-61. As well as this aircraft, it was agreed that the main carrier should be the Mosquito.

It will be recalled that the original night-fighter Mosquito II had been fitted with AI.IV. On 22 July 1942 one of these aircraft, DD715, was modified on the assembly line to carry AI.VIII, with a thimble nose. (Its original nose, with four Brownings, was later fitted to MP469, the pressurized development Mosquito, to produce an emergency high-altitude fighter; later this was refined into the first definitive long-span Mk XV with AI.VIII, which reached 44,600 feet with 85 Squadron, then commanded by John Cunningham.) After trials at Defford the converted Mosquito II with AI.VIII now encased in a 'bull nose' was accepted for Fighter Command as the Mosquito NF.XII, and 97 were quickly converted by Marshall's at Cambridge, entering service with 85 Squadron at Hunsdon in March 1943. They were followed by 270 Mosquito NF.XIIIs, which were new aircraft with AI.VIII, based on the fighter/bomber airframe of the Mk VI with increased fuel capacity. Meanwhile Western Electric was beginning quantity production of AI-10 with minor changes for British use. In late January 1943 the white-painted Wellington used for SCR-720 trials was used as a transport to ferry from Defford to Hatfield a second set, a TRE installation crew and a small team of US experts headed by Walter Pree of Western Electric. The American radar was fitted in Mosquito II DZ659 in eight weeks, and flown to FIU at Ford for testing on 1 April 1943. Here it was evaluated against DD715 (AI.VIII) and the superiority of the US radar was confirmed. Derek Jackson again officiated at Window trials at Coltishall, which were encouraging. Air Marshal Sir Trafford Leigh-Mallory merely asked for small changes to the strobe width on the elevation scale, and suggested that all controls should be made instantly identifiable by touch alone. General McClelland, USAAF Director of Technical Services, called DZ659 'a crackerjack of an airplane' and said its radar was 'the most accessible installation of any American equipment I have ever seen'. So AI-10 became the RAF's main night-fighter radar for the next thirteen years. Though Jackson later found false ground returns that did not manifest themselves in trials, he could always demonstrate to the doubters a clear range exceeding 4.5 miles at an altitude of only 500 feet.

So ten Wellingtons were equipped as AI-10 classrooms, while as soon as Marshall's had finished turning Mosquito IIs into XIIs it started on a new batch of IIs and turned them into XVIIs, the first to be fitted with AI-10. New production with the 'basic wing' (more fuel) and a new Universal Nose capable of accepting either British AI.VIII or AI-10, and powered by the Merlin 25, received the mark number XIX. The final wartime fighter was the Mk 30, basically a XIX with two-stage Merlin 72, 76 or 113 engines. After VJ-day de Havilland produced the Mosquito 36, the RAF's standard post-war fighter until 1951, and the Mk 38 for Yugoslavia in which AI-10 was replaced by the British Mk IX radar, which had, after all, been put into small-scale production in Britain to keep the industry's hand in and avoid total reliance on a transatlantic source.

Exploits of the Mozzie are legion, and it was also the chief carrier of experimental or short-run 'special devices'. Fighter versions racked up a score of more than 600 *Luftwaffe* aircraft destroyed, the bulk of them by night over Germany, as described in the next chapter. They also destroyed nearly 600 flying bombs, of which 428 fell to Mosquitos of Fighter Command (181 by 96 Squadron alone). This was the first attack by cruise missiles in history. The weapon, actually the Fieseler Fi 103, but called (as a cover) FZG 76, and known to the recipients as the V-1, doodlebug or buzz-bomb, had a devastating warhead. It was guided in an essentially straight line by an autopilot at a cruise height of 1,000–2,500 feet. It was propelled by a spring-flap-valve pulsejet, which from a wide arc ahead or astern could easily be seen on a clear night from many miles away, as a bright yellow dot. The problem was not so much finding the bomb, which in any case would be surrounded by AA shell-bursts, but its speed. Soon after being launched (by a catapult ramp in northern France) it was travelling at about 385 mph, and as fuel was consumed, the speed gradually rose to over 400 mph.

This was right on the limit, as far as defending fighters were concerned. All the fighters had supercharged engines, so that their maximum speed rose as they climbed from sea level, reaching a maximum at full-throttle height. Put another way, a fighter such as the Mosquito, with a published maximum speed of about 400 mph, would be unable to exceed about 340 mph at sea level. The fastest defending fighter was the Mustang III (USAAF P-51B), which could reach just over 370 mph. Not far behind were the Spitfire XIV and Tempest V, both on about 365 mph. Almost overnight, defending aircraft were moved to south-east England and modified for maximum speed at low altitude. Removal of the Spitfire's rear-view mirror gave an extra 8–9 mph, but the greatest gain was achieved by over-boosting the engines, using 150-grade fuel. Indeed, by August 1944 special synthetic mixtures were being used, enabling even the Mosquito NF.XXX to exceed 400 mph 'on the deck'. In the final phase of the campaign, from October 1944, flying bombs were carried by night to launch locations off England's east coast slung under the right wing root of He 111s. Night fighters found the Heinkels difficult to intercept, because with the bomb attached they were flying at well under 2,000 feet at barely 170 mph. The biggest attack, on Christmas Eve, was actually against Manchester, when fifty bombs were launched; twenty were destroyed before reaching the British coast and only one reached the city. Of over 2,400 bombs air-launched, only sixty-two reached London, and seventy-seven Heinkels never returned, sixteen of them being destroyed by Mosquitos.

Mosquitos with special electronics served notably with 100 Group, and with the US Army Air Force in the Mediterranean even after arrival of the first P-61s in that theatre. As an exciting 'pilot's aeroplane' it had few equals, though some might claim that a single-engined overshoot was almost too exciting. Contrary to what the very first Mosquito bomber crews had rumoured, the wood not only stayed properly glued but proved outstandingly well able to hold together after severe battle damage. And there were many cases of Mosquito night fighters flying through the intense heat of an exploding aircraft, or even the detonation of a V-1 warhead, with no worse damage than superficial charring, blistering, and stripped fabric on control surfaces. Altogether 7,781 were built, nearly half of them fighters and about 1,500 being night fighters with AI radar. It was by a wide margin the chief Allied night fighter of the Second World War.

Though the ubiquitous Mosquito eventually went to sea, it did so in the torpedo/reconnaissance/strike role. It was never a naval fighter, and in this field the leadership rested squarely with the US Navy, which in comparison with the Royal Navy had far superior aircraft and enjoyed generally better and bolder long-range planning. In 1941, when the Royal Navy appeared to have little interest in airborne radar beyond preliminary work with ASV, the US Navy drafted a detailed specification for AI radar for single-seat carrier-based fighters. This was a development of the utmost importance, boldly carried to fruition to a timescale only a few months later than the 10 cm programme for the Army Air Corps. As described in Chapter 7, it led to a completely new species of night fighter that differed from single-seat day fighters only in being fitted with radar: at last they put the radar display in front of the pilot.

It has never been explained why the British Air Staff continued to show so little interest in the radar-equipped single-seat fighter. As far as I know, apart from the very successful twelve Hurricanes, only one British single-seater carried radar in the Second World War: Typhoon IB R7881, which in 1942 was fitted with a trial installation of AI Mk VI. It was a neat installation, many of the drawings being done by the future editor of *Jane's All The World's Aircraft*, John W.R. Taylor. Hawker Technical Director Sydney (later Sir Sydney) Camm was cool about the idea, and so was the RAF; FIU decided it was 'too difficult to fly at night', though why this should have been so remains unexplained. This established a rigid rule in Britain that fighters had to have a crew of two in order to fly at night or in bad weather. The tradition endured while the US forces successfully operated fourteen types of radar-equipped single-seater, under every conceivable kind of operational situation from airfields and carriers.

The story of how the US Navy and Marine Corps pioneered the single-seat night fighter is told in Chapter 7. Meanwhile, the scene shifts to Germany, where took place the biggest, longest and bloodiest air battles in all history. The giant role played by the US Army Air Forces in daylight is known to all, but has little place in this book about night fighters. Increasingly the night air battle became a battle of technology. At the same time, technology was often self-defeating, and some surprising successes were gained by the 'pilot's eyeball, Mk I'.

# Six

# Battle for Germany

At the outbreak of the Second World War the British and French governments were still living in cloud-cuckoo-land. Among other things they had agreed that they would not authorize the bombing of German soil, because they did not want to anger the enemy and provoke reprisals! So the RAF was forced to spend the winter of 1939–40 flying long and arduous missions deep into the Reich dropping nothing more deadly than leaflets. The only bombing attacks had been on units of the German fleet, and nobody could claim that these had been successful. On the second day of the war a force of Blenheims and Wellingtons had suffered a loss rate of 37 per cent, and (though they did not know it) about one-third of their bombs failed to detonate. On 18 December 1939 a nice formation of twenty-two Wellingtons, each armed by three power-driven gun turrets, looked for targets off Wilhelmshaven and in the Schillig Roads. On the homeward journey, with bombs still on board, they were intercepted by thirty-two Bf 109Es and 15 Bf 110s. In a few minutes twelve Wellingtons were shot down and three more badly damaged.

Apart from forcing on the RAF belated recognition that even a tight formation of bombers could not survive in daylight, so that future attacks were mainly at night, the one-sided encounter did not teach either side very much. Certainly the RAF did not suspect that that particular formation had been detected at a range of seventy miles by a *Freya* radar on the island of Wangerooge. There was a delay of twenty minutes before the Messerschmitts took off from Jever to intercept, and by this time the Wellingtons had crossed the coast near Wilhelmshaven. So the RAF continued in its smug belief that radar was exclusively a British invention.

Likewise, there was not the slightest suspicion that the bomber crews of the *Luftwaffe* were being trained to perform accurate blind bombing using radio beams. British bombers relied entirely upon their full-time navigators, who laboriously plotted their course and airspeed, wind velocity, and track and groundspeed (the classic triangle of velocities) on charts, using pencils and rulers. In between times they took sightings on stars using a sextant, standing under an astrodome of Perspex on top of the fuselage. Near this dome a streamlined body, carried above the fuselage on a strut, housed a D/F loop aerial, a radio receiver aerial which could be rotated until the received signal was a maximum; with a bit of luck and foreknowledge of where the radio signal was coming from, this gave a position line. Two D/F loop bearings in quick succession gave a fix – but once the war had begun enemy radio stations tried to avoid helping in this way.

Altogether, the night navigation of RAF bombers seemed adequate. On 19 March 1940, for example, forty-one out of fifty crews reported that they had found and bombed the seaplane base on the island of Sylt. Unfortunately reconnaissance photographs taken shortly afterwards showed that virtually no bombs had fallen anywhere near the target. Something did not add up, and the bomber crews increasingly realized that they were ineffectual. With the system as it existed, not all the courage and dedication in the world could make up for the fact that they could not find the target. Suddenly, on 10 May 1940, the Phoney War ended, as all hell was let loose in the West. On 14 May the *Luftwaffe* set out to break the dogged Dutch hold on the north bank of the Maas by a mass attack on Rotterdam. As the bombers neared their target, the Dutch opened negotiations for surrender. The *Luftwaffe* recalled its bombers, but one unit – the fifty-seven Heinkels of KG 54 – had already done its work and started fires which gutted the heart of the Old City. Far worse attacks had been made on Polish cities, and later on Belgrade, but for some reason this incident made the Allied leaders recoil in horror. On the following day Winston Churchill, just appointed British Prime Minister, announced that henceforth the RAF could bomb Germany. That night ninety-six heavies set out against specific oil and rail targets in the Ruhr. Only twenty-four even claimed to have located their objectives.

Later, a bomber pilot visiting TRE said, 'They used to tell us to bomb Krupps, but we were lost as soon as we left the aerodrome.' Clearly, Bomber Command had a long and difficult road ahead; but so did the *Luftwaffe*. Reichsmarschall Hermann Goering, the famed head of the *Luftwaffe*, had promised in August 1939, 'We will not expose the Ruhr to a single bomb dropped by enemy aircraft.' He had just inspected some of the *Luftwaffe*'s heavy *Flak* emplacements near Essen, with 88, 105 and 128 mm guns radar-directed by the new *Würzburg*s. By a very wide margin indeed, it was the best AA artillery in the world. But radar-directed *Flak* took a long time to come into general use, and the *Luftwaffe* had no night-fighter aircraft at all. In its first four months of unrestricted bombing of Germany between May and mid-September 1940 the RAF lost only 163 aircraft, about two per cent of the 8,000-odd sorties. Goering was bothered, because the occasional bomb was falling on the Ruhr; one or two even hit their intended targets. In July 1940 he instructed Colonel Josef Kammhuber to form a special force of night fighters.

Kammhuber was not impressed by the existing German defence system. The *Würzburg*s and heavy *Flak* formed a formidable combination, but there were still only 450 guns and a mere handful of radars. Night fighters were another story. Nobody in the *Luftwaffe* had even dreamed

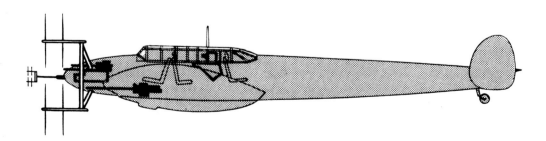

*Messerschmitt Bf 110G-4 with FuG 212 and FuG 220; four 20 mm MG 151 and four 7.92 mm MG 17. Later G-4 sub-types had 30 mm guns and 20 mm MG FF in* Schräge Musik *installation.*

*The 25th Messerschmitt Bf 110C-1 to be built by Focke-Wulf at Bremen was painted with pre-war Balkankreuz markings. Such aircraft equipped the first NJG units.*

of putting radar into a fighter, and the only method of operation was *Helle Nachtjagd* (illuminated night fighting). A few day fighters, nearly all Bf 109s flown by bolder or more experienced pilots, would take off on radar early-warning of a British raid and orbit a radio beacon. Often they would keep their navigation lights on to avoid a mid-air collision, and sometimes they would have to fly to a second beacon and orbit again. Interceptions were achieved solely by watching the searchlights and trying to see the enemy bombers. Throughout the summer this method resulted in just one success: on 9 July 1940 *Feldwebel* Foerster of JG 2 managed to shoot down a Whitley. He would probably have admitted that this was mainly by luck.

Kammhuber could see the need for bigger twin-engined night fighters, with adequate endurance for the long night patrols. The Bf 110 was an obvious choice, but an even better one might be the Ju 88C. This sub-type had begun life as a long-range day and anti-shipping fighter, with the Ju 88V7 prototype flown on 27 September 1938, which had an unglazed nose mounting two cannon and two machine-guns. Some pre-production C-0 fighters were used for ground attack during the Polish campaign, but plans to build the fast C-1, with two BMW 801 radials, were shelved to enable all effort to be applied to building A-series bomber versions. In 1940 the BMW 801 went into production, but with priority for the Fw 190 single-seater, so the C-1 was abandoned and instead the *Luftwaffe* began to receive the Ju 88C-2, a rather hasty conversion of the A-1 bomber with Jumo 211 engines and a nose armament of one cannon and three machine-guns. Instead of being ordinary day *Zerstörer* (destroyer) fighters, these were now regarded as primarily for use by night. They were the forerunners of the aircraft that were to play the biggest part in the biggest night air battle in history.

While giving much thought to the last long-term system for the night defence of the German-controlled continent, Kammhuber acted quickly to create a night-fighter force. On the day of his appointment he picked the premier Bf 110 *Staffel*, I/ZG 1 commanded by Major Wolfgang Falck, and transferred it to Düsseldorf to serve as the nucleus of a night-fighter research and training school, with the unit designation of NVS 1 (*Nacht und Versuchs Staffel*). Three days later it was redesignated I/NJG 1 (*Nacht jagdgeschwader* = night fighter wing), on 20 July

1940. Falck was promoted *Geschwaderkommodore* of NJG 1, and a second squadron, II/NJG 1, was formed with twenty newly delivered Ju 88C-2s. Hauptmann Gunther Radusch took over I/NJG 1, and the force swiftly expanded by adding III/NJG 1 with Bf 110Cs from IV(N)/JG 2, and IV/NJG 1 from Zerst Sta/KG 30 with Bf 110Ds; a fifth staffel was also added, partly based on a special unit that had been formed to operate the first Dornier night-fighter conversions, the Do 17Z-6 *Kauz* 1 (Screech Owl I) and Do 215B-5. On 11 September II/NJG 1 was redesignated as the nucleus of the second wing, I/NJG 2, and a new II/NJG 1 was promptly formed from I/ZG 76, one of the most famous Bf 110 units (they shot down the twelve Wellingtons in December 1939) under Hauptman Graf von Stillfried. Another unit became the nucleus of a third wing, I/NJG 3, with Radusch taking over as *Kommodore*.

Kammhuber was eventually promoted Major-General and set up his HQ in the beautiful castle at Zeist in Holland. He reported to Colonel-General Hubert Weise, in overall command of the German air-defence organization. With constant changes and improvements, the main effect in the first few months, in the autumn of 1940, was the rapid build-up of a well-equipped force of large night fighters, each with a pilot and observer (and gunner, in the case of the Ju 88s and Dorniers), heavy nose armament and endurance of seven hours. In general, the Bf 110 units were deployed geographically to intercept bombers already over Germany, and were alerted by *Freya* early warning and guided to their targets by the *Freya*s and the searchlights. The bigger Ju 88 and Dornier aircraft operated around the periphery of Europe in the intruder role, unhesitatingly following bombers right back to their English bases if necessary, and using bombs as well as guns. At this time the *Luftwaffe* was indisputably the supreme air force in the world. It was easily the best equipped, and the unpalatable failure to subdue the RAF by day had not noticeably affected its morale. It had an abundance of skilled crews, and it was still conditioned to believe in a succession of swift victories (one of its few shortcomings was that no provision had been made for a long war). Not least, it had the backing of a large and competent equipment and radio industry, and by a rapidly increasing margin the world's best aircraft guns.

What was less good was the makeshift night interception system. None of the fighters yet carried their own radar, so they were strongly dependent upon the searchlights. The latter were grouped around the target cities, so not much could be done to intercept the bombers on their flight to and from their targets except as they crossed the belt of searchlights along the coastline. Over the target the sky was full of *Flak*, and at that time there was no way for the German *Flak* to tell which were RAF bombers and which were NJG fighters. Accordingly, during September 1940 Kammhuber took the bold decision to move nearly all his searchlights from the cities to a single dense belt stretching from Liège (Belgium) to Schleswig-Holstein (near Denmark). Virtually all RAF bombers had to pass through this belt, within which no German aircraft were permitted after dark except NJG fighters on patrol. This immediately stopped the wastage of night fighters shot down by their own *Flak*, but it was by no means a complete solution. The *Flak* gunners now had hardly any searchlights, and were still waiting for their *Würzburg* radars. And it needed only a thin cloud layer to wreck the whole system.

It was obvious that what was required was a more sophisticated defence using *Würzburg*s not only to direct the *Flak* but also to direct individual night fighters. This radar sent out a fine pencil beam focused by a large circular dish reflector. Nothing like it had been seen before, and as the movable dishes gradually appeared all over northern Europe they excited much comment, most of it concerned with 'giant mirrors'. The bearing and elevation of the aerial could be read off with great accuracy, and the discrimination was good enough to distinguish two aircraft less than 500 feet apart at over 20,000 feet. On the other hand *Würzburg*'s extreme limit of range of 25 miles meant that *Freya* would be needed to give early warning, and get the *Würzburg* and night fighter into the right positions beforehand. Perhaps the biggest problem was the inability of *Freya* to indicate the hostile target's altitude. The night fighter would therefore have to scramble and climb up to a likely altitude by guesswork. In 1940 a good attacking height for a Wellington or Hampden was 15,000 feet, with a Whitley appreciably lower. Only in the final few minutes could the *Würzburg* suddenly pass an accurate height.

In September 1940 the first trials took place using night fighters directed by a ground controller. *Luftwaffe* fighter pilots argued heatedly about the supposed loss of initiative and freedom of action in accepting such control – a psychological problem that was much less evident in Britain at this time – and the record shows that the Germans were at first far from eager to accept any of the new radar methods. The first GCI radar tried by the *Luftwaffe* was a *Freya*, excellent for early warning but hopeless in the GCI role, because no controller could separate the fighter's blip from that of the bomber once the range had closed within a mile. Despite this, it was a *Freya* that was rigged up near Zwolle, Holland, together with a naval height-finding radar, and trials began against 'Auntie Ju' (Ju 52/3m) transports. On the whole they were as unsuccessful as those in Britain at this time, but on 16 October 1940 Leutnant Ludwig Becker of IV/NJG 1 suddenly found himself in visual contact with an unidentified aircraft flying east over Holland. Flying a Do 215B from Gilze-Rijen, Becker closed slowly and identified the aircraft as a Wellington. With little difficulty he hit it hard in a five- or six-second burst and watched the bomber eventually spin into the ground. But this was the exception that proved the rule, and it was gained in bright moonlight.

By 1941 Kammhuber had masterminded a completely new defence system, and his organization had placed large orders for an improved GCI radar, *Gigant* (giant) *Würzburg*. The need for such a radar was obvious, because *Freya* had inadequate accuracy and discrimination, and *Würzburg* had inadequate range. It was not uncommon for RAF bombers to pass through the defence belt while the NJG fighters were still trying to reach the same approximate position and height. A further problem with *Würzburg* was that reflections from the ground began to mask the target blip at flight levels lower than 6,000 feet (though, of course, few RAF night attacks came down as low as this). *Gigant Würzburg* accordingly had a much larger aerial dish, roughly twenty-five feet in diameter compared with *Würzburg*'s ten feet, which concentrated the energy into a narrower beam capable of giving a clear blip at a range of more than forty miles with typical aircraft targets. Telefunken hurried the improved set into production at the end of 1941, by which time the *Luftwaffe* had placed large orders.

Kammhuber needed several hundred *Gigant Würzburg*s to equip his grand design to defend the Reich, which became popularly known to the RAF as the Kammhuber Line but was officially designated *Himmelbett* (heavenly bed, i.e., a four-poster). This code-name stemmed from the fact that Kammhuber divided up the airspace round the north and west sides of Germany into notional boxes, each having a rectilinear shape like an old four-poster. Each box was about twenty miles wide, and there were 750 of them strung in a vast curve from Denmark round the north of Germany, across the Low Countries and south through eastern France to Switzerland. Somewhere in each box was a GCI station equipped with a *Freya* early-warning radar, a *Gigant Würzburg* to track a chosen bomber, and a second *Gigant Würzburg* to track the NJG fighter assigned to that box. At least, that was the intention; the tracking radars were mainly earlier *Würzburg*s until well into 1942.

*Himmelbett* had many good features. First, each box was a definite functioning system, technically capable of putting a night fighter very accurately onto the tail of a hostile bomber. It had enough width, something like 150 miles of electronically guarded sky, for there to be plenty of time to set up the interception long before the raider had passed out of the box, let alone out of radar range. And as Kammhuber set up the line just outside his searchlights, the latter were ready to take care of any bombers that the night fighters missed under GCI. By this time the searchlights were arranged in groups of five, one of which was a radar-directed master. The latter, with a brilliant beam having a bluish tinge, was alight all the time, normally pointing straight upwards. Once the associated *Würzburg* had locked-on to the bomber, the master searchlight would suddenly swing right onto it, much too fast to be dodged. At once the other four beams would snap on and light up the unfortunate bomber; then the master would return to the vertical, waiting for the next customer. Whether this was done to aid fighters or *Flak*, it was heartily disliked by the Bomber Command crews. Only an exceptional pilot could shake off the cone of beams on a clear night, and it made night-fighter interception almost easy.

On the other hand, there were plenty of shortcomings in the system. It could handle only one bomber at a time per box, and the most rapid interception rate a skilled set of *Himmelbett* and night-fighter crews could possibly hope for was six aircraft per hour for any single box. In 1941 this was not a serious problem, because the lumbering twin-engined heavies crossed enemy territory at about 165 mph in a thin stream, often many miles apart, generally unsure of their position, and often having to spend as long as an hour taking astro shots, working out revised winds and searching for their target. One crew in a Whitley actually spent over 2¾ hours in the general target area trying to find the place they had been sent to bomb (München-Gladbach). In its first eighteen months the Kammhuber Line was able to pay close attention to the majority of the RAF bombers that attempted to cross it, but the situation was to change dramatically.

A less apparent drawback was that, almost unbelievably, the *Gigant Würzburg* perpetuated a basic feature of the earlier radar which made it unsuitable for the GCI function. The original *Würzburg* had been designed for directing *Flak*, and accordingly gave its information in the form of numerical bearings and ranges. This could easily have been converted in *Gigant Würzburg* into the ideal form of presentation, the PPI, such as was being used in Britain. Such a display had been developed between 1936 and 1939 by Baron Manfred von Ardenne in his laboratory at Lichterfelde (Berlin) under the name *Panorama Sicht Gerät* (panorama display equipment). By 1940 he and the short-wave expert Dr Hollmann had prepared this for production with the Radio-Loewe company, and at Christmas in that year a deputation made a presentation to Goering. They explained it in such simple terms that even Goering – the epitome of the technology illiterate, whose opinion of radar was that, 'It consists of boxes with coils . . . I do not like boxes with coils' – could not fail to see the advantages. With PPI a controller has a perfect real-time picture, with the aid of which he can use his judgement to tell the night-fighter pilot exactly when to turn, onto what heading, and at what rate, to bring him up astern of the bomber. Goering gradually saw how it worked and what it did, and even he was forced to admit that it was better than a mere list of ranges and bearings. But it was Christmas 1940, and he told the electronics expert, 'Such a comprehensive development is no longer worth while; the war is already as good as won!' So *Gigant Würzburg* provided nothing but ranges and bearings. To provide a PPI picture for the controller, a clumsy device called a *Seeburg* table was necessary. An operator was told the ranges and bearings of the bomber by telephone, set them up on a rotary and sliding scale in front of him and, in doing so, moved a red spotlight on a large ground-glass table at an upper level. A second operator, connected by telephone to the radar tracking the fighter, moved a spot of blue light in the same way. At the upper level, a third operator with red and blue wax crayons marked the tracks of the two aircraft. The mind boggles at the number of places where errors and inaccuracies could be introduced.

Despite this, the *Himmelbett* system worked. By the end of March 1942 Kammhuber had about half his initial order for 185 *Gigant Würzburg*s, and Telefunken was delivering thirty a month. But by this time, in a single bold stroke, the British had made up for their amazingly inept radar intelligence, and learned all they needed to know about the original *Würzburg*. Though a slight digression from night fighters, it is a thrilling story. For years the British learned nothing about German radar, despite the valuable clues in the Oslo Report. In February 1941 a low-flying reconnaissance Spitfire brought back pictures of circular objects at Auderville, west of Cherbourg, and an interpreter noticed that a narrow object in one of the circles had changed its bearing between one exposure and the next. The British had at last discovered *Freya*. In November 1941, when a number of *Freya*s had been pinpointed, interpreters became interested in a small black blob on a path trodden between the cliffs and a large house, at another *Freya* station at Bruneval, north of Le Havre. Flight Lieutenant Tony Hill went and took pictures at low level with his Spitfire (twice, because the cameras failed the first time) and also had a good look himself. The upshot was one of the earliest and most successful Commando raids ever mounted. On 27 February 1942 twelve Whitleys dropped 119 paratroopers near Bruneval. Next day the 111 survivors, seven of them injured, landed back in Britain with all the vital parts of the *Würzburg*, plus three prisoners, one of whom was a skilled radar operator. In subsequent weeks the *Luftwaffe* showed the British the locations of all its other coast radars by surrounding them with masses of barbed wire, which showed up beautifully in reconnaissance photographs. (The Bruneval raid alerted the British to the exposed position of the vital TRE, and it was accordingly moved to Malvern.)

Of course, by this time *Würzburg* was an old set, fast being supplemented or replaced by the *Gigant* variety. For better early warning, *Freya* was being supplemented by a huge new radar called, appropriately, *Mammut*. This had an aerial like two bedsteads back-to-back measuring 45 feet high and 90 feet wide, with electronic switching through an arc of 100°. This rapid switching, which was much later to become a feature of night-fighter radars, allowed the beam to sweep across the sky while the aerial stayed fixed. The other early-warning set was *Wassermann*, with a rotating aerial about 130 feet high and 30 feet wide. Both the new sets had narrow beams enabling them to see aircraft 150 to 200 miles away. In most respects, they were superior to Britain's prehistoric CH system, though neither was a patch on the monster MEW (Microwave Early Warning) radar developed in the USA. This was first installed at Start Point, Devon, where it could see every aircraft in southern England and northern France on D-Day.

German prowess in big radars was thus unquestioned, but what about AI? Work in this field started years later than in Britain and was generally not inspired, as was that of the Allies with their magnetron. It was in December 1940 that Kammhuber gave orders to Telefunken to begin

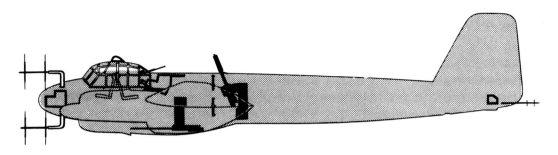

*Junkers Ju 88G-6b with FuG 220 with tail-warning aerial, Naxos Z homer (cabin roof) and Flensburg homer (wings); four (rarely, six) 20 mm MG 151, with two additional MG 151 in* Schräge Musik *installation.*

work on an AI radar, and the company's answer was an interesting compromise. It chose a wavelength of about 62 cm, corresponding to a frequency of 490 MHz, and used an aerial system comprising four double pairs of vertical dipoles in an array carried on struts on the fighter's nose. Under good conditions – and the installation was found to give a rather variable and unpredictable performance – the two display scopes gave useful blips between ranges from about 3½ miles down to about 600 feet. The dipoles were fixed, but by means of a high-speed commutating (rotating phase) switch the emissions and received signals could be channelled through the four sets of dipoles in rapid succession, thus giving a useful indication of target bearing and relative height, which appeared as up/down and left/right deflections on the blip positions. In some ways the results were rather like those of early British AI: they were marred by distortion, fading, spurious blips and plain unserviceability. Unlike the RAF night-fighter crews, most *Luftwaffe* NJG crews scorned the new device, and showed something almost akin to hostility. This suggests a communications failure between the supplier and user, of the kind that TRE had so effectively overcome.

Telefunken called its AI radar *Lichtenstein*, and the name was retained for several subsequent installations. The original pre-production set was designated FuG 202 *Lichtenstein* BC (FuG meaning *funkgerät*, radio equipment). Flight trials began in July 1941, using Bf 110, Ju 88 and Do 17Z carrier aircraft. Even the trials pilots, whose technology-oriented outlook by no means paralleled the supposed blend of unaided courage and individualism of the fighter pilots, looked askance at the FuG 202 aerial arrays, which appeared to be cumbersome and insecure. In cruising flight the bristling dipoles had surprisingly little effect, and the well-designed array showed no tendency to judder or vibrate. Only by brutal application of rudder could the dipoles be made to flap laterally, and then not enough to cause trouble. The maximum speed, however, was cut by an average of 40 km/h (25 mph) and there was also a significant adverse effect on rate of climb and ceiling. It is remarkable that subsequent German night fighters, even the Bf 110, nevertheless managed to reach their targets, despite an often marginal difference in performance. Bomber Command never investigated the effect of cruising at maximum weak-mixture power and accepting the resulting penalty in engine overhaul life and fuel consumption. On most missions this would not have cut into the bomb load, and raising the speed (with a Lancaster, from about 200 mph to about 260 mph) would undoubtedly have had a marked effect on the number of successful night interceptions.

During 1942 Kammhuber's four NJG wings increased their aircraft strength from about 242 to almost 500. Numerically the leading type was the Bf 110, which, despite its failure in the Battle of Britain, was being kept in production because of the interminable delays with the Me 210. Later, in 1943–4, the Me 410 was to be likewise rejected, and production of the old Bf 110 was stepped up to unprecedented levels. This was one of the most remarkable examples in history of an obsolescent aircraft becoming far more important than its intended replacements. The first non-experimental night-fighter version was the Bf 110E-1/U-1, used for training in 1941. The production NF versions for combat use began with the Bf 110F-4, with 1,300-hp DB 601F engines and the heavy forward-firing armament of two 30 mm MK 108s, two 20-mm MG FFs and four rifle-calibre MG 17s. It had a third crew member because, for some extraordinary reason, it was judged important to retain the occupant of the rearmost seat as a defensive gunner, with a single MG 17. The middle man, the observer, was seated immediately behind the pilot facing rearwards. In nearly all subsequent Bf 110 versions he faced the display scopes of AI radar, the *Lichtenstein* BC being first introduced into NJG units in October 1942 with the specially designed Bf 110G-4.

The G-4 was one of the new G-family of Bf 110 models powered by the 1,475-hp DB 605B, introduced as a stop-gap upon the abandonment of the Me 210 in 1941 and continued in production to near the end of the war. They were cramped and very limited machines, yet they continued to play a major role in the night battle for Germany while burdened by ever-greater loads. The G-4 was significant in that it marked the first victory for Kammhuber in his fight to have a large fraction of *Zerstörer* (heavy fighter) output specially reserved as radar-equipped night fighters. In 1941 the High Command had flatly refused, but by 1942 the fact that there was going to be a long war was inescapable, and the need for such aircraft had become urgent.

*This Bf 110G-4d/R3 has the usual eight Lichtenstein SN-2 dipoles replaced by 32 sized to half-wavelength. Compared with the Bf 110C, DB 605 engines partly made up for the 55 per cent increase in gross weight.*

*By 1943 the Do 217J-2 became operational, with FuG 202 and, under the cockpit, four MG FF cannon and four MG 17. One J-2 fired 125,000 rounds of 20 mm without a stoppage.*

To become even more important than the Bf 110, the Junkers Ju 88 was perhaps the most valuable single weapon in the entire Nazi armoury. It played a major role in Telefunken's *Lichtenstein* BC development, and entered service equipped with the production set in NJG 1 in February 1942. The first sub-type to carry radar was the Ju 88C-4, the original fighter Ju 88 with long-span wings of the type introduced with the A-4 bomber, strengthened airframe and landing gear, more crew armour and, in most sub-types, the 1,410-hp Jumo 211J engines that were more powerful than those of early 88s. Here was the basis for what in the course of two years was arguably to become the most formidable night fighter in the world. Such a bold claim is justified by the results, even though, as will be explained, this was partly because of the policy of the RAF. Produced as a mere trickle in 1941, in defiance of the High Command's wishes, the Ju 88 night fighter was pouring off the assembly lines in a flood by late 1942. The initial production versions built with radar from the start were the C-6b and C-6c, the latter having a simpler aerial array with only two sets of quad dipoles.

The point has been made that most *Luftwaffe* NJG crews disliked the aerial-cluttered night fighters, and went on using the non-radar machines in the traditional manner, with *Würzburgs* and *Seeburg*-table plotters doing their best to guide them close enough for visual contact with the bombers. That they had success at all says much for the accuracy of the ground radar and for the skill of the men involved. It is also relevant to point out that, even in 1942, the density of British bombers per thousand cubic miles of airspace over Germany was appreciably greater than in most *Luftwaffe* night raids on Britain in 1940–1. A handful of pilots chose to persist in using a radar-equipped fighter; one was Ludwig Becker, by now a Hauptmann (captain) and a most experienced night operator whose opinions carried considerable weight. He was the first NJG pilot to be officially judged an '*Experte*'. To the surprise and chagrin of many of his colleagues, Becker continued to score with his FuG 202 Ju 88C-6b and ascribed much of the credit to the radar. As a result the 'Christmas tree' night fighters were grudgingly accepted, and used by more and more NJG crews. Once pilots and radar observers had learned how to work with the equipment there was no question of turning back; even the earliest *Lichtenstein* sets were found to be much better than nothing.

During 1942 Dornier delivered about ten Do 17Z-10s with early *Lichtenstein*, as well as the first night-fighter versions of the larger and more powerful Do 217. The first Do 217E bombers had gone into service in 1941, and in 1942 Dornier converted 157 of them on the assembly line into Do 217J-1 intruders (with bomb bays) and J-2 night fighters (with FuG 202 and no bomb bay). Painted black, the 217J-2 was one of the largest and most powerful night fighters of its day, but it perhaps looked more formidable than it really was. When the *Regia Aeronautica* (Italian Air Force) formed its *Forza Aerea Intercettori* in 1943 to defend Turin, Milan and other industrial cities, it asked the Germans for night fighters, and promptly received 217J-2s. They went into service with the 2°, 59° and 60° *Gruppi*, still black but with Italian markings. Reports of fighter interceptions over Italy by night continued to be almost non-existent, possibly reflecting poor ground control. In 1943, while a few 217J-2s continued to be produced, the main Dornier night fighter was the 217N-1, a conversion of the 217M bomber with bulbous nose and 1,750 hp DB 603A engines. Altogether 364 Do 217 night fighters were delivered, including intruder versions.

It is necessary at this point to turn to their increasingly powerful enemy, RAF Bomber Command. Partly owing to the basic Trenchardist doctrine of the RAF, which laid the highest priority of all on strategic bombing of enemy heartlands, and partly owing to the forceful personality of the AOC-in-C, Air Chief Marshal Bert 'Bomber' Harris, Bomber Command was built up during the Second World War to become an enormous and very hard-hitting force, despite tremendous losses. That it was able to grow as it did depended on a truly heroic sustained effort by the British aircraft industry, which had become the biggest industry in the nation, and the overseas aircrew training schools whose output reached more than 500 crews per month. During the crucial years 1941–4 another big factor working for Bomber Command was that it was Britain's only direct way of hitting at the enemy, as distinct from attacking his troops in distant Africa or Italy or his U-boats in the far Atlantic. Countless arguments can be sustained about the rights and wrongs of the case, and to what extent the nation's industrial potential and fighting aircrew might have been better used; the fact remains, it happened. And with this mighty build-up came new methods and new tools.

Not much need be said about the new bombers. The first of the four-engined heavies was the Short Stirling, introduced in August 1940 and on operations from February 1941. Though powered by four Hercules, it was structurally unnecessarily heavy, and thanks to a ridiculous requirement related to pre-war hangars that its span be less than 100 feet it had poor wing efficiency which seriously reduced range and ceiling. It was mainly the Stirling's depressed ceiling that made its crews into poor relations deserving of every sympathy for their short life expectancy. The Handley Page Halifax, first sent over Europe in March 1941, was a superior aircraft which later grew much better still by a succession of changes of which the most important were an increase in span, enlargement of the fins, removal of the front turret and a switch to Hercules engines. The twin-engined Manchester had grossly unsatisfactory engines, but from it stemmed the four-engined Lancaster, usually powered by Merlin liquid-cooled engines, which is generally regarded as the best RAF bomber of the war. An idea of relative merit is afforded by the production totals of 1,759 Stirling bomber versions, 6,176 Halifaxes and 7,377 Lancasters.

Backing up this formidable force were new techniques, of which the most important was to concentrate the attack in space and time. This was prompted by the *Himmelbett* system, sketchy details of which began to be pieced together during 1941, mainly from prisoners of war. The fact that each of Kammhuber's boxes could deal with only one bomber at a time was crucial. If bombers passed overhead at the rate of one every ten minutes then, in theory, each could be shot down. But if they passed overhead at the rate of 1,000 every ten minutes, then, unless some were unlucky enough to collide, 999 out of the thousand would be bound to come through unscathed because the box could not pay any attention to them. Such a concentration at night was not possible, but the RAF went a long way towards it. To do so, they had to have new ways of navigating.

In 1940 the pioneer of night-fighter infra-red sensors, Dr R.V. Jones, had belatedly been asked to find out about the mysterious German radio beams mentioned in the Oslo Report. When he had done so there was brief discussion by the Air Staff of the possibility of sending RAF bombers equipped with *Knickebein* receivers out to Germany along the same beams – either to bomb the transmitters or so that their navigators could start their dead-reckoning from a point much nearer the target. But British electronics could do far better than this. It was one of the old hands at Bawdsey, R.J. Dippy, who came up with the first answer. In 1940 he reminded the TRE Superintendent, A.P. Rowe, that three years earlier he had proposed a blind-landing system involving two pulse transmitters about ten miles apart, with the received signals displayed on a CRT in the approaching aircraft. By suitably siting the transmitters, and making them send out pulses that were keyed precisely together, it was possible to offer the aircraft very accurate guidance. If each pair of pulses was received by the aircraft at exactly the same instant, the aircraft knew that it was equidistant from the two transmitters, and all that had to be done to create a useful bad-weather landing system was to make this position line pass along the centre of the runway. With a fixed time difference between the two pulses, the aircraft would follow a hyperbolic trajectory passing between the stations. Future ILS (instrument landing system) installations to close parallel runways may work in this way, so that aircraft do not have to make a long straight approach, with a considerable time separation between them. In 1937 Dippy's potentially brilliant scheme was put on ice (there were no 'boffins' available to work on it), but in 1940 he told Rowe it could also serve as a primary navigation aid (navaid) over enemy territory. To cut a long story short, the result was Gee (G from grid), with a master and three slave stations in south-east England sending out pulses, all exactly in step, day and night. Bombers over Germany, with a Gee receiver, compared the blip positions and read off a hyperbolic projection chart exactly where they were.

Though not the first electronic navaid, Gee was the first not to rely on continuous-wave (CW) radios and instead to use what might also be called digital techniques. It was certainly the first to give area coverage. From it stemmed a vast profusion of military and civil navaids which are today used all over the world by aircraft, ships and even land vehicles. From the start, this wholly British system was completely successful. The operational Gee stations were ready in July 1941, and in August the first trials were flown by Wellingtons of 115 Squadron, mostly over the North Sea. Then, unbelievably, secret Gee-equipped Wellingtons were allowed to fly over Germany. Two went out and one came back. The full Bomber Command use of Gee was still six months off, and now the idea had probably been handed to the Germans on a plate. As a 'cover' Gee was styled TR.1335, so that when the Germans found the new cables and mountings in shot-down aircraft they would think that these were to service a mere communications transmitter/receiver. And a spurious J-beam system, just like *Knickebein*, was set up as a double-bluff. In fact the Germans did not discover Gee for months, and were surprisingly late even in finding out anything about the deliberately planted J-beams. At this stage of the war their intelligence performance was unimpressive.

In March 1942 a heavy attack was mounted on Lübeck and Rostock, and though these cities were just beyond normal line-of-sight Gee coverage the fact that every navigator knew exactly where he was until he was near the target allowed every aircraft to go straight in, bomb and get out. It was the first attack with a concentrated 'bomber stream' where there was a distinct danger from collision or friendly bombs. Unlike the future American daylight formations, the bombers could not help to protect each other by gunfire, but the sheer concentration defeated the *Himmelbett* system completely. Later that month 120 bombers hit Cologne within fifteen minutes, and on 31 May 1942 Harris mounted his first and most famous 'thousand-bomber raid' on Cologne. Despite scraping the barrel and sending not only the new four-engined heavies but also hundreds of old twins from OTUs (Operational Training Units), more than eighty per cent bombed accurately, and with a concentration that, for the first time, smothered the *Himmelbett* system. For every bomber the *Würzburg*s tracked, forty or fifty droned past unmolested. From then, on, Gee was the prime navaid of Bomber Command, though from the late summer of 1942 it was usually jammed by the *Luftwaffe* in the airspace over German-occupied territory. Later, in 1943, Bomber Command introduced a combined system, Gee-H, in which the 'H' portion was an extremely accurate final position-fix involving brief interrogation by each aircraft of two fixed beacons in England. Gee-H was first used to attack the Mannesmann steelworks at Düsseldorf on November 4 1943, when half the Gee-H bombs hit within half a mile of the aiming point.

For even greater accuracy, the RAF used a completely different system, Oboe. This was conceived by A.H. Reeves at the TRE from November 1940, helped by F.E. Jones (later the Managing Director of Mullard). For some reason the ignorant VIPs in London persistently scorned or criticized Oboe, whereas in fact it was absolutely crucial to the success of Bomber Command in the final three years of the war. It could hardly have been simpler, and it bore a strong resemblance to the original *Luftwaffe* beam, the *X-Gerät* of the mid-1930s. There were just two special radar stations, each sending out a stream of pulses: the Cat station was near Dover and the Mouse station on the Norfolk coast at Cromer. Their pulses followed a line-of-sight sheet sloping up away from the curvature of the earth, so that a bomber at 15,000 feet could just pick them up nearly 200 miles away, while one at 28,000 feet could still use them at over 270 miles. As each pulse passed the bomber it triggered a small transmitter, a 'secondary radar' in modern parlance, which sent a different pulse back to the Cat and Mouse operators. In their blacked-out caravans they could watch the progress of the distant bomber, while sending it signals heard in the crew's headsets. It was the Cat station's job to measure the exact distance of the bomber, and keep it flying along a very gradual curve at precisely the same radius from the Cat station as the target. As in the familiar radio range, the pilot heard dashes on one side of the desired trajectory (on the far side) and dots on the other. It was his job to fly the accurate circular path, with a radius of maybe 250 miles and centred on the Cat station, that gave him a steady note. Over the Ruhr the path was almost due north-to-south. Eight minutes from the target the navigator, listening to the Mouse station, heard a B in morse; five minutes out he heard a C; three minutes out he heard a D. Finally he heard five dots at half-second intervals followed by a 2½-second dash. At the end of the dash he let go the load.

Of course, the Mouse operators at Cromer might have released the load themselves, with greater accuracy, but it was thought better to let the navigator do it. For some reason that today is obscure, it was this feature of Oboe – that people sitting in England could know the position of a distant aircraft better than its own crew – that made many important people think the idea nonsensical. In fact, the only obvious snag was that it required the two ground stations to devote all their attention to a single aircraft for about ten minutes, while the aircraft flew an almost straight and exactly predictable path. Had the German *Flak* or fighters taken the trouble to plot that path exactly, shooting down an Oboe aircraft could have become almost routine (though not, perhaps, quite so routine when the aircraft was a Mosquito). Why Oboe was so vital was that it was the key to most of the future major attacks of Bomber Command. Once the exact positions of German targets had been worked out in relation to England – by carefully removing the errors at the interfaces between the different national mapping survey systems – it was possible to bomb on Oboe at night or through cloud much more accurately than by using the best visual bombsight. With hindsight, the answer was obvious, though it was not thought of for three years. At last the Pathfinder Force (PFF) was set up by Air Vice-Marshal Don Bennett to use Oboe aircraft carrying special target indicators (TIs) and other markers. It is worth looking a little closer, because from that time onwards the *Luftwaffe* night fighters did not have to contend with a lot of bombers slouching along aimlessly, as they had in 1940–2, but with large forces proceeding in a dense stream, thundering through the German night to targets that had been already marked out for them. Indeed, by late 1943 markers were even put down along the outbound route and at all changes of heading.

Bennett's birthplace was Parramatta, near Sydney, and the basic marking was called a Musical Parramatta. As the main force neared the target, at about 20,000 feet, Oboe Mosquitos flew at about 350 mph at 28,000 feet, often in the opposite direction, at first at intervals of about ten minutes but later, when more Oboe stations were in use, at five-minute intervals. Each would very accurately drop a TI, usually giving sixty bright pink-red markers like a huge chrysanthemum; the appearance of these later became quite cunning, to defeat German efforts to fire misleading false ones nearby. At first there was no guarantee that the second TI would be in place before the first had burned out, after about six minutes, so a small proportion of the main force would visually drop green secondary markers, which were used as the aiming point if no red one could be seen. If there was dense cloud cover the answer was a Musical Wanganui (from the New Zealand birthplace of Artie Ashworth, a PFF staff officer): allowing for drift due to wind, the Oboe Mosquitos would mark the target with flares just above the cloud. Despite the obvious problems, even a Wanganui marker was usually more accurate than the best previous visual bombing on a clear night.

Oboe Mosquitos, of 109 Squadron, first went into action on the night of 21 December 1942 against the mighty Krupp works at Essen. This target had often figured in BBC news bulletins, but what the British public did not know was that on 20 December 1942 it was still almost completely undamaged. The Ruhr, besides being extremely heavily guarded, was a perpetually misty valley that seemed to be impossible to find even on a moonlit night. From 21 December everything was changed. The four high-flying Mosquitos just listened to the Cat and Mouse stations and released their bombs, and more than half the bombs actually hit the works (this was before the era of Oboe marking for a main force). By 1943, in heavier attacks against much greater opposition, a fair average was for half the Oboe-guided bombs, markers and other stores to hit within 150 yards. The climax at Krupp's came on 25 July 1943, when 627 heavies let go 2,032 tons on the markers of Oboe Mosquitos. Virtually every bomb hit, and when Dr Gustave Krupp von Bohlen und Halbach came to his works next morning he fell down in a fit, and never recovered (which saved him from standing trial in 1946 as a war criminal).

It was Oboe that guided the bombs that laid waste most of the German arms industry, but the radar aid that excited the VIPs was a totally different one called $H_2S$. This happens to be the chemical formula of a gas that smells like rotten eggs, but the name actually derived from 'Home, sweet home', crews having been told to tell their German captors that the wiring and mountings for the unfitted device were in readiness for an aid to help their return to base. Why $H_2S$ excited the technology illiterates was because it painted a PPI picture of the land or sea beneath; the VIPs could understand this, but could not comprehend Oboe. Each set comprised a large and powerful centimetric radar, containing a magnetron, sending out a vertically polarized beam that swept round and round, painting a picture in bright green light of all the areas that strongly reflected the energy back to the bomber's receiver. Calm water behaved like a mirror, reflecting the energy away from the bomber and looking black. Land sent back diffuse and scattered reflections, standing out clearly against the black water. Buildings reflected strongest of all, so cities stood out brightly even against the land. Lord Cherwell (Lindemann) forcefully backed $H_2S$ because it could go anywhere the bomber went, and thus did not have a range-limitation as did Oboe. There was such political pressure behind it that it was hurriedly bulldozed through, despite the need to disrupt bomber production to accommodate it, the need to cut a quarter-ton off loads to carry its weight, the need to accept a reduced speed because of the drag of the big blister radome, the fact that it burdened each bomber with an airborne lighthouse which advertised its presence from many miles away, and, not least, because magnetrons proved to be practically indestructible so that using $H_2S$ meant giving the enemy a present of the highly secret centimetric technology.

The birth of $H_2S$ was one of the first flights of AI radar, in the old Heyford in 1937. Ed Bowen had taken S/L (later Air Marshal Sir Raymund) Hart for a ride, and Hart commented on the fact that the crude CRT gave recognizable reflections from a ship, from the harbour at Harwich, and even from the railway station. The same thing was noticed by TRE boffin P.I. Dee in October 1941, and this time things moved fast. A primitive converted AI flew on 1 November 1941, and the first purpose-designed $H_2S$ in a Halifax on 16 April 1942. In June this Halifax (V9977) tragically crashed in Wales, killing five of the team, including the brilliant Blumlein. Head of the team, at Swanage and then Malvern, was A.C.B. (later Sir Bernard) Lovell, whose public fame came after the war as a radio-astronomer; and the first $H_2S$ operator was Dr B.J. O'Kane, who needs no introduction to anyone in today's field of navaids.

It was partly from the designation $H_2S$ that the 10 cm waveband became called the S-band. Subsequently, in late 1943, PFF Lancasters began using $H_2X$ working on X-band radiation at 3 cm – an American radar used by the B-17 and B-24. This Mk III equipment was then supplemented in 1944 by $H_2S$ Mk VI operating on K-band radiation at only 1.5 cm, giving a marvellously sharp picture with fine definition. The supposed wonder aid needed no 'selling' to

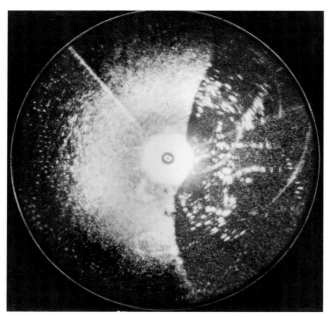

*Shipping off the Normandy coast on 6 June 1944 (D-Day) made what an H₂S operator would consider a clear picture. The aircraft is almost exactly over the coastline.*

the crews, who were tickled pink at seeing the ground on the darkest or cloudiest night. H$_2$S went into action over Hamburg, a very suitable target, on the night of 30 January 1943. The radar-equipped Stirlings and Halifaxes marked for the Main Force, though most of the sets that kept working were fooled by ground decoys that included false lakes. In any case, H$_2$S was useless as a sole aid to precision bombing, because its circular error was many times greater than that of bombing on the despised Oboe. It was never intended to fulfil such a role, but merely to aid navigation.

There was one other important device fitted progressively to all the vast fleet of Bomber Command heavies in 1943. This was a baby radar called Monica, the world's first example of rear-warning radar (RWR). Just below the tail turret of each bomber was fitted a horizontal arrowhead aerial like a miniature AI Mk IV turned through 90°. It sent out signals in a 45° cone, and if anything reflected the energy within 1,000 yards the crew heard an urgent bleeping in their headphones. If the target came closer the bleeper increased in rapidity, virtually forcing the crew to take evasive action. It had the advantage that one sensed the presence of any hostile aircraft, even if the wavelength of its AI radar was unknown. It had the grave disadvantage that it also sensed friendly heavies even better, and in a dense bomber stream the incidence of false alarms was so high that Monica bleeps were soon almost ignored.

This would have been no great loss if it had merely put the clock back to pre-Monica days. Unfortunately, the two new devices which had been thrust forward with such urgency, and fitted to every RAF heavy bomber, were the most suicidal things that could possibly have been contrived. The subject of night flying was obviously still largely misunderstood by the decision-takers in Britain. Yet the basic rules are so simple they ought to be obvious. Suppose two men each carrying a torch and a pistol are stalking each other in the dark. There will be a strong inclination to turn on the torch and try to see the enemy, but the first man to do so will almost certainly regret it. He would be better advised to rely on his ears and unaided eyes, because these are 'passive' sensors that emit no tell-tale radiation. With H$_2$S and Monica the RAF had taken to using torches, and it did not take the *Luftwaffe* long to latch on to the fact.

German night fighters became a real menace towards the end of 1942. Virtually all of them by this time were large twins carrying the first major production version of *Lichtenstein*, FuG 212 *Lichtenstein* C-1. This differed only in detail – gain, time-base deflection and CRT display – from FuG 202, and had an equally large aerial array, and until late 1943 both were in wide use. As far as technology and results went these sets were primitive, and no better than British

AI.IV of 1940. Indeed, in one respect they were worse, because their azimuth range was only ±25°. This was partly because of the late start, in 1940–1 when the German leaders grudgingly conceded that the war was not yet actually over, and partly because of the basic excellence of Kammhuber's *Himmelbett* system with its pinpoint *Würzburg*s. Nevertheless the RAF naturally became jumpy at the prospect of facing AI-equipped night fighters. What wavelength did they operate on? That was the first question to answer. Indeed, there was a chance the fighters might not use radar at all, but an IR (infra-red) detector. Unknown to Britain, the very first *Luftwaffe* night-fighter sensor had indeed been an IR device, named *Spanner-anlage*, carried by Do 17Z-10 and Bf 110D-1/U1 trials aircraft in early 1941. It did not just sense a bomber's exhausts; instead a spotlight 'illuminated' with so-called 'black light' any aircraft closer than 650 feet in front, the image being seen on a *Q-rohr* screen, and IFF display built into the standard Revi gunsight. As had been decided in Britain four years earlier, this scheme was dropped as having too short a range, and being too prone to misleading indications.

All the RAF knew was that the *Luftwaffe* night-fighter crews were increasingly mentioning a device called *Emil-Emil*. Until 1943 all R/T traffic between the *Himmelbett* controllers and the NJG crews was in plain language – for example, 'The enemy is now only two kilometres in front of you, can't you see him on *Emil-Emil*?' – and everything was recorded by the monitoring stations in Britain. The very first search for '*Emil-Emil*' seemed to be successful; a monitoring receiver in Norfolk, specially sited on low ground where all German surface transmitters were below the horizon, soon picked up busy streams of airborne pulses at 490 MHz. Was this the *Luftwaffe* night-fighter force looking for its prey, or was it some quite different lot of aircraft? The only way to be sure was to send out an aircraft equipped with a 490 MHz receiver and get it to trail its coat past the night fighters. I do not suppose a more courageous thing has ever been done. A Wellington IC (DV819) flew the world's first electronic ferret mission on the night of 3 December 1942. It ditched off Kent a shattered wreck, with four of the six men on board grievously injured. Picked up by a small boat, they learned that their frantic signals had been received. They had actually seen their attacker, a Ju 88C, and knew every detail of *Emil-Emil*'s emissions. Six months later a *Luftwaffe* crew defected – a remarkable thing, indicative of exceptionally intimate understanding and trust between the three crew members – and flew their nearly new Ju 88R-2 to RAF Dyce, now Aberdeen airport. On board was *Emil-Emil*, in the form of FuG 212.

All through 1942 and the first weeks of 1943 the RAF and *Luftwaffe* sat on their growing stocks of aluminium foil, one side calling it Window and the other *Düppel*, each scared to use it and half wishing that they had never thought of it in case the other side got to hear about it. In May the Japanese, who had done the obvious and not only hit on the idea but decided to use it, began strewing the sky over the Solomon Islands with *Giman-shi* (deceiving paper) foil strips which sorely bothered the American AA gunners and cut the Japanese night-bomber losses. This intelligence doubtless reached Washington, but it never got through to London, and the RAF heavies continued to suffer severe attrition from the serenely working *Himmelbett* system. The *Luftwaffe* was naturally surprised at the absence of any British attempt to jam the vital *Würzburg*s. Night after night, RAF bombers fell as flaming wrecks all over northern Europe. Next morning the pieces were carefully raked over to see what could be found. In 1943 the *Luftwaffe* began to find plenty. It was the start of an air battle unparalleled in duration, in ferocity, in geographical extent and, above all, in electronics, counter-electronics and counter-counter-electronics.

After exhaustive trials the British gave up trying to fit the H2S magnetron with a destruct system, so discovery was just a matter of time. The *Luftwaffe* first noticed a strange device in a Stirling near Rotterdam on 2 February 1943, and they code-named it Rotterdam. Though deeply concerned at the unexpected British progress with centimetric radar, the *Luftwaffe* made no immediate attempt to use magnetrons itself, but instead swiftly developed passive sets specifically to detect H2S. One type of detector was ground-based, called *Korfu*. These monitored Bomber Command's give-away emissions *en masse*, enabling the Main Force bomber stream to be plotted. More to the point was a directional receiver, *Naxos*. Hundreds were fitted to old *Würzburg* dishes to create *Naxburg*, a ground tracker that gave precise elevation and bearing on every British bomber from as far away as Yorkshire! Even more dangerous was the airborne FuG 350 *Naxos*-Z, with which a night fighter could fly straight towards a bomber from a distance of twenty-five to thirty miles. Inevitably, as *Naxos*-Z was progressively fitted to all NJG fighters, Bomber Command losses rose. Had the British crews been made aware of the danger of H2S and been told to use it for, say, five seconds in each two minutes, the result might have been a little better. As it was, this 'king of the pack of TRE devices' (as Rowe put it) was serving simply as a constantly switched-on lighthouse telling the German fighters exactly where their targets were. What made the situation even more ludicrous, with Gee navigation, and Oboe-guided target marking visible for many miles, H2S was no longer serving much useful purpose.

On 1 March 1943 the *Luftwaffe* Signals Service received another new device, taken from a Lancaster destroyed over Berlin. It was clearly a receiver that operated in the same waveband as *Würzburg* and *Lichtenstein*. Indeed, further investigation showed it to be tuned to exactly the same wavelength. Prisoners eventually confirmed that it was Boozer, a useful and popular aid that flashed an orange warning on the pilot's coaming if the aircraft was illuminated by a *Würzburg*, and a red light if the bomber was tracked by an AI-equipped night fighter. Now the *Luftwaffe* was really stumped. How could the RAF do all this, yet completely fail to interfere with these vital German radars? It continued to be puzzled until late in the summer, and by this time the *Luftwaffe* had a potent new night-fighter force that was so primitive that clever electronics could not hinder it.

Major Hajo Herrmann had been one of the most famous of the *Luftwaffe* bomber pilots, with an already incredible record of accomplishment. In early 1943 he was at staff college, fuming at the fact that each night the *Reich* was being defended by grossly overworked night fighters while hundreds of single-seaters stayed on the ground. He made out to Kammhuber a powerfully argued case for what was virtually a return to the old *Helle Nachtjagd* system. Herrmann was a man of influence far above his rank, and he explained how readily he could build a potent night force of single-seat fighters that would not be part of the regular day (JG) wings but manned by skilled former bomber pilots, all men used to flying at night and toughened by years of action. In his view such a man flying a 109 or 190 could find enemy bombers at night, especially over the glow of a burning city. Searchlights would be invaluable, and he considered that such experienced pilots ought to be able to destroy every bomber held in a searchlight cone for as long as two minutes. But Kammhuber had patiently constructed a formidable defence based on close GCI *Himmelbett* control. Fighters ranging uncontrolled among the *Flak* bursts seemed a terrible idea, even though Herrmann stressed that he wanted to fight not in place of the NJG force but in addition to it.

Getting nowhere with Kammhuber, he did not give up; he just went over his head, straight to Generaloberst Weise. Weise had no vested interest in the *Himmelbett* system, and felt that every little helped, especially as Herrmann had secured a verbal agreement from the Berlin *Flak* commander to restrict gunfire to below an altitude of 5 km (16,404 feet), giving the fighters a safe region above; and presumably other *Flak* divisions might do the same. Weise gave permission for trial operations, and Herrmann gathered his forces to practise what he called the *Wilde Sau* (wild boar) method. It was intended to be simple and effective. The single-seaters would be standard except for carefully flame-damped exhausts and, in some cases, the fitting of *Naxos*-Z homers. The main *Wilde Sau* fighters were the Bf 109G-6/U4N and Fw 190A-5/U2N. The name of the unit was the *Kommando Herrmann*, and there is no doubt that – quite apart from whatever else it achieved – it exerted an inspiring effect on the regular NJG forces. Herrmann's ex-bomber pilots were imbued with their leader's fanaticism. One way in which this was manifest was in their flight planning, which was based on continuing each mission until the tanks had practically run dry. The heavily armed single-seaters carried no external fuel, and endurance was very limited. It may have been deliberate policy to eschew such a nicety as being bothered about the fuel state, because in the course of the winter 1943–4 this became increasingly the general policy among the NJG units as well. Night fighters were now pouring off the assembly lines. So long as the crew got away with it, a dead-stick landing in the dark that destroyed the aircraft was of little consequence. Indeed, the most remarkable factor was the high proportion of pilots who did manage to regain an airfield runway.

The *Kommando Herrmann* began operations in the Essen/Duisburg area in June 1943, and had their first big chance on 3 July, when the target was Cologne. Undeterred by the fact that he had not notified the local *Flak* division, Herrmann and eleven of his pilots spent two hours among the intense shell bursts and shot down twelve bombers. Next day Herrmann found himself a national hero; he was instantly summoned to Karinhalle, where Goering authorized him to form a full *Wilde Sau* wing, designated JG 300 (not, it will be noted, NJG). It put Kammhuber in a difficult position. In the Nazi environment of constant intrigue it might have served him best to decide that, if he couldn't beat Herrmann, he would join him (by publicly joining in the chorus of adulation). He chose instead to stick to his rigid and narrow doctrine of close radar control, and to call for a further increase in radar production. Little did he know what was just around the corner.

On the afternoon of 24 July 1943 the crews of over 800 RAF bombers were briefed to attack Hamburg. During the briefing they were at last told about Window, and that night the 746 aircraft that bombed also released about 92 million strips of foil. The result was chaos. Ground controllers, night fighters, master searchlights and *Flak* were thrown into frantic confusion. Only twelve aircraft were lost, and those tended to be either low-flying Stirlings or the highest-flying Lancasters, cruising outside the main Window cloud. Just a few *Himmelbett* stations and NJG operators managed, partly by luck, to pick off from their crowded and flickering display screens the vital blip that appeared to have a motion different from the rest. But Window made no difference to Herrmann. In subsequent attacks in the ten-day battle that destroyed Hamburg, his single-seaters moved to the area and destroyed more than fifteen bombers, while others fell to NJG crews operating in the same freelance way. Some of the bombers were seen from below, dimly reflecting the light of the burning city. Some were seen from above, silhouetted against the fires, while others were spotted against the numerous searchlight beams pointing out the bombers' track almost horizontally along the ground. It says much for the courage and tenacity of the German pilots that they were able to inflict many casualties by the same crude methods that had proved so ineffectual over Britain in 1917 and 1940. But one is not comparing like with like: over Germany in 1943 the bombers were bigger and much more numerous, and the amount of illumination on the ground and in the sky was immeasurably greater. Both RAF and *Luftwaffe* aircrew were hard-put to retain their night-adapted vision in the midst of such an inferno. (It was in theory a court-martial offence for Bomber Command aircrew to look at the glowing target.)

Great as was the confusion caused by Window, it was not the only countermeasure used by the RAF. The awareness, ingenuity and fast action of the TRE, Bomber Support Development Unit and other organizations had already begun a succession of ECM developments that henceforth kept the *Luftwaffe* perpetually off-balance. One of the first was Mandrel, a powerful airborne radio transmitter that broadcast intense noise interference on the exact frequency of *Freya*. Defiants, pensioned-off from night fighting, orbited bravely near the outer reaches of the Kammhuber Line with Mandrel instead of armament, taking out a section up to 200 miles wide during major RAF attacks. The heavies themselves were able to carry the jamming across Germany, because a Mandrel transmitter was installed in an average of one bomber in every squadron. To blot out GCI communication between the *Himmelbett* stations and the NJG fighters most bombers also carried Tinsel. This was simple and effective: the ordinary TR 1154/1155 radio was tuned to the German controller's wavelength and arranged to broadcast from a microphone bolted inside one of the bomber's engine nacelles. With *Wilde Sau* tactics, in a sky full of Window, everything depended on guiding the fighter in among the bombers. The *Luftwaffe* reacted violently to Mandrel and Tinsel, investigating ways of making the newer *Mammut* and *Wassermann* early-warning radars resistant to jamming, and building powerful new HF and VHF radio stations for broadcasting to the night fighters – all of them, not just the single-seaters. The RAF responded with Special Tinsel; monitors in England listened to the GCI traffic and radioed each new frequency to the attacking force, which then jammed it as before. To smother the VHF frequencies, 101 Squadron Lancasters sprouted tall mast aerials to broadcast jamming from ABC – Airborne Cigar – an extremely powerful VHF transmitter manned by a special German-speaking operator who listened to all VHF transmissions until he or she found the GCI frequency.

This was still only the beginning, for there was even more that the RAF could do. For months the possibility of sending the RAF's own night fighters over Germany had been discussed, but as the majority of possible targets they might find were RAF heavies there were obvious snags. Of course IFF would help, but how could they be made to home on to the *Luftwaffe* night fighters? The answer was provided by TRE within a week of laying hands on the *Lichtenstein*-equipped Ju 88 that landed at Aberdeen. They devised Serrate, a small receiver tuned to 490 MHz and displaying any received signals on a cockpit CRT. The observer saw a display like a gappy herringbone; the bones became longer as the range closed, and moved up or down the display. When the fighter was heading straight for the German night fighter the bones were equal in numbers and length on each side of the vertical time-base. Serrate was issued first to 141 Squadron at Wittering, equipped with early Beaufighter VIF aircraft that still used AI.IV radar. Radar was essential, because Serrate did not positively indicate range. Under aggressive Bob Braham No. 141 began a few weeks of startlingly successful intruder operations, mostly over Holland, but after destroying 23 *Luftwaffe* night fighters the work was halted in

September, because there were insufficient customers. By this time No. 141 was achieving a kill every 35 sorties, on average.

I suspect the real problem was bringing Braham's men and their quarry together. One of the snags was that the rather tired Beaufighters were almost always slower than the German night fighters. Another was that, in a chaotic electronic environment, the *Luftwaffe* night fighters were operating freelance all over Germany. A leading *Experte*, Oberst Viktor von Lossberg, had argued for NJG units to infiltrate into the bomber stream before the heavies even reached the coast, and he transferred several squadrons to the Scheldt estuary and north German coast. Under the name *Zahme Sau* (Tame Boar) he proposed a freelance running fight with the NJG force to partner Herrmann's *Wilde Sau* single-seaters which concentrated over the target. An integral part of *Zahme Sau* was to use the RAF's own Window to confirm the position and track of the bomber stream. The technique recognized that under the new circumstances the *Himmelbett* system was useless, except to get the odd straggler that strayed out of Window protection. The answer seemed to be loose control, with fighters flying perhaps right across Germany, instead of staying in a neat little box, and fighting until they ran out of fuel. It was essential for the GCI controller to use every wile and sixth sense to try to divine the bombers' target in advance, and to note every turn made by the leading sections in the bomber stream. Co-operation with *Flak* was essential, and one of the recurrent problems was that the free-ranging fighters were often running into intense *Flak*.

They also began increasingly to run into something else that struck even greater fear into the hearts of the bravest *Luftwaffe* crews: the Mosquito. This aircraft had long been playing a vital role with its Oboe-guided target marking. Now, in 1943, the radar-equipped fighter versions also began to invade the German night sky, and with their speed and manoeuvrability they exacted a serious toll upon the hard-pressed night fighters. Many fell to the Mosquitos' guns, and many more – possibly as many as 200 – crashed because of the dangerous procedures they were forced to adopt. *Luftwaffe* night fighters took to flying cross-country at 'nought feet' in the dark, landing without fuel in bad weather on unlit airfields, and adopting a host of personal tricks and unconventional procedures. These desperate measures often kept the Mosquitos at bay, but at the cost of an eventual fatal accident. Offensive patrols with Mosquitos, code-named Mahmoud, began in August 1943, the pilot on the first mission being none other than Chisholm, who had been promoted to command FIU at Ford. As the AI.VIII was not allowed to fly over enemy territory the Mahmoud sorties had to be flown by old Mosquito IIs with AI Mk IV (and, with some of the most 'tired' aircraft, engines that seemed to cut either on take-off or on landing, or both). Not until D-Day (6 June 1944) were centimetric radars, of all kinds, released for operations over Europe; after that the Mozzies ranged the length and breadth of Germany. Almost imperceptibly, night after night, the RAF began to get on top of the *Luftwaffe* in every sense except the one that mattered: though harried from pillar to post, the NJG fighters still slaughtered the RAF heavies, which continued to be complete sitting ducks. By August 1944 the Mosquitos often outnumbered the enemy night fighters. Fortunately there were plenty of ways of avoiding mistaken interceptions. The SCR-729 miniature radar receiver could tune in to beacons and IFFs and pass the result to the main AI, visually identifying each blip as friendly or hostile. Coded IR lamps facing to the rear could not be seen by the enemy, but could be detected from several miles' range by an IR detector mounted directly in front of the suspicious Mosquito observer, just like modern night-vision telescopes.

*Heinkel He 219A-7/R1 with FuG 220; two 30 mm MK 108 in wing roots, two 30 mm MK 103 and two 20 mm MG 151 in ventral tray, and two 30 mm MK 108 in* Schräge Musik *installation.*

Most Mosquitos flying over Germany also carried a version of Monica, which was made in great numbers in many forms. Mosquito Monicas usually had a separate CRT display for the pilot, and these were probably the only aircraft in which Monica was not suicidal. Indeed it became standard practice to try to look like a Lancaster and attract an enemy night fighter. Mosquito pilots had to become expert at knowing just when to turn the tables, and it needed icy nerves. When the Bf 110 or Ju 88 was about to open fire, it needed just a few vicious manoeuvres (not necessarily in the horizontal plane) to reposition the Mosquito nicely behind the enemy, before the latter could work out where his blip had gone.

Few aircraft did as much to win the war as the Mosquito. I feel I am letting the side down in daring to criticize it, but my personal view was that it needed a shade more wing – especially in single-engined overshoots at gross weight – and that it was a pity that de Havilland never made its powerful petal-frill airbrakes work, tried on W4073, the first production fighter. From the NF.30 onwards the performance at altitude was improved by fitting two-stage Merlin 60- or 70-series engines with paddle-blade propellers. Unfortunately, the new engines received a redesigned exhaust system, for reasons which are far from clear either to me or to Rolls-Royce. The old Mozzie exhausts had worked perfectly well and rarely showed a trace of flame at night, but the new double-layer shrouds of the Mk 30 caused endless trouble, and kept the new mark out of action for much of the second half of 1944. By this time the earlier night fighters were running at up to 24 lb boost chasing flying bombs by night and day. They then turned their attention to the He 111 carriers that continued this aimless bombardment of London and other cities after the original missile launch sites had been overrun. As noted earlier, the lumbering Heinkels hugged the sea, and were extremely difficult to spot by radar. They were even harder to shoot down, and several pilots spent up to half an hour trying to get lined up in pitch blackness on a Heinkel doing 125 knots at under 500 feet. The FIU pioneered a new form of GCI, with the fighter directed by a Wellington orbiting low over the sea using a modified ASV radar. Despite such help, a number of night-fighter Mosquitos were lost in these extremely difficult interceptions, probably through trying to pull turns while too low and too slow. In contrast, the defence of south-east England against the frequent *Luftwaffe* raids by the fastest and latest fighters and bombers throughout 1944 was almost simple. Even though the usual procedure was for Ju 88s, Ju 188s, He 177s, Me 410s and Fw 190s to cross the coast at a great height and then scream across in a long

400 mph power dive, the Mosquitos made the game highly unprofitable (on the night of 13 June 1943 John Cunningham shot down an Fw 190 near London with twenty rounds). Between 21 January 1944 and D-day on 6 June defensive Mosquitos destroyed 129 of these raiders, a high proportion of the attacking force.

Over Germany, however, one aircraft could meet the Mosquito on even terms. The He 219 had been proposed by Heinkel in December 1940 and rejected as unnecessary. But eventually the need for a purpose-designed night fighter penetrated even to Goering, and the He 219V1 flew on 15 November 1942. There followed a seemingly interminable succession of He 219 prototypes, but there were also a few that got into combat service and made their mark. Usually powered by two DB 603 engines, the He 219 *Uhu* (Owl) was bigger than a Bf 110, roughly as large as a Ju 88, and it stood high off the ground on a tricycle landing gear. Pilot and observer sat back-to-back, and there was a typical *Lichtenstein* (usually FuG 212) installation and very heavy cannon armament. In January 1943 the second prototype was flown in evaluation against a Do 217N, which soon gave up, and against a new Ju 188S flown by von Lossberg. Despite all this *Experte* could do, he was outflown by the He 219, flown by another very experienced pilot, Major Werner Streib, *Kommodore* of NJG 1. Streib was so impressed he asked for some of the He 219A-0 pre-production aircraft, and in April 1943 these began to arrive at 1/NJG 1 at Venlo. Streib himself flew the first mission on the night of June 11; when he landed, he and his radar operator had notched up another five RAF bombers! During the subsequent ten days the undeveloped He 219s of 1/NJG 1 accounted for a further twenty RAF aircraft, including the first six Mosquitos to be destroyed over Germany in close combat at night. As the Mosquito had by this time become a kind of supernatural spectre, the incredible debut of this new fighter ran through the *Luftwaffe* grapevine like wildfire.

Thanks to political vacillation, and to Heinkel's own industrial problems and unpopularity with the Nazi hierarchy, only about 290 of all sub-types of He 219 were built, and no fewer

*The Ju 88G-1 of 7/NJG2 which on the night of 13 July 1944 (one month after D-Day) landed by mistake at RAF Woodbridge, Suffolk – the navigator set the reciprocal on his compass! It was one of the greatest prizes the RAF ever received, because of its SN-2 and, especially, Flensburg.*

than sixty of these were test or development aircraft. The much-vaunted Focke-Wulf Ta 154 *Moskito* was a failure, the Me 410 little better, and the main *Luftwaffe* night fighters in the final eighteen months of the war continued to be the Bf 110 and Ju 88. Both were well-tried machines, though the 88 was fundamentally superior to the 110. The Messerschmitt twin had been planned in 1934 to carry two people and a few guns, at a gross weight of 11,790 lb. By 1943 the Bf 110G family included night-fighter versions carrying four men, over a ton of cannon and ammunition, nearly a ton of radar and other sensors, and with a gross weight exceeding 20,000 lb. The radar aerials did nothing to help performance, and neither did the large exhaust flame-dampers with their double sets of cold-air ram intakes to cool and mix the gases. Like the Bf 109G, likewise powered by the DB 605, the ultimate Bf 110 was formidable only in that it was the end product of ten years of lash-up additions. Its only redeeming feature was that it was viceless and willing, and easier to fly than any other *Luftwaffe* fighter; but performance of the final night versions was often marginal at gross weight, even using the MW50 or GM-1 (nitrous oxide) power-boosting system. To put it mildly, the night fighters were also crowded – though, from the earliest days of the *Luftwaffe*, packing men close together was considered to improve morale.

With the Ju 88, the bigger airframe lent itself better to successive extra burdens. Most people judge the 88 as one of the greatest combat aircraft of all time, and certainly its versatility was unsurpassed. Even the difficult requirements of night fighting were met by the 88 better than by any of the many other German types converted for the role, and during 1943 steps were at last taken to produce a Ju 88 night fighter that was not just a lash-up but an optimized design. To the chagrin of the Nazi leaders, defensive fighting over Germany had by this time become the most important role of the *Luftwaffe*, and Kammhuber had built up his night forces into the largest and most efficient arm of the entire *Luftwaffe*, with an inventory strength of more than 600 twin-engined fighters. These aircraft were needed almost every night, and many were pressed into service by day also, with different crews, to keep up the pressure on the massed formations of the US 8th Air Force. The Junkers design team eased off their work on the 188, 288 and 388, and produced what many consider the best 88 of all, the G-series.

Superficially this was immediately distinguished by its vertical tail, which was the larger, squarish tail of the 188. Poor directional stability, and generally bad control qualities, had been an adverse feature of the earlier 88C and 88R night fighters, especially when operating at maximum weight as they nearly always did. In the first six months of 1943 more than seventy Ju 88 night fighters had been written off as a result, and, with the steady attrition of the *Luftwaffe*'s irreplaceable experienced pilots, the situation was getting worse. The G, however, could be safely flown at all weights, even by a novice with only 150 hours. It finally eliminated the offset under-nose gondola, and instead introduced a large cannon bulge under the mid-fuselage. This bulge was necessary because Telefunken had developed a new and more powerful AI radar which needed the whole nose. It was FuG 220, *Lichtenstein* SN-2.

SN-2 was an odd and yet lucky choice. Its design had been started in late 1942, long before the RAF had played its high card and used Window. It might have been expected to operate on shorter wavelengths than the previous sets, to use a small dish aerial, get better resolution, a concentrated beam and fine discrimination. On the contrary, it used a longer wavelength, greater than 3 m, which meant another cumbersome aerial array (called *Hirschgeweigh*, antlers) and a very long minimum range of some 1,200 feet. Maximum range was about four miles, and the angular coverage was excellent, but for a long time the excessive minimum range was to be a great drawback, if not positive grounds for rejecting the set entirely. It was only after the massive use of Window had thrown the German night-defence system into chaos that it was realized that SN-2 was a fully developed AI radar that was almost unaffected by the foil strips. Thanks to its long wavelength, it could still 'see' in the presence of dense Window clouds almost as well as before. Goering at once ordered a crash programme for 1,000 sets from Telefunken, and these were installed in both new and existing Ju 88G and Bf 110G night fighters. Soon the SN-2 was being supplemented by a simplified version of the old FuG 202 served by a single quad dipole aerial, to take care of the final closure of visual acquisition at a range of less than 300 feet.

In the autumn of 1943 the German night-defence force stood at a crossroads. It had been reeling under crushing blows, but had never failed to hit back hard – largely thanks to Herrmann and his infectious spirit of cool ferocity which relied on the unjammable human eye. With new sensors, it was on the verge of making a giant come-back and inflicting on Bomber Command losses so painful that, had the night onslaught not been switched to different targets for reasons connected with the forthcoming invasion, Bert Harris would have been forced to take agonizing decisions (no matter what decisions he actually took, they would have been agonizing). But, at one stroke, Goering knocked the defence force askew again: he sacked Kammhuber. He had long thought Kammhuber's reliance on electronics nitpicking and tiresome; the débâcle at Hamburg made the sacking inevitable. In his place he appointed Generalmajor Josef Schmid. Though Schmid did his best, he was no long-term strategist and could not plan as had his predecessor. The rest of the Battle for Germany was an endless series of improvizations, with one inevitable outcome. And of course, though this book is concerned with the night battle, at least as big a contribution to that outcome was made by the US 8th Air Force in daylight, which not only gained air superiority all the way to its targets but also destroyed quite a few night fighters, which were used by day because of their endurance.

Towards the end of 1943 Herrmann's single-seat pilots began to suffer sorely from casualties – far more in crashes than in combat, and no new experienced pilots were available to take their place. The few aircraft that were left carried Naxos-Z, and so did almost all the regular NJG fighters. By the end of 1943 a majority of the twins also carried FuG 228 Flensburg. This was the passive receiver that homed onto the RAF bombers' Monica tail-warning radar. It worked like a dream. From now on, the NJG crews cared little for Window or close ground control. All they needed was some idea from the controllers of where the bombers were, and the Zahme Sau principle of looking for the Window clouds paid off here. The loose freelancing technique became still looser, as the controllers merely gave a general running commentary, broadcast to all and sundry. The Flensburg/Naxos-Z combination was amply good enough for a closure to visual range, but increasingly the SN-2 was also coming into use to make an interception still more certain.

Once the German night fighters could see their target, shooting it down had become considerably easier. They were using a new type of cannon installation which they called Schräge Musik ('slanting music', or jazz), in which the guns were fixed to fire obliquely upwards. Several are the stories of how this horribly effective armament came to be used. Many schemes for oblique upward-firing armament had been patented, and many actually tested, from about 1913 onwards. In Germany an excellent scheme was proposed in 1938 by Fritz

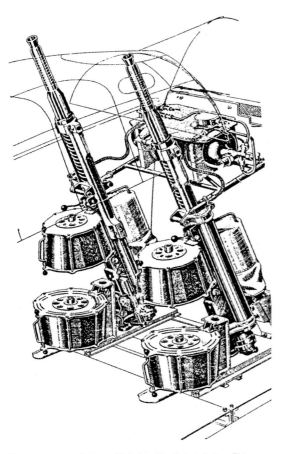

There were several types of Schräge Musik installation. This version, with two MG FF at an inclination of 70°, was fitted to the Bf 110G, which later used the MG151 or MK108.

Thiede. This was never tested, but in early 1941 future NJG *Experte* Rudolf Schönert began experimenting with upward-firing guns, starting with a single MG 17 installed at an angle of about 70° in his Do 17Z-10. This was despite a complete lack of enthusiasm by Kammhuber, but in July 1942 Schönert received the *Ritterkreuz* (knight's cross) from Kammhuber, and took the opportunity to tell him that careful trials of the upward-firing guns at the armament test establishment at Tarnewitz had been impressive. As a result, in December 1942 Kammhuber sanctioned the installation of twin oblique MG 151/20 cannon at 70° behind the pilot in three Do 217J night fighters. The installation worked excellently, the main problem being the installation of the Revi C/12D reflector sight in the front of the cockpit roof, and getting its position correct in relation to the pilot's head.

At about this time a senior *Luftwaffe* armourer, Paul Mahle, studied the installation at Tarnewitz, and it may have been he who called it *Schräge Musik*. Certainly it was Mahle who, after being posted to II/NJG 5, organized the installation of twin MK 108 cannon at an angle of about 75° in a Bf 110F-4, the installation adding /U1 to the aircraft's designation. Though it fired much more devastating ammunition than 20 mm, the MK 108 was a basically short-range weapon, shorter and much lighter than the massive MK 101 and 103 of the same calibre. Thus, it fitted almost completely inside the Bf 110 between the two crew above the wing spars. The Bf 110F-4/U1 had no radar, and the rear gun was deleted, the backseater being tasked mainly with keeping a watch to the rear and keeping an eye on the upward-firing guns (sometimes the feed-belt broke). The axis of the guns was arranged to pass only a very short distance aft of the aircraft's c.g., causing a very mild nose-up tilt when the guns were fired. The NJG 5 crews are said to have regarded the armament with some amusement, becoming completely converted when, on 17/18 August 1943 Gefreiter Hölker of 5/NJG 5 used the aircraft to shoot down two bombers on the raid on Peenemünde. The same installation was used by Leutnant Erhardt of 6/NJG 5 to destroy four bombers within forty minutes.

Schönert himself also opened his own score with *Schräge Musik* on the night of the Peenemünde raid, but his aircraft was a Bf 110G. One account states that his upward-firing guns were MG 151/20s, and twin MG FF 20 mm guns were also installed in this way. One authoritative account states that, from mid-1943, this type of gun installation accounted for eighty per cent of all kills by *Luftwaffe* night fighters. Certainly, from this time onwards, there was no argument. Using *Schräge Musik* was universally agreed to be easier than the traditional stern chase. In the conventional attack the target was against the horizon, usually the darkest part of the night sky. One's own fighter was centred in the horizontal cone of the bomber's Monica tail-warning radar. Even if the bomber stayed straight and level, and its crew were apparently asleep, it presented a difficult end-on target, and any relative motion required an aim-off deflection shot. Even if the Monica was unserviceable, the rear gunner, and sometimes the mid-upper, often caught sight of the much-feared fighter as it closed for the kill, especially if moonlight or searchlight beams were reflected from the fighter's canopy. To overcome some of the problems many NJG pilots closed the range at a lower level, below the Monica zone of coverage, until they could see the bomber above; then they pulled up into a climb with all front guns blazing. But this demanded fine judgement, gave only a second or two of firing time, and almost immediately brought the fighter up behind the bomber's tail turret.

What a contrast with *Schräge Musik*! Again the technique was to approach deliberately at a lower level, but this time all the night-fighter pilot had to do was slow up a little, rise up below the bomber and hold formation. An NJG *Experte* could follow his observer's direction, acquire the bomber visually, close and destroy it within sixty seconds. The firing position, with the bomber 65° to 70° above the fighter, was an almost ideal one. The fighter could see the bomber clearly, as a darker silhouette either blotting out the stars or against paler sky or high cloud. It presented the biggest possible target, and reflected any light from searchlights, ground fires or TIs. With the two aircraft in close formation, there was an ideal no-deflection shot. And the fighter was perfectly safe, because it was well below the beam of the Monica and could not be seen by any member of the bomber's crew. The only snag was that the *Luftwaffe*'s guns were so effective that the night fighter usually had to get out of the way very quickly. It was rather like 1916, except that a Lancaster with one wing blown off tumbled downwards and backwards faster than an ignited airship.

*The upward-firing* Schräge Musik *guns of this Ju 88C-6c can be seen pointing up from the mid-fuselage. Lacking radar, this was an armament-test aircraft. Later installations had the guns at the back of the crew compartment.*

By December 1943 all the NJG *Experten* were using *Schräge Musik* as their primary armament, though invariably the slanting guns were an extra and the forward-firing armament was retained and loaded ready for immediate use. The big twins frequently patrolled for six hours, and with a skilled crew might make several interceptions. The usual *Schräge Musik* installation in the Bf 110G-4 family comprised two 20 mm MG 151 or MG FF cannon, the former with 200 rounds each and the latter with manually changed sixty-round drums, arranged at 70°, 72° or 78°. The Ju 88C-6c had two MG 151s, each with 200 rounds; so did most of the Ju 88G series, though a few had two 30 mm MK 108s. The He 219A-5/R1 and A-7/R1 had the 30-mm MK 108 installation, each fed by a large 180-round tank, the usual angle being 65° or 72°. An incidental advantage of *Schräge Musik* was that it did not blind the pilot (and the observer could keep his eyes shut), whereas some of the forward-firing installations did.

Though this deadly armament was used by the *Luftwaffe* night fighters from August 1943, non-tracer ammunition was used exclusively, and in most interceptions the bomber crew never knew what had hit them. The *Experte* could usually destroy a Lancaster or Halifax with an economical two-second burst. Aiming was so straightforward that it was possible to choose the right place to hit, the main wing spars between the engines being a favoured spot. The bomb bay was carefully avoided! The result was that RAF heavies began to blow up, catch fire or break into pieces for no obvious reason. Many of the early such incidents, often witnessed by a score or more of other aircraft in the stream, were put down to *Flak*; but it often happened when *Flak* was light or non-existent. Not until well into 1944 did the RAF at last tumble to what was happening, and then only by a lot of hard thinking after studying the very few bombers that had, by great good fortune, managed to break out of the rain of shells and bring back to Britain evidence of air-to-air strikes all at the same near-vertical angle. I happened to be at Manston in early 1944 and woke to find a damaged Lancaster outside. One propeller was feathered, and there were marks of several 20 mm strikes, at least one of which had gone clean through the rear fuselage. It had blown a great hole in the top, and made a mess of the four ammunition belts for the rear turret, but what shocked the crew was the angle. They were Australians, and seemed to think this was renewed evidence of a *Luftwaffe* secret weapon; tales of strange upward-firing night fighters had begun to get about.

This strangeness was itself very strange, because oblique upward-firing guns had been common in the First World War, tested in several RAF aircraft between the wars, and experimented with at great length with RAF night fighters – mainly Havocs – as recently as 1941. I believe that none of the upward-firing Havocs carried cannon, a typical armament being six oblique Browning 0.303s. At the conclusion of apparently successful trials, a full report was written and handed to the Fighter Command AOC-in-C. Almost the next day he, 'Stuffy' Dowding, was replaced by Sholto Douglas. Thus, nothing was done. So runs a much-quoted report, but Dowding was sacked (many consider unjustly) in 1940, and I am certain the Havoc trials were not completed until much later. FIU did not evaluate the Havoc until 1945. In any case, there is still no explanation of why this promising armament should have been subsequently ignored, nor of why the adoption of the same technique by the *Luftwaffe* should have caused such amazement. Indeed, one could argue further that it was odd that *Schräge Musik* should have been so deadly in *Luftwaffe* hands and so completely ignored, both before and afterwards, by the Allies. When the RAF finally got round to ordering jet night fighters, it bought cannon in the outer wings, firing ahead, which was an even less satisfactory scheme than having them under the nose.

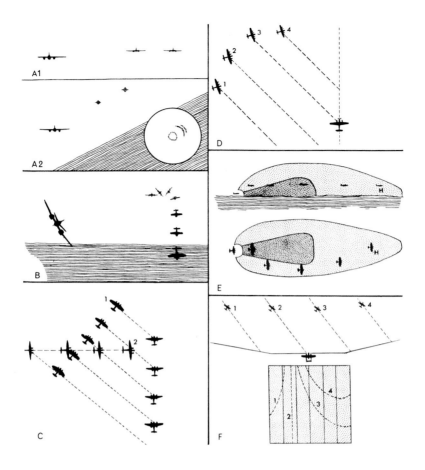

Most Second World War situations called for skill and experience. At A1 a Mosquito has acquired two contacts way off to the right. It turns towards them, and the banked turn makes them appear now to be above the fighter (A2). Only the positions of the contacts are shown in A2, because their attitudes are invisible. The radar observer, looking into his Mk VIII circular display, now sees a target well above to the right, and a second, slightly further away, even higher. What does he say, in his highly excited state? In B a Beaufighter is racing at full throttle after an Fw 190. Suddenly the radar observer sees the target moving rapidly off his screen to the right. What does he tell the pilot to do? Does he recognise that the target has actually half-rolled into a vertical dive? At C a Mosquito flying at 240 knots has a contact closing at the same level from port. How does the observer know it is a lumbering old He 111 at 168 knots (1), instead of the seemingly identical Ju 88 on a totally different course at 240 knots (2)? To the man in the fighter both 1 and 2 have exactly the same relative motion, their blip movements are the same. What does he tell his pilot to do, and when? At D a Bf 110 spots a contact off to the left. At 1 the Lancaster would be invisible; at 2 it would eventually pass behind the fighter; at 3 it would collide with the Bf 110; at 4 it is perfectly placed. The German observer cannot see which way the Lanc is heading, yet must know exactly what to do in each case. At E we have a Mosquito with AI Mk VIII chasing a hostile at low level. Eventually its observer picks up a juicy fat Heinkel dead ahead at H. How does he keep it in radar vision, avoiding the part of the sky obliterated by the ground return (shaded darker)? He has to keep the target at 11 o'clock or 2 o'clock, edging it nearer until it can once more be lined up (but at a higher level). Then he commands his pilot to climb (telling him how many feet), confident they will get a visual. They must avoid the target's slipstream at such a low level, and must on no account come up directly under or ahead of it. Finally, at F a P-61 with SCR-720 spots a Bf 110. If it is at 1 the hostile blip will move down the square 'B-scope' as in broken line 1. Likewise targets 3 and 4 will leave blip paths which eventually curve away. But the blip of Bf 110 No 2 will travel straight down the display. At the bottom there will be a mid-air collision, unless the observer recognises the situation. One could never relax in the night-fighter game.

*Schräge Musik* was just one extra item that increased the lethality of the NJG fighters in the final phases of the giant battle. *Lichtenstein* SN-2 was a godsend in seeing through the too-short strips of Window, and *Naxos*-Z could home on to the helpful H2S beacons from a distance of about twelve miles. But without doubt the most useful aid of all was *Flensburg*, the receiver tuned to the Monica tail-warning radar. As it was a passive device it could not itself give any indication of its presence, nor could it give false warnings caused by friendly aircraft. It still used dipole aerials out in the airstream, but these were small and had little effect on flight performance. These three highly effective and reliable sensors were all in production by the autumn of 1943; they completely transformed the German night fighters, and the Ju 88G in particular. This aircraft, of which more than 2,000 were delivered in 1944, was in my opinion the most useful night fighter of the Second World War, save for the little-used He 219. Capable of speeds between 380 and 405 mph, depending on sub-type, it had excellent manoeuvrability, an endurance in excess of seven hours, and formidable forward-firing and oblique armament. Just how easily it could hunt down its prey was not, however, to be immediately revealed to the RAF.

Throughout the winter Bomber Command's losses mounted, and they reached a daunting climax on the crystal-clear night of 30 March 1944, when an admitted 94 out of 795 heavies raiding Nürnberg were shot down (the *Luftwaffe* claimed 'at least 102'), with almost as many written off from other causes. It so happened that this was the last massive assault on a German city for many months; Bomber Command's main efforts were already planned to be switched to the Low Countries and France ready for the invasion just two months distant, and never again were there such great air battles by night. But there was no let-up on either side, and the frantic efforts to find out about SN-2, *Naxos*-Z and *Flensburg* – all known by name from the conversations of *Luftwaffe* prisoners – continued unabated. These efforts were crowned by a singular lack of success. By 1944 the RAF had become extremely skilled at finding such things out, and since November 1943 it had deployed a large and clever force, 100 Group, specifically to gather electronic intelligence and confuse the enemy. The aircraft of this unique group included Stirlings, Halifaxes, Wellingtons, Mosquitos and, at first, the special Defiants and Beaufighters of 515 Squadron, as well as both types of US heavy bomber, the Fortress and Liberator. All were fitted with special equipment, and many were so grossly modified that in the daytime they attracted attention even from a distance. In the air their presence sometimes exerted a fantastic electronic effect.

For example, some of the four-engined aircraft carried Jostle transmitters, which until many years later were the most powerful jammers ever built. There were several species, with different radiative power and frequency-spread, but some had a total output, on a continuous basis, of 2.5 kW. They could jam not just single channels but the entire spread of frequencies used by the German GCI controllers. Backing up these and other jammers were the Corona operators, in England, who tuned in to each night's *Luftwaffe* GCI frequencies and broadcast false instructions. The *Luftwaffe* thought the maddening voices were coming from the bombers, and changed to using girls of the *Luftwaffehelferinnen*; so the RAF countered with fluent German-speaking WAAFs! Despite bluff and double-bluff, this part of the game aimed mostly at just making the *Luftwaffe* angry and rattled. The German controllers became increasingly frustrated, took to repeating short, previously coded messages, and then worked out a scheme of broadcasting different kinds of music, each type meaning the night fighters should orbit a particular beacon or go to a particular target. When this was jammed or falsely copied, the

*Luftwaffe* tried powerful Morse, and finally, too late for the war, commissioned extremely powerful transmitters which radiated a rotating beam of digital teleprinter signals, giving an output on tape in the cockpit. This final system, *Bernhard*, would have been very difficult to jam, but it meant yet another special receiver in the overloaded night fighters.

British courage, technical expertise and capacity for hard work has never been manifest more abundantly than in the stirring final year of the night battle over Germany. Its cumulative effect on the morale of the *Luftwaffe*, from Goering down to the lowliest hangar-sweeper, was enormous. The entire NJG force gradually came to feel that the British were simply cleverer, or quicker off the mark, and thus were perpetually one jump ahead. But in fact this was not true. For a whole year every conceivable method had been tried to find out the frequency of *Lichtenstein* SN-2 and details of *Naxos*-Z and *Flensburg*, without success. No trace could be found of a new night-fighter radar emission (so that a fair conclusion would have been that SN-2 emitted signals similar to those of some previous set, which in fact happened to be the advanced forms of *Freya*). The other sensors emitted no radiation at all, and the numerous night fighters shot down by Mosquitos all fell on German soil. Prospects were extremely discouraging. Then, before dawn on 13 July 1944, a single aircraft orbited RAF Woodbridge, Suffolk, got a green and landed. The crew bus ambled out to collect what was expected to be the pilot and observer from a Mosquito. Instead it collected three men, in *Luftwaffe* gear. Having set the reciprocal course by mistake, they had brought one of the latest Ju 88G-7 night fighters.

In a matter of hours Bomber Command had set in motion actions which were to remove the last advantages enjoyed by the German night fighters. It learned all about SN-2, checked that it was unaffected by standard Window, but found that its vision was seriously impaired by a special long concertina-form Window that Bomber Command had used during the invasion to simulate a non-existent fleet of surface ships. Design was begun, on a crash basis, on Serrate IV, to home on to the German radar, and Pipe-rack, to jam it. Another cunning device, Perfectos, harping still further on the cigar theme, was carried by the intruder Mosquitos to interrogate the latest *Luftwaffe* night-fighter IFF sets and give the bearing and range of the replies! But perhaps the most urgently needed result of all came as soon as the Ju 88's almost empty tanks were refilled.

Derek Jackson headed the probe into the previously unknown *Flensburg*. He began by trying the passive homer against the Monica radar of a single Lancaster, and found that it gave clear bearings out to a range of at least 130 miles. He then tried it against five Lancasters flying in a loose gaggle, and found that he could home the big night fighter immediately onto any one of the five. Still Bomber Command argued, so at the end of August 1944 he managed the final evaluation against a 'bomber stream' of seventy-one Lancasters orbiting between Cambridge and Gloucester. Far from being smothered or confused, the *Flensburg* continued to give crystal-clear indication of the exact positions of the nearest bombers. Clearly, this one aid alone could guide a night-fighter crew straight to any bomber using its tail-warning radar. At once Bert Harris ordered the Monica sets not to be switched on, and to have their frequency changed at the earliest opportunity. At last the RAF bombers stopped telling the dreaded night fighters precisely where they were.

Of course, Monica was not an entirely misguided device, any more than was $H_2S$. Both did achieve their objective of providing information for the bomber crew, and in a very small minority of cases – especially those in which the fighter used forward-firing armament, and thus

*This Me 262B-1a/U1 served with 10/NJG11. It became the property of the RAF, and was then handed to the USA, which applied the serial FE (Foreign Equipment) 610. It was then falsely repainted, and eventually scrapped. A superb B-1a/U1 survives in Johannesburg.*

closed from dead astern – the bomber crew detected the fighter's presence in time to do something about it. By far the best thing to do was to corkscrew: to open the throttles wide and fly a very large horizontal corkscrew path that kept the bomber something like 500 feet away from the original straight and level trajectory. It was a strenuous sick-making manoeuvre, best performed without bombs (though from 1942 onwards it was extremely rare for an RAF bomber to jettison its load short of the target unless a night fighter had shown itself to be unusually skilled and aggressive). In daytime a corkscrew would not seriously inconvenience an experienced fighter pilot, but at night it was a different matter. The greatest *Luftwaffe Experte* of all, Major Heinz-Wolfgang Schnaufer, gained three of his 121 confirmed night victories with *Schräge Musik* cannon while he was actually formating with a corkscrewing bomber; but he also had some fruitless encounters because of this manoeuvre and once followed a corkscrewing Lancaster for forty-five minutes without being able to get it in his sights (he vowed he would never again waste time in this way; there would always be other, easier pickings).

In the final year of the battle great changes were afoot. At the Junkers development centre at Dessau plans were well advanced with night-fighter versions of the Ju 388J, some of which had two monster 50 mm BK 5 guns and were intended to be armed with the experimental 50 mm

MK 114 cannon. At several Messerschmitt factories were to be seen the two-seat Me 262 twin-jet, which had originally been intended as the 262B-1a conversion trainer but was eventually, in late 1944, ordered to be developed into a series of night fighters. Indestructible Major Herrmann, by now an Oberst (colonel), had been extremely favourably impressed by a solitary NF conversion of the original single-seat Me 262A-1a. On this speedy machine the top speed was cut by about 37 mph by fitting a slightly simplified SN-2 aerial installation, which also had a distinctly adverse effect on rate of climb. Yet the 262 had such a tremendous performance, such sweet handling qualities, and such a devastating punch from its four 30 mm cannon that it promised to make a superb night fighter which the Allies could not match. Ultimately only a handful of radar-equipped Me 262B-1a two-seaters became operational, beginning with III/EJG 2 at Lechfeld in November 1944, followed by I/KG(J) 54 near Würzburg whose crews had previously flown bombers. They accomplished little, but did manage several interceptions without operative radar. Operationally, while at the end there was a desperate shortage of high-octane petrol (gasoline) for piston engines, there was no shortage of fuel for the jets. The problem was that the whole country was devastated, and the last operating bases for the jets were straight sections of *Autobahn* highway.

In the Oberammergau plant were the first pieces of metal for the B-2a with more fuel and two *Schräge Musik* MK 108s, as well as a more powerful three-seat night-fighter version, and plans for a completely new jet night fighter. Ultimately all *Luftwaffe* night fighters would have had new centimetric radar and a very effective infra-red homing system. Pioneer work with cooled detectors had led to a series of IR sensors which promised to be ideal, but none reached the production stage. Even bigger effort went into new radars, a natural result of forming a special High-Frequency Research organization on a nationwide scale in July 1943 which swiftly grew under Plendl to employ over 3,000 scientific staff alone. FuG 228 *Lichtenstein* SN-3 was a replacement for SN-2, using the same aerials, with the ability to vary its operative frequency to sidestep hostile active jamming and slightly improve the view through Window. FuG 217 and 218 *Neptun* was a family of more advanced radars operating at shorter wavelength and widely variable frequency. These used the *Hirschgeweih* 'toasting fork' or the new *Morgenstern*

*Messerschmitt Me 262B-1a with FuG 218 with rear-warning aerial, Naxos ZC homer and blind-approach aid; four 30 mm MK 108.*

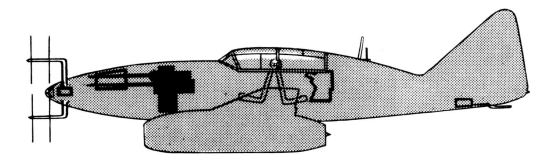

(morning star) aerial with a central pole carrying two pairs of crossed-X dipoles, often enclosed by a streamlined cone through which the dipole tips protruded. Most advanced of all were the centimetric sets based on the British magnetron and in many cases actually using magnetrons from crashed RAF bombers. The 9 cm FuG 240 *Berlin* was the commonest, ten actually getting as far as installation in the specially arranged Ju 88G-7c with a wooden nose radome. FuG 245 *Bremen* was a variant intended for the several projected night-fighter versions of the four-jet Arado Ar 234C.

Yet even these formidable developments could be largely countered by switching off H2S and Monica, keeping a sharp lookout, and having the patience and dogged persistence to corkscrew better than the *Luftwaffe* fighter. The night battle over Germany was one of increasingly clever technology, but courage and skill still played a large part, and the element of sheer chance also assumed frighteningly large proportions. Heavies would carefully fly low, or high, to escape the worst of the *Flak* – and be hit by a shell incorrectly fused. They would turn every fifteen seconds or so when running through the most intense radar-directed *Flak* – and run into a badly aimed shot. They would keep their eyes peeled for a night fighter but be physically unable to look below, where the fighter was most likely to be. Others would keep such a jittery lookout that when they saw another Lancaster or Halifax loom close they shot it down. Others lost out through collisions, or from a rain of friendly bombs from above. Over 55,000 aircrew failed to return.

Yet it was far from being a one-sided battle. From mid-1943 no *Luftwaffe* night-fighter pilot ever felt safe in his own night sky, and far more were killed in crashes (often caused by fear of the omnipotent Mosquito) than in combat. Many were shot down by their own *Flak*, and once Perfectos had made them switch off their IFF this happened frequently. In the end, along with the rest of the *Luftwaffe*, the remnants of the once proud and formidable night-fighter wings just ground to a halt. Their airfields were blasted, their organization in chaos, and, worst of all, piston-engine fuel had become an almost non-existent commodity. This was because of the destruction of the German oil refineries, synthetic oil processing plant and storage tanks, by the bombers that got through.

# Seven

# Other Theatres

Though at the time of Pearl Harbor, on 7 December 1941, the Europeans had vastly greater experience of air warfare than the Americans, the close collaboration between Britain and the United States from mid-1940 had gone far to put the United States well in the picture. With characteristic energy the US Army and Navy re-thought their day-fighter procurement, buying aircraft with the much more powerful R-2800 engine and much heavier firepower. Planned mainly for night use, the Army P-70 and P-61 saw limited action in the Pacific war against Japan. But the most immediate burden of the Japanese war fell upon the US Navy and Marine Corps. Both deployed large and important forces of combat aircraft, the most basic difference between the two services being that the Marine Corps squadrons were nominally all land-based and trained to operate chiefly in support of amphibious assaults on land targets.

Both the Army and the Navy took a keen interest in Britain's struggle in the winter of 1940–1 to defeat the night bomber. It is worth emphasizing that neither adopted an isolationist policy, nor said that it could see no threat to the United States. Though it did not at first collaborate with the British with quite the same affinity as the Army, the US Navy – which handled procurement and technical development for the Marine Corps also – gradually came to recognize that the need to be able to intercept enemy aircraft at any time of day or night was a pressing one. In collaboration with the Army Air Corps (Army Air Force from March 1942) it organized the nationwide Aircraft Warning Service, with equal attention paid to both the Atlantic and Pacific coastal areas. The defence problem was alleviated by the geographical remoteness from any enemy, other than carrier-based forces such as had crippled the Pacific Fleet at Pearl Harbor; but it was exacerbated by the sheer size of the territory to be defended, and the absence of any US night fighters. Fortunately the development by the Radiation Laboratory of advanced and powerful microwave surveillance radars had been started in 1940, and small numbers of pre-microwave sets had been used by the Army Signal Corps as early as 1938. By December 1940 the Navy was working with its own team at the Radiation Laboratory on large shipboard radars, not only for air and surface warning but also for GCI by the fleet's own fighters. By February 1941 American microwave ASV radar was being designed, and a different team then began the challenging task of developing an AI radar that would fit into a single-seat carrier-based fighter.

Though the British had been unable to build much research hardware on this wavelength, they had conducted limited studies into 3 cm radar from the spring of 1940, and were able to give the Radiation Laboratory a lot of useful information. On virtually no evidence, they had believed that this extremely short wavelength was a prerequisite to radar being satisfactory in a single-seat fighter. The US Navy was persuaded to the same conclusion, and in January 1941 it requested a 3-cm AI radar that was light, compact, simple, difficult to jam, operable by the pilot, and useful in night air interception with secondary capability in attack on surface vessels. By August 1941 sufficient success had been achieved with 3 cm components for design to begin on a complete radar, called AI-3 (SCR-537). The complete installation was proposed to the Navy on 2 November 1941. Six days later the Navy requested from the Chance Vought company a study for a night-fighter version of the Corsair, the XF4U-2. In December Sperry received a contract for AI-3 development and production, with the Radiation Lab serving as consultant. On 28 January 1942 the mock-up review board accepted the proposal for the XF4U-2. The radar was contained in the fuselage behind the pilot's seat, with a waveguide running out along the right wing to a scanner in a fairing near the tip. Spiral scan was used for search (120° cone at fifteen scans per minute) and a 10° conical scan for the second phase, then called 'sight', in which accurate aiming was needed for a blind firing attack. The single CRT display in front of the pilot showed a Type G (Az-El) presentation with 'wings' growing on the target blip in inverse ratio to range.

Flight trials began in a JRB (Twin Beech) in April 1942, with the scanner in the nose. Soon the pointing error had been refined to less than 0.25°, though problems were met with sea return, with humidity and with performance above 20,000 feet. In June the set was taken to Marine Corps Air Station Quonset Point, Rhode Island, for tests and training, while a second set flew in an F4U. This was delivered as an operable night fighter in October 1942, but by this time extreme pressure on the F4U-1 programme had unfortunately caused Chance Vought to drop work on the F4U-2. By late 1942 the first Sperry set, the AIA, was in production for the Grumman F6F Hellcat. A total of 604 were delivered, and installed in F6F-3E and -5N Hellcats, as described later, and the AI Mk XIVA (ASH) in British NF Fireflies and TF Sea Mosquitos. In 1943 this radar was given the new Army/Navy designation of APS-4.

In January 1943 work began on an improved radar, with a new Dalmo Victor scanner, Westinghouse pressurized RF head (this did away with the long waveguide from the fuselage to the wing pod) and Stromberg Mk II modulator. This radar was completed in October 1943, and flight-tested in an SNB-1 (Beech Kansan). Westinghouse began to deliver production sets, designated APS-6, in April 1944. A few months earlier deliveries had begun of the APS-6A in which, because of difficulties with the new RF head, the receiver was the Philco APS-4 type. Many modifications were made, including changing the polarization of the aerial feed through 90° to improve beacon reception, before production APS-6 sets were cleared for use. Sea clutter remained a major problem, but on the whole this challenging miniaturized set worked well even at heights above 30,000 feet and in combat manoeuvres. It could paint coastlines at forty miles, and dependable search range was rarely less than five miles. Minimum range was a mere 360 feet. In the search mode the well-balanced 17 in scanner rotated at no less than 1,200 rpm in sweeping through a 60° spiral scan. No tremors were felt in the cockpit, and the fighter's stability and manoeuvrability were unchanged, though in a sideslip the pod falsely increased the airspeed reading. The whole installation weighed 242 lb, and was priced at $10,936. Altogether the enormous total of 5,260 were delivered, 2,161 of them by 1 August 1945.

*Last of the night-fighter Corsairs, the F4U-5N had an uprated R-2800 engine giving a placard speed of 470 mph. Armament was four 20 mm and two 1,000 lb bombs.*

All the first deliveries were installed in Corsairs and Hellcats. The very first Navy night fighters were 12 F4U-1 Corsairs converted by MCAS Quonset Point and the Philadelphia Navy Yard. The 'hand-built' conversion installed the APS-4, usually removed the outermost of the three 0.50 in guns in the right wing, and rearranged the cockpit to accommodate pilot radar controls, a viewing scope and an autopilot. These dozen aircraft saw a fantastic amount of action. Six went to VF(N)-75 at Munda, New Georgia, where Lieutenant-Commander Widhelm and his experienced pilots – all said to have logged over 2,000 hours – slaughtered the Japanese bombers that had previously come over every night mainly to deny the exhausted Americans any sleep. Their first combat mission, and first kill, was on 31 October 1943. Thereafter every 'washing-machine Charlie' that approached New Georgia was destroyed. Indeed, Lieutenant O'Neill (so the story goes, and the Navy confirms it) shot down a Japanese bomber that unexpectedly got in the way as he tested his guns one night over Bougainville! The other six aircraft served with VF(N)-101 under Lieutenant-Commander R.E. Harmer aboard *Essex*, *Hornet* and *Intrepid*, and then were assigned to Marine Corps VMF(N)-532. So single-seaters were too difficult to fly at night? It is doubly significant, because until a short time earlier the Navy had insisted that the Corsair could not be operated from carriers even in the daytime.

These arduous missions from pitching carrier decks and island airstrips pioneered a big US Navy and Marine Corps night-fighter effort. Numerically the most important night fighter in the Pacific was the Grumman Hellcat, designed and developed with amazing rapidity long after the start of the Corsair programme, and produced to the tune of 12,274 aircraft in just over two years! The two fighters were both powered by the mighty R-2800 Double Wasp engine, both were large and strong, and both were extremely capable and popular. The main snag with the Hellcat was night vision, and the first NF version, the F6F-3E, was a conversion of the ordinary -3 with APS-4, red cockpit lighting and no curved Plexiglas windscreen in front of the bullet-proof front panel. These eighteen conversions were followed by 149 F6F-3Ns with APS-6, a radio altimeter and IFF, and finally by 1,434 F6F-5Ns (one of which had a scanner pod on both wings) plus eighty designated Hellcat NF.II for the British Fleet Air Arm. It was an officer in the Royal Marines, Major 'Skeets' Harris, who almost singlehandedly set up a naval FIU, equipped with Fulmars, Fireflies and Hellcats. In the Pacific, partly because of their faster climb, a Navy F6F-5N squadron replaced an AAF P-61 squadron in the defence of Leyte in early 1945. The NF Hellcats and Corsairs were usually painted midnight blue or jet black, and operated by day as well as by night in defence of the fleet and shore bases, and in escorting Avengers and other attack aircraft. At the end of the war Vought produced the more powerful F4U-4E (APS-4) and -4N (APS-6), which served in Korea together with the final NF Corsair, the -5N, which had, among other things, a rearranged cockpit. Total F4U production (which did not end until 1952) was 12,571.

Creating an all-weather day and night air defence for the fleet was a task comparable in magnitude to that on land. Thanks to British help, the US Navy immediately had available VHF radio and IFF, and the Radiation Laboratory developed a superb GCI radar for Fleet carriers, and installed the prototype in the *Lexington*, which perpetuated the name of the earlier carrier lost a year previously in the Coral Sea. Designated SM, this radar had a large dish that scanned conically to give the azimuth, elevation, altitude and range of multiple targets. Production SM radars were made by General Electric, the first coming off the line at Syracuse in August 1943. But there was a serious delay in the 3-cm airborne radar, leading to a variety of temporary

*The Grumman F6F Hellcat was a superb fighter, despite the remarkable fact that, with the same basic engine as the F4U-5N, it was 90 mph slower! Like its rival, this F6F-5N has APS-6 radar on the starboard wing, which folded back manually on a skewed hinge.*

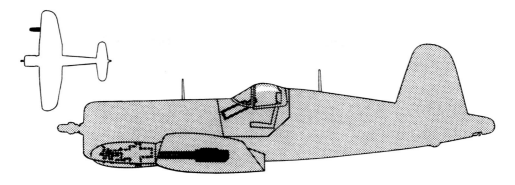

*Vought-Sikorsky F4U-4N with APS-6; six .50-inch Browning or four 20 mm M-2.*

expedients. These included close GCI control of day fighters used at night, use of day fighters in conjunction with radar-directed searchlights, and even brief trials (in the United States) of searchlight-equipped night fighters reminiscent of the RAF's Turbinlites. The only scheme that was widely used in combat service was to operate as a two- to four-aircraft team, with from one to three fighters co-operating with a larger aircraft fitted with radar. The usual sensor aircraft was either the Grumman TBF Avenger with ASV or the Douglas SBD Dauntless with Westinghouse ASB. The team would hold tight formation, if possible without showing any lights, while the big surveillance radar(s) of the fleet scanned the sky from horizon to horizon. Upon a hostile force being spotted, the GCI controller would vector the team towards it until the airborne radar, used in the air-to-air search mode, had gained a good contact. The observer watching his scope would then guide the formation until the Japanese aircraft were close enough to be seen visually. After combat, the aircraft returned to the carrier individually.

Though seemingly cumbersome, the system worked quite well, and was perpetuated for many years in an even more complex form in the hunter/killer teams used in anti-submarine warfare. American losses were minimal, though one early casualty was 'Butch' O'Hare, after whom the world's busiest airport (Chicago) is named. Chatting after the war with Tommy Blackburn, one-time commander of the famed VF-17, the first operational Corsair squadron and later Head of Fighter Branch in BuAer in Washington, I reached the opinion that this form of CAP (Combat Air Patrol) might even have been extended to include larger formations. Right up to the present day the 'lead ship' concept has remained competitive in attacks on surface targets, and in the Pacific war at night there was often the need to intercept Japanese night attacks by as many as thirty or forty aircraft. In the earliest such engagements the use of IFF had not yet been introduced into the Navy and Marine Corps. This made it imperative to recognize the target before opening fire, whereas after mid-1944 it was by no means unusual for pilots of AI-equipped Hellcats to open fire on a hostile aircraft they had not even seen, and to hit it first time. This was an authorized practice, whereas in the European conflict night-fighter crews were required to identify their targets visually – or at least to do their best to do so.

*The Kawasaki Ki-45 KAIc had twin 20 mm Ho-5 cannon installed at an angle of about 40°. A 37 mm Ho-203 was mounted under the fuselage, but the nose was left free for radar, which most aircraft of this type never received. Note the fabric main-wheel covers.*

In the Imperial Japanese Army and Navy there was no alternative to visual recognition, because until early 1944 neither service used any avionics apart from communications radio and DF loops. AI radar and IFF were slow to come into Japanese service, though preliminary information on FuG 202 *Lichtenstein* was sent by submarine from Germany in 1942. But it would be misleading to picture Japan as a land of technology illiterates, able only to copy Western innovations. This image may have comforted the Allies until the first few days after Pearl Harbor, but it was knocked for six by the superior combat performance of the A6M (Zero) fighter, and it never had much basis in fact. In 1928 Okabe in Tokyo had been the first microwave worker to generate enough power for communications in this band of new centimetric wavelengths, and at about the same time Professor Yagi had devised the short-wave directional aerial that bears his name. Comprising a linear array of dipoles, the Yagi aerial is today seen on many millions of rooftops around the world, and it was this type of aerial that was used in the first Japanese AI installation.

Though their development was slow and often troublesome, no fewer than five types of airborne radar were worked on by the Japanese in the Second World War. At first the main effort went into ASV (air-to-surface vessel) sets, which by 1944 were operational in several types of Navy aircraft down to the familiar B5N ('Kate') torpedo-bomber. The three types of AI radar for night fighters were less successful. One was an Army copy of FuG 202, and though it was tested in an obsolescent Mitsubishi Ki-21 bomber in 1943 it either never reached combat units or made only an insignificant impact on operations. The much more important Army set was the E-1, operating in the S-band at near 11 cm wavelength, the main carrier of which was the Kawasaki Type 2 heavy fighter, also called Ki-45 *Toryu* (dragon-killer) and known to the

*First of the specially equipped black-painted Japanese night fighters, the Nakajima J1N1-C KAI (Gekko Model 11) had cannon firing obliquely above and below (see illustration on p. 135). This example served at Maiji airbase.*

Allies as 'Nick'. Originally a day long-range fighter, with forward-firing guns, the Ki-45-*Kai*-C (modification C) version appeared in June 1944 with two 20 mm guns mounted obliquely in the mid-fuselage and, in some aircraft until October 1944, a searchlight in the nose. Gradually the AI radar was fitted and operators trained, but there is no evidence that radar played the central role in the occasional successes scored by these aircraft defending Japan against the B-29. At least the Ki-45 could reach the B-29 attack height of around 31,000 feet, and at full throttle could just overtake the speedy American bombers. Over Japan there was often chaotic radio communication, and no GCI system at all. Night fighters were thus left to their own devices, and the few successful night interceptions that took place were usually on moonlit nights when the B-29 contrails showed up from a considerable distance.

Intercepting a B-29 formation called for great courage. Whereas a *Luftwaffe* NJG pilot had nothing to fear from 99 per cent of the RAF heavies, the B-29 had no blind spots and carried heavy armament covering every possible direction of attack. Downwards and to the rear a fighter could be seen from three sighting stations and fired upon by six 0.5 in guns and a 20 mm cannon, and as these great bombers held tighter formation than the RAF bomber stream it was probable that, if one bomber opened fire, several others would open up on the same target. Added to the fact that head-on attacks were impractical at night, one is left with a situation in which a single fighter is faced with withering heavy-calibre fire in a stern chase at a closing speed hardly more than walking pace. A few Ki-45 night fighters attempted to get more speed and altitude by fitting only two 12.7 mm (0.5 in) oblique guns, a totally inadequate armament for the task of bringing down a B-29. Typical Ki-45-*Kai*-C forward-firing armament comprised a single heavy cannon of 37, 50 or 75 mm calibre, but these fired slowly and carried a very limited number of rounds. How eight of these fighters managed to bring down seven of a force of B-29s attacking northern Kyushu on the night of 15 June 1944 remains a mystery: there may have been some deliberate collisions.

The equivalent of the Ki-45 in the Imperial Navy was the Nakajima J1N1 *Gekko* (moonlight), called 'Irving' by the Allies. Planned as an escort fighter in 1940, the original J1N1-C failed to make the grade, but eventually entered service as a reconnaissance aircraft. It first operated in late 1942 in the area of New Guinea and the Solomon Islands, and though it had inadequate performance for day fighting it was locally judged to be a possible answer to the US Army heavy bombers that were making life a misery at night. The initiative to turn the J1N1-C into a night fighter stemmed from the commander of the 251st Air Corps at Rabaul, Yasuna Kozono, who proposed the same upward-firing armament as was being experimented with by the *Luftwaffe*. He went further, and suggested two pairs of 20 mm Type 99 Model 2 cannon, one pair firing obliquely up and the other pair obliquely down. Compared with the *Luftwaffe Schräge Musik* installations the inclination was less steep, a typical angle being 30°.

In March 1943 Kozono received permission for the proposed modification, and two aircraft were returned to Japan for this purpose. At the same time the Navy Bureau of Aeronautics in Tokyo recognized that the basic aircraft was eminently suitable for use as a night fighter, a category of aircraft then non-existent in the Imperial Navy. Work began on a specialized sub-type, the J1N1-S. Meanwhile the first two night-fighter conversions, designated J1N1-C-*Kai*, returned to Rabaul in May 1943 and soon proved their worth by shooting down two B-17s, following the next night by a B-24. This was no mean achievement, as the C-*Kai* had long exhaust stacks discharging above the wing, without flame dampers, and maximum speed not higher than 300 mph. At one time one of them had a trainable searchlight in the nose. They retained a crew of three, the pilot being assisted by a navigator and a gunner, the latter being needed to change ammunition drums.

These successes, the first ever gained by Japanese night fighters, were followed by others until both the original C-*Kai* conversions had been destroyed. But by August 1943 the definitive J1N1-S *Gekko* was in production, and most of the 479 of all J1N versions built were of this sub-type. The new Type 99 Model 2 guns had belt feeds, so no gunner was needed, and the previously lumpy rear fuselage was made more streamlined. From December 1944 the *Gekko* was the chief Navy night fighter, but its success against the B-17 and B-24 could not be repeated against the B-29; it could not climb high enough nor fly fast enough, despite the speed being increased to 315 mph at the best height of about 16,000 feet and 272 mph at 30,000 feet. In the final versions produced in 1945 a Navy-developed AI radar was fitted, again using *Yagi*-type aerials in a neat quadruple array and being under the control of the observer. There is no record of successful B-29 interceptions, and these aircraft either languished on the ground or were used for *Kamikaze* attacks.

The Army's success with the Ki-45 led to a successor, the Ki-96, first flown in September 1943. Much more powerful, it had a speed of 373 mph and carried a 37 mm cannon and two 20 mm guns. The Army could not make up their minds whether it should have one seat or two. Eventually the Ki-96 was redesigned into the Ki-102 two-seater, flown in March 1944. One of its guns had a calibre of 57 mm, and a single shell blew an engine off a B-29 in the course of a prototype test flight with loaded guns. Only a handful of different types of Ki-102 were built, the last two being Ki-102c night fighters with two oblique 20 mm Ho-5 cannon and two forward-

*This belly-landed J I N 1-C KAI Gekko shows the four 20 mm Type 99 cannon, two firing obliquely up and the other two obliquely down.*

firing 30 mm Ho-105s. All these were new guns marking a great improvement on the old patterns used previously. The Ki-102c also carried AI radar, almost certainly E-1, and its crew comprised a pilot and radar observer. The Allied name for all Ki-102 versions was 'Randy'.

It so happened that the best of all Japanese night fighters was a converted bomber extremely similar to the Ju 88 in character. Though many years later in conception than the German aircraft, the Yokosuka P1Y1 had precisely the same wing span, almost identical weights and engine power, a close-grouped crew of three and very similar flight performance. Like the Ju 88 it was big, tough, durable and could be flung round the sky like a single-seater. So good was it that the Navy instructed the Kawanishi company to redesign it into the P1Y1-s *Kyokko* (Aurora), known to the Allies as 'Frances'. The tricky airframe was made simpler to build, the troublesome Homare engines were replaced by robust Kaseis, and the interior was rearranged with the navigator in the nose, the pilot in the centre and the rear gunner in the aft cockpit. The usual armament comprised two oblique 20 mm guns (said to be Type 99 but almost certainly Ho-5s) and a third gun of the same type in the rear cockpit for defence. Radar was fitted, related to that of the J1N1-S but derived from the widely used ASV installation with a completely different dipole aerial array, there being a single large *Yagi* array in the nose and an axial trio of dipoles along each side of the rear fuselage. About ninety-seven *Kyokkos* were built, a few having a twin 20 mm dorsal turret. It was perhaps fortunate for the Allies that protracted trials were still going on when the war ended.

There were many other 'heavy fighter' programmes in Japan which might have yielded a useful night defender. Among these were the Ki-46-III-*Kai* version of an established reconnaissance machine, with an oblique 37 mm cannon; the big Mitsubishi Ki-109 with a forward-firing 75 mm gun; the Nakajima J5N-1 *Tenrai* (heavenly thunder), designed to replace the J1N1-S; the Kawasaki Ki-108 with twin turbocharged engines and a pressure cabin; the

*This Kawasaki Ki-102b was captured intact. Armament comprised an awesome 57 mm Ho-401 in the nose and twin 20 mm Ho-5 underneath, plus a 12.7 mm aimed by the backseater. The radar-equipped Ki-102c never entered production.*

Rikugun Ki-93, with two six-blade single-rotation propellers; and the Mitsubishi Ki-83, which was one of the best combat aircraft the Japanese produced in the Second World War. None of these played any part in the war, owing to a combination of muddled administration, severe technical snags, crippling shortages, and the catastrophic effect on Japanese industry of the devastating B-29 raids. Unlike the air battles in the German night sky, those over Japan – if they took place at all, which was very seldom – were one-sided. The general objective of the Japanese was not so much to develop a better fighter that would destroy the B-29 faster, as to develop one that could actually get within firing range. There was quite a difference between a Lancaster cruising at 200 mph at 22,000 feet and a B-29 cruising at 300 mph at 32,000 feet. This must be borne in mind when reflecting on the Japanese lack of success.

It so happened that the last type mentioned above, the Ki-83, bore a startling resemblance to the final US Navy night fighter of the Second World War, the Grumman F7F Tigercat. The Long Island company began its adventure into fighters twice as powerful as their contemporaries with the XF5F-1 Skyrocket flown on 1 April 1940. It continued with the Army XP-50, with nosewheel landing gear, flown on February 18 1941. This led to the XF7F-1 flown in December 1943. Powered by two 2,100 hp Double Wasps, this impressive single-seater suffered from carrier incompatibility, but went into production in April 1944 as a close-support fighter for the Marines. At the thirty-fifth aircraft, in October 1944, production abruptly switched to the F7F-2N, a two-seat night fighter with a back-seat operator for the APS-6 radar with the scanner in the tip of the nose. It had to give up the four 0.50 in guns in the nose of the -1, but still had four 20 mm cannon in the wings. The main production version was the F7F-3, with more powerful engines and built in six sub-types. The -3N night fighter was immediately distinguished by its long, knobbly nose housing the SCR-720 radar – a very different set from the little APS-6. The -4N, of which thirteen were built in 1946, was structurally strengthened and had a more streamlined nose (see next chapter).

It is seldom wise to predict the course of human conflict. Certainly nobody at Grumman's Bethpage, NY, plant would have dreamed that the awesome F7F would never fire on a Jap, would spend years patrolling deep in China and would finally go into action against Koreans and America's former allies, the Russians. Indeed, the great and – at the level of individual soldiers and pilots, genuine – alliance forged in war between the USSR and the Western Allies was to be rent asunder as soon as the fighting was over. There were deep-seated problems on both sides, but the most intractable one was the professed belief of the Soviet Union that the Capitalist nations were forever seeking to destroy it. The world became polarized into East and West; and, while the West begrudged every penny and cent spent on armaments, the East multiplied its budget for weapons over and over again. The Soviet Union was especially eager to become proficient in radar, which, apart from nuclear weapons, was the most important area of military technology in which the Communist bloc countries were seriously behind the West. During the war – called the Great Patriotic War by the Soviet Union – this had been a source of endless worry, mainly to Britain. The Soviet government had asked for 'full information' on every kind of radar, and in March 1942 made an explicit request for airborne RDF. This was

*One of four Mitsubishi Ki-83 prototypes, seen after capture. Fitted with two 30 mm and two 20 mm, it was (apart from the Me 262B-1a) the fastest two-seater of the Second World War.*

The two-seat Grumman F7F-3N had an elongated nose housing SCR-720, a powerful and versatile radar, instead of the four 'fifty-caliber' guns of the single-seaters. This still left four 20 mm in the wing roots. Note underwing weapon attachments.

highly secret, and not allowed at that time to fly over Europe. What fouled things up was that the Russians demonstrated that, in practice, they did not really wish to learn from their Allies. The RAF sent a large team of radio, radar and GCI experts, called '30 Mission', to Moscow in April 1942. This brought mobile GCI units, VHF/RT and a lot of other equipment, and looked forward to instructing the Soviet air forces. There followed months of utter frustration, and 30 Mission repeatedly signalled to London their inability to get the Russians to use any of the equipment properly, or even show an interest. There appeared, said one signal, to be 'bad faith', and by early September the Director of Radar at the Air Ministry was authorized to disclose to the Soviet Union all radar information down to 50 cm wavelength (which meant many equipments used by all three services), and to invite the Russians to send a mission to London to discuss the sensitive subject of AI radar. No mission was ever sent.

I have only the British view of things, and it may be that the Russian view would be slanted very differently. But my own opinion is that the Russians were thrown off-balance by finding Britain and the United States as their Allies. They appeared to be so crippled by ideological hang-ups that they were unable to work, openly and efficiently, with the Capitalist nations to defeat their common enemy. The only exceptions were with fragments of the Capitalist nations that actually came to fight on the Eastern Front, such as the *Normandie-Niemen* squadron from France and 151 Wing, RAF. Had the Capitalists really wished to see the Soviet Union defeated they would not have poured such enormous quantities of armaments in through Iran and by Arctic convoys, which ran the gauntlet of U-boats and the *Luftwaffe* despite a lamentable failure by the Soviet naval and air forces ever to co-operate in providing protection. To the end the Russians continued, tragically, to distrust their Allies. They appeared never to understand the very real reluctance of the British to hand over their technology in AI radar to people who, going by their record, would show no interest in using it properly and would probably compromise it. Later, in 1943, a way out of the impasse was sought by asking the Soviet Union whether it would welcome a wing (two or three squadrons) of RAF Havocs to operate on the Eastern Front as detached units of the RAF under Soviet tactical command, as 151 Wing had done by day. The only problem appeared to be incompatibility of the nosewheel-equipped Havoc with soggy fields and rough wooden board airstrips, but as thousands of P-39 Airacobras, B-25 Mitchells and other versions of the Havoc (DB-7) were already in use on the Eastern Front this did not appear an insuperable difficulty. In the event the Russians did not reply, despite the fact that, had the radar-equipped squadrons been dispatched, the aircraft would undoubtedly have been given to the Russians when their crews finally returned home, as had been the case with the Hurricanes of 151 Wing.

I must emphasize that the above is written from a British perspective. At the same time, several Russian historians have told me that it pretty well reflects the way it happened. Almost no work was done on the development of Russian night fighters until after the war, and the story is picked up again in the next chapter.

# EIGHT

# THE POST-WAR ERA

To continue with the Soviet Union's story, in 1945 the USSR found itself in possession of not only vast new tracts of land, where it swiftly set up puppet governments, but also thousands of German engineers and scientists, and countless previously unknown items of hardware. Many of the latter were Allied developments, but the greatest effort was put on finding out about German jet and rocket engines. New electronics, especially radar, came a close second. Tens of thousands of prisoners were screened to separate out those with knowledge of these subjects. Very little had been done on radar prior to VE-Day (8 May 1945); Russians told me, 'We were too busy fighting'.

By 1946 substantial research and design teams had been organised to make up for the deficiency, and these naturally made the maximum use of existing German hardware and projects. By the end of that year various radars had flown in Pe-2 and Tu-2 aircraft, and on 22 March 1947 flight-testing began on the Tupolev 63P (P for *Perekhvachik*, interceptor), with Service designation Tu-1. Distantly derived from the Tu-2S, this impressive three-seater had the awesome armament of two devastating NS-45s under the forward fuselage and two NS-23s in

*This Tu-1 can fairly claim to have been the first night fighter in the Soviet Union. Powered by 1,900 hp AM-43VS engines, it had devastating firepower. Note the tail-warning aerial which was part of the PNB-1 radar, derived from the German FuG 220.*

the wing roots, plus upper and lower 12.7 mm UBTs for rear defence. The 63P was the first Soviet aircraft designed to carry AI radar, the installation (called PNB-1 *Gneiss*-7, gneiss the same word in English) being based on the German FuG 220, with tail warning.

By January 1948 the V-VS (air force) and PVO (air-defence forces) firmed up a long and detailed specification for a jet-propelled night and all-weather interceptor, to be fitted with radar and have the highest possible flight performance (maximum speed was to be not less than 1,000 km/h (621 mph). To support this effort, on 7 December 1948 the Council of Ministers issued a decree calling for the development of the radar, leading to high-priority effort by three specially formed OKBs (experimental design bureaux). Meanwhile, the four principal fighter OKBs also beavered away on the aircraft. Predictably, they all chose to use the imported Rolls-Royce Nene turbojet, which was the most powerful fully developed and flight-cleared engine available. With the Soviet designation RD-45, it had been rushed into production at a complex which originally grew to include five major factories.

Remarkably, three of the OKBs settled on a unique aircraft configuration, which enabled them to use two engines on the centreline. The Lavochkin, MiG and Sukhoi prototypes all had a nose inlet feeding one engine low in the front fuselage, with the jet nozzle under the wing, and a second engine behind the wing with the jet nozzle at the tail. All three used the *Toriy* (thorium) radar, developed by the KB of A.V. Slepushkin, which provided search, track and gun-ranging using a single mechanically scanned antenna. A minor problem was that the first examples of this radar could not operate at the $8g$ design limit set for these aircraft. Lavochkin designed the La-200, with the scanner in the centre of a circular nose inlet. Wing sweep was 40°. The MiG R, or I-320, and Sukhoi P, or Su-15 (no relation to a later Su-15), both had an almost untapered wing swept at 35° and the radar scanner in the 12-o'clock position at the top of the nose, above the inlet. Yakovlev used the derived *Korshun* (kite) radar, and boldly put it above the nose of a small single-seater which was also bold in having bicycle landing gear (like a Harrier) and wing sweep of 45°.

Before any of these prototypes could fly, Mikoyan put prototypes of the *Toriy* radar into a modified MiG-15bis, and got it on flight test on 23 April 1949. MiG-factory pilots Col. Gregoriy Sedov and A.N. Chernoburov later also tested five more conversions with the improved *Toriy*-M, but NII-VVS (air force) testing resulted in the conclusion that a single-seat interceptor was simply too difficult, pilot workload being excessive. Mikoyan suggested to Slepushkin that he should work on automatic lock-follow radars, and meanwhile switched his aircraft designers to the *Izumrud* (emerald), a 60 kW radar with one dish for search and a second for locked-on target tracking, gun aiming and ranging. Meanwhile, the specially designed interceptors were on flight test, the Su-15 on 11 January 1949, the MiG R-1 (first I-320) on 16 April, the Yak-50-I on 15 July and the La-200-01 (without radar) on 9 September 1949. Each had good and bad points, the most serious problems being that, having had to abandon the Su-15 in flight because of violent flutter, the very experienced LII-VVS pilot Sergei Anokhin found that the neat little Yak-50 suffered severe Dutch roll (an uncontrollable oscillation) above Mach 0.92, and in a crosswind or on an icy runway it was uncontrollable.

In any case, none of this first generation went into production, and the first interceptors to do so were SP-7 versions of the single-seat MiG-17, their service designation being MiG-17P (*perekhvatchik*). These were fitted with the RP-1 *Izumrud*, with the scanning antenna in the upper lip of the nose inlet and the tracking/ranging dish in a small radome in the centre. Used

*Called P by Sukhoi (and officially designated Su-15, later used for a totally different aircraft), this odd machine had two Nene-derived engines discharging in different places on the centreline, and a pilot offset to the left, as in the D.H.110/Sea Vixen.*

as trainers by the PVO and AV-MF (naval aviation), they posed the pilot with the problem of a high and sustained workload, and the upper scanner made the view ahead on landing marginally worse. Armament was two NR-23s, each with muzzle horsepower 5.5 times that of a 20 mm Hispano and almost ten times that of a 0.50 in Browning. By 1951 the MiG-15 had been replaced by the 15bis, with the more powerful VK-1A engine, in turn replaced by the completely redesigned MiG-17. In 1953 the MiG bureau rolled out the SP-6, a MiG-17 prototype filled with RP-1U *Izumrud* which had the capability of providing a circularly polarized beam, locked-on to the target. Along this beam could fly K-5 AAMs (air-to-air missiles) developed by P.D. Grushin's OKB-2 *Almaz* (diamond) bureau. Four of these were carried on underwing rails. In 1955 the missile went into production as the RS-1U, and these equipped a small series of production SP-6 aircraft, which received the Service designation MiG-17PFU. These had no guns, and, after upgrading with the RS-2US missile, served as trainers for pilots selected for the MiG-19PM.

The MiG-19 was a completely new design, made possible by slim axial-compressor turbojets designed by S.K. Tumanskiy. He was working in the engine KB of Aleksander Mikulin, so the first of this engine family was designated AM-5. First tested in early 1950, it was rated at 1,900 kg (4,189 lb), and a side-by-side pair were used in the MiG SM-1, or I-340. This was basically a MiG-17, and it reached Mach 0.997 in level flight. Mikoyan's team were by this time building the SM-2, or I-360. This was a totally fresh design, with a longer fuselage, slim wings swept at

*Powered by the afterburning VK-1F engine, the MiG-17PF was a good performer despite the weight of RP-1 Izumrud radar and several other extras. This LSK (East German) example probably had just two NR-23 guns, one on each side.*

55° and a high T-tail. Fitted with twin AM-5A engines, it flew on 24 May 1952, and led to the production MiG-19, with many changes, including a low-mounted tailplane. The MiG-19S introduced an all-moving (so-called 'slab') tailplane, and by 1954 it had led to a series of SM-7 prototypes which in turn led to the production MiG-19P. These were gun-armed interceptors with RP-5 *Izumrud* radar and two of the devastating NR-30 guns, the engines being the AM-9 each rated at 3,250 kg (7,165 lb) with afterburner. Level speed was Mach 1.35. By 1957 surviving aircraft were brought up to the standard of the MiG-19PM, fitted with RP-2U *Izumrud* 2 and four RS-2U missiles. By this time newer interceptors were available, and only about 260 MiG-19PM aircraft were delivered, of which half went to Warsaw Pact countries. More significantly, five were sent in crates to China, where such aircraft were to become much more important.

By 1951 the need for a night and all-weather interceptor had become urgent, to counter the menace of the USAF Strategic Air Command with jet bombers carrying thermonuclear weapons. On 10 August of that year the Council of Ministers, accepting that the first crop of

*From 1960 most surviving MiG-19P interceptors were fitted with outer-wing launchers for R-3S (K-13) missiles, based on the AIM-9B Sidewinder. Two NR-23 guns were retained.*

such aircraft (described previously) were inadequate, issued a decree calling for a superior aircraft. Tupolev's OKB was overloaded with large strategic aircraft, Sukhoi's had been closed, and Mikoyan was fully occupied with the small aircraft already described, and with plans for much faster aircraft with delta (triangular) wings. Lavochkin persisted with the La-200B, with the engine installation modified with three inlets (the bottom one feeding the front engine, the side inlets serving the rear engine) leaving the nose free for a large radome housing the 1 m scanner of the RP-6 *Sokol* (falcon) radar. First flown on 3 July 1952, it could be seen from the start to be a basic design developed too far, and not in the same class as its Yakovlev rival.

The Yak-120 was virtually the little Yak-50 scaled up, retaining the same arrangement of nose radar, mid-mounted wing and bicycle landing gear. The differences were that under the wings were two of the slim AM-5 engines, each rated at 2,000 kg (4,410 lb), and behind the pilot was a second cockpit for a radar operator. The ailerons and elevators were hydraulically boosted, and fuel capacity was no less than 3,445 litres (758 Imp. gallons). The radar was to be RP-1 *Izumrud*, and there was a most comprehensive fit of all-weather avionics for navigation and blind landing. Armament comprised two of the awesome N-37L cannon. The first of two prototypes flew on 19 June 1952, and by late 1954 the production aircraft had entered PVO service, with the designation Yak-25 (a designation which had been used previously for a much smaller jet fighter). After delivering sixty-seven aircraft, production switched in 1956 to the Yak-25M, with RP-6 *Sokol* radar, RD-5A engines (AM-5A redesignated after Mikulin's

*This Yak-120 (Yak-25 development aircraft) is in the Monino museum. It is externally similar to early production aircraft.*

departure) rated at 2,600 kg (5,732 lb) and various other changes. The production plant (GAZ-292, at Saratov) delivered 406 Yak-25M aircraft by early 1957.

Apart from the Soviet Union, AI radar suffered a partial hiatus in development in 1945–8. The only completely new airborne radar was airborne early-warning (AEW), which was logical enough. Ground-based surveillance radars are limited in the distance they can see by the curvature of the Earth. The distance in miles to the horizon is roughly the square root of 1.5 times the height in feet of the observation point. Thus, discounting clutter, a radar scanner sixty-six feet above the ground can see a sea-skimming attacker ten miles away, which with jet aircraft means less than a minute's warning. But if the same radar is put into an aircraft and lifted to a height of 27,000 feet it could spot the intruder at a distance of more than 200 miles, provided that it was sufficiently powerful and had good enough discrimination. So on 8 August 1945, just before the end of the war, Hazeltine and General Electric began to work on Project Cadillac, the world's first AEW radar. It was to be able to see individual aircraft in a close group of three or four, at a range of 170–200 miles. Height accuracy was to be ±1,000 feet at 70 miles, and gapless all-weather surveillance was mandatory.

At such long ranges p.r.f. becomes a problem, because the speed of light is finite. A 100-mile timebase cannot be run faster than 1 ms (one-thousandth of a second) per sweep, so the p.r.f. has to be below 1,000. There are severe problems with sidelobes, because even with a large reflector dish not all the energy goes into the principal lobe or main beam. This is especially annoying at low altitudes, and another difficulty arises from overwhelming clutter whenever the powerful beam touches the Earth's land or sea surface. In the early days such problems were major technical challenges, but gradually the handmade APS-20 Cadillac equipment was made to give useful results. It flew on 13 November 1946 in a TBM-3W Avenger, and a bigger installation followed in a version of the B-17 called PB-1W. There followed a production set, the APS-20A, giving one megawatt in the S-band, with an eight-foot elliptical aerial rotating inside a huge glassfibre ventral radome. This graced many aircraft, but is today obsolescent despite a variety of attempts to update it. One batch had a life history almost beyond belief. Made in 1949–50, they were delivered to Douglas at El Segundo and installed in Skyraider AD-4W 'Guppy' early-warning aircraft of the US Navy. In 1951 a batch of fifty were supplied to the UK under the Mutual Defense Assistance Program. These aircraft were redesignated as Skyraider AEW.1 and used by the Fleet Air Arm, operationally by 849 Squadron. From 1960 these aircraft were replaced by the Westland (ex-Fairey) Gannet AEW.3, the same radars being transferred to the British aircraft. From 1969 the carrier-based Fleet Air Arm was phased out as unnecessary, nobody stopping to think that airborne early-warning radar might be useful, for example, in retaking the Falklands. The same radars were upgraded to APS-20F(I) standard and bolted into well-worn Shackletons of the RAF, to produce a force (soon reduced to eight) called Shackleton AEW.2. These served No. 8 Squadron until 1992, when they were replaced by another US aircraft, the Boeing Sentry (development of the British Nimrod AEW.3, which in some ways was significantly superior to the Sentry, having been abandoned and the airframes thoughtlessly destroyed).

By the end of the Second World War both the big SCR-720 and little APS-4 and -6 were all fully developed and in wide use. One of the most interesting and impressive new American combat aircraft was the P-82 (later F-82) Twin Mustang, a highly successful attempt to

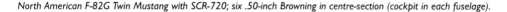

*North American F-82G Twin Mustang with SCR-720; six .50-inch Browning in centre-section (cockpit in each fuselage).*

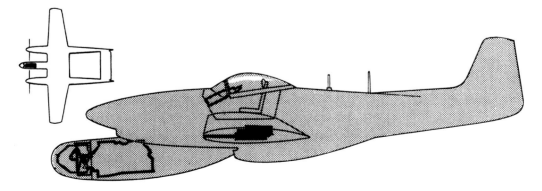

*This Twin Mustang was built as a P-82B, with Packard V-1650 engines, and converted into the unique P-82C night fighter, painted black and with a gaint SCR-720 radar pod. It served as the prototype for 100 F-82Fs, with the Allison V-1710 engine.*

combine P-51 performance with even longer range, with two pilots to share the long mission. In 1945 two of the first batch, with Merlin engines, were converted into night fighters, the P-82C having an SCR-720 in a large centreline pod and the P-82D a small APS-4. To replace the P-61, which had never been a real winner, the USAAF bought 100 P-82Fs with SCR-720 and 50 P-82Gs with APS-4. These were the last piston-engined fighters ordered by the AAF. They were Allison-powered, painted black, and entered service with Air Defense Command in 1947, the year in which the USAF was formed. The last nine F and five G models were delivered as Alaskan F-82H versions, with special cold-start provisions.

At the start of the Korean War the F-82F and G were the chief USAF night fighters. In 1950 a G of the 68th Fighter (All Weather) Squadron of the 8th FB Wing shot down an Il-10 at night. This was the first aerial victory of that war, and also the first gained by the USAF. The main feeling engendered by the Twin Mustang is one of regret that this outstanding aircraft was not developed earlier. It could have served throughout the US participation in the Second World War, had it been proceeded with in 1940. North American Aviation's President, Lee Atwood, told me in 1955 that they had, in fact, thought of such an aircraft at about that time, and literally sketched it on the proverbial back of an envelope, but had been far too busy even to make a proposal to Wright Field.

At the end of the war jets were all the rage, and the Inglewood design staff, by now numbering over 2,800, quickly schemed the NA-134, which became the FJ-1 Fury carrier-based jet fighter for the Navy. By this time, however, German swept-wing data were available, and cutting a long story short, NAA's design team redesigned the Army Air Force version of the FJ-1 and turned it into the NA-140, with wings and tail swept back at 35°. This was ordered as the XP-86. The first XP-86, by this time named Sabre, flew on 1 October 1947. Before long Los Angeles was being startled by what were eventually identified as sonic bangs, made when a jet aircraft is dived faster than sound. Though initially an uncompromised day fighter, the Sabre was to become of outstanding importance, some versions having radar.

In the United Kingdom progress was at a different pace. The only new fighter equipped with radar was the de Havilland Sea Hornet NF.21, a carrier-based derivative of what was possibly the most beautiful, and certainly one of the fastest, piston-engined fighters ever built. The beauty of the single-seat RAF Hornet was destroyed by adding a large pimple on the nose housing ASH radar (the American 3 cm set previously called AI Mk XV), managed by a crew-member whom the Royal Navy still called an observer seated in the slender rear fuselage under a bulging Perspex canopy. This quart in a pint pot equipped only one Fleet Air Arm squadron, No. 809, and this was not sent to Korea (whereas single-engined Seafires, Sea Furies and Fireflies were).

After the Second World War a foolish British government blandly decided there would be no need for new weapons until 1957, and while allowing advanced designs of aircraft to go ahead did little to keep the RAF properly equipped. In 1947 Specification F.44/46 was issued for an all-weather (i.e. including night) fighter, with two engines and two seats. This important specification was re-issued several times with refined requirements, which by late 1947 included four forward-firing 30 mm guns with ammunition for fifteen seconds, a speed not less than 525 knots at 25,000 feet, and various then-challenging times for start-up, takeoff and climb. Many manufacturers tried to meet it, but at first without success. So as a stop-gap the RAF bought a version of the Gloster Meteor, its main day fighter and reconnaissance aircraft.

The 'Meatbox' was even then swiftly becoming obsolete, having been designed to a specification of 1940. Gloster proposed a minimum-modification NF version of the tandem-seat T.7 trainer version in 1947, and again in 1948. Apart from American AI.10, the only modern radar was the British AI.IX, which after its suspension in early 1943 had ticked over gently and become available for production in 1945. But eventually the choice fell on AI.10, plenty of which were available in stores and pensioned-off Mosquitos. This completely filled the lengthened nose, displacing the four 20 mm Hispano guns to the outer wings. In the original Gloster proposal it was planned to pressurize the radar for high-altitude operation, but the aircraft the RAF actually got did not even have a pressurized cockpit, nor ejection seats. Its directional stability was marginal, and the wing-mounted 20 mm guns archaic. Armstrong Whitworth did the conversion design, and managed production of the NF.11 Meteor, which reached No. 29 Squadron in 1951.

As a passenger, I flew several instructive missions in NF Meteors, which at the time seemed impressive but which on reflection were an inadequate compromise. Waiting to take off with 85

PX230 was a de Havilland Hornet F.1 which was later fitted with ASH radar and a cramped observer cockpit as the first Sea Hornet NF.21. First flown in this form on 9 July 1946, it still lacked a dorsal fin and folding wings. Note the handed (opposite-rotation) propellers.

*Developed and built by Armstrong Whitworth, the Meteor NF.14 was at least a great improvement over earlier NF versions, but in comparison with its American or Russian counterparts, it was primitive and ill-equipped. This example served with 85 Sqn (black/red checkerboard markings) at West Malling.*

Squadron at West Malling I watched an NF.11 crash inverted on the approach through inadvertent opening of the airbrakes. Visiting 141 Squadron at Coltishall I flew with the CO, Major Merle Adams, USAF, whose jet time exceeded the aggregate of all the rest of the squadron. A tropicalized NF.11 was the NF.13, while the NF.12 had the American Westinghouse APS-57 (called AI.21 in Britain) in an even longer nose. The final mark of Meteor was the NF.14, again with APS-57 and fitted with a beautiful bubble canopy sliding to the rear instead of the heavily framed side-opening hood inherited from the T.7. Even more important, the '14' had spring-tab ailerons and two-axis autostabilization, and was so much better than its predecessors that it was almost adequate for the job. The last NF.14 first flew on 31 May 1954, closing out 547 night-fighter versions (preceded by 2,920 Meteors built in Britain without radar).

*In true British style, the Vampire NF.10 was not only inadequately equipped, but it was also a death trap, because it was thought that the cockpit was too narrow for ejection seats. Compared with single-seaters, it had an extended tailplane and taller rudders. This example served (like the Meteor NF.14, at West Malling) with No 25 Sqn.*

My last job in the RAF had been flying a Vampire F.3 in June 1948. This was a delightful little day fighter which enjoyed a long period of service in many air forces. In 1947 de Havilland decided, despite official lack of interest, to build a night-fighter version. The D.H.113 prototype was flown by Geoffrey Pike in August 1949, and appeared the following week at the SBAC show. I doubt if many who saw it there noticed that it bore no service roundels. In fact the only customer was Egypt, though India and other nations were in the process of negotiating for what looked like the most cost-effective night fighter in the world. To a remarkable degree it was the cockpit and nose of a Mosquito NF.36 stuck on a standard Vampire. The AI.10 was better-streamlined, and the four cannon remained underneath. But in 1950 arms for Egypt were suddenly banned, and the D.H.113, which had been carefully evaluated at Boscombe Down, was diverted into the RAF. Some ninety-five were delivered, and their main fault was what Boscombe rightly called the 'grossly inadequate' facilities for crew escape. Pilot and navigator, who were squeezed in side by side, had to try to climb out through a hinged hatch in the roof.

De Havilland followed the Vampire with the much more powerful Ghost-engined Venom, whose thin wing gave it potentially higher performance. Like the Vampire, the first Venoms were single-seat fighter-bombers unable to operate at night, and these had a thin wing so structurally weak they were painted with broad red bands to remind the pilots to make only gentle manoeuvres! They were followed by a two-seat night fighter which again was built as a private venture in the absence of official interest. But by the time this flew, on 22 August 1950, the Korean War had broken out, and the Whitehall politicians decided to remove their heads from the sand. Eventually the RAF received sixty Venom NF.2s, similar to the Vampire NF.10 except that they went faster; I managed to avoid becoming airborne in either type. The Venom NF.3, of which 129 were built, was somewhat better; it had Westinghouse APQ-43 radar (called AI.21, like its near-relative in Meteors), powered ailerons, a better tail, and a clear-view canopy with quick-jettison bolts (but still no ejection seats). The Royal Navy followed with its own variant, the Sea Venom FAW.20, with the same American maker's APQ-43. The FAW.21 introduced powered ailerons and Maxaret brakes, and the FAW.22 had a more powerful engine and could carry two Firestreak air-to-air missiles as described in the next chapter. To help spend taxpayers' money more liberally, no ejection seats were fitted until after delivery; then the Mks 21 and 22

*Flying over a few of the houses built in the 1930s, this Sea Venom FAW.21 did at least have ejection seats, as well as a good American radar. The vertical tails were again modified, and it was found that the tailplane extensions were not needed.*

were rebuilt with Martin-Baker Mk 4 seats, making them more popular with their crews.

In 1949 the *Aéronavale*, the air arm of the French Navy, adopted the Sea Venom as its first night and all-weather fighter. The SNCASE group built a modified version under licence as the *Aquilon* (sea eagle), most versions having a Fiat-built Ghost engine, two seats and Westinghouse APQ-65 radar. The final variant was a single-seater, with sliding canopy, and armed like one earlier version with four cannon and two Nord 5103 air-to-air missiles.

None of these European aircraft saw action, except for participation in the ill-starred Suez campaign in November 1956. But in the United States the years 1945–50 were not wasted, and modern jet night fighters were developed in time to serve in Korea. The F-82 was an AAF machine, but two of its rivals in the Korean night sky bore the new 'midnight blue' livery of the US Navy and Marine Corps – singularly appropriate to a night fighter. While the RAF and Royal Navy did nothing about a modern night fighter, the US Navy bought an excellent radar-equipped version of an established carrier-based jet (another thing the British lacked) and also got another company to build a radically unconventional machine designed as a night fighter from the start.

The conversion was the McDonnell Banshee, the first really successful aircraft produced by a young and enthusiastic company which was to go on to become perhaps No. 1 in the world of combat aircraft. The first McDonnell jet, the FD-1 Phantom flown in January 1945, was

*Just arrested aboard* Clémenceau, *the 77th SNCASE Aquilon was a Mk 203, the final single-seat version. Aquilons were painted in US Navy Midnight Blue. In the background, destroyer* Maillé Brézé.

the first jet fighter ever designed for carrier operation. The F2D-1 (later F2H-1) Banshee, flown on 11 January 1947, was bigger and faster. In May 1948 the Navy bought fourteen night-fighter versions, designated F2H-2N. These remained single-seaters, but had a Westinghouse APS-46 radar, a refined derivative of the pioneer 3 cm sets, snugly installed in the nose between the two pairs of M-2 cannon. A further 146 -2N versions were bought in 1950, and many of these tractable and well-liked machines flew night patrol in Korea. In 1952–3 McDonnell delivered 175 of a completely redesigned version, the F2H-3 (later restyled F-2C), with no less than 88 inches added to the fuselage to accommodate extra fuel and the completely different Westinghouse APQ-41 radar. The final Banshee, the F2H-4 (F-2D), had different radar, more powerful engines and other changes. Later fitted with a flight-refuelling probe, these were standard night fighters with the US Navy, Marines and Royal Canadian Navy until after 1960.

The reader cannot have failed to notice that the name Westinghouse has appeared frequently as supplier of radar to nearly all these US, British and French aircraft. Unlike Sperry, Westinghouse kept in the 3 cm radar business after the Second World War, and retained its position as No. 1 at this wavelength. By far its biggest job at this time was providing the radar

*In Korea, VMF(N)-542 had a distinguished career with the F4U Corsair. Then they converted to a dramatically different aircraft, the F3D-1 Skyknight. Here the penultimate aircraft of the first F3D-1 batch (123767) from El Segundo is seen during the Marine unit's type-conversion. It then deployed to Korea with F3D-2s.*

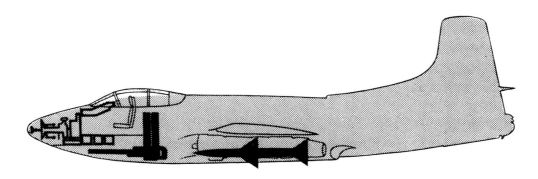

*Douglas F3D-2M (MF-10B) Skyknight with APQ-35 or -36; two AIM-7A Sparrow I and four 20 mm M-2.*

for the other Navy fighter, the one designed explicitly for night fighting. It was because of its eventual success with this radar, the APQ-35, that it was able to supply all the other installations. The aircraft for which the APQ-35 was designed was the F3D (later F-10) Skyknight. Never in the public limelight, it was one of the most important night fighters in history.

This is because it was the first jet, and the first carrier-based aircraft, to be planned from the start as a night and all-weather fighter. Ed Heinemann, chief engineer of the Douglas plant at El Segundo, was a legend in his own time. No designer has ever exercised more stringent control over weight, been more cunning in pruning unnecessary items, or racked up such a diverse list of famous aircraft (including the DB-7/Havoc). It was his team that beat Curtiss, Grumman and Fleetwings to build the Skyknight to a BuAer specification of August 1945. With the advent of jets it was clearly only a matter of time before the Navy had to defend itself against jet bombers, and the requirement was for detection of typical targets 125 miles distant at 40,000 feet at a target speed of 500+ mph, with the interception completed in fifteen minutes. This demanded a radar with better range and discrimination than SCR-720, a crew of two, and a combat radius of 600 miles. According to Heinemann, 'This was quite a shock to us. The performance seemed incompatible with the need for a crew of two and a heavy load of electronics.'

Eventually he arrived at a satisfactory layout. Not least of the unusual choices was side-by-side seats, with an optically flat windscreen. Such a screen had been used in the fighter Mosquitos, but it was remarkable that it should be aerodynamically acceptable to a jet. All normal fuel was in fuselage cells above the easily exchanged Westinghouse J34 engines. Instead of ejection seats the crew could abandon the aircraft by a very neat belly chute. In the nose was the extremely challenging APQ-35, and Marine Corps flightline crews often spent all day and all night rectifying faults and fitting individually matched tubes (valves) by hand. They did this in trailers and huts in the severe Korean weather, while Navy men toiled at these unfamiliar tasks aboard carriers. The twenty-eight F3D-1 Skyknights, all delivered by April 1951, were followed by 237 slightly more powerful F3D-2s of various sub-types, the last entering service in October 1953. Standard armament was four 20 mm cannon, but two -1s and sixteen -2s were modified to carry APQ-36 and four Sparrow I beam-riding missiles as well.

In Korea VMF(N)-513 converted from a mix of F7Fs and F4U-4Ns to the Skyknight during 1952. On 3 November Major William T. Stratton Jr and his R/O, MSgt Hans C. Hoglind, shot down what was thought to be a Yak-15: 'Contact was made on radar, same altitude, speed 320 knots. First contact was lost, but was again established at the same distance. We closed until a visual was obtained . . . I opened fire at 12,000 feet altitude. The first burst hit the left wing, the second the fuselage and the third entered the tailpipe, exploding therein. Three explosions were observed, and the plane smoked heavily as it went down.' This was the first known night jet-v-jet kill in history. Five days later Captain R.O. Davis and W/O D.F. Fessler were on night combat air patrol when they were notified of

Bogey, 12 o'clock, 10 miles, 12,500 feet . . . I began a dive from 19,000 feet . . . my R/O got the contact, ordered a gentle starboard but lost it immediately. I requested further help from the ground controller . . . As we closed I got a visual and a jet exhaust. I requested the controller to distinguish it as friendly or bandit; he replied, 'Bag it! Bag it!' I was about a quarter-mile from the exhaust and closing rapidly. I popped the speed brakes. The exhaust was so bright it was hard to make out the airframe outline. The bandit began a hard starboard. I turned with him and fired a short burst of about 20 rounds of 20-mm into the tailpipe. There was an explosion and parts flew past. I was closing dangerously. I pulled hard back, and as I was already in a hard starboard turn I passed the enemy to his right. I observed flames and black smoke . . . After reversing my turn I picked up a visual on the flaming craft as it descended and crashed. I had opened fire at 0136 and the plane crashed at 0137.

This renowned Marine unit destroyed ten aircraft in Korea, six while flying the Skyknight. Their main duty became flying barrier patrols ahead of B-29 bombers, and while they were present not one B-29 was lost to enemy fighters. In 1955 a Navy outfit, VF(AW)-3, based at North Island (San Diego), became the only Navy squadron forming part of the Norad (North American Air Defense) system. In 1962 the ageing Skyknight was redesignated F-10, surviving F3 D-2 versions being rebuilt as 131 F-10Bs, 16 MF-10Bs (missile), 55 TF-10Bs (trainer) and 35 EF-10Bs (countermeasures). The change in designation was not bothersome, because by this time the Skyknight was universally known as 'Willy the Whale'. On 10 April 1965, more than seventeen years after its first flight, the Skyknight went to war a second time. VMCJ-1, based at Iwakuni (Japan), was detached to Da Nang, a base that was to become one of the world's busiest and best known in an ill-starred war that on many counts was bigger than the Second World War. The old 'Whale' EF-10B was, in the words of General Homer S. Hill of the Marine Corps, 'the only aircraft in the entire US arsenal ready for tactical active and passive countermeasure missions, and proved most valuable to all services'. The EF-10B had previously been the platform that first detected Chinese fire-control radar during the Quemoy/Formosa crisis in 1957–8, and first detected Russian radar emissions in Cuba in 1962, as a result of which reconnaissance coverage was stepped up until it discovered the Russian ballistic missiles. In their twilight years these bulging boxes of electronics served until 1969 escorting strikes into North Vietnam, jamming entry radars, and on the return journey using their sensors to find targets of opportunity for their guns.

Heinemann was proud of the fact that his aircraft invariably weighed about half as much as those of his rivals (indeed, with the A-4 Skyhawk the Navy angrily proclaimed that his weight

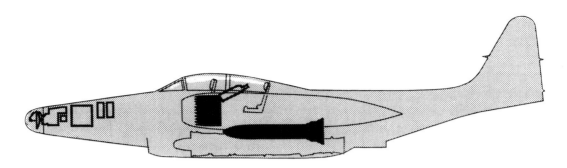

*Northrop F-89J Scorpion with E-9 fire-control updated to MG-12 standard; two AIR-2A Genie (can also carry four AIM-4A radar or AIM-4C IR Falcon) and 104 FFAR of 2.75-inch calibre.*

calculations were not serious, an inadvisable thing to say where EEH was concerned). His big twin-engined, two-crew night fighter, burdened with extra equipment for carrier operation, weighed *half as much* as the rival night fighters for the US Air Force. In fact, compared with one of the USAF contenders, the Skyknight had *the same type of engines but half as many*. Actual gross-weight figures for the three aircraft (prototypes) are: Douglas XF3D-1, 21,500 lb; Curtiss XP-87, 49,900 lb; Northrop XF-89, 43,910 lb.

The once-mighty Curtiss company spent the Second World War producing a succession of unsuccessful prototypes. On 5 March 1948 they began flight testing the XP-87 Blackhawk night fighter. Painted black, it was impressive, with a span of 60 feet and length of almost 63 feet. The pilot and radar observer were seated side by side, and an unusual (but not unique) feature was that in the nose were four 20 mm guns mounted on a pivoted platform so that they could be aimed over a limited range of elevation angles. Well out on the wings were the four Westinghouse XJ34 turbojets. In June 1948 the vast factory echoed to cheers with the news that the newly formed Air Force had ordered eighty-eight F-87A Blackhawks. Precisely four months later the order was cancelled.

It was cancelled because Northrop's XP-89, first flown on 16 August 1946, was better. Later it was restyled XF-89, and named the Scorpion, a predator to which, on the ground, it had an uncanny resemblance. Throughout its life this big interceptor was handicapped by its engines, which were primitive fuel-hungry axial turbojets designed in 1942 as the General Electric J35 and mass-produced as the Allison J35. Even with the crude afterburner lit the J35 gave only 7,200 lb thrust, and a total sea-level thrust of 14,400 lb for an aircraft which in later versions weighed 46,780 lb resulted in a near-record poor ratio of thrust to weight. Despite this, the USAF said it had plenty of long runways, and it put the F-89 on a lot of them around the world.

John K. Northrop's team always showed exceptional interest in wing efficiency and the attainment of high lift coefficients. This was strongly evident in the P-61, and with the F-89 this was matched with a thin profile for 600 mph speed. In turn, the decision to house the retracted main landing gears in this thin wing resulted in wheels of unprecedented diameter for a fighter, which somebody insisted were taken from scrapped steam locomotives from the Atchison,

Topeka and Santa Fé railroad. Another unusual feature was patented Decelerons: ailerons which could split into upper and lower halves, forming powerful airbrakes. (One wondered how so many Mosquito crews had managed, storming up behind their invisible targets with no means of slowing down, and landing gear red-lined at 180 knots.) Unlike the Skyknight, the pilot and RO were seated in tandem, and they did have ejection seats, though fairly primitive ones. The rear fuselage, which sloped up to the high tail to give the aircraft its predatory resemblance to a scorpion, was extremely slender, and did not contain the rear-warning scanner and other gear found in most Skyknights. The nose, however, was extremely capacious, and was designed to accommodate six 20 mm cannon and a completely new radar.

This radar came from a source which surprised many: Hughes Aircraft. Texan Howard Hughes was known to be one of the world's richest men, a brilliant and courageous pilot, and many other things, including a producer of gigantic Hollywood epics. Hughes Aircraft had built only a few aircraft, but these included the world's fastest landplane of 1935 and the world's biggest aeroplane of any kind. The company had a good record of war production, and was known to be building up strength in all branches of what are today called avionics. In 1947 Hughes demonstrated a radar-based system for transport aircraft which today would be called a ground-proximity warning system (GPWS); in other words, it warned pilots not to fly into mountains or other obstructions. The only thing wrong was that Hughes was nearly thirty years ahead of the market. Many observers, including Top Brass of the US armed forces, tended to dismiss Hughes Aircraft as a mere plaything of its founder. But in 1948, when the Air Force asked US industry for a completely new radar-based system for future interceptors, such a superficial opinion could no longer be sustained. Hughes was in deadly earnest, as was the Air Force, and the talent he had gathered sent in a bid that stood alongside those from the giants such as GE, Westinghouse, RCA and other formidable opponents. In round-table discussion the men from Hughes showed themselves to be anything but 'playthings'; they inspired confidence in a challenging field in which the Air Force needed all the confidence it could get.

When the Air Force picked Hughes, many – indeed most – of the unsuccessful bidders thought the upstart California team would fall down on the job. They knew Hughes had been the only bidder to agree to the Air Force request for a flying installation in one year; most said it would take at least two. After five months, the Russian troops in East Germany suddenly sealed off all surface communications to Berlin, in the belief that the Western allies would have no option but to back down and get out. How the Berlin Airlift sustained the city for almost a year, so that – to their considerable surprise – it was the Soviet Union that had to back down, is now part of history. What is less familiar is the profound influence this brash act had on the US government, and the fastest reaction of all came from the Air Force. On the day after the Russians shut the barriers Hughes Aircraft was asked, 'Can you give us a flight test in four months, and production six months later?' Hughes was also asked if it was willing to invest millions in expanded facilities. The answer in both cases was positive. Hughes recalls, 'Technicians slept on their work-benches, shaved and ate at the job. No one was forcing them. They were driving themselves to beat this deadline.' They met the flight-test schedule, and beat the production schedule by two days. A little later, at Eglin AFB, Florida, an Air Force F-94A interceptor equipped with the Hughes E-1 fire-control successfully located, intercepted and shot down with gunfire a target drone without the crew ever seeing it.

This was the beginning of a new era in air defence. It has proved to be an era in which the young Hughes team has not only survived but flourished, and virtually all US Air Force interceptors have been fitted with Hughes radars and fire-control systems. A further characteristic of this new era has been that the fire-control system has increasingly tended to take over from the pilot, leaving the latter somewhat in the role of supervisory manager. Another characteristic is that the traditional chase from behind, and prolonged attack with gunfire, was rather suddenly replaced by a 'collision course' attack from quite different directions, during which rockets or guided missiles would be released at a single brief moment. Perhaps the most fundamental change of all was that henceforth there would be no 'night fighters', if by that is meant a special rather exotic species distinguished by extra equipment from run-of-the-mill fighters. Today very few air forces would even consider buying a fighter that could not operate at night or in bad weather. The ability to seek out targets and destroy them almost automatically is something that is now taken for granted. As the next chapter shows, the main problems today stem from the fact that to most weapons there are antidotes, and the modern interceptor is no exception.

Walking round the nose of the first production F-89 Scorpion in June 1950, nothing looked very different. Closer study of the array of black boxes would have revealed an extra pair of rather large ones. They were the airborne computer, which marked the first major change in the new era of interceptor equipment. Though this was still firmly in the days of thermionic valves, meaning that electronics were large, heavy, consumed a lot of power and needed a lot of cooling, it was marginally possible to build a radar and a computer that would fit into a fighter and give useful results. Though it was still possible for a malfunction to ruin the whole exercise – and there was now more to go wrong – the objective was to harness the obedient electrons and made them do the calculations and take at least some of the decisions, easing the strain on the crew's cerebral cells and probably reducing the errors.

While the F-89 was being developed, the whole technique of air interception underwent two further radical revisions, though both had been foreseen long beforehand. In each case the change was associated with a new kind of armament, and it is no more than historical fact to note that both these new weapons were pioneered by the *Luftwaffe*. The first new weapon was the air-to-air rocket, unguided but stabilized by spinning rapidly in flight. The second was the air-to-air guided missile. These, coupled with the changed methods of interception, were to suggest that the future lay in increasing automaticity. Fighters tended to be developed with all-missile armament, and to fly at higher and higher speeds. Some experts saw that the obvious next step would be to leave out the pilot, and either use surface-to-air missiles or convert the fighter into an automatic re-usable missile launcher. This kind of thinking reached its apparently logical pinnacle in Britain during the 1950s, as a result of which that country cancelled all its fighters but one, and severely held back the development of that lone survivor until it realized that this thinking was grossly mistaken. Only since 1960 has the pilot returned to his former position of unchallenged mastery in air combat. With this about-face in views has come a return to close dogfighting and close-range missiles and guns. With today's fire-control systems it is theoretically possible to indulge in such close combat at night or in thick cloud, which was impossible with the technique of 1950.

With the early F-89, such as the F-89C of 1952 (the first major production version), the initial stages of an interception were traditional. The GCI controller transmitted vectors to steer

A standard work on the F3D (see picture on p. 156) calls it 'a large and heavy aircraft'. Compared with its Air Force counterpart, the Northrop F-89, it was not only much smaller but its gross weight was much less than the empty weight of the F-89J. The final F-89 version to leave the Hawthorne factory was the F-89D, with Hughes MG-12 fire control, and Falcon missiles mounted on the tip pods housing FFAR rockets or fuel, Falcons moved under the wing and extra racks added for two awesome Genies. Painted white, the Genies had no guidance, but they did have a nuclear warhead!

and a height at which to fly. The scanner in the nose of the fighter swept from side to side, and up and down, searching in a series of parallel scans rather like the lines across a TV screen. As soon as the RO saw a blip, in the place where the GCI controller had predicted, he would guide a small ring of light on the radar scope by means of a cockpit pistol-grip until it was centred over the blip. Then, with a switch or button, he would lock the radar onto the target. The scanner would cease its search mode and would point at the target, no matter what manoeuvres the target or the fighter might perform (provided that the target sightline was kept within the cone limits of the scanner). In fact the fighter pilot would aim to steer almost directly towards the target, and he would be assisted by a major new development. Instead of the RO having to watch the blip, try and work out what the target was doing and tell the pilot which way to steer, the Hughes radar worked all this out instantly. Locking-on the radar to the target changed the operating mode. Instead of presenting target azimuth, elevation and range, the pilot display now showed merely the steering dot and the surrounding circle. All the pilot had to do was keep the dot centred in the circle. If he let it wander off, to say, 10 o'clock, the pilot merely had to roll slightly to the left while hauling back on the stick to bring it back to the centre. For an attack with guns, the computer had to control the steering dot to bring the pilot into a 'lead-pursuit' path behind the target. When the range was close enough he could open fire. The system worked. I recall seeing towed-banner targets at Yuma positively riddled with F-89C passes with only two of the six guns loaded. The holes were assignable to each aircraft involved, because their 20 mm shells were doped in contrasting colours.

In 1953 Northrop began to deliver the next version of the Scorpion, the F-89D. This introduced a substantially different Hughes fire-control system, a modified computer and rocket armament instead of guns. The F-89C had slim 253 gal (300 US gal) tanks on each wing tip. In the D these were replaced by much fatter tanks which, in their forward section, incorporated launch tubes for fifty-two Mighty Mouse rockets, or 104 for the whole aircraft. Each rocket had a calibre of 2.75 inches, folding fins which flicked open as the missile left the tube, canted motor nozzles to impart spin, and such warhead power that a hit anywhere on a large bomber was likely to be lethal. The official term was FFAR, for folding-fin aircraft rocket. The original FFAR had been the *Luftwaffe*'s R4/M, of 55 mm calibre (just over two inches), which was salvoed against US 8th Air Force heavies in the daytime. The reason behind the R4/M was the difficulty of hitting a bomber hard enough without being shot to pieces by the bombers' massed defensive fire. The same argument lay behind the Mighty Mouse. With a traditional lead-pursuit interception the fighter had to close in from behind the bomber, and stay closed in long enough to bring it down with gunfire. Most bombers, other than those of the RAF, were being equipped with radar-directed tail guns which were deadly to a fighter at such close range. The Mighty Mouse promised to put the interceptor back on top.

It promised to do so partly because of the destructive power of each rocket. The F-89D could salvo all 104 in a split-second, 'blanketing an area of sky bigger than a football field'. Thus it needed to be in firing position only for that brief moment. So the firing position did not have to be from astern. The computer that was installed in the F-89D, to calculate the release position and time, could release the interceptor from the severe constraints of the traditional lead-pursuit attack, in which the fighter had to close from astern, always aiming slightly ahead of the target, and inevitably getting closer all the time to the dead-astern position. With a computer on board, the interceptor could automatically calculate the target's exact speed and heading, and thus its likely position at any time in the near future. All the fire-control system then needed to do was steer the fighter, or direct its pilot, so that it flew in a straight line directly towards that place. At the correct moment the salvo of rockets would be launched. In a great blast of flame and smoke they would streak to the predicted target position, arriving there at the same moment as the target. The latter would be seen not from the rear but from the side, or some other favourable angle offering a large cross-section, easy to hit. In contrast, the fighter would be seen by the target almost head-on, several hundred yards away, and changing its apparent direction rapidly all the time. This 'lead-collision' interception had much to commend it.

In 1955 the USAF Air (from January 1968 Aerospace) Defense Command received the final models of Scorpion, the F-89H and J. These had further revised radar fire-control and many smaller changes, but again the main difference concerned the armament. Though a few Mighty Mouse FFARs were still carried, the chief weapons were four or six Falcon guided missiles and, in the J model, two Genie rockets. The Genie, originally known by the code-name Ding Dong, was only a plain rocket but it had a nuclear warhead. It could thus destroy a bomber even if it missed, the proximity-fused head being lethal within a radius of several hundred feet. Despite several self-evident problems with such a weapon, the Genie was to be carried right up to the 1970s by a number of important types of USAF interceptor.

In comparison with Genie, Falcon was much smaller. Whereas Genie weighed 830 lb, a typical early Falcon weighed but 100 lb, and was smaller than a man, being about six feet long but only six inches in body diameter. Its warhead, though many times more powerful even than that of a Mighty Mouse, nevertheless had to be triggered on or extremely close to the target for it to be lethal. Where Falcon was different was that it steered itself automatically towards the target. Provided it worked properly, nothing in 1955 could deflect it from its course, and no aircraft could manoeuvre out of its way. It was the first air-to-air guided missile to go into service.

As in so many fields of armaments, the first air-to-air guided missiles were developed in Germany during the Second World War. The Ruhrstahl AG produced over 1,000 transonic X-4 wire-guided missiles capable of being launched from the Me 262 jet fighter over ranges between one and 2.2 miles. The fighter 'stood off' while the pilot steered the missile with a small joystick which generated electrical control signals transmitted through wires paid out from bobbins in the missile's wing-tips. Henschel built the radio-controlled Hs 117H and Hs 298. Large numbers of test firings took place of all three missiles, but none reached the *Luftwaffe*. Information on German missiles was studied by all the victorious Allies, but only the Soviet Union decided to carry on where the Germans had left off. In the United States the bold decision was taken to go straight to supersonic missiles that did not need any steering by a human operator. In 1947 the brilliant young Hughes company began work on a missile for the US Air Force that became the Falcon. In 1949 Sperry started work on a larger missile that became the Sparrow. In 1951 the Naval Ordnance Test Station let a handful of engineers develop a simple and cheap missile that became the most cost-effective weapon of modern times: Sidewinder.

These missiles were subsequently developed in many different forms, with improved reliability, increased performance, greater lethality and contrasting kinds of guidance. Some homed on infra-red emission from the target, some were semi-active radar homers that steered towards reflections from the target of the fighter's own radar, and there were also other

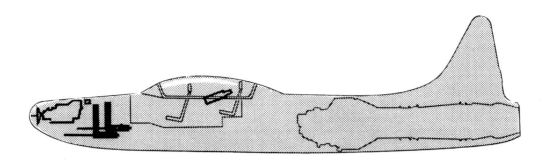

*Lockheed F-94B Starfire with APG-32 forming part of E-1 fire-control system; four .50-inch Browning.*

methods such as riding the centre of a coded radar beam from the fighter locked-on to the target. The main promise of guided missiles was improved lethality, but secondary advantages were the ability to engage at greater ranges, the ability to get in a killing shot in a split second, and the ability to hit an unseen target in the dark or in cloud. They entered service with the US Air Force and Navy in 1956, about four years later than Mighty Mouse.

Between the two, in 1954, arrived a better 20 mm gun, with a higher rate of fire made possible by a revolving multi-chambered feed cylinder. This gun, the M-39, was developed by the Pontiac Division of General Motors from the German Mauser MG 213 of 1944. In Britain the MG 213 led to the 30 mm Aden, while France, Switzerland, Sweden and the Soviet Union all produced similar 'revolver cannon'. The ultimate in guns appeared to be reached when, in 1953, the butts at Burlington, Vermont, echoed to a kind of explosion that went on without stopping. General Electric had begun firing the six-barrel 'Gatling' known as Project Vulcan and today called the M61, firing high-velocity 20 mm shells at the rate of 100 per second.

All these weapons were of benefit to day fighters as much as to night fighters, but gradually the very concept of the day fighter had to be rethought. By 1950 fighter designers were planning future aircraft to fly at speeds exceeding Mach 1, the speed of sound, and within a further two years Mach 2 had become attainable. Coupled with this dramatic increase in speed had come a similar multiplication in rate of climb and operational ceiling. When these factors, combined with extreme difficulty of conducting a visual search for the enemy in the stratosphere, were added to the introduction of long-range air-to-air missiles, it was self-evident that interceptions by fighters not equipped with radar would no longer be practicable. No matter how accurate the GCI control might be, the fighter of the future was going to need not only comprehensive AI radar but also a means of linking the radar display with the pilot's gunsight, and with such basic flight information as roll attitude, all projected on to the pilot's windscreen.

Thus, the concept of the fighter itself underwent a revolution. It had already gone through one in the 1940s with the advent of jet propulsion. This in turn had so increased flight performance that the concept of the (day) fighter was no longer viable. All fighters had to be equipped with radar to enable them to search a large volume of sky, so all fighters henceforth had to be capable of operating at night. However, this took a while to sink in. In the Korean

War the appearance of the MiG-15 gave people on the other side, notably the United States, a severe shock. It was bad enough when the shiny swept-wing enemies were flown by inexperienced Chinese, who could flee across the Yalu river with no hope of being caught even by an F-86. When Russian instructors began flying combat missions, they did not flee and the situation became serious. At the time the true state of affairs was kept secret, and the USAF claimed a kill:loss ratio for the F-86 Sabre against the MiG-15 of 'better than 14:1'. The true figure was just under 3.5:1, and this was entirely due to the skill and experience of the US pilots, compared with the Chinese. If the MiG pilot was also skilled the results were very different. The top-scoring Russian, Evgeny Pepelyaev, said, 'The fifty-calibre bullets rattled on the MiG like peas . . . The MiG, and especially its engine, could take damage far better than the Sabre.' His personal score was nineteen US fighters destroyed.

The fact that the MiG-15 was evenly matched in a close turning fight against an F-86, and had far more devastating armament, was not communicated to America's allies. Britain's top fighter designer, Sydney (about to become Sir Sydney) Camm, told the author he was intrigued by the MiG's seemingly disastrous 1:14 showing against the F-86, which was at odds with the fact that the US government was desperate to find out about the Russian fighter and was offering $100,000 (equivalent to several million today) to any pilot who would fly one to Kimpo, a US base in Korea (in September 1953 a Korean pilot took the bait). Somehow, British fighter designers felt that all this was a long way away, whereas, in contrast, several US fighter designers actually went to Korea to talk first-hand with pilots who had engaged the MiG-15 in close combat.

One who took the trouble was Clarence L. 'Kelly' Johnson, Chief Engineer of Lockheed. He found that every pilot he spoke to was saying, 'I want more performance, more speed, more height, faster climb. . . .' The top USAF wartime ace, Colonel 'Gabby' Gabreski, even said, 'I'd gladly throw out the massive gunsight and aim with a piece of gum stuck on the windscreen if it meant I could outfly the MiG.' Johnson returned to California and, with the most careful planning and support, created the Lockheed Model 83, which became the F-104 Starfighter. It was the ultimate expression of the interceptor, with fantastic rate of climb, Mach 2.2 speed and just enough armament to bring down an opponent (one of the new Project Vulcan guns and two Sidewinders). In the needle-like nose was an ASG-14 radar to feed target range to the MA-10 gunsight. With its tiny sharp-edged wing, the F-104 certainly merited its maker's title of 'the missile with a man in it'. On the other hand, as a fighter it was of extremely limited value. Later versions found more effective employment carrying reconnaissance cameras or nuclear bombs, but even the ultimate F-104S version, with Sparrow missiles, was too limited to be what was really needed: an equally fast night and all-weather fighter.

The world is a funny place, and the F-104's opposite number in the USSR, while dramatically better in a tightly turning dogfight, was initially to be every bit as limited in capability. Mikoyan's designers had studied the results of the Korean War, and so had the Kremlin. The central result was that three months after the Korean armistice of July 1953 a requirement was issued for 'a frontal fighter . . . with a level speed of Mach 2 at an altitude of 20 km [65,617 ft] while carrying guns and a radar-ranging sight'. This was precisely the same objective that Kelly had set himself with the F-104. 'Frontal' meant that the new fighter was to be used by Soviet tactical aviation, which was a different service from the PVO air-defence force. The result, after most careful evaluation of swept wings and deltas (but in every case with a horizontal tail) was to become the MiG-21. It is surely ironic that a fighter deliberately designed to be limited in

*Lockheed's advertising lauded the F-104 Starfighter as 'the missile with a man in it'. A joke in the Luftwaffe was 'Optimist: an F-104 pilot who gives up smoking because he's afraid of dying of lung cancer'. In contrast, Italy's Aeronautica Militare had few problems with the ultimate version, the F-104S. This had upgraded radar and Sparrow missiles.*

capability, initially without AI radar, should have sustained a production run of more than 13,400, for fifty-six air forces, and to have participated in more than thirty shooting wars. No other post-1945 fighter comes close.

Brief details of post-1945 fighters, and a selection of earlier fighters, appear in the Appendix. Some, such as the Vought F-8 Crusader and Dassault Mirage, began life as simple aircraft designed solely for flight performance, and quickly acquired all-weather capability. However, as aircraft grew larger and much more expensive, it became obvious even to the most 'gung-ho' customers that there was not much point in buying fighters that could operate only on a nice day, in the daytime. Even today there are plenty of simple so-called light fighters, but they are really advanced trainers. For example, when I am told that RAF Hawk trainers can carry Sidewinders, and that the UK's Flying Training Schools have a dual role in a time of national emergency as fighter squadrons to defend the United Kingdom – for example, 7 FTS doubles as two former Lightning-Phantom squadrons, Nos 19 and 92 – my only comment is 'pull the other one'. Good thing we didn't have Tiger Moths pretending to provide defence in 1940.

To return to serious all-weather and night defence, during the early 1950s Hughes delivered all-weather interception systems at an increasing rate. The basic E-1, already described, entered

*The F-104S placed heavy demands on its pilots. Everything happened at very high speed, and in an era of dial instruments it was not easy to pay constant attention to the radar display seen behind the control stick (which itself had as many controls as a clarinet).*

service first with the Lockheed F-94A Starfire, the rather limited night fighter produced by converting the F-80C Shooting Star day fighter. The F-94B had more fuel but still only four 0.5 in guns. Another aircraft equipped with the E-1 was the Avro CF-100 Mk 3, a large Canadian aircraft fitted with eight 0.5 in guns. But, as related in the history of the F-89 Scorpion, the USAF decided to adopt collision-course interception using FFAR rockets, and Hughes accordingly developed a series of more complex fire-control systems incorporating a computer, to determine the lead-collision attack trajectory and fire the armament automatically. The first of the new systems, the E-4, incorporated a radar five times as powerful (250 kW) as that of the

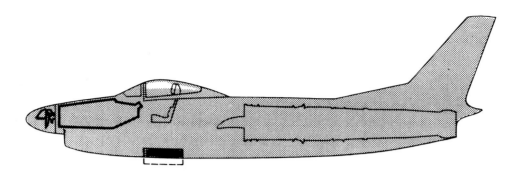

*North American F-86D Sabre with APG-36 forming part of fire-control/autopilot system; 24 FFARs of 2.75-inch calibre in retractable tray.*

E-1, with a 200-mile ground-mapping display mode to assist navigation, and an added ground-beacon interrogation facility.

A dramatic breakthrough was achieved in planning the E-4 initially for a single-seater, the F-86D Sabre. Instantly identifiable by its nose radome and 'chin' air inlet, the 'Dogship Sabre' was the successor to the wartime radar-equipped single-seaters of the Navy and the forerunner of the single-seat fighter of today. Much heavier than earlier Sabres, it yet had excellent performance as a result of adding an afterburner to boost the J47 engine. Its only failing was in having no guns, but just a belly pack of twenty-four FFARs which were pushed down into the airstream and 'rippled' away in less than one second. The pilot could previously select whether the system would fire six, twelve or all twenty-four. It was a system extremely advanced for its day, and I believe the technology almost over-reached itself. In the days of thermionic radio valves (vacuum tubes in American parlance) even a simple radar or computer was a formidable proposition. Development problems meant that at one time in 1952 there were 380 otherwise complete dogships still at LA airport waiting for their fire-control system, and even as late as 1955 the serviceability with the USAF squadrons was little short of a disaster by modern standards. On the other hand no fewer than 2,504 Dogships were built, and when they worked they were unbeatable. I was amused at the impossible situation into which the British defence chiefs got themselves with their public insistence that any single-seat night and all-weather interceptor would be 'absolutely useless for British conditions', because the USAF 406th Fighter Interceptor Wing had two squadrons of single-seat D-models based at Manston in Kent and they scored close to 100 per cent in night and all-weather exercises.

Hughes then reworked the E-4 for a two-man crew for the rocket-armed F-94C (48 FFARs, E-5 fire-control), F-89D (104 FFARs, E-6) and CF-100 Mk 4 (57 FFARs, MG-2). The next stage was to adapt the growing system to the Falcon missile, the first result being the E-9 of 1955. This had a more powerful, longer-ranged radar, a more complex computer system for the fire-control calculations needed by guns, FFARs or Falcons, and armament auxiliaries to prepare the Falcons for automatic launch locked-on to home on the correct target. The E-9 was fitted to the F-89H, armed with six radar-homing Falcons and forty-two FFARs. Meanwhile, Hughes' backroom engineers had been working on a completely new system, the MG-10,

*The MiG-21F-13 (second production version, with broad fin), was still only marginally a night fighter. Despite having just one gun, and later two simple K-13A missiles, it sold like hot cakes – in this case to Czechoslovakia, which licence-built 194.*

*After 17 years, the primitive MiG-21F had become the MiG-21bis, which was a totally different species. Major changes included the R-25 engine, upgraded avionics, including RP-22 Sapfir multi-mode radar, and a choice of various R-3 or R-60 missiles. Note: to hold formation, No. 55 is using a touch of airbrake on takeoff!*

*Avro CF-100 Mk 4B serial 389 (actually 18389) really was No 389 off the Malton assembly line. This example mated the Hughes MG-2 radar with the original armament of eight 0.5 in guns. Note the black rubber Goodrich de-icer boots on the leading edges, a unique feature on an aircraft that could dive beyond Mach 1.*

*Powered by an afterburning J47 engine, the Sabre F-86K was an F-86D with all the sensitive (i.e., new) parts left out, so that it could be made by licensee Fiat at Turin for various NATO allies. North American did the basic design and prototype testing. The Inglewood plant then quickly delivered 120, and also sent 50 kits of parts to Turin, where Fiat produced 221 of this gun-armed version. The last 45 had slatted wings, as seen here.*

forming the next generation in interceptor fire controls. To avoid the desperate problems encountered with the F-86D, the MG-10 was planned in parallel with the interceptor that was to carry it, the Convair F-102. When the first YF-102 flew in October 1953 its handling seemed satisfactory, but during 1954 the unpalatable fact emerged that the new interceptor, planned to be highly supersonic, would not exceed Mach 0.997. In 117 days the entire F-102 was redesigned, in one of the biggest panics I can recall, and eventually emerged a different shape with the same engine giving Mach 1.25 in level flight.

Convair never expected the troubles to lie in the basic shape of the F-102 but in its complex equipment. Though miniaturized to only 52 per cent of the bulk of the F-86D system, the MG-10 was much more powerful and automatic. One of the new features of the F-102 was a large internal weapon bay, from which Falcon missiles could be flicked out on powered arms before release. Another was that the new IR-homing Falcon was included, and the MG-10 was matched to the needs of these as well as to the radar kind. (Later a special IR seeker was added above the F-102 nose to give better IR lock-on at greater ranges.) Another new feature was that

The USAF caption said 'Alert crews run to their F-102A Delta Daggers to investigate an unidentified aircraft . . .', but the only pilot is in the furthest aircraft. At a time when most USAF aircraft were unpainted, the Daggers were painted battleship grey. Later they were camouflaged, and given two drop tanks and an infra-red sensor above the nose. What nobody expected was that in 1974 secondhand Greek and Turkish 'Deuces' would engage each other (for real) over Cyprus!

the MG-10 incorporated a digital data-link receiving target vectoring commands from a ground station; it then translated these signals into analog form for display to the pilot. Briefly, digital means a succession of discrete 'bits' of information, as in calculating with an abacus or with plain numbers. In contrast, analog means that information is conveyed by selecting points along continuous scales, as in a slide-rule, or particular voltages which can vary without any jumps or steps, as in an analog computer. A fundamental feature of modern society has been increasing importance of digital methods, and fighter aircraft are no exception.

Yet another radical innovation in the F-102 was what Hughes called CSTI, for control-surface tie-in. The MG-10 was linked to the interceptor's autopilot so that it could automatically steer the aircraft to any desired heading, pitch attitude or altitude, during either the attack on an aerial target or the recovery at the home airfield. Compared with previous systems MG-10 was more capable and more reliable, and it enabled a lone pilot to manage an interception by night or in any weather with virtually 100 per cent certainty against any target the F-102 could catch. During the final phases the pilot flew with his eyes looking into the vizor

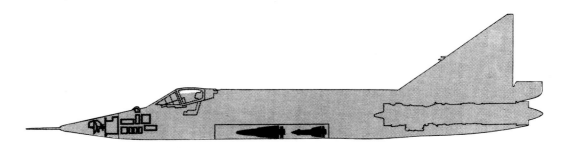

*General Dynamics (Convair) F-102A Delta Dagger with MG-10 fire-control system with added IR seeker; various missile options, such as AIM-26A Nuclear Falcon and (in rear of bay) three AIM-4C IR Falcon.*

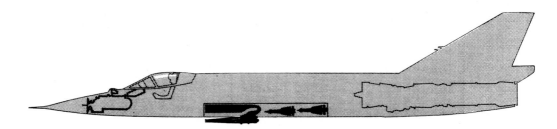

*General Dynamics (Convair) F-106A Delta Dart with MA-1 fire-control system with added IR seeker; two AIM-4F radar Super Falcon and two AIM-4G IR Super Falcon, plus 20 mm M61 gun.*

of the display, his right hand flying the aircraft and his left controlling the radar with an auxiliary stick governing scanner elevation limits and arranging to lock-on at the appropriate moment. The fact that his canopy and windscreen were transparent was immaterial!

Originally the F-102A, which was named Delta Dagger and painted a pearl grey, was usually armed with three radar and three IR Falcons, the pilot selecting which to use depending on the nature of the target and the weather conditions. Additionally, twelve FFARs were carried in tubes in the missile-bay doors. Continued development of the Falcon missile family led in 1960 to release for service of the AIM-26 Nuclear Falcon, and the standard F-102 fit was changed to one of these costly weapons and three AIM-4C IR Falcons. Further changes gave the F-102A a flight-refuelling receptacle and drop tanks. After long USAF service surviving Daggers were passed to the Air National Guard, the highly professional part-time air defence force run on a state-by-state basis, and to the air forces of Greece and Turkey. A considerable number were later used as remotely piloted drones simulating possible hostile aircraft in missile and other research programmes.

By 1953 the US Air Force had begun to plan a nationwide ground defence system to monitor the entire airspace with powerful radars and incorporate large computers to select defensive weapons (fighters, SAMs and even guns) and guide them onto the enemy. In 1956–9 this

*Designed to the same tailless-delta formula as the F-102, Convair almost succeeded in creating a multirole all-weather fighter seaplane. Here the first YF2Y-1 Sea Dart thunders across San Diego Bay on the power of its two Westinghouse J46 engines. The second YF was the first water-based aircraft to exceed the speed of sound. The most intractable problems were the skis and the Westinghouse engines.*

system, known as Sage, from the initials SAGE (Semi-Automatic Ground Environment), came into operational use. A vast system, it was masterminded partly by MIT, which had remained in the business of advanced defence electronics, and incorporated twenty-one of the most powerful computers that had been built up to that time. It was the first of other 'automatic ground environments' that today cover all the home territory of the developed countries. Fighter aircraft are automatically linked by digital data networks to these systems so that, normally, there is no longer any need for manual plotting or for anyone picking up a telephone. There simply is no time, especially in crowded regions such as Western Europe, which could be crossed at Mach 2 in a few minutes.

To partner SAGE, the USAF considered various interceptors, some highly unconventional but all of them large, powerful and with unprecedented flight performance. Perhaps the most 'far out' was the Republic XF-103. Back in 1946 Republic's design team had schemed what became the XF-91 Thunderceptor, an extraordinary aircraft with an F-84-type fuselage housing a turbojet and a liquid-propellant rocket engine with four thrust chambers, and a unique inverse-taper (so-called 'butterfly') swept-back wing whose tips housed the tandem-wheel main landing gears. It was exciting and supersonic, but, having no radar, was quite useless.

Undaunted, Republic's design team, led by the creator of the famous wartime P-47 Thunderbolt, Alex Kartveli, set about creating the interceptor to blow away all competition, the XF-103. By 1951 the design was complete and two prototypes were ordered. The giant fuselage, over 77 feet long, housed a monster turbojet with afterburner, used for take-off. At high speed and high altitude the pilot, seated in the needle-like nose with no view except through small side windows (possibly plus a periscope for landing) could switch the airflow to a huge ramjet. With this in operation, the titanium and steel manned missile could hurtle towards its enemies at Mach 3.7, 2,446 mph. At such a speed a manned aircraft has to travel in an essentially straight line, and after many design changes this futuristic project was terminated in 1957.

In its place Kartveli schemed the F-105 Thunderchief. This more conventional aircraft could have been a useful radar-equipped all-weather interceptor, with an M61 gun and many missiles, but in fact it found its niche as a bomb truck and electronic-warfare platform. This was the end of the road for Republic fighters, but over in California North American Aviation (NAA) followed the Sabre with a succession of much more powerful fighters.

*As it remained on paper, the shape of the 2,446 mph Republic XF-103 kept changing. This impression dates from mid-1956, showing pivoted wingtip ailerons, four rocket compartments and a circular (instead of square) propulsion nozzle.*

The massive Pratt & Whitney J57 engine enabled NAA to create the F-100 Super Sabre, which went supersonic on the level on its first flight. This never had all-weather radar, but the derived F-107 did. A striking feature of the F-107 was that the even bigger J75 engine was fed from a mighty inlet on top of the fuselage behind the cockpit, leaving room for the radar element of the XMA-12 fire-control system in the nose. The F-107 was an outstanding aircraft, but Republic needed the work, so the F-105 was ordered.

For the Navy, NAA created the A3J (later redesignated A-5) Vigilante, a brilliant Mach-2 carrier-based attack aircraft, which incorporated more new innovations than any other aircraft in history. NAA studied interceptor derivatives, but eventually, in 1957, set to work on a totally new aircraft, the F-108 Rapier. This, the ultimate interceptor for the USAF, was very like the Vigilante in layout, with a slim cobra-like fuselage merging into a wide box-like rear section housing two afterburning engines, fed with high-energy 'zip fuel', and with a broad swept wing mounted on top. It was also like the Navy attack aircraft in having two vertical tails, later replaced by a single all-moving fin on the centreline. It was even bigger, heavier and much more powerful than the Navy attack aircraft, and it was intended to fly long distances even while adding the odd dash at 2,000 mph (Mach 3).

In the event, in September 1959 the whole F-108 programme was cancelled. This was not because a long-range Mach-3 interceptor was no longer needed, but because even the mighty US Air Force was unable to fund such an aircraft in parallel with a range of fantastic ICBMs (intercontinental ballistic missiles), IRBMs (intermediate-range ballistic missiles) and a growing

*Unlike the XF-103, the F-107A was actually flown – indeed, five were. They were exciting times. Designed less than ten years after VJ-Day, the 107 had a variable engine inlet, powered spoilers for lateral control, and three all-moving tail surfaces! A USAF general told the author 'The 107 was better than the F-105, but Republic needed the work'.*

*An eminent North American designer told the author 'The F-108 would have been bigger, more powerful, faster, more agile, longer-ranged and more heavily armed than the F-15 Eagle, but it would also have cost more and been an inferior fighter!' This shows the mock-up in its final form in 1959.*

range of satellites and spacecraft. It had also been influenced by its advice to the Canadians to kill their own fighter and buy US missiles instead.

The Canadian fighter was the Avro CF-105 Arrow. As noted earlier, in the immediate post-war era Avro Aircraft, at Malton, outside Toronto, produced 692 CF-100 long-range fighters designed to cope with the vast distances and severe weather of the world's second-largest country. The CF-100 began with guns, but quickly embraced the Hughes collision-course doctrine based on radar, a computer and batteries of spin-stabilized but unguided rockets. In 1953 the RCAF issued a specification for a much more advanced replacement.

Cutting a long story short, this emerged as the CF-105, which began its flight-test programme on 25 March 1958, watched by the proud workforce, numbering over 14,000. It was by a wide margin the most advanced night and all-weather interceptor in the world. A tailless delta (triangular-wing) two-seat aircraft, it was powered by two of the most powerful

*The Canadian public were taught to think of the CF-105 as an expensive white elephant, just like the British public's view of TSR.2 eight years later. The fact that Canadian airspace never had to be defended in no way invalidates the belief that its defence ought to be possible. Here the J75-engined first prototype shows its enormous missile bay, stretching from the inlets back to the open airbrakes.*

afterburning engines (locally made Orenda Iroquois in the production Mk 2 version) to enable it to sustain Mach 2.5 for long distances. An internal bay wider than the bomb bay of a Superfortress housed a mix of Sparrow 2 and Falcon missiles.

Most unfortunately, this outstanding aircraft emerged just as the British had proclaimed that manned fighters were obsolete and the USAF was on the point of cancelling the F-108 (on purely financial grounds). Desperate to win votes by offering a better price to Canadian farmers, the Canadian Prime Minister curtly announced cancellation of the CF-105 on 20 February 1959.

This marked the end of any serious attempt to defend Canada against attack by manned aircraft. To replace the CF-105, Canada did as the USAF had wished and bought Bomarc missiles made by Boeing. The futility of these can be seen by drawing their effective radius as a ring round the two launch sites: the result looks like coins placed on a living-room carpet. These did not last long, and in 1961 they were replaced by another US import, the McDonnell F-101 Voodoo. The original F-101 had been a single-seat long-range fighter for USAF Tactical Air Command, with the capability of dropping tactical nuclear bombs. The most numerous version was the F-101B two-seat night and all-weather interceptor, able to carry a variety of weapons, including the Genie nuclear-warhead rocket. Electronically, however, it was a generation earlier than the F-108 or CF-105, the fire-control being the MG-13, which was essentially the old MG-10 modified for a two-seat aircraft. Moreover, the Canadians received second-hand aircraft, which they called the CF-101, with classified electronics removed and no provision even for Genie.

Thus, it was left to a smaller single-engined aircraft to take over where the F-102 left off. Indeed, the Convair F-106 Delta Dart was originally called the F-102B, but in the course of development it became much more than just an F-102 with the powerful J75 engine. By 1956 Convair knew how to design supersonic aircraft, and with a redesigned fuselage the F-106A was almost twice as fast as its predecessor.

The key to the F-106 as it finally emerged in 1959 was a completely new Hughes system, the MA-1. This used the new technology of digital microelectronics. The main panel display was an 8 in screen on which the aircraft appeared as a tiny triangle driven across a projected map, the main navigation input being Tacan. In theory the pilot could just sit there and watch the MA-1 intercept the hostile aircraft, fire the Genie or Falcon missile(s) and then bring the aircraft back to its base and make a smooth landing. In practice, the pilot had to do more than just keep an eye on the fuel state.

In 1963 an IR seeker was added ahead of the windscreen, and from 1971 – in a totally unexpected move – most F-106As were fitted with an M61 gun in a semi-retractable cradle

*Dated 12 July 1967, this photo shows two of the F-101B aircraft that were transferred to Canada as CF-101s after service with USAF Air (later Aerospace) Defense Command. Before handover, classified items and nuclear-warhead Genies were removed.*

extended below the weapon bay. By the 1970s it was becoming evident that not even the USAF could afford a new generation of aircraft every three or four years, and in fact the F-106, and its tandem-seat TF-106B trainer version, remained in front-line service with the Air National Guard until August 1988.

In other countries in the 1950s and 1960s development was less purposeful. The RAF finally issued a specification (F.4/48) for a night fighter in 1949. It was a pedestrian specification, showing none of the forward-thinking that had led to the USAF/Hughes fire-control systems; it mainly called for 'AI radar . . . and an armament of four 30 mm Aden guns.' Two aircraft competed for the expected RAF order. The first to fly was the de Havilland D.H.110, flown in September 1951. This was an outstanding machine with quite a thin swept wing, two Avon engines in a central nacelle and twin tail booms carrying a high tailplane. The pilot sat on the left under a raised canopy, while the navigator was placed lower down on the right inside the nacelle. As there was at that time no modern fighter of any kind even approaching service with the RAF (except the American F-86), the D.H.110 was clearly one of the most important aircraft in Britain. Chief test pilot John Cunningham – who, of course, had the most profound knowledge of night fighting – thought it potentially a world-beater, and certainly superior to the somewhat earlier F-89.

*The D.H.110 was such a good design that, even though five years were wasted in its development, the ultimate Sea Vixen FAW.2 version could still do a useful job in the 1960s. These are XN655 and 696, from HMS Eagle, built at Christchurch as FAW.1s and converted for Red Top missiles, and with a grotesque fuel tank on the front of each tail boom.*

Tragically, the first prototype suffered a disastrous structural failure at an air display, and the British government customer was so inept that it simply took no action at all during the following year. Then, with painful slowness, this good but gradually obsolescing machine was turned into the Sea Vixen all-weather fighter for the Royal Navy, with GEC AI.18 and the four 30 mm guns replaced by four Firestreak IR missiles. A Mk 2 Vixen had greater fuel capacity and Red Top collision-course missiles with greater flight performance.

Instead of this fine aircraft, the RAF chose the Gloster G.A.5, flown in November 1951 and later named Javelin. Though big and in some ways capable, this reflected Britain's difficulty in designing good modern airframes to match the nation's superb engines. It began life as a primitive tailed delta of odd proportions, and its early development was marred by fatal crashes. Eventually the Javelin FAW.1 reached the RAF in 1956, but this was only the start of a process of development that never let any mark get into its stride before it was succeeded by another. More fuel, changed radar (Westinghouse APQ-43, alias AI.22, in place of British AI.17), cambered leading edge, flight refuelling, higher elevator boost ratio, all-moving tailplane, powered ailerons, fewer guns, no guns, Firestreak missiles, yaw damper, Sperry autopilot, and modestly afterburning engines all matured somewhere along the line, leading

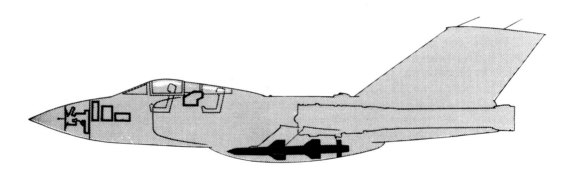

*Hawker Siddeley (Gloster) Javelin FAW 9R with AI 17; four Firestreak IR missiles.*

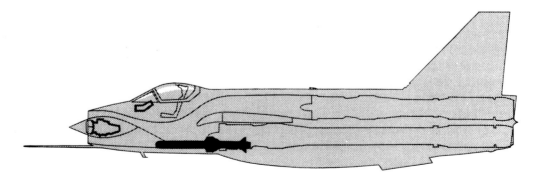

*BAC (English Electric) Lightning F6 with AI 23; two Red Top IR missiles (optional addition, two 30 mm Aden).*

*Typically primitive, the Javelin FAW.1 at last reached the RAF in the spring of 1956, among the first being these from 46 Sqn. at Odiham. They had Sapphire 102/103 engines rated at 8,000 lb thrust, fixed tailplanes, A1.17 radar and four 30 mm guns in the wings.*

eventually to the FAW.9R which was perhaps adequate for its missions. A supersonic development was cancelled in 1957.

One of the reasons for cancelling this successor to the Javelin was the attractive belief of the Minister of Defence of the day that all fighters were obsolete. The Minister was Duncan Sandys. During the Second World War he had served in the Royal Artillery, as commander of a Z-battery. These units fired unguided rockets into the night sky in a misguided attempt to bring down *Luftwaffe* bombers. Any more ridiculous way of trying to counter the night Blitz would be hard to imagine, and it was the author's belief that Z-batteries were provided to encourage the local civilian population. Be that as it may, firing off aimless rockets gave Mr Sandys the idea that all you had to do was give a rocket a guidance system and you had a supreme weapon that would make fighters and bombers obsolete.

By 1957 he was Minister of Defence, and his idea that manned military aircraft could simply be dispensed with was naturally enormously popular with the Chancellor of the Exchequer. On 4 April 1957 Sandys issued a famous White Paper on future defence policy. In it he publicly proclaimed that development work on new fighters and bombers would stop. It seemed eminently logical that, as in his view bombers were fast being replaced by missiles, especially ICBMs (intercontinental ballistic missiles), there was no point in developing ever better and more expensive fighters, which could not provide any defence against such a threat. Nobody dared to point out that to eliminate the RAF's fighting aircraft might be the act of a lunatic, and because of his bold forward-looking policy Mr Sandys soon became Lord DuncanSandys.

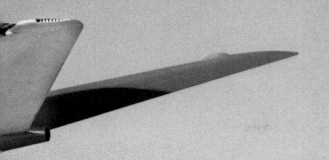

Lingering beliefs that a 'fighter, all-weather' had to have a backseater made the RAF designate the Lightning just as a 'fighter', with letter F. The first squadron to get the F.1 was No 74 'Tiger', at Coltishall. By February 1967, when this photo was taken, they were flying from Leuchars with the F.6, as seen here taking fuel from a 55 Sqn Victor K.1. Note the 260-gal. overwing ferry tanks, Red Top missiles and primitive refuelling probe.

On the very day that the crazy policy was proclaimed, the English Electric company began the flight-test programme of the P.1B. This was the first supersonic aircraft to be developed for the RAF; indeed, almost unbelievably, it was the *only* British supersonic military aircraft ever to go into service. Test-pilot R.P. 'Bee' Beamont exceeded Mach 1 on the first flight, but the fact that he had a potentially outstanding aircraft was clouded by the fact that the official view was that the P.1B had 'unfortunately already gone too far to cancel'. Only with the very greatest difficulty was the harassed design and test team permitted to continue, always with the proviso that the smallest amount of money must be spent, and that any upgrading of the aircraft – such as a steerable nosewheel – would not be permitted.

Eventually, renamed the BAC Lightning, this outstanding interceptor entered service with 74 Squadron in July 1960. As a flying machine it was outstanding, having two powerful engines, superb handling qualities and a forgiving nature. In the streamlined centrebody of the nose inlet was the AI.23 radar, which with a hand controller, pilot attack sight and other units formed Ferranti's first integrated airborne radar system. AI.23 was Britain's first post-war AI radar, and it was a neat X-band set weighing 287 lb, with four overlapping beams (two azimuth, two elevation), so that when the target was in the centre the output voltage was zero. This so-called monopulse technique was quite new when the set first operated, in early 1950, and it enabled the Lightning to have a compact and simple interception system that was later known by the happy name Airpass (AI radar, pilot attack sight system). There was no radar scope to clutter the cockpit; the PAS (sight) projected different illuminated displays in the search, acquisition and track phrases combined with gunsight information, while a computer drove the aiming mark in such a way that the pilot had only to keep this over the target spot (or the actual target, should this become visible) for a perfect interception. Different marks of Lightning carried Firestreak or Red Top IR missiles, while other options included guns and air-to-air rockets.

Of course, prior to what has gone down in history as 'the Sandystorm', there were several other advanced aircraft under development by British design teams. The Olympus-powered Gloster G.50 'thin-wing Javelin', to Specification F.155D, had already been cancelled, in July 1956. Its main armament would have been a formidable guided missile, Red Dean. Instead, development went ahead on the all-new Fairey F.155T to meet RAF Operational Requirement 329. It was to have two Rolls-Royce RB.128 engines, and carry Red Deans, later replaced or augmented by Red Hebes with CW (continuous-wave) guidance. On 1 April 1957 Fairey was officially informed that it had won the development contract. Three days later, 'the Sandystorm' burst on the scene.

Another programme it destroyed was the SR.177. In February 1952 the Ministry had issued a specification called F.124T for a fast-climbing interceptor powered by a rocket engine. This was sent to the established fighter firms. On the Isle of Wight Saunders-Roe had built and flown prototypes of a remarkable jet flying-boat fighter, but it was not sent the specification. The company requested a copy, and Chief Designer Maurice Brennan showed me the insulting refusal it received. It persisted, and to cut a convoluted story short they were one of two firms which won the contract for prototypes (the other was Avro, with the 720).

The Saunders-Roe SR.53 was an attractive little aircraft, with a powerful D.H. Spectre rocket engine, plus a small Armstrong Siddeley Viper turbojet to provide 'get you home' power, and drive pumps and generators. The Spectre took three years longer to develop than planned, but in 1957 the white-painted SR.53s put on brilliant flying displays. By this time Saunders-Roe was

*Ed Heinemann's 'Ford' – so-called from its original designation F4D – is remembered with affection by its pilots. In 1953, despite having carrier equipment, it shocked the USAF by setting a world speed record. The design requirement had been to reach 40,000 feet in five minutes; in 1958 a Marine pilot passed that level in 61 seconds. This 1959 photo shows a VMF-114 aircraft about to depart CVA-42 Franklin D Roosevelt in the Mediterranean.*

well advanced with a slightly larger and much more powerful production aircraft, the SR.177, with two de Havilland engines, an upgraded Spectre and a Gyron Junior afterburning turbojet.

The SR.177 was quickly developed in slightly different versions for the RAF (OR.337) and for carrier operation with the Royal Navy (NA.47). Both would have had full night and all-weather capability, the radar being the AI.23, as in the Lightning. In terms of rate and angle of climb, combat ceiling and turn rate at high altitudes, the 177 would have been in a class of its own. For example, the time for the RAF version from brakes release on the runway to Mach 1.6 at 60,000 feet would have been 3.59 minutes. Having been curtly cancelled by 'the Sandystorm', Britain then had the crass effrontery to try to sell the SR.177 to Germany's *Luftwaffe*!

In the United States the monopoly of Hughes in Air Force interceptors was matched by the Navy's loyalty to Westinghouse. From the host of offshoots of the APQ-35, that company derived the AERO-13 radar for the curious F4D-1 (later redesignated F-6A) Skyray transonic tailless interceptor of the Navy and Marine Corps. The Skyray, which in 1953 shocked its Air Force rivals by setting a new world speed record, was designed by Heinemann just after the Second World War using Lippisch aerodynamics for minimum transonic drag. One of its unusual features was a control column that could be extended to give the pilot more leverage if he should ever have to fly without hydraulic control power; another was a skin made of two thin layers joined by spot-welded dimples. It was the steepest- and fastest-climbing interceptor of its day, and it saw front-line service, popularly called the Ford (from F4D), until 1964.

Douglas went on to test an even better derivative, the F5D Skylancer, but the Navy couldn't let Heinemann's team win everything, so it bought two totally different fighters instead. The first was the McDonnell F3H Demon. An outstanding design, it was crippled by the total failure of Westinghouse to perfect its powerful single engine, the J40. In 1955, four years after the start of flight-testing, the St Louis plant had completed the fifty-six F3H-1N fighters. Of these six had crashed, twenty-one were used for 'ground instruction' (most were just taken away by barge and scrapped) and twenty-nine were re-engined with the Allison J71 engine. The new engine made all the difference, and by 1959 McDonnell had delivered 519 F3H-2 Demons with Hughes APG-51A radar and four Sparrow III missiles.

The other new fighter was even better. Designed to a Navy BuAer requirement of September 1952, the Chance Vought F8U Crusader bristled with odd features yet outperformed even the best fighters able to use 10,000-foot runways. For example, compared with the USAF's F-100 Super Sabre, which was fitted with an almost identical J57 engine, it carried a greater weapon load further, and was 300 mph faster. The Crusader's most unusual feature was that the wing was placed at the top of the fuselage and mounted on hinges. Thus, approaching the carrier, the wing could be pivoted up while the fuselage was tilted slightly down to give the pilot a perfect view of the deck.

Even the first production version of 1955 had an advanced Martin-Baker seat, a wide choice of guns and missiles, excellent radar, and a neat retractable flight-refuelling probe. In the

*A famous quote in the US Navy was 'when you're out of F-8s you're out of fighters'. The last outfit to go 'out of fighters' was France's Aéronavale, whose squadron 12F finally stood down, to convert to the Rafale, in December 1999. Their aircraft were midnight blue, but this photo was taken when the F-8E(FN) was new, and painted medium sea grey.*

following ten years the Dallas plant delivered 1,259 Crusaders, designated F-8 from 1962, the last batch of forty-two being F-8(FN) for the French *Aéronavale*, which remained in front-line service until December 1999!

Russ Clark's design team at Dallas went on to produce an even more striking successor, the XF8U-3, or Crusader III. Powered by a monster J75 engine, and with folding underfins, this was so good it seemed almost impossible to beat. One cannot help noting that at the same time Britain's equivalent under development was the Scimitar, which had no radar, and a speed at 35,000 feet of 635 mph compared with the XF8U-3's 1,580 mph. To Chance Vought's astonishment, a rival produced a design that consigned the Crusader III to history: the McDonnell (later McDonnell Douglas) F-4 Phantom II.

From the start this had a Westinghouse radar, the original set being the APQ-72 with a 24 in dish (F-4A), which soon changed to a 36 in dish in the bulging-nose F-4B. Under the nose was an IR sensor in a separate fairing, giving a two-pronged appearance. During the 1950s IR

*Making a free take-off (not catapulted) from USS* Ranger, *this early-production F-4B Phantom II shows its essential drooped leading-edge surfaces. The small fairing under the nose houses the AAA-4 infra-red seeker.*

*In some ways the F-111B was the best of the swing-wing F-111s. Features included AWG-9 radar fire control, and a weapon bay big enough to accommodate AIM-54 Phoenix missiles. Altogether, however, it was far from being what the Navy wanted (which was the F-14). Here the second YF-111B, BuAer 151971, formates with auxiliary engine inlets open.*

technology was transformed, mainly under the pressure of air-defence problems, into a broad and versatile array of devices capable of serving reliably in fighters and even inside small guided missiles such as Firestreak and Sidewinder. Not all modern fighters carry an IR detector; when one is fitted it contains a highly sensitive cell, usually cooled by liquid nitrogen so that the least trace of heat focused upon it will energize electrons out of the low-energy 'bound state' into the conduction band and thus cause a small current to flow. Basically an IR detector is just another string to the fighter's bow, because as it works at far shorter wavelengths than radars it is unaffected by ECM (other than explicit IR countermeasures such as flares). The detector can be more sensitive in discrimination than a radar, being able to determine (for example) if a formation of aircraft sixty miles away is made up of four aircraft or five.

Few readers will need much briefing on the F-4 Phantom, which from 1960 until 1975 was the world's pre-eminent fighter. At first all the emphasis was on air-to-air missiles, maximum load being four large Sparrows in fuselage recesses and two more (or four Sidewinders) on wing pylons. In 1962 the Phantom was found to be so superior that it was bought by the US Air Force, an unprecedented honour for a Navy/Marines combat aircraft. The emphasis then shifted to air-to-ground operations and multi-sensor reconnaissance, but it returned to the air dogfight mission in the F-4E version with a slatted wing, solid-state APQ-120 radar and M61 gun built into the nose. Indeed in 1965–9 there was nearly a single-seat version. Total production, including aircraft assembled or manufactured in Japan, amounted to 5,197.

Another Phantom that did not come off was a swing-wing model proposed to replace various failed or cancelled aircraft of other types. Aircraft need to be different shapes for different missions. A low-level attacker needs to have the smallest wing area and, in particular, the smallest span, whereas a subsonic long-range machine needs the most slender long-span

*Mindful of the problems of the F-111B, Grumman were determined not to let the F-14 Tomcat's weight get out of hand. Unlike its predecessor, the F-14 had tandem seats and no internal missile bay, but it retained pivoted wings (seen here at maximum sweep) and TF30 engines. The latter caused severe problems, and were eventually replaced by the F110.*

wings for high cruise efficiency. The dogfighter, on the other hand, needs the biggest and broadest wing possible, but with short span. In the General Dynamics F-111 an attempt was made to build an aircraft with pivoted 'swing-wings' able to go most of the way to satisfying the conflicting demands, but technical difficulties were severe and the F-111B Navy fighter version was cancelled. The remaining Air Force models were strictly bombers, though retaining an 'F' designation.

To replace the F-111B the Navy contracted with Grumman for the most versatile and capable combat aircraft of modern times, the F-14A Tomcat. This swing-wing two-seater combined the West's most powerful fighter radar, an advanced IR detector, the most powerful

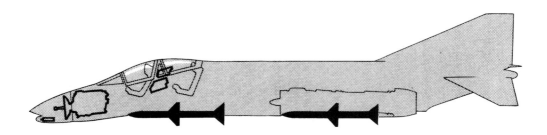

*McDonnell Douglas F-4B Phantom II as originally delivered, with APQ-72; four (or six) AIM-7C Sparrow III (plus many other armament options).*

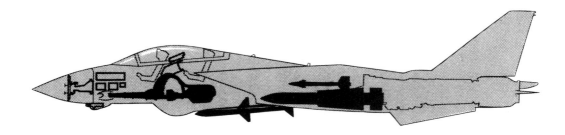

*Grumman F-14A Tomcat with AWG-9 fire-control; various missile options including six AIM-54A Phoenix (fuselage pallets) or four AIM-7F Advanced Sparrow (fuselage recesses) plus four AIM-9H or -9L Sidewinder on wing pylons (or two AIM-54A and two AIM-9), plus 20 mm M61 gun.*

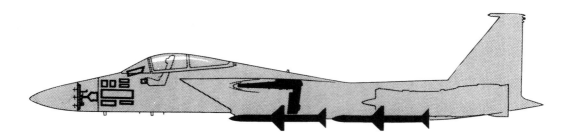

*McDonnell Douglas F-15A Eagle with APG-63 fire-control; four AIM-7F Sparrow on angles of fuselage (also SRM option of AIM-9H or -9L pairs on wing pylons) plus 20 mm M61 gun.*

AAM (Phoenix), a medium-range missile, short-range missile and gun. Unlike some 'all-can-do' aircraft it had no significant shortcomings, and even at prices in the range of $14 to $19 million an F-14A represented such enormous air-defence capability that it was good value. Its AWG-9 radar, originally designed for the F-111B along with the related Phoenix missile, was representative of the latest techniques in the mid-1960s, and incorporates two things I have not yet discussed: pulse-doppler and software control. These take us into the final chapter.

# NINE

# THE MODERN ERA

Everyone knows the analogy of the whistling train rushing through a station to illustrate the Doppler effect, the apparent shift of frequency of a wave motion if the source is moving with respect to the observer. Doppler naturally applies to radar. If a fighter detects another aircraft coming head-on, the received signals from the target will have a frequency higher than the true frequency of the fighter's radar; similarly, the frequency will be reduced if the two aircraft are moving apart. This shift in frequency can be used to separate a target return from a background of clutter. In most traditional-type interceptions there is little clutter, except that caused by chaff or heavy rain, but today non-stealth attacking aircraft would invariably penetrate hostile territory at treetop height to try to get under the defending radar coverage. A fighter would therefore see them from above, against the Earth's surface. Except in stark mountain or desert areas, the Earth's surface is moving: sea waves, trees and even grass are constantly in motion, causing clutter that shows as interference on the radar display. The fighter's radar is itself moving with respect to the Earth.

With a PD (pulse Doppler) radar the received RF signal is processed by mixers and band-pass filters that cleverly eliminate everything except targets of real interest. (The reader will note that targets may be flying in such a way that the radial distance from the fighter is constant, i.e. they seem to have no relative speed; they too can be distinguished, but it needs radars with very small 'sidelobes' and other advanced features.) The returns from these real targets are converted into streams of digital pulses which are fed to a computer and thence to the pilot's display. On the latter, nothing appears except real targets and inserted information. Instead of being a mere CRT, the modern display is a synthetic picture made up of target spots and pictures, sightlines, impact points, velocity vectors, markers, range scales and a host of alphanumeric information.

Some of the most challenging radar problems of all are met with 'overland downlook radar' of this type, especially those having power to search beyond the visual horizon out to a radius of about 245 miles. Such a radar is fitted to the AWACS (Airborne Warning And Control System), the aircraft platform being the Boeing E-3 Sentry. This can pick out hedgehopping aircraft coming head-on, trying to protect themselves with every hostile ruse, even though the signal pulses have to travel for scores of miles right along the surface of the Earth. Only a few years ago this would have been quite impossible. AWACS and the Russian Il-78 are airborne stations which, among other things, serve as the main GCI directors for all modern fighters in the same airspace. Of course, there is no need to talk, because all data and even radar pictures are transmitted from computer to computer across perhaps 150 miles of airspace by high-speed digital links. Thus, today's fighter may well know precisely what is coming long before any target gets within the range of its own radar.

As for software control, this simply means the control by digital computer I have been describing. The computer has to be digital, small, fast and completely reliable. As in many fields, the compact digital computer has revolutionized airborne radar (we no longer talk about 'AI').

To a considerable degree today's radar is designed as a collection of standard modules, each equipped with automatic fault diagnosis, and capable of being pulled from its racking and replaced in about two minutes by a man at an Arctic base wearing fur mitts. The actual collection of modules assembled into the fighter depends on what the customer wants and can pay for. Even then the characteristics can be grossly changed, either with a screwdriver or on pilot command, by the software programmed into the computer. The computer can change the p.r.f. (pulse-repetition frequency) or the wavelength; it can change the characteristics of the signal or the pulses; it can change basic parameters according to flight-test results or different kinds of expected targets; it can change the radar 'signature' (how the radar's emissions look to an enemy) between peace and war, or even hour by hour, to defeat hostile intelligence (electronic intelligence, or Elint) or countermeasures.

Countermeasures is a gigantic subject today, but it still embraces passive jammers such as chaff (which is now automatically cut to length on board the ECM aircraft or fighter by a system that listens to the hostile radars and sizes the chaff to match it) and plain noise jammers which blot out the hostile radar frequencies. One obvious way of making the noise-jammer's life more difficult is to work your own fighter radar on changing frequencies. Modern magnetrons and TWTs (travelling-wave tubes, another potent source of microwaves) can operate over a frequency spread of more than 1 GHz, instead of being tuned exactly to a central frequency. It is possible in modern software-controlled radars, if they are switched out of the PD mode, to make their operating frequency vary rapidly and seemingly randomly all over the available range. Thus a hostile jammer has to jam on all these frequencies, so instead of using a small transmitter he needs something coupled to the National Grid. All fighters, of course, carry simple dispensers for chaff, flares or active RF-jammer payloads, and most also have passive warning receivers on the fin and many other ECM systems.

Typical of the best Western practice of the 1970 period is the F-15 Eagle. This big twin-engined aircraft was designed by a team at St Louis which still thought of itself as McDonnell, creator of the Phantom, but which in 1966 had become McDonnell Douglas. Most of them were shocked to find themselves in August 1997 part of Boeing; thus, today it is the Boeing F-15. When it was being planned, a popular slogan in USAF corridors of power was 'Not a pound for air-to-ground!'. This meant that the F-15 was to be absolutely uncompromised as an air-combat fighter, with no thought of carrying bombs or similar uncouth stores. Of course, the winds of fashion often reverse direction, and before long the F-15E was in production, with a maximum bomb load of 24,500 lb!

From the outset, the F-15's avionics were 'state of the art'. The original radar was the Hughes APG-63, with a flat-plate mechanically driven scanner (such scanners are discussed later). The basic ECM system, the Loral ALR-56, was based on low-band and high-band tuners fed by a blade aerial and by small spiral receiver aerials on the tips of the wings and vertical tails to give all-round coverage. It served several functions, the most crucial being to warn the

*Taken in October 1984, this shows F-15A 76- (i.e. 1976) 099 firing a Sparrow medium-range AAM. Just as the F-14 replaced the F-111B, so did the F-15 replace the F-111 by an aircraft with twin vertical tails, no internal weapon bay and, in two-seat versions, tandem seating. The F-15 went even further, and used a fixed wing.*

pilot if his aircraft was being illuminated by a hostile radar. It also provided steering directions for the ALQ-135 internal jamming system. 'Internal' does not mean the system jams the fighter's own systems, but that the equipment is an integral part of the aircraft, not contained in an external pod.

This was typical of the EW (electronic-warfare) suites fitted to fighters of the 1970s. At least, such equipment was fitted to the fighters of most countries. In Britain the purse-strings were clamped so tightly by the Treasury that most British warplanes were worse equipped than they had been back in the Second World War. When, in April 1982, a task force had to be assembled to retake the Falkland Islands from the Argentine invaders, the last Fleet carrier had been withdrawn and there was no seagoing airpower except for Harriers and helicopters. With no sense of urgency, British Aerospace was delivering Sea Harriers, which had some air-combat capability. Suddenly, these aircraft were seen as absolutely crucial. It was then discovered that no money had been voted to equip them with any electronic-warfare system. Harriers and Sea Harriers went into action with bundles of chaff jammed under the airbrake; thus, to release chaff, the pilot had to open the airbrake just at the time when he wanted maximum performance! Frantic orders for chaff and flare cartridge dispensers were placed with the

American Tracor company, to bring the Harriers and Sea Harriers almost half-way to the standard of fighters in other countries.

Even in the twenty-first century, Britain is so unwilling to give its fighting personnel proper tools that it is the only major country to announce that, in any time of national emergency, pilot-training schools would become front-line air-defence squadrons. They are not equipped with fighters, but with advanced trainers. The Hawk T.1A, superb as a trainer, was never designed to have a fighter's flight performance, and it is totally lacking in all-weather electronic weapon systems.

Indeed, the story gets worse! Despite several welcome upgrades, the RAF's Harriers are among the swiftly dwindling group of 'fighter-type' aircraft that, though in front-line service, have no multimode radar, and thus cannot be considered to be 'fighters' within the accepted meaning of the word. The Sea Harriers, on the other hand, have had radar from the start, and indeed were recently upgraded to FRS.2 standard with the dramatically superior Blue Vixen multimode radar and AIM-120A Amraam missiles. It can only be the action of imbeciles to take the decision – which the British government has taken – to withdraw the Sea Harriers from use, purely to save money, in 2005–6. Somehow, their role will be taken over by the RAF's Harriers, which are being flown jointly by the RAF and Royal Navy. How can these aircraft, which have no capability as fighters, defend the Fleet? Well, apparently the defence of the Royal Navy against air attack will be provided entirely *by destroyers*! Did Britain learn *nothing* from trying to do this in the Falklands campaign?

Almost everywhere one looks, the British procurement scene appears to be a shambles. For years a bitter rearguard action was fought against the very idea of what was then called 'the Eurofighter' having vectored thrust. We have yet to see whether the excellent vectoring nozzle developed by the Spanish partner on the EJ200 engine will be permitted on the RAF Typhoon. The author was repeatedly censured for publicly daring to suggest that such a feature was worth having. As for the RAF Typhoon having a gun, the UK actually spent a considerable sum not only making sure that a gun was not fitted, but actually having the local fuselage and wing-root structure modified so that fitting the gun was impossible! Eventually it was discovered that this modification would be so costly that the structure had to be left ready for a gun, and that it would be cheaper not to design special ballast but to fit the gun and carry it as ballast to keep the centre of gravity in the right place. So, the British attitude is a petulant 'Oh dear, we have to install the gun, but we're certainly *not going to buy any ammunition*'. Did nobody talk to anyone who flew gunless Phantoms in Vietnam? Have the words of Col. Robin Olds, USAF, who flew in 'the big show', then in Korea and finally in Vietnam, been forgotten already? He said, 'A fighter without a gun is like a bird without a wing.' Did nobody think for a few seconds about all the situations in which a gun is not just useful but essential?

Of course, it may be that the Treasury's attitude was, 'We know a gun is essential, but we just can't afford it.' If so, such parsimony contrasts with the situation which obtained in the Soviet Union. Western intelligence appears to have been so bad that most of the profusion of equipments fitted to the Soviet Union's night and all-weather interceptors went unrecorded. If the electronic equipment of RAF fighters was the most meagre in the world, that of Russian interceptors was unquestionably the best. The on-board systems were tailor-made for each aircraft, each *Kompleks* having its own designation. Thus, the Yak-28P, a supersonic successor to the Yak-25, was designed in partnership with *Kompleks* K-8M. This included RP-11 *Oryol*-D

*In its day, which was 1961-83, the Yak-28P was an important Interceptor in the USSR's PVO (air-defence force). Features included powerful Oryol (Eagle) radar, and both radar and IR versions of the K-8 (R-98) and K-13 (R-3) missiles. The Irkutsk plant delivered 435, plus 183 trainers with separate stepped cockpits.*

(Eagle) radar and various species of R-8M missile. Factory 153 at Novosibirsk delivered 435 of these aircraft, which entered PVO service from 1962.

In the 1950s the Moscow-based Central Aero and Hydrodynamics Institute (CAHI, often rendered as TsAGI) had refined a configuration for Mach-2 aircraft with a triangular delta wing and swept tailplanes. This shape was used by Mikoyan for the MiG-21 family, and by Sukhoi for the significantly larger Su-9 all-weather interceptor. By 1962 this had been developed into the Su-11, with a more powerful radar and better missiles. By this time the Sukhoi bureau was working on a much more powerful twin-engined design, the T-58, which matured as the Su-15. Production aircraft followed the Yak-28P at Novosibirsk, the final batches being of the Su-15TM version with R13-300 engines, later radar and additional weapon options including externally hung UPK-23-250 gun pods. Called 'Flagon' by NATO, these attractive aircraft had a wing extended in span to just over 30 feet, but a fuselage no less than 69 feet long. They achieved the rare distinction of shooting down unidentified targets that turned out to be civil airliners that had strayed far from their authorised track: a 707 on 20 April 1978 and a 747 on 1 September 1983, both of Korean Air Lines.

In 1966 PVO regiments began receiving the biggest fighter in history. The sheer size of the Soviet Union made it almost impossible to defend against the multiple threats from USAF Strategic Air Command, partnered by US Navy carriers on which were A-3 Skywarriors carrying nuclear weapons. Thus, defence had to be provided even along the 15,000 km

*Yakolev Yak-28P with augmented RP-11 Oryol radar; two R-8M radar/IR missiles (some aircraft have one 30 mm gun).*

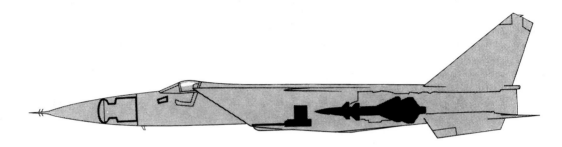

*Mikoyan MiG-25P with Smerch-25 look-down radar; two R-40R radar and two R-40T IR missiles. The MiG-25PD had improved radar, engines and missiles.*

northern frontier. The job called for big aircraft with big radar and big missiles. For a start, in January 1958 work began on *Kompleks* K-80, which included the RLS *Smerch* (waterspout) radar and PR-S-80 sighting system. Biesnovat worked on the K-80S missiles, which in production became the R-4. Cutting a long story short, the aircraft part of the system was the Tupolev Tu-128. Prototypes puzzled the West, which called them 'Fiddler'. Powered by two AL-7F engines, the mighty interceptor could reach over 1,200 mph, Mach 1.96, even though it was almost 100 feet long (the upgraded Tu-128M just exceeded 100 ft) and carried four giant missiles externally. Factory 18 at Voronezh delivered 189 of the initial version, plus eleven trainers with stepped cockpits.

The threats from Strategic Air Command continued to escalate. According to legend, Artyom Mikoyan, who had previously concentrated on quite small fighters, was instantly impressed by the (secret) intelligence on the North American project which became the A-5 Vigilante. He liked the broad box-like fuselage with sharp supersonic inlets to the two engines, high-mounted thin wing with sweep replaced by leading-edge taper, and (an innovation) twin vertical tails. In late 1959 he authorized project design of a similar aircraft, with the range of the Tu-128 but greater speed and altitude. He calculated that two R-15B engines would give a speed of 3,000 km/h (Mach 3, 1,864 mph) and a sustained ceiling of 26 km (85,300 ft).

While Britain was regretting that the primitive Lightning had already reached a stage where it would be difficult to cancel, but certainly was not going to be permitted a steerable

*Loosely, the second aircraft to be designated Su-15 was the Su-11 given an extra engine, more powerful radar, twice as much fuel and twice as many missiles! This shows the final version, the Su-15TM, the only type of aircraft to have shot down two Boeing jetliners, a 707 and a 747! Both belonged to Korean Air Lines, and both had departed wildly from their filed flight plan and flown over one of the most sensitive parts of the USSR.*

nosewheel, the Soviet Aviation Ministry urged development of a series of Ye-155 prototypes, which began flight-testing from 6 March 1964. The first to fly was actually the Ye-155R-1, to lead to a reconnaissance aircraft, the MiG-25R. The Ye-155P-1 first flew on 9 September 1964, leading to production of the MiG-25P interceptor. These amazing aircraft were to sustain the biggest development programme in history, leading to forty-nine versions, of which thirty-three flew and more than twenty entered service. Production of the two basic sub-families, the MiG-25P and the MiG-25R reconnaissance aircraft, amounted to 1,186, all from the enormous Factory 21 at Gorkiy (today called Nizhni-Novgorod).

Apart from the SR-71 'Blackbird', a specialized unarmed reconnaissance aircraft, no other country had aircraft with anything even approaching the speed/altitude/range capability of the MiG-25. The United States decided against offering a bribe to the first MiG-25 pilot to defect, so it was with astonished delight that a team of US experts arrived at Hakodate airbase in Japan to examine a MiG-25P which had been flown there (undetected by Japanese defences) by a defecting PVO pilot on 6 September 1976. This event spurred development on the next

*This Su-15TM was fitted with an RP-15M (Oryol-D58M) radar, with a traditional mechanically steered Cassegrain aerial. It could provide guidance for R-8MR missiles against targets at altitudes from 656 to 79,000 feet.*

generation, which had been launched in 1968 when the Council of Ministers ordered Mikoyan to build the Ye-155M.

The Mikoyan experimental factory built two prototypes, called *Izdeliye* (product) 83. Aircraft 831 began flight testing on 16 September 1975, and the fully equipped 832 followed in May 1976. These led to the production at the Gorkiy factory of 500 MiG-31s. At first glance a MiG-31 might be mistaken for a MiG-25, but in fact in order to find common parts one has to come down to the level of rivets and pipe-joints. It would be inappropriate here to list all the equipment carried by even the original MiG-31, prior to ongoing upgrades, but in my book on MiG aircraft I list thirty-three different items of fire-control and navigation electronics. The biggest item is the SBI-16 *Zaslon* (barrier) multimode radar, which has electronic scanning and can track ten targets simultaneously while guiding four R-33 missiles against those posing the greatest threat. On-board computers and secure data transmitters can link a finger-four formation to defend a front 900 km (560 miles) wide, the outer members of the formation being 600 km (373 miles) apart. In 1990 the MiG-31 was replaced in production by the MiG-31B, with improved avionics and R-33S missiles, but the largely redesigned MiG-31M came after the collapse of the Soviet Union and was never funded.

To defend a country as big as the USSR takes big fighters, and the Tu-128M was 30.49 m (just over 100 ft) long. Wing pylons carried two R-4R and two R-4T missiles. Without them the two AL-7F-4 engines could propel the 43-tonne aircraft at Mach 1.96. In theory, intercepting a target over 700 miles away should have posed no problem.

The MiG-25 was the fastest fighter ever to go into service anywhere. This MiG-25PD has the slightly longer nose required by Sapfir-25M radar, matched with R-40RD and TD missiles. On the outer pylons are pairs of R-60s.

This MiG-31B has its 8TP infra-red search/tracker extended under the nose. It is carrying a full complement of missiles: four upgraded R-33S and four super-agile R-60M. The devastating gun is hidden in shadow.

This MiG-31 has several features (such as the rear canopy) of the MiG-31M, but the MiG-31M has the flight-refuelling probe on the other side of the windscreen. The inner pylon carries a Kh-31A long-range ramjet missile. Boeing is converting these into M-31 targets for the US Navy.

In 1989 Sukhoi was cleared to send Su-27s to Paris, Singapore and North American airshows, where their displays – especially the Cobra manoeuvre – caused a sensation. In 1990 two came to Farnborough, where Su-27UB two-seater 388 is seen landing. At that time the aerodynamic shape and mass distribution, repeated on a smaller scale in the MiG-29, was unrivalled anywhere in the world.

Until the F/A-22 arrived, a decade later, one could hardly have imagined a more formidable fighter than the Su-27 carrying a mix of R-27R, R-27T, R-73 and R-73E missiles – and, of course, a gun even more devastating than the USAF's M61.

To round off the former Soviet scene, in the late 1960s design began on two engines for a future generation of fighters. As before, MiG was (at this stage only verbally) tasked with a smaller aircraft and Sukhoi with a larger edition. By 1974 both the new engines were on test. The Klimov RD-33 and Lyul'ka AL-31 are turbofans with large afterburners and advanced variable nozzles. Each of the new fighters was planned around two of the new engines mounted wide apart in a broad fuselage that merged imperceptibly into a broad wing tapered on the leading edge. A vertical tail was mounted above each engine, while a snake-like forward fuselage projected ahead from between the engine inlets. In partnership with the Central Aero and Hydrodynamics Institute, this shape was refined until it was perfect.

As in the 1950s, Sukhoi was assigned the bigger aircraft. The T-10-1 prototype flew before the first MiG, on 20 May 1977. Powered by AL-21F-3 engines, almost identical to those of later Tu-128s, it was impressive, but as testing of later T-10s progressed they ran into severe and sometimes fatal problems. Some redesign was necessary, and General Designer Simonov told the author, 'In the end, we managed to retain the main wheels and ejection seat' (he was not really joking). What followed, starting with the T-10S, became the Su-27, perhaps the most beautiful, and certainly most impressive, fighter ever built. When it appeared, Western analysts predictably wrote things like, 'A cross between the F-15 and F/A-18'. Simonov said, 'You can't win if you just copy.' Once Western pilots were allowed to fly the Su-27 one heard comments like 'What an airplane! If only I could afford to buy one.' Most production versions have the

*Despite the side number, this was not prototype 9-01 but a production MiG-29. The inboard pylons have R-27R1 missiles, while the outers have paired R-60s, which from the mid-1980s were replaced by various types of R-73.*

*Shortage of money has prevented the ANPK MiG complex from making more than two flights with the impressive 1.44 prototype of the projected 1.42. Russians call this layout a triplane, for obvious reasons.*

outstanding AL-31F engine, which among other things can tolerate having its inlet rotate nose-up through up to 135° in what is called the Cobra manoeuvre (which no Western fighter has yet been able to do). Later Su-27 versions, including the Su-30, 33, 35 and 37 (note, *not* the S-37), have later engine versions, some of which have a fully vectoring engine nozzle, and in many cases canard foreplanes. Virtually all production today is for export, though small numbers of naval and land-based bomber versions have been delivered, and advanced variants are being produced under licence in China and India.

In terms of numbers, the smaller rival MiG has done ever better. First flown as the '901' on 6 October 1977, virtually no redesign was needed and production aircraft were delivered from 1982. The initial production version, called *Izdellye* (product) 9-12 for the Soviet Union, 9-12A for the Warsaw Pact countries and 9-12B for export, is much better known as the MiG-29. For some reason NATO gives it an extra name, 'Fulcrum'. There have since been almost twenty versions, all similar externally apart from some later variants having canards, like certain Su-27 derivatives. Crippling lack of money meant that the Russian Air Force could no longer buy fighters after the 1980s, and production of MiG-29s tapered off in the early 1990s with a large number of aircraft not quite finished. Fortunately for what is now the MiG Aviation Scientific/Industrial Complex, many air forces (thirty at the most recent count) have enabled these aircraft to be completed, and have also bought used MiG-29s. This brought the number of completions by 1997 to 1,257. Since then the only immediate prospect of new construction has rested on Indian Navy adoption of the MiG-29K carrier-based version.

Income from these sales enabled MiG to design and build a single example of a supposed next-generation aircraft, the impressive 1.44, also known as the MFI. This big aircraft, with both foreplanes and tailplanes and with a huge chin inlet feeding two of Viktor Chepkin's superb AL-41 engines, made two flights in early 2000. Slightly less strapped for cash, Sukhoi conducted an extended test programme with the even more astonishing black-painted Su-47

*Few aircraft could hold an audience as spellbound as Sukhoi's black-painted Su-47 (originally S-37) Berkut (golden eagle). The writing says 'OKB (design bureau) Sukhoi'. This aircraft has assisted the creation of Russia's next-generation fighter.*

*Today's multirole fighters need special flying testbeds to assist development of their integrated avionics. This British-built One-Eleven was used by the Northrop/McDonnell Douglas team from July 1989 to fly the all-new sensors of the YF-23. The Westinghouse radar was in the nose, with infra-red and electro-optical sensors above and below.*

Dated 6 May 1988, this shows the start of testing of the McDonnell Douglas (now Boeing) Night Attack F/A-18D. The stick and throttles were removed from the rear cockpit, and replaced by two controls for three displays and various sensors, the latter including the FLIR pod seen under the engine duct.

(originally, confusingly designated S-37) *Berkut* (eagle), which has a forward-swept wing and two D-30F6M engines almost identical to those of the MiG-31. An extended test programme with this aircraft has helped underpin the only funded programme for a new Russian fighter, the Sukhoi LFS (light frontal aeroplane). Possibly to fly in 2005, this will be powered by two AL-41F engines, and have a predictably outstanding suite of electronics.

Turning now to the USA, in April 1972 the US Air Force picked General Dynamics and Northrop to build prototypes, respectively called YF-16 and YF-17, of an LWF, standing for Lightweight Fighter. Restyled ACF, for Air Combat Fighter, the F-16 was selected. At a USAF briefing, the author was told, 'It's an exercise in seeing what can be done using one F100 engine instead of two. We expect our allies will buy it, but there's no question of it becoming an important type in the Air Force inventory – why buy a Volkswagen when you can have a Cadillac [the speaker meant the F-15]?' Allies did indeed buy it, starting with 306 aircraft for Belgium, Denmark, the Netherlands and Norway. By the end of the twentieth century they had been joined by sixteen other countries, but what the 1975 spokesman would have found amazing is that, of the current total of 4,347 F-16s, no fewer than 2,230 are for the USAF, plus another twenty-six for the Navy!

The loser in the ACF competition was the Northrop YF-17, which differed in having two engines. In a unique about-face, this was metamorphosed into the F/A-18 Hornet for the US Navy, a McDonnell Douglas aeroplane with Northrop reduced to the role of mere forty-per cent associate contractor. Compared with the F-17, the F/A-18 was marginally bigger, and had a stronger and heavier airframe suitable for carrier operation. Unlike the F-16, the Hornet had a large multimode radar, the Hughes APG-65, and thus could be armed with big medium-range missiles such as Sparrow and later the AIM-120 Amraam. While McDonnell Douglas got on with the US Navy order, Northrop tried to sell a simpler version, 2,600 lb lighter, and with significantly higher performance and anything up to double the payload/range. To its astonishment, all the export customers (who had to go to McDonnell Douglas, not Northrop) chose to buy the heavier and supposedly inferior carrier-based version, even though they were going to operate from airfields. The situation led to an unprecedented lawsuit between the two partners. This led to the F/A-18 becoming an all-McDonnell Douglas product. By 1996 the original F/A-18 versions had been developed into the F/A-18E/F Super Hornet, which is more of an upgrade than it looks (see Appendix). But Boeing had the last laugh; in 1997 it bought McDonnell Douglas.

By the 1970s the technology of what was officially called LO (low observables), but became better known as 'stealth', appeared likely to revolutionize the whole of warfare. Few commentators recalled that in 1936 Watson-Watt had pointed out how important it would be in future for all weapons, even small ones, to be designed to minimize their signature on hostile

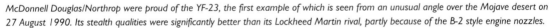

*McDonnell Douglas/Northrop were proud of the YF-23, the first example of which is seen from an unusual angle over the Mojave desert on 27 August 1990. Its stealth qualities were significantly better than its Lockheed Martin rival, partly because of the B-2 style engine nozzles.*

*Lockheed Martin's F-22 won over the stealthy YF-23, and Pratt and Whitney's F119 engine was picked over the rival GE F120. This air-to-air shows the first YF-22 Raptor, with USAF serial 91–4001, first flown on 7 September 1997.*

radars. Certainly nobody cared to offer an explanation of why this advice had been ignored, and then regarded as if it were something new. Cutting a long story short, the LO technology was first put to use in a dedicated attack aircraft, the F-117 Nighthawk. Astonishingly, the even more stealthy Navy counterpart, the A-12A Avenger II, was cancelled in 1991, so in the twenty-first century the Navy/Marines still fly the venerable A-6. Obviously, stealth also applies to fighters, so in 1991 the USAF launched the programme for an ATF (advanced tactical fighter).

Prototype contracts were awarded to Lockheed Martin for the YF-22 and to Northrop Grumman for the YF-23. Two examples of each were ordered, one to be powered by the Pratt & Whitney YF119 and the other by the General Electric YF120. Though the YF-23 was judged stealthier, and the YF120 the more powerful engine, the winner was the YF-22 powered by the Pratt & Whitney engine. Among many other challenging requirements was the ability to supercruise, to sustain supersonic speed with the two engines in dry (non-afterburning) thrust. Cutting a huge story short, while the engine was refined into the F119-PW-100, with rectangular vectoring nozzles, the aircraft was almost completely redesigned into the F-22A Raptor. The enormous wing (840 square feet is roughly the same as five Bf 109s!) has sharp taper but no sweepback. As far apart as possible, the twin vertical tails are canted outward and are fixed, incorporating powered rudders in the traditional way. In contrast, the tailplanes are fully powered and incorporate some sweepback. Overall the shape is very like that of the Russians of the previous generation, but an innovation is to preserve stealth by carrying missiles in three internal bays, a big one underneath between the engine air ducts and a shallow

In the immediate post-Second World War era some air forces became hooked on the idea of fast-climbing interceptors to defend particular point targets. One French answer was the Sud-Ouest S.O.9000 Trident, which had a three-barrel rocket engine in the tail and, to provide some get-you-home power, a small turbojet on each wingtip. First flown in 1953, it was the first aircraft to have three fully powered tail surfaces, with no fixed portion.

In 1957, when Britain said it would build no more fighters, France stepped smartly in and began marketing the Dassault Mirage III. A tailless delta, assisted by the British Fairey F.D.2, the first production version was the Mirage IIIC, powered by an afterburning Atar 9B. Equipment included Cyrano 1bis radar, a single primitive R.511 missile and either a rocket pack or two 30 mm guns. Like the rival MiG-21, it was just what many air forces wanted, and 1,422 were built. This IIIC served with the first squadron, No. 2 Cicogne (stork).

*Having extolled the virtues of the tailless-delta configuration, Dassault then not only explored the variable-geometry 'swing wing' but also went into production with the Mirage F1, with a tail and a conventional fixed wing mounted high on the fuselage! Powered by the Atar 9K50, 731 were built for many air forces. This F1-CR-200 served with Escadre 33 at Strasbourg.*

*Powered by a Snecma M53-P2 engine, rated at 21,385 lb thrust, the Mirage 2000 returned to the tailless-delta formula, but in a more advanced form with relaxed longitudinal stability (for rapid manoeuvres) and powerful leading-edge droops and slats. This is a Mirage 2000N, with full flight controls for the backseater, who is concerned mainly with navigation and weapon preparation. The small missiles are Matra Magics. Production by 2003 totalled 614.*

Powered by two M88-2 augmented turbofans, the Rafale (squall) takes the Dassault tailless formula to a new high level. This two-seat Rafale B is carrying Magic missiles, four GBU-12 laser-guided bombs and over 2,000 Imp. gal. of external fuel. There are 14 store attachments, and a 30 mm gun.

*Bigger than it looked, the Saab J32B was the ultimate operational (as distinct from training and target-towing) version of the* Lansen *(lance). It had an Avon engine with a fully modulated afterburner five years before such an engine was in service in Britain.*

bay on each side outboard of the duct. When stealth does not matter, two pylons can be attached under each wing, each rated at 5,000 lb, principally for air-to-ground stores. The planned initial buy of 648 F-22As had by 2003 been reduced to 339, with the prospect that it might be increased again by funding for a Naval variant and for an enlarged attack version. Price of the latest batch in production in 2003 was US$3,920 million for thirteen aircraft.

Such aircraft are too costly for all but a handful of nations, but in the late 1980s several US teams began studying smaller and more affordable aircraft, which included jet-lift Stovl (short-take-off, vertical landing) versions to replace the AV-8B (Harrier). After the merger of several studies the result in 1995 was the JSF (joint strike fighter). Following competitive tests of very different prototypes made by Lockheed Martin and Boeing, the former was chosen in October 2001 to develop three versions of JSF with the designation F-35. These are the F-35A, a conventional long-runway aircraft for the USAF; the F-35B, a jet-lift Stovl aircraft for the Marine Corps, RAF and Royal Navy; and the F-35C, a big-wing carrier-based version for the USN. The original partners require 3,002, and it is expected that this number will be doubled by other customers, which are expected eventually to include about half the world's air forces.

In Western Europe the only consistent developers of fighters have been France and Sweden. In the absence of competition from Britain, the former developed a long succession of Mirages. Some, the Mirage F1 family, have a high-mounted swept wing and horizontal tail, but the final version is the considerably upgraded Mirage 2000, which in the new century remains in production for Abu Dhabi, Greece and India. First flown in 1986, the totally redesigned twin-engined *Rafale* (Hurricane) was in 2003 in full service with *l'Armée de l'Air* and in a carrier-based version with *l'Aéronavale*, but maker Dassault had come to accept that export orders were going to be hard to achieve.

In contrast, Sweden has moved in the reverse direction. Initially, it was Swedish policy never to manufacture military aircraft for export, though two batches of J29Fs (never a true night fighter) were sold to Austria after serving with the Swedish Air Force. The outstanding J32 *Lansen* (lance) included a very successful night-fighter version, and the Mach-2 J35 *Draken* (dragon-kite), one of the most striking aircraft ever to fly, achieved both new and used export sales. Next came the Saab-37 *Viggen* (Thor's hammer), a powerful aircraft specifically designed with a canard foreplane, large wing, tandem-wheel landing gears and a thrust reverser to fit it for operations from short rough airstrips, including stretches of public highway. Unlike the USAF, the Swedes realized that in war against any significant power conventional airfields would be wiped off the map. Today Saab, assisted by BAE Systems, are in production with the JAS-39 *Gripen* (griffin), which repeats the canard formula in a smaller airframe. No other aircraft promises to offer twenty-first-century night and all-weather multirole capability so affordably, and while South Africa has a firm order other air forces are likely to follow suit.

The only other major producer of fighters is China. Having gained experience by mass-production of derivatives of the MiG-19 and MiG-21, several Chinese companies have boldly developed what can only be regarded as Chinese aircraft. The Shenyang Aircraft Corporation has delivered large numbers of both air force and naval versions of the J-8 twin-jet all-weather multirole fighter. The Xian company XAC has likewise delivered substantial numbers of the JH-7, a multirole aircraft looking like a greatly enlarged Jaguar with all-weather radar. Biggest group of all, the Chengdu-based CAC, has followed MiG-21 derivatives with the F-7MF, with multirole radar made possible by a chin engine inlet, the neat FC-1 with lateral inlets feeding a single imported RD-93 (derived from the MiG-29 engine) and the potentially very important J-10 family, a larger aircraft with a chin inlet feeding a single AL-31F, so far with a fixed-direction nozzle.

Israel's *Kfir* upgrade of the Mirage was never specifically intended for night and all-weather use, and the IAI *Lavi* was terminated during development. In contrast, though it is taking a very long time, India's LCA (light combat aircraft) remains in full development, with the first of several prototypes having been on test since 4 January 2001. The Indian radar features what house agents call 'all mod cons': doppler beam sharpening, coherent pulse-doppler TWS (track while scan), ground mapping, look-up/look-down modes, MTI (moving-target indication), missile guidance, the lot!

This leaves just the aircraft produced by international groups. The Anglo-French Jaguar was designed in the 1960s purely for attack and reconnaissance, though some later Indian versions

*In an environment where failed programmes were unheard of, it took courage for Saab and the Swedish air board to go ahead with such a bold design as the J35 Draken (dragon-kite). This J35A, one of the first production aircraft, is carrying Bofors 13.5 cm rockets. Guns were reloaded through the panels ahead of the national markings. Later examples carried Swedish versions of Sidewinder and Falcon.*

*Bigger and much more powerful than the Draken, the JA37 Viggen (Thor's hammer) was the first fighter in service with a thrust-reverser. This was essential when operating from dispersed stretches of closed-off highway. Normal armament comprised Sidewinders and big RB71 (British Aerospace Sky Flash) missiles, plus a powerful gun mounted internally.*

*Powered by an uprated version of the General Electric F404 (without a reverser), the sleek Gripen (griffen) proves that fighters do not have to get ever-larger. By mid-2003 over 140 had been delivered, including two-seat trainers and quite different two-seat command and control aircraft. First of the export customers is South Africa.*

*Although it has a specification closely similar to that of the abandoned Israeli Lavi, China's CAC J-10 is in many respects a later design, with a more powerful engine (an imported AL-31FN rated at 28,218 lb). In late-2003 the author did not yet know if the main radar is Russian or Israeli; the missiles on this pre-production aircraft (still in primer paint) are PL-2B or PL-8, based on the Israeli Python.*

are fitted with French or Israeli multimode radar. First flown in 1974, the Panavia Tornado is a slightly larger and considerably more powerful aircraft, conceived jointly by Germany, the UK and Italy when a variable-sweep 'swing wing' was all the rage (the author is puzzled that it ever went out of fashion). Though the original title was MRCA, meaning multirole combat aircraft, it was eventually decided that a considerably modified version should be developed to fly the all-weather and night interception role. The same three partners were joined by France and Spain to create a successor. France soon pulled out, to build the *Rafale*, leaving four partners in a company called Eurofighter GmbH (the suffix showing it is registered in Germany) to create an aircraft that was at first just called Eurofighter. Powered by outstanding EJ200 engines fed by a ventral inlet, it is yet another canard-equipped delta, and probably the best of the lot. Eventually it was recognized that, the company being Eurofighter, the aircraft had to have a name, and the choice fell on Typhoon, or *Taifun*. By 2003 the four partner air forces had all received production aircraft, which – like most of today's fighters – also comes in a two-seat version.

There is always unlimited scope for new possibilities and new problems in ECM. For example, several SAMs are guided not by pulsed radar but by CW (continuous-wave) illuminating sets. So are several AAMs, such as Sparrow. Not until the CW-guided lethality of the Soviet 'SA-6 Straight Flush' SAM radar became apparent in the Middle East war in October

*The more pointed radome for the AI.24 Foxhunter radar makes the Tornado F.3 better-looking than the attack versions. While the latter have two 27 mm Mauser guns, the F.3 has only one, with its muzzle centred in the black patch behind the radar. AMRAAM, Sky Flash, Active Sky Flash and ASRAAM missiles can be carried under the fuselage and wings. Here, without missiles, are aircraft of 56 RAF Sqn.*

*ZJ699, a British-assembled two-seater, was the first production Eurofighter Typhoon. Assigned to defensive-aids trials, it is seen with two AMRAAM missiles, chaff dispensers and wingtip ESM/towed-decoy pods.*

1973 did the United States suddenly wake up to the fact it had no ECM capability except against pulsed radars. Today even quite small tactical aircraft are being outfitted with complex passive warning receivers, active jammers, IR deceivers, and RF deception jammers which send back hostile radar signals with steadily increasing delay on each pulse to make the enemy think the aircraft is further away and moving faster than is actually the case.

Some of the later illustrations in this book show that modern fighter radars no longer have parabolic or Cassegrain dish reflectors, but flat 'planar arrays'. These make better use of available space, have a lower moment of inertia and, for a given gimbal geometry and radome size, have about ten to twelve per cent bigger aperture (ie, the scanner can be larger). They should not be confused with phased-array radars, which are exceedingly complex though they also have flat faces. Unlike the phased array, the planar aerial is still scanned mechanically.

We have come a long way in fighter radars in thirty years. The number of electronic components per cubic foot in AI.IV was about 198. In SCR-720 it was about 600, and in AI.IX

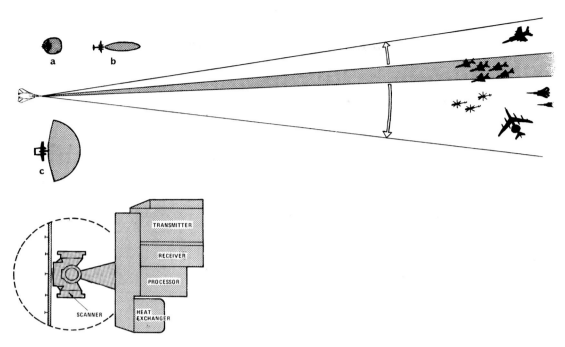

*Top: During the past 30 years fantastic advances have been made in the power and data-handling capacity of fighter radars. The AWG-9 of the Grumman F-14A Tomcat can simultaneously track 26 targets, twice as many as are shown, at ranges to 130 miles despite hostile ECM. To the same scale are shown the coverage patterns of (a) AI IV of 1940, (b) AI VIII of 1942 and (c) SCR-720 of 1943–4. Above: Basic elements of a simple modern multi-mode radar, the Ferranti Blue Fox of the Harrier FRS 1. Features include a small size, modular construction, a flat scanner with an electronically scanned aerial array, and built-in fault diagnosis. Details of the array on the scanner are deliberately not representative.*

it reached 3,300. In the Hughes E-1 and Westinghouse APQ-35 the figure rose to over 60,000. In the MG-10 it went to 330,000, and in MA-1 it almost reached a million. The AWG-9 of the F-14 hit 3 million, and the APQ-63 of the F-15 reached 7 million. Today's radars, such as the Westinghouse chosen for the F-16, invariably use LSI (large-scale integration) and advanced constructional forms in which the circuit forms the structure and also serves as a cooling duct, and 20 million components per cubic foot is now a good figure. This is the main factor underlying the sheer cleverness of today's radars. Earlier sets had 'blind velocities' like radial spokes along which targets could not be seen. They were unable to see moving targets against clutter; or, having got MTI (moving-target indication), they were unable to see hostile aircraft against any background of fast vehicle traffic on the ground. STAE (second-time-around echoes) and MTAE (multiple-time-around echoes) kept on appearing at two, three or more times the true range, causing more clutter. Even rain clutter was often a severe problem. But with 20 million components per cubic foot, today's night-fighter pilot can see a picture on which positively nothing appears except the precise items he needs.

*One of the most advanced electronically scanned phased-array fighter radars is the Bars (panther), one of the outstanding two-band (X and L) series from the Tikhomirov bureau. Angular coverage from the fixed metre-diameter array is ±40° in azimuth and ±70° in elevation. It is standard on the Su-30M MKI in production for the Indian Air Force.*

But we would do well not to get cocky. To every radar there is appropriate ECM. To every ECM – if we can quickly find out all about it – there is the appropriate ECCM. It is the situation of weapon and counter-weapon that has characterized the history of warfare, and which re-emphasizes its ultimate futility. I like the story about the *Luftwaffe* night-fighter pilot who in 1944 was posted from the Soviet Union to Germany to help shoot down the lavishly equipped RAF heavy bombers. He found it a marvellous change from the Eastern Front. 'The task there', he said, 'was terribly difficult. The Russians were so backward they had no radar.'

# GLOSSARY

It is probably impossible to write a book on such a technology-based subject as night fighters without using a lot of jargon and abbreviations. The following are offered to assist the reader:

**AAM** Air-to-air missile.

**ABC** Airborne Cigar, RAF active jammer carried by special Lancasters to jam *Luftwaffe* GCI frequencies.

**Active jamming** Jamming with powerful transmissions of the enemy's radar or communications frequencies.

**AEW** Airborne Early Warning.

**AGLT** Airborne gun-laying turret.

**AI** Airborne interception (radar).

**AIF** AI-follow (lock-on).

**AIM** Air Interception missile.

**AIS** AI-scanner (search mode).

**AMRE** Air Ministry Research Establishment (Orfordness-Bawdsey-Dundee/Leighton Buzzard-St Athan-Worth Matravers); became TRE.

**AMSR** Air Member for Scientific Research.

**AMTI** Aerial moving-target indication.

**ANG** US Air National Guard.

**AOC** Air Office, Commanding.

**APG** US radar designation: carried in piloted aircraft, a radar, used for fire control.

**APQ** US radar designation: carried in piloted aircraft, a radar used for a combination of purposes.

**ARI** UK designation prefix: Airborne Radio Installation.

**ASV** Air-to-surface-vessel.

**AW** All-weather.

**AWACS** Airborne Warning and Control System.

**AWG** US radar designation: carried in piloted aircraft, armament, fire-control.

**Az-el** Radar display of Cartesian form with two axes giving azimuth and elevation.

*Berlin* *Luftwaffe* centimetric AI radar.
*Bernhard* *Luftwaffe* GCI communications transmitter to beat jamming.
**Blip** Small illuminated spike or spot on a radar display denoting a target.

*Blitz* German for lightning, this became the English name for German air attacks on the UK in the Second World War.

**Boozer** RAF passive receiver turned to *Lichtenstein/Würzburg* frequencies.

*Bremen Luftwaffe* centimetric AI radar.

**BUIC** Back-up interceptor control.

**Carpet** Active jammer carried by RAF/USAAF heavy bombers to jam Würzburg.

**CFAR** Constant False-Alarm Rate.

**CH** Chain Home (original British coastal warning chain).

**Chaff** Modern name for Window.

**CHEL** Chain Home, Extra Low.

**CHL** Chain Home, Low (low-level coverage).

**Clutter** Unwanted background 'noise' pictured by radars, tending to mask real target returns.

**Corona** Transmission from Britain of misleading or diverting instructions or information on *Luftwaffe* GCI frequencies.

**CRT** Cathode-ray tube.

**CW** Continuous-wave (i.e. not pulsed).

**Deception jamming** Active jamming that, while hiding the true target, broadcasts to the enemy false positions and velocities.

**D/F** Direction finding (by radio).

**Doppler** Changed frequency due to relative motion between wave phenomena (e.g. sound or radar emissions) and a target.

**EAR** Electronically agile radar (e.g. FA).

**ECCM** Electronic counter-countermeasures.

**ECM** Electronic countermeasures.

**Electronic scanning** Radar transmitter in which outgoing signals are divided into many parts subjected to progressive shifts of phase and each emitted from a different part of the aerial.

**ELINT** Electronic intelligence.

**EM** Electromagnetic (wave having electrical and magnetic components and, depending on wavelength, being classed as heat, light, microwave, UV, etc.).

**ES** Electronic scanning.

**ESM** Electronic surveillance measures.

**EWS** Electronic warfare system.

**FA** Frequency-agile.

**FFAR** Free-flight (spin-stabilized) or folding-fin aircraft rocket.

**Fishpond** All-round warning system for RAF heavy bombers, used in conjunction with $H_2S$ and AGLT.

**FIU** Fighter Interception Unit, RAF centre for fighter research, later merged into the Central Fighter Establishment.

*Flensburg Luftwaffe* passive receiver for homing on to Monica radars.

**Frequency agility** Ability to operate at constantly, and seemingly randomly, changing frequency to defeat ECM.

*Freya Luftwaffe* surveillance radar.

**FuG** *Luftwaffe* airborne radio prefix (*Funk Gerät*).

**GCI** Ground control of interception.

**Gee** RAF and Allied area-coverage navaid of pulsed hyperbolic type.

**GHz** Gigaherz, thousands of millions of cycles per second.

**Glint** Erratic changes in the apparent radar centre of a target, fluctuating between the major reflective areas, the apparent centre of other places, and sometimes going off the target altogether.

**GMT** Ground moving target, such as road or rail vehicles, which an airborne radar may wish to include or eliminate.

*Helle Nachtjagd* Illuminated night fighting, *Luftwaffe* technique for night use of fighters without radar or any sensors.

*Himmelbett* Heavenly (i.e. four-poster) bed, subdivision of defence airspace around Germany into rectilinear boxes.

*Hirschgeweih* Stag's antlers, *Luftwaffe* AI radar aerial array.

**HPD** High-p.r.f. pulse-doppler.

**H2S** Ground mapping radar originally used by the RAF (H2X, used mainly by the USAAF, similar but shorter wavelength).

**HUD** Head-up display, projecting information onto pilot's windscreen.

**IFF** Identification friend or foe, automatic radio transponder giving coded reply if friendly.

**Interceptor** Aircraft intended to intercept, identify and if necessary destroy unidentified aircraft.

**Intruder** Night fighter operating over enemy territory.

**IR** Infra-red, i.e. heat.

**Jamming** Powerful emissions or a blanket of reflective material intended to deny the enemy a radar picture or intelligible communications.

**JG** *Jagdgeschwader, Luftwaffe* fighter wing (day).

**Jostle** Very powerful RAF active jammer 1943–5.

*Korfu Luftwaffe* ground receiver giving bearing on RAF H2S.

**kW** Kilowatt, thousand watts.

**LAM** Long Aerial Mine.

*Lichtenstein Luftwaffe* family of AI radars.

**Lookdown radar** Capable of detecting and tracking moving targets against a land or clutter background.

**LPD** Low-p.r.f. pulse-doppler.

**LRM** Long-range missile (air-to-air).

**Lucero** Facility for tracking and measuring distance from 1.5 m ground beacons (often used in conjunction with AI radar).

*Mammut Luftwaffe* surveillance radar.

**Mandrel** Active jammer carried in RAF aircraft to blot out *Freya/Wassermann*.

**MDAP** Mutual Defense Assistance Program, funded by US taxpayers.

**MHz** Megaherz, millions of cycles per second.

**MIT** Massachusetts Institute of Technology.

**Monica** Family of RAF active radars for rear warning.

*Morgenstern Luftwaffe* aerial array for AI radars to replace *Hirschgeweih*.

**MPD** Medium-p.r.f. pulse-doppler.

**MRM** Medium-range missile (air-to-air).

**MTAE** Multiple-time-around echoes, from targets at distances which are exact multiples of the radar unambiguous range.

**MTI** Moving-target indication (by eliminating all radar returns from apparently fixed targets).

**Mutton** RAF code-name for LAM trials.

**MW** Megawatts, millions of watts.


**NATO** North Atlantic Treaty Organization.

*Naxos* Family of *Luftwaffe* passive receivers for ground and airborne use giving bearing on RAF H$_2$S.

**NDRC** National Defense Research Council (USA).

*Neptun Luftwaffe* AI radar in metre waveband (1945).

**NF** Night fighter.

**NJG** Nachtjagdgeschwader, night-fighter wing.


**Oboe** RAF precision navaid for target marking or bombing.

**ODT** Overland downlook technology.

**OKB** Russian shorthand for an experimental design bureau.


**Pandora** Colloquial name for LAM-equipped Havoc aircraft.

**Passive** Not emitting RF (e.g. Window jamming, *Flensburg* receiver).

**PD** Pulse doppler.

**Perfectos** RAF night intruder radio for triggering hostile IFF and homing on the response.

**PFF** Pathfinder Force.

**PPI** Plan-position indicator, radar display painting a map-like picture.

**p.r.f.** Pulse-repetition frequency.

**Pulse** Very short burst of RF energy.

**PWR** Passive warning radar.


**Radar** Device for transmitting radio emissions, receiving part of those emissions diffused or reflected from a target, and giving consequent information on the position of that target (from Radio Direction And Range).

**Radome** Streamlined enclosure over a radar aerial system, made of dielectric material transparent to the chosen wavelength.

**RDF** Radio Direction Finding, original British code-name for radar. Thus RDF 1 for ground-based radar and RDF 2 for airborne radar.

**RF** Radio frequency.

**RFC** Royal Flying Corps (1912–18).

**RIO** Radar Intercept Officer (US Navy, Marine Corps).

**RLM** *Reichsluftfahrtministerium* (German air ministry).

**RNAS** Royal Naval Air Service (1912–18).

**RO** Radio/radar observer/operator/officer.

**ROC** Royal Observer Corps.

**RRE** Royal Radar Establishment (Malvern); previously TRE.

**RT** Radiotelephone.

**RWR** Rear-warning radar.

**SAGE** Semi-automatic ground environment (USA).

**Scanner** Radar aerial and reflector, usually either parabolic (Cassegrain) dish or planar emitter, mechanically driven to radiate in different controlled directions.

*Schräge Musik* Slanting music, *Luftwaffe* system of fixed oblique gun armament for night fighters.

**SCR** US Army equipment designation, Signal Corps Radio.

**Serrate** RAF passive receiver for RAF night intruders tuned to *Lichtenstein* radars and giving directional information.

**SN-2** Most important of the *Lichtenstein* AI radars.

**SRM** Short-range missile (air-to-air).

**STAE** Second-time-around echo, from target at exactly double the radar unambiguous range.

**Target** Among other things, anything seen by a radar.

**TFU** Telecommunications Flying Unit (Christchurch-Defford/Pershore).

**Tinsel** Crude noise jammer carried by RAF heavy bombers to jam *Luftwaffe* GCI frequencies.

**TRE** Telecommunications Research Establishment (Worth Matravers-Malvern); previously AMRE, later RRE.

**Turbinlite** Powerful visual searchlight carried in some RAF night fighters.

**TWR** Tail-warning radar.

**TWS** Track-while-scan.

**UHF** Ultra-high frequency.

**UV** Ultra-violet.

**VHF** Very high frequency.

**WAAF** Women's Auxiliary Air Force.

*Wassermann Luftwaffe* surveillance radar.

*Wilde Sau* Wild boar, Luftwaffe technique for using non-AI single-seat fighters to intercept over the bombers' target.

**Window** Basic passive jamming system with clouds of reflective foil, today called chaff.

**WSO** Weapon-System Officer (USAF).

*Würzburg Luftwaffe* ground radar for aiming *Flak* or searchlights.

*Zahme Sau* Tame boar, *Luftwaffe* technique for feeding fighters into the bomber stream en route to the target.

**Zombie** Western term for Soviet electronic reconnaissance aircraft.

# APPENDIX

A summary of aircraft designed or specially equipped as night fighters.

## AUSTRALIA

**CAC CA-12 Boomerang** This primitive yet manoeuvrable fighter was designed and put into production in Australia in the first weeks of 1942. Powered by a 1,200 hp Pratt & Whitney R-1830 Twin Wasp, it could exceed 290 mph and carried an armament of two 20 mm Hispano cannon and four 0.303 in Brownings. Though not designed as a night fighter, its docile handling and good pilot view fitted it well for the role, and several successful night interceptions were made in 1942–3, especially in the New Guinea campaign.

## CANADA

**Avro CF-100** In October 1945 the Defence Staff in Ottawa issued an RCAF specification for an extremely advanced long-range all-weather and night fighter, with jet propulsion. Among the varied demands were fast reaction to any threat, short field-length, rapid climb and advanced AI radar managed by the second crew member. The Avon-powered prototype flew on 19 January 1950, at a time when no comparable aircraft was even under construction or on order in Britain. The first production CF-100 Mk 2, powered by 6,000 lb Orenda engines, was delivered on 17 October 1951 and exceeded Mach 1 in a shallow dive on 18 December 1952. The first quantity production version was the Mk 3, armed with eight 0.5 in guns in a belly pack, delivered to 445 Squadron at North Bay in 1953. The Mk 4A was completely redesigned to accommodate a Hughes MG-2 collision-course fire-control system, generally similar to that fitted to the USAF Northrop F-89D. The guns were removed, and on each wing tip was added a pod housing thirty Mighty Mouse 2.7 -in rockets. The Mk 4B had an additional belly pack of forty-eight rockets, and was powered by 7,275 lb Orenda 11 engines with full anti-icing. The final version, bringing production up to 692, was the long-span Mk 5, with larger tip pods, each housing fifty-two rockets. The CF-100 could have been made compatible with the AIM-4C and -4D Falcon guided missile, but was expected to be replaced by the extremely formidable CF-105. Many aircraft were converted to serve in ECM roles.

**Avro CF-105 Arrow** To replace the CF-100, Avro Aircraft created an aircraft that today, fifty years later, still has no equal apart from the MiG-31. Among other things, the CF-105 was required to have a mission radius of 691 miles despite 1½ min at over Mach 1.5, the ability to sustain a 2 g turn at 50,000 ft, and an internal weapons bay bigger than the bomb bay of a B-29. With the world's most powerful AI radar and two seats, the first aircraft, temporarily fitted with Pratt & Whitney J75 engines (26,500 lb thrust each in full afterburner) began testing on 4 October 1957. The production engine was the Orenda Iroquois, an outstanding engine which made unprecedented use of titanium. By far the most advanced all-weather interceptor in the world at that time, it fell victim to a government which took its cue from Britain in thinking manned military aircraft should be replaced by American missiles, enabling money to be transferred to politically important farmers. On 20 February 1959 the whole programme was axed acrimoniously.

## FRANCE

**Dassault Mystère IVN** Dassault's successful line of early jet fighters drew their technical inspiration mainly from North American Aviation. Just as the basic Mystère resulted from a keen study of the F-86 Sabre day fighter, so did the IVN version stem from study of the F-86D all-weather and night interceptor. It had a redesigned nose, with a chin intake surmounted by a large radome (though no radar was available in France). In the belly was a pack containing 128 Hotchkiss-Brandt rockets, a much larger number than the load of FFARs carried by the F-86D. The engine was an imported Rolls-Royce Avon RA.7R. Eventually the *Armée de l'Air* chose two engines and two crew with the Vautour.

**Dassault Mirage IIIC** Dassault's original Mirage MD 550 was a small low-powered point-defence interceptor, devoid of radar and operated under ground control. Dassault increasingly doubted the validity of this *intercepteur léger* and instead planned a larger aircraft powered by an afterburning SNECMA Atar turbojet. This machine, the Mirage IIIC, was the forerunner of one of the world's most successful combat aircraft, which, with little competition, has sold 1,422 examples in more than twenty countries. This original version was a supersonic night and all-weather interceptor, fitted with CSF Cyrano Ibis radar and armed by two 30 mm DEFA cannon and a variety of externally hung ordnance, including a Matra R 530 air-to-air missile. Most IIIC aircraft of the Catac (fighter command, *Armée de l'Air*) were also equipped with an SEP 844 rocket engine to increase rate of climb and high-altitude acceleration. Other Mirage delta fighters were supplied to South Africa and Israel, and the completely redesigned Mirage III-S was built under licence in Switzerland, with Hughes Taran radar and HM-55 Falcon missiles supplied from Sweden. Other Mirages were all configured primarily for the ground-attack role.

**Dassault-Breguet Mirage F1.C** This completely redesigned aircraft, derived by scaling down the Mirage F2 of 1964, entered service in March 1973 as the new standard all-weather interceptor of the *Armée de l'Air*. Powered by an Atar 9K-50 engine of 15,873 lb thrust (about sixteen per cent more powerful than the Mirage III series), the F1.C has a more efficient non-delta wing, integral tankage of much greater capacity and greatly improved systems. The radar is the

Cyrano IV, considerably updated in comparison with the Ibis but still an old-fashioned pre-Doppler type. Weapons include the same two 30 mm guns and the R530, Super 530 or close-range Matra 550 Magic missiles. Dassault-Breguet has sold many similar aircraft to South Africa, Spain and Arab countries. In 1973–5 it mounted a major campaign to sell the F1.E with the newer M53 engine, but in 1976 abandoned this objective. Production totalled 745.

**Dassault-Breguet Mirage 2000** This 1976 project has a long history beginning with the swing-wing Mirage G of the mid-1960s, extending through the GB and fixed-wing GBA to the *Avion de Combat Futur* (Super Mirage), abandoned in early 1976, and ultimately led to a new all-weather interceptor for the *Armée de l'Air* in 1982. It is a simple tailless delta, but with an airframe much more advanced aerodynamically and structurally than that of existing Mirage IIIs. The engine is the M53-P2 rated at 21,385 lb with afterburner. EMD and Thomson-CSF (now Thales) supplied the first modern (pulse-Doppler) radar for any French aircraft. Production by 2003 totalled 601, for eight countries.

**Dassault Rafale** Having pulled out of the Eurofighter programme (partly because France wanted a carrier-based version), Dassault began flight testing the first ACT (*Avion de Combat Tactique*) on 4 July 1986. Subsequently Dassault developed the Rafale (hurricane, or squall) type B dual trainer, Rafale C single-seat fighter, Rafale M carrier-based naval fighter, Rafale N two-seat multirole naval version and Rafale 2 for export. Powered by two Snecma M88-2 engines, each rated at 16,400 lb in full afterburner, the Rafale can carry no fewer than thirty-seven types of missile, bomb, tank or sensor store on its thirteen external pylons. Maximum Mach number (clean) is 1.8. The programme slipped in timing, but in 2003–8 it is planned to deliver fifty-seven to the *Armée de l'Air* and nineteen to the Aéronavale.

**Les Mureaux ANF 114** One of a large family of closely related combat types with large parasol monoplane wings, the Mureaux 114-CN2 was (as its designation CN2, *chasse nuit 2*, reveals) a two-seat night fighter. The 114 entered *Armée de l'Air* service in 1933, and despite being unable to exceed 194 mph on its 690 hp Hispano vee-12 water-cooled engine, many survived right up to the Second World War. Most Mureaux, however, served in the reconnaissance role, one being the first Allied victim of the conflict.

**Morane-Saulnier 408** The only reasonably modern French fighter to be available in large numbers in the Second World War was the M-S 406, derived from the similar 405. The thirteenth of the numerous M-S 405 prototypes was completed in November 1939 as the first 408, a night fighter with four retractable landing lights. Powered like other versions by an 850 hp Hispano 12Y-31 engine, it just reached 300 mph, and was armed with one 20 mm Hispano cannon and two machine-guns. It was used as the prototype of the Swiss D 3800.

**Potez 631** One of the first twin-engined cantilever monoplane fighters, the Potez 630 family were designed to a 1934 specification, the prototype flying in April 1936. Powered by two 670 hp Gnome-Rhône GR14M3/M4 Mars two-row radials, the 631 was available in large numbers by 1940 despite crippling shortages of guns and propellers. The intended armament was two 20 mm Hispano Type 9 cannon in the nose and a single MAC 1934 machine-gun in the rear cockpit, but often the nose carried four machine-guns instead. In February 1940 six MAC 1934 machine-guns were added under the wings of over 200 aircraft. The 631 equipped squadrons ECMJ1/16, ECN1/13, II/13, III/13, IV/13 and V/13 (away at Lyons), and GAM5/50 and GC1/7. In daylight it was no match for the Bf 109E, but in the week following 10 May 1940 the Potez squadrons did much good work by day and night.

**Sud-Est Aquilon** To meet the need for a carrier-based night fighter for the Aéronavale, SNCASE (later Sud-Aviation, later Aérospatiale) built a series of French versions of the de Havilland Sea Venom under licence. The first twenty-five were land-based night fighters, with a Fiat-built Ghost engine. Then followed twenty-five Aquilon 202s, with carrier equipment, a sliding canopy (unlike British Sea Venoms) and armament of four 20-mm and eight rockets. These were followed by forty Aquilon 203 single-seaters, armed with the Nord 5103 command-guidance air-to-air missile, and ten Aquilon 204 dual trainers. All Aquilons had ejection seats and Westinghouse APQ-65 radar, supplied by the MDAP. Aquilons were used by Flotilles 11F, 16F, 17F, 2S, 10S, 54S and 59S.

**Sud-Ouest Vautour** Undoubtedly one of the best French military aircraft since 1939, the SO 4050 Vautour was a compact all-swept machine powered by two early 7,720 lb Atar 101E3 turbojets, and identical in layout to the Yak-25 with bicycle landing gear and crew of two in tandem. There were three main versions, and no fewer than 140 were originally ordered of the Vautour IIN night and all-weather fighter version, with US radar, four 30 mm DEFA guns, pylons for up to four guided air-to-air missiles (such as the Matra R 510) and provision for internal boxes of rockets. This order was cut back to seventy in 1958, but the Vautour IIN force served until replacement by the Mirage F1.C in 1973–6. The Israeli Air Force also operated twenty-five Vautour IIA fighter and attack aircraft without AI radar.

## GERMANY

**Dornier Do 217** First flown in 1938 as a potent bomber, the 217 was one of the first aircraft picked on in 1942 to meet the urgent shortage of night fighters for the *Luftwaffe*. The first night fighters were 157 Do 217E-2 bombers, powered by 1,600 hp BMW 801A engines, which were hurriedly converted into 217J night fighters. There were two versions, the J-1 intruder with the bomb bay retained for carrying 50 kg (110 lb) and other small bombs, and the J-2 night fighter with the bomb bay sealed and with *Lichtenstein* AI radar. Standard nose armament was four 20 mm MG FF cannon and four 7.92 mm MG 17s, all firing forward. Many of these aircraft served in Italy in 1943, and in this year the second NF version appeared, when about 220 Do 217M versions were modified on the assembly line into 217N night fighters. Powered by 1,750 hp DB 603A engines, the N-1 had four 20 mm MG 151/20s and four MG 17s or MG 81s, all in the nose but differing considerably from the nose of the J. A few of the N-2 sub-type, which differed in having the defensive ventral MG 81 guns removed and the position faired over, were modified after delivery to have one of the first *Schräge Musik* installations with two or, more often, four MG 151/20s mounted obliquely behind the rear spar above the bomb bay.

**Do 335** *Pfeil* **(Arrow)** One of the more radical of the many unconventional *Luftwaffe* aircraft, the 335 was a large and powerful fighter powered by two engines – usually 1,800 hp DB 603E – mounted in front of and behind the cockpit, driving propellers at each end of the fuselage. Though no version went into mass production, there were many sub-types, most of them fighters. The 335A-0, of which ten were built in the autumn of 1944, was an interim fighter with a 30 mm MK 103 firing through the hub of the front propeller and two 20 mm MG 151s on the front cowl; light bombs were also carried. Then followed twelve Do 335A-1s, with the 1,900 hp DB 603G. The Do 335V-10 prototype had SN-2 radar, and was the prototype for the 335B series of night fighters, with either one or two seats and normal armament of three MK 103s and two MG 151/20s. Another prototype, the V-4, was intended to lead to a yet later specialized night fighter, the Do 435.

**Focke-Wulf Fw 189** Powered by two 410 hp Argus aircooled inverted-V engines, this distinctive twin-boom reconnaissance aircraft, made principally by French companies, was pressed into service as a night fighter. The principal unit was I/NJG 100, which operated against Po-2 biplanes, and other tactical aircraft on the Eastern Front which carried out nuisance bombing raids at night.

**Focke-Wulf Fw 190** An outstandingly efficient and formidable single-seat day fighter-bomber, the Fw 190 was inevitably turned into a night fighter in late 1942. In many respects it was superior to the Bf 109 in this role, having improved pilot view, much better controllability (especially at high speeds) and wide-track landing gear. Typical early NF versions were produced from the Fw 190A-4 and A-4/R-6, the latter having the original armament of four 20 mm guns and two MGs supplemented by two 210 mm rocket launch tubes under the wings. In 1943 the NJG force was expanding swiftly, and to it were assigned more than three-quarters of the Fw 190A-5 output in that year, many being the A-5/U-2 sub-type with flame-damped exhausts so successfully and boldly used by Hajo Herrmann's *Wilde Sau* pilots. There were several further specialized NF variants, such as the A-8/U-11 with an autopilot, additional communications and IFF/ECM for trying to counter the RAF's spoofing and jamming tactics.

**Focke-Wulf Ta 154** *Moskito* It was perhaps natural that this twin-engined night fighter should be so named, especially as it was built largely of wood; but it was as unsuccessful as the Mosquito was successful. Built to a 1942 RLM specification calling for an antidote to the Mosquito, to be made of non-strategic materials and developed rapidly, the 154 had a nosewheel landing gear and came in single- and two-seat versions. The first prototype, underpowered with 1,440-hp Jumo 211 engines, flew on 7 July 1943; the second prototype reached 435 mph and the third was fitted with *Lichtenstein* C-1 radar, but such progress belied the true state of the programme. In November 1943 an initial 250 were coming into production at a fully tooled plant at Poznan, Poland, the Ta 154A-1 being powered by 1,776 hp Jumo 213A engines and having a normal armament of two 30 mm MK 108s and two 20 mm MG 151s. Unfortunately for the *Luftwaffe*, the engine problems were rivalled by the structural failures, and the only examples of this much-publicized aircraft ever to see combat were the eight pre-production A-0 batch in the summer of 1944.

**Heinkel He 219** *Uhu* **(Owl)** Ernst Heinkel proposed this twin-engined *Zerstörer* in August 1940, but the RLM – thinking of a quick *Blitzkrieg* war – was totally uninterested. In January 1942, however, it viewed the war somewhat differently, and told Heinkel to go ahead. This the planemaker did, to such effect that the prototype flew on 15 November 1942. Reaching about 420 mph on its two 1,750 hp DB 603As, it went to Peenemünde in December 1942 for armament trials. It was hardly a 'Zerstörer' with a tray of two 20 -mm MG 151, plus two 13 mm MG 131s manually aimed from the rear cockpit; but that was just the beginning. Its main attribute was superb all-round performance and handling, and the initial order for 100 was soon trebled, the deciding factor being a thrilling competitive fly-off in January 1943 between the 219V-2, flown by Major Streib, and Oberst von Lossberg's Ju 188S. Though Heinkel had droves of enemies in the RLM, the inescapable fact gradually seeped through that the He 219, forcefully pushed from the start by *General der Nachtjagd* Kammhuber, was by far the greatest night fighter in prospect for the *Luftwaffe* (or, so one can say with the benefit of hindsight, any other air force in the Second World War). By the spring of 1943 the armament had been greatly increased, the pre-production A-0 series usually having four of the shattering 30 mm MK 103s (or 108s) in a belly tray and two 20 mm MG 151s in the wing roots. To try to speed up service introduction – in view of Heinkel's dismal inability to build faster than ten per month – a handful of A-0 versions were assigned to I/NJG-1. Streib himself flew the first combat mission, on the night of 11/12 June 1943, and destroyed five Lancasters in two hours! By 21 June this tiny force (never more than five aircraft) flown by I/NJG 1 had destroyed twenty-five RAF bombers, of which six were the previously seemingly immune and almost supernatural Mosquitos. There followed months of political wrangling and confusion, with Chief of Staff Milch trying to cancel the 219 in favour of more Ju 88Gs. Later He 219A-2 versions belatedly went into service with two extra MK 108 cannon in a *Schräge Musik* installation that was possibly more lethal than the heavy forward-firing armament. Ultimately only 268 of the He 219A series were produced, the profusion of later versions mostly not even being built.

**Junkers Ju 88** Ranking with the Bf 109 as the most important combat type of the wartime *Luftwaffe*, the outstandingly robust and versatile Ju 88 was by far the best of all the night fighters produced by converting an existing aircraft. The first Ju 88 *Zerstörer* version was the C-series, the first examples of which were delivered to the embryo NJG 1 in December 1940 (this unit having since July operated Ju 88A series bombers with or without extra forward-firing armament). Powered by 1,200 hp Jumo 211B engines, the C-2 was a conversion of existing A-1 (short-span) bombers, a typical nose armament being one 20 mm MG FF and three MG 17s. Much more formidable was the C-6b, with 1,410 hp Jumo 211J engines and typical forward-firing armament of three MG FFs and three MG 17s, but still not fitted with AI radar until about February 1942. By this time work was well advanced on the Ju 88R series powered by BMW 801 radials of 1,600 or 1,700 hp, but in late 1943 all earlier night-fighter versions were replaced in production by the specially designed Ju 88G. This was completely revised to eliminate many earlier deficiencies in equipment, performance and handling, the most obvious change being the larger Ju 188-type tail to improve directional stability at low speeds which had been marginal with the R and caused many accidents. Though the nose was now filled with *Lichtenstein* AI radar, there was heavy forward-firing armament, usually including four 20 mm MG 151s in a ventral tray, and in many versions two 20 mm or (rarely) 30 mm cannon were fitted in a *Schräge Musik* installation. The G-1 had BMW 801D engines, the G-6 the 801G or the Jumo 213A, and the best mass-produced night-fighter sub-type of all, the G-6c of December 1944, had 1,880 hp Jumo 213E engines and reached about 390 mph with MW50 (methanol/water) power boosting. About 7,000 of the 16,900-odd Ju 88s of all versions were night fighters, outnumbering all other types.

**Ju 188 and 388** Neither of these potentially superior aircraft succeeded in replacing the evergreen 88, but both served in small numbers, including a few night-fighter variants. The main 188 night fighter was the R series, but there is no evidence that any reached combat units. Likewise, only three examples were completed of the impressive Ju 388J *Störtebeker*, the first (J-1) sub-type having 1,980 hp turbocharged BMW 801TJ engines, and the J-2 and J-3 having the Jumo 213E. Both were fitted with two 30 mm MK 108s and two 20 mm MG 151s firing forward, while leaving the nose free for the new FuG 228 *Lichtenstein* SN-3 with a *Morgenstern* aerial faired inside a wooden nosecone, as on the final Ju 88 fighters. Most of the handful of 388J-3 models had two 20 mm MG 151 guns in a *Schräge Musik* installation.

**Messerschmitt Bf 109** Built in greater numbers than any other warplane in history, except for the Ilyushin Il-2/Il-10 *Stormovik*, the ubiquitous 109 played a major role in defending Germany by night, though the basic aircraft was ill-suited to the task. Early models were reasonably pleasant to fly, though the lateral control stiffened up at high speeds and the slats tended to flick open and shut when pulling g in turns, making aiming difficult. By 1942, however, when the RAF night onslaught began to hurt, the sole production series was the G (Gustav), a heavy, sluggish beast powered by the DB 605 engine rated initially at 1,475 hp and later giving 2,000 hp with MW50 injection. Large numbers of Gustavs were used by NJG units in *Wilde Sau* tactics, with little to help them but courage, searchlights and whatever night-flying skill the pilot happened to possess. Typical armament was one 30 mm MK 108 firing through the propeller hub, two 20 mm MG 151s (or 30 mm MK 108s) under the wings and two 13 mm MG 131s above the engine. The only specialized night variant was the G-6/U4N, equipped with the *Naxos* Z (H2S homer), which was of little help to the lone pilot once he had reached the proximity of his quarry on a dark night.

**Messerschmitt Bf 110** The original *Zerstörer*, built to a 1934 specification for a heavy escort fighter, the prototype of this twin-engined machine flew on 12 May 1936, and in RLM testing in 1937 reached 316 mph. This was impressive, but its success in Poland in September 1939 was misleading. In the Battle of Britain the 110 itself had to be defended by the Bf 109(!); it was outclassed in air combat, and was considered sluggish and tiring to fly. Hastily sent away to the Eastern Front and North Africa, it ceased to appear in Western Europe until the sudden expansion of the NJG force in 1941, when the Bf 110 was restored to its front rank and production rapidly increased. The first specialized NF version was the 110F-4, with 1,300 hp DB 601 engines, early *Lichtenstein* radar, a crew of three and two 30 mm MK 108 cannon firing ahead. By the end of 1942 the intended replacement, the Me 210, was faltering and production concentrated on the 110G with the 1,475 hp DB 605B. Important versions included the G-4 with two or four 20 mm MG 151s and four MG 17s, or two 30 mm MK 108s and two 20 mm MG 151s. Many G-series were operated with a crew of two, but most of those fitted with *Lichtenstein* SN-2 radar had a third man. More than 1,500 of all versions were built in 1943, more than three times the 1942 output, and about the same number (all night fighters) were delivered in 1944. But the 110 was an old aircraft by this time.

**Messerschmitt Me 210 and 410** Intended as replacements for the Bf 110, neither of these twin-engined fighter/bomber/reconnaissance aircraft was an unqualified success.

**Messerschmitt Me 262** This very advanced twin-jet fighter was a far bolder design than the corresponding British Meteor, and had Hitler personally not insisted on its conversion for use as a bomber, might have exerted an even greater influence than it did in the final year of the war. First flown on a Jumo 210 piston engine on 4 April 1941, it flew with the same engine plus two BMW 003 turbojets on 25 November of that year. Finally the third prototype flew as a twin-jet fighter with two 1,980 lb Jumo 004 engines on 18 July 1942. The single-seat A series were fighter-bombers, usually armed with the devastating punch of four 30 mm MK 108 cannon, while the tandem-seat B series led to the B-1a/U-1 night fighter, with two crew and *Neptun* radar. This was a most formidable aircraft, but only a handful became operational with Welter's special *Gruppe* in the closing days of the European war.

## INDIA

**Aeronautical Development Agency LCA** Named Tejas, The Light Combat Aircraft, India's second indigenous multirole fighter, is a tailless delta powered in the production version by the Kaveri turbofan. Armament includes various missiles and a Russian GSh-23L twin-barrel gun.

## INTERNATIONAL

**Eurofighter Typhoon** In 1983 Britain, France, Germany, Italy and Spain issued an outline target for a collaborative fighter to enter service in the mid-1990s. In 1985 France withdrew, but the other countries developed what became the Eurofighter. In 1998, recognizing that 'Eurofighter Eurofighter' sounded silly, it was decided to name the aircraft Typhoon, or in German *Taifun*. Powered by two Eurojet EJ200 afterburning turbofans of 20,250 lb maximum thrust each, the resulting aircraft has a delta wing and swept foreplane, and is in production in single- and two-seat forms. Wingtip pods house ECM/ESM and a towed decoy, while up to 8 tonnes (17,637 lb) of stores can be hung on eleven attachments. The original partners have a requirement for 620, and began taking delivery of inventory aircraft in winter 2002–3.

**Boeing (previously McDonnell Douglas)/BAE Systems Harrier II Plus** This long title identifies the only version of the land-based Harrier to have full night and all-weather capability in the fighter role. The St Louis plant manufactured 389 AV-8B Harrier II aircraft (not including forty dual trainer TAV-8Bs), and in 1990 agreed with Italy and Spain to fund a version equipped with the APG-65 multimode radar, as fitted to the F/A-18A/B Hornet. A total of twenty-seven Harrier II Plus were delivered to the Marine Corps, plus seventy-three rebuilds of early Harrier IIs, to provide a total of 100 to equip the three wings VMA-223, -231 and -542. A further sixteen were produced for the Italian Navy, and eight for the Spanish Navy.

**Panavia Tornado (MRCA)** From its initials, signifying Multi-Role Combat Aircraft, it can be deduced that this versatile three-nation aircraft could serve in the night-fighter role. Developed jointly by Britain, Federal Germany and Italy, and powered in its initial version by two RB 199-34R three-shaft turbofans giving a thrust with full afterburning of about 14,500 lb, the swing-wing MRCA is efficient in almost every tactical role, including day and night air superiority, bombing, reconnaissance and interdiction. The basic aircraft is fitted with two 27 mm cannon by IKWA-Mauser, with very high muzzle velocity and rate of fire. It has Texas Instruments pulse-doppler forward-looking radar, suitable for multi-mode use, and can carry a wide range of air-to-air and air-to-ground missiles. In addition, the RAF purchased 165 of a specialized air-defence version (ADV) fitted with a different forward-looking radar by Marconi-Elliott/Ferranti, matched with weapons and fire-control optimized for the air-to-air mode. One batch has been loaned to Italy.

## ITALY

**Aeritalia F-104S** Built under licence from Lockheed, the F-104S was the final variant of the Starfighter to be developed, and the first since the original F-104A to be optimized for the air-to-air role. The designation signifies Sparrow, this large all-weather radar-guided missile forming the principal armament, one being carried on a pylon under each wing. Two Sidewinders can be carried under the fuselage, and two more (in lieu of tanks) on the wing tips. The radar was originally the R21G Nasarr, but in 1974 work began to update this by providing MTI and improved ECM capability. The 20 mm M-61 gun is a standard fitment. Total production for the *Regia Aeronautica*, in 1969–76, amounted to 205. Turkey added a further thirty-two.

**Fiat biplanes** Rapidly outmoded by monoplanes in the early years of the Second World War, the CR 32 and CR 42 were extensively used as night fighters over North Africa and Greece in 1941–3, the 42N having special night gear.

## JAPAN

**Kawasaki Ki-45 *Toryu* (Dragon Killer)** Designed to an Imperial Army specification of March 1937, calling for a twin-engined escort fighter, this fine and manoeuvrable fighter first flew in January 1939. After protracted engine trouble the first (day) version was in production by September 1941, powered by 1,080 hp Ha-102 engines and reaching about 335 mph. Typical armament comprised a 20 mm Type 99 cannon and two 12.7 mm (0.5 in) guns, all in the nose, firing ahead, and a machine-gun aimed by the navigator. By February 1942 night raids by B-17s and other bombers had prompted the Army to try to convert this aircraft into a night fighter, though no AI radar then existed in Japan. The outcome, flown in the summer of 1942, was the Ki-45 *Kai* (modification) C, with a searchlight in the tip of the nose and the forward-firing armament augmented by a 37 mm cannon under the fuselage. By the time *Kai* C was in production, in 1943, the 37 mm was the sole forward-firing armament, but two 20 mm cannon had been fixed obliquely in the fuselage between the two crew, copying the idea claimed to have been invented by the Navy. Code-named Nick by the Allies (who had to devise slick, instantly identifiable designations for Japanese aircraft) the Ki-45 night fighters were the only specially designed Army aircraft in this category able to resist the Allied onslaught back across the Pacific and over Japan itself. Despite being obsolescent, they scored at least sixty victories over the B-17, B-24 and B-29, mainly over Tokyo and Osaka.

**Kawasaki Ki-102** Having acquired in the Ki-45 a sound high-performance twin, the Imperial Army modified it into many versions, one of which was the Ki-102B anti-shipping attack fighter, with heavy armament including a 57 mm cannon. During a test flight a Ki-102B encountered a formation of B-29s and blew an engine off one of the bombers with a single shot from the heavy gun. As the most desperate need was for night fighters the Ki-102C was urgently built in this role, with imperfect AI radar in the nose, twin 20 mm cannon mounted obliquely in the mid-fuselage and two 1,500 hp Ha-112 engines giving a speed of about 360 mph. But the B-29 raids the Ki-102C was intended to stop so completely disrupted Japanese industry the new night fighter never got into production.

**Mitsubishi A6M** By far the best-known Japanese aircraft, popularly called the Zero, this fighter was such a shock to the Allies – almost entirely because of its combination of outstanding manoeuvrability and cannon armament – that it took a long time before it was, in effect, cut down to size. Towards the end of production of 10,449 examples A6M5s were pressed into urgent use as home-defence night fighters, though they found it difficult to reach and destroy B-29s. Some of these, hastily fitted with an oblique upward-firing cannon behind the cockpit, were unofficially designated A6M5d-S.

**Mitsubishi J2M *Raiden* (Thunderbolt)** Code-named Jack by the Allies, this diminutive single-seat fighter marked the sudden recognition by the Imperial Navy that there might be some advantage in a fighter having not merely good manoeuvrability but also high speed and rapid climb. Though comparatively 'hot' compared with its predecessors, so that it needed skilful handling and a good runway, a number of *Raiden*s were converted for use as land-based night fighters in the defence of Japan. These J2M5 conversions had a single 20 mm cannon mounted obliquely behind the cockpit in the left side of the fuselage. They operated freely, like the German *Wilde Sau* pilots, but without the benefit of ground vectoring by a controller watching a radar plot.

**Mitsubishi Ki-83** Whereas the A6M was an aircraft of the Navy, the Ki-83 was an Army type. Powered by two 2,200 hp Ha-211 engines, it was very similar to the Grumman F7F, though its speed of 438 mph was even greater, and the nose housed two 20 mm and two powerful 30 mm guns. A radar-equipped night-fighter version was never completed.

**Nakajima J1N1-S *Gekko* (Moonlight)** The Navy counterpart of the Ki-45, this highly manoeuvrable twin-engined machine was built to a 1938 fighter specification and first flew in May 1941. But the Navy judged it too big and heavy for use as a fighter and consigned it to the reconnaissance role, the J1N1-C entering service in this duty in 1942 with a speed of about 320 mph on two 1,130 hp Sakae 21 engines. But, as related in the text, a local commander suggested the fitting of cannon fixed at an oblique angle as an experiment to find the most effective night fighter. The result was the J1N1-S, the first aircraft ever to go into service with the form of armament which proved more effective than any other in the pre-missile age. It had the rather strange armament of two 20 mm Type 99 cannon firing obliquely upward at 30° and a second pair firing down at the same angle, all aft of the crew compartment. Put into use in the Rabaul area of New Guinea in May 1943, they proved lethal against even the best-protected US heavies. Nose guns were usually removed, but a few *Gekko*s had a manually aimed dorsal turret with a 20 mm gun. About eighteen months later *Gekko*s in Japan were fitted with AI radar and operated by night against B-29 raids, but – like almost all other Japanese aircraft except small single-seaters – they were hard pressed to reach the big bombers, which were too high and too fast.

**Nakajima Ki-84 *Hayate* (Hurricane)** Generally regarded as the best of all the Japanese single-seat fighters, the Ki-84 was a contemporary of the US Navy F6F Hellcat, and (called Frank by the Allies) was virtually the only combat aircraft in use in numbers that posed real problems to the Allied fighters. In the final defence of Japan more than 400 operated by day and night, though industrial destruction was such that fuel, ammunition and spares were often unavailable. It had no trouble in climbing up to B-29 formations, but serviceability was poor and in night operations the weak landing gear often failed, the main cause being attributed to faulty steels.

**Yokosuka D4Y *Suisei* (Comet)** A carrier-based dive-bomber with an internal bomb bay, the D4Y flew in November 1940 with an imported DB 601 liquid-cooled engine and saw service with the Japanese *Atsuta* vee-12 and 1,560 hp *Kinsei* 62 radial. In the early weeks of 1945 the situation in Japan became so desperate that even these rather unlikely machines were urgently turned into night fighters, with the designation D4Y2-S and D4Y3-S. As there was no radar the observer was often left on the ground, and the armament comprised one (occasionally two) 20 mm cannon obliquely mounted in the rear fuselage.

## SWEDEN

**Saab 32 *Lansen*** Svenska Aeroplan Aktiebolaget has since 1945 emerged as the most consistently successful producer of military aircraft in the world (every one of its projects having gone into service in large numbers), which really reflects chiefly upon the outstanding Swedish procurement organization which has yet to make a major mistake. The Saab 32 began life as a rather uninspired attack aircraft powered by two Ghost turbojets, but this was changed on the drawing board to a far better aircraft with a single Rolls-Royce Avon. The first A32A attack version was followed by the redesigned J32B night and all-weather fighter, with powerful RM6A engine (Swedish-built Avon 200 with SFA afterburner) giving a maximum thrust of 15,190 lb. This gave a level speed of about 710 mph, but *Lansen*s in clean condition were supersonic in a shallow dive. The J32B had Ericsson radar, Saab S6 fire control, four internal 30 mm Aden cannon, four Rb 324 (Sidewinder) missiles and optional heavy loads of other ordnance. Delivery to seven RSAF squadrons, beginning with F12, took place in 1958–60.

**Saab 35 _Draken_** While the _Lansen_ was impressive, the _Draken_ was truly outstanding, and it resulted in the RSAF being equipped with a Mach 2 night and all-weather fighter earlier than any other country in Western Europe and at a unit price lower than that of any other Mach 2 aircraft in the non-Communist world. Notable for its radical 'double delta' shape which enabled everything to be packaged in a supersonically efficient front-to-rear arrangement, the J35 was developed in 1952–8 and proved extremely pleasant to fly (almost too responsive in pitch at high speed, until modified) and virtually unbreakable even in harsh supersonic manoeuvres. The J35A was a basic version to achieve early service-clearance at a high flying rate. Powered by a 15,200 lb RM6B (Swedish Avon with SFA afterburner), it had an Ericsson radar derived from an early French CSF _Cyrano_ design, the same S6 fire control as the J32B providing for simple radar-only lead-pursuit sighting, and armament of two 30 mm Aden cannon. Operational service began in 1959, about ninety being in service by 1960, and in 1961 the RSAF began to receive the locally produced Rb 24 and 324 Sidewinder missile that was supplied first to F13, the original J35A squadron, the aircraft being retrofitted with the S6B sight with infra-red capability. In 1962 the J35A, by now called the _Adam_, was either relegated to trials and training or converted into the next version, the J35B _Bertil_. This was fitted with S7 fire control to fit into the new STRIL 60 automatic air-defence system that henceforth provided an integrated electronic airspace over Sweden. _Bertil_ also carried a wide assortment of external ordnance, and by 1963 equipped F16 at Uppsala and F18 at Tullinge. After the Sk35C (_Caesar_) dual trainer the next combat variant was the J35D (_David_), with speed raised to Mach 2 or slightly higher by virtue of the 17,650-lb RM6C engine (a more powerful Avon with yet another SFA afterburner). _David_ also introduced the S7 fire control, Ericsson PS-Ø3 radar and advanced FH5 autopilot. In service from December 1963 at F13 and with F10 at Angelholm, the J35D was soon operating from assorted lengths of straight highway in remote country districts even in wet or icy weather (and later, with portable ILS, by night). Next came the S35E (_Erik_) reconnaissance version and finally the greatest _Draken_ of all, the J35F (_Filip_). Wholly automatic, it had the extremely powerful and reliable PS-Ø1 radar, under-nose Hughes IR sensor and prime armament of Swedish-built Hughes Falcon guided missiles. Two versions of the latter were carried, the Rb 27 fat-bodied radar homing type, and Rb 28, the slim IR-seeker (neither of which had a US counterpart, though both were supplied to Switzerland for that country's Mirage IIIS). Pairs of both missiles were carried on wing pylons and have been repeatedly proved lethal even in intense ECM or at tree-top height. Total _Draken_ production was 606, final versions being supplied to Denmark and Finland.

**Saab 37 _Viggen_** While the English translations of _Lansen_ and _Draken_ are pretty obvious, _Viggen_ bears no relation to its English meaning of 'Thunderbolt'. Likewise the aircraft bears little relation to the _Draken_, which it replaces, though in one way it could be thought another 'double delta'. It has a huge delta wing and small delta foreplane, working together in a unique configuration designed not only for outstanding flight manoeuvrability but also good performance from short rough airstrips that could not be safely used by any other supersonic aircraft now flying. The first of six single-seat prototypes flew on 8 February 1967, and the AJ37 attack version entered RSAF service in June 1971. Powered by an RM8A (Swedish Pratt & Whitney JT8D redesigned for supersonic flight and added to an SFA afterburner) rated at 25,970 lb thrust, this version has an advanced Ericsson radar and extremely comprehensive digital fire control, navigation and head-up display system contained in fifty avionics packages weighing about 1,325 lb. Though primarily an attack aircraft, the AJ37 has secondary all-weather intercept capability using a variety of air-to-air missiles. In 1968 design began on the JA37 fighter *Viggen*, about 200 of which were followed on behind the 180 *Viggens* of four earlier types, for RSAF service in eight squadrons beginning in 1978. Powered by the new RM8B engine, of 28,085 lb thrust, the JA37 was as good as any interceptor in the world in the 1980s. In the nose is a completely new Ericsson X-band pulse-Doppler radar, the first in service in Europe. Partly as a result of a technical agreement with Hughes, Ericsson has been able to make this UAP 1023 radar one of the new class of software-controlled types. In the JA37 it is linked with completely new head-up and head-down displays, comprehensive digital computers and digital flight control, and a new armament system. Slung under the centreline is a 30 mm KCA cannon by the Swiss Oerlikon company, which Saab chose after carefully studying a wide range of guns, with high muzzle velocity, high rate of fire and a large projectile. Under the wings and fuselage are seven (optionally nine) pylons for 13,200 lb of ordnance, including air-to-air missiles of new types for both short- and long-range attack, and ECM pods. The JA37 air vehicle naturally is compatible with the nationwide STRIL 60 system.

**Saab JAS 39** *Gripen* First flown in December 1988, the *Gripen* (Griffin) continues the Swedish company's record of never putting a foot wrong and never being late. Like the *Viggen*, the *Gripen* is a canard delta, but it is much smaller, and the Volvo RM12 turbofan (derived from the General Electric F404 and rated at 18,100 lb in full afterburner) does not have a thrust-reverser. Up to six tons of various stores can be carried on nine hardpoints, and a Mauser BK 27 gun is fitted in the nose. Single- and two-seat versions have been in service since 1993, and what could well be a significant list of export customers began in 1998 with South Africa.

## UNITED KINGDOM

**Avro 504** One of the best of the earliest generation of military aircraft that were available at the start of First World War, the 504 served in many versions until 1936. The two most important early combat versions were the 504C of the RNAS and the 504K of the RFC. Both were often flown as single-seat fighters, and they were especially suitable for night operations in view of their docile handling, good view and high reliability. Typical armament included a Lewis machine-gun above the upper wing (sometimes manually aimed, but usually fixed, often on a Foster mount), small bombs on underwing racks, Le Prieur rockets for use against balloons and Zeppelins, and Ranken free-fall darts in boxes of 24.

**BAC Lightning** After very long development (1947–60) this high-performance all-weather interceptor became the only type of all-British supersonic aircraft in history to go into production, a total of 338 being built. Handicapped by faulty procurement at the start, which called for very limited range and endurance, the Lightning F. 1 was powered by two afterburning Rolls-Royce Avons, each rated at 14,430 lb, and could exceed Mach 2 for a brief period. Outstanding features were rate of climb, ceiling and manoeuvrability at all altitudes. In the fixed-intake centrebody was a Ferranti AI-23 radar, and standard armament comprised two 30 mm Aden cannon and two Firestreak pursuit-type IR-homing missiles. The improved F. 2

and 2A followed, and the next version, the greatly altered F.3, was subsequently updated to the standard of the final version, the F.6. Powered by 16,360 lb Avon engines, this had roughly double the internal fuel capacity, and could also carry overwing tanks and refuelling probe and thus fly useful missions (for example, scrambling to identify Soviet long-range aircraft probing NATO defences). Unfortunately the nose guns were foolishly omitted from these aircraft, but two 30 mm guns could be fitted in the forward section of the ventral bulge. Two Red Top collision-course missiles were also usually carried, in preference to the very limited Firestreak.

**Boulton Paul Defiant** Designed to an Air Ministry specification of 1935, this attractive monoplane fighter was radical in having no fixed guns; instead the second crew-member operated a power-driven turret containing four 0.303 in Brownings (which could, if necessary, be locked to fire ahead, with the guns synchronized). Two marks were produced, I with the 1,030 hp Merlin III and II with the 1,260 hp Merlin 20. Entering combat service in May 1940, the Defiant suffered very mixed fortunes, sometimes appearing to slaughter the best *Luftwaffe* aircraft and on other occasions being so mauled that only single machines limped back to tell what happened. Certainly the whole concept was nonsensical for a day fighter (though it briefly contained an element of surprise to any enemy pilots who had not read their magazines reporting on it before the war), but as a night fighter it had a great deal to commend it. Transferred to this role in August 1940, it was in the following year fitted with AI Mk V or Mk VI, the equipment fitting snugly into the fuselage and wing, and with the vital scope not in the turret but in the pilot's cockpit, where he could himself interpret it and then tell the gunner where to look. During the night Blitz of 1940–1 the Defiants, painted matt black and with flame-damped exhausts, shot down more enemy aircraft than any other type. They also had more kills per interception and more interceptions per 100 sorties. Curiously, nothing was done to develop either the NF Defiant itself nor the valuable attribute of upward-firing armament.

**Bristol F2B Fighter** Probably the best two-seat combat aircraft of the First World War, the 'Brisfit' was fast, robust and extremely efficient in many roles. It equipped many of the RFC's Home Defence fighter squadrons, but was not ideal for such duty. The water-cooled engine took as long as ten minutes to start and warm up, while at night its bulk impaired the pilot's view ahead for landing.

**Bristol Bulldog** Standard RAF fighter from 1929 until 1937, this popular biplane, powered by a 490 hp Jupiter radial, was equipped from the outset for night operations. However, the equipment was rudimentary, as related in the text. The same is true of other fighters prior to about 1941.

**Bristol Blenheim I** As the first stressed-skin monoplane multi-engined aircraft ever bought by the RAF, the Blenheim seemed outstandingly modern when it entered service as a light bomber in 1937, but by the summer of 1940 it had, like the Battle, taken a terrible beating whenever it had met the *Luftwaffe* in daylight. On the other hand it had all the attributes of a night fighter, save for the equipment and armament to do the job. From 1938 many bombers were modified into Mk IF fighters, fitted with a belly tray containing four 0.303 in Brownings firing ahead. From July 1939 some of these aircraft received the highly secret AI radar. AI Mk III was soon followed by AI.IV, both being easily accommodated in the Blenheim and causing 'no measurable change in flying qualities'; on the other hand, the maximum speed of about 260 mph was only just high enough to catch typical enemy bombers, and reliability of the AI was poor. These were the first radar-equipped night fighters in the world.

**Bristol Beaufighter** Planned as a private venture, the Beaufighter was a natural development of the Beaufort torpedo-bomber, but powered by the more powerful Hercules sleeve-valve engine initially rated at 1,590 hp. It went into production in early 1940 after rapid development, and thus happened to be available in precisely the form needed to become the first really formidable night fighter. Amply big enough to carry AI Mk IV radar, it had everything the Blenheim IF lacked: a tougher airframe, a speed of over 320 mph, and the devastating forward-firing armament of four 20 mm Hispano cannon and six 0.303 in Brownings. Its only shortcoming was a tendency to swing on take-off or landing, which much later was cured by fitting a long dorsal fin and a dihedralled tailplane. These modifications were not thought of during the 'Beau"s finest hour in 1940–1. First delivery (without AI) comprised single aircraft to 25 and 29 Squadrons in September 1940. By the end of October Fighter Command had forty aircraft, nearly all fitted with radar. As related in the text, these gradually managed to achieve mastery over both the night sky and the enemy. The Beaufighter I with AI.IV radar was without doubt the biggest single reason – next, perhaps, to the invasion of the Soviet Union – for the *Luftwaffe*'s abandonment of the night Blitz in May 1941. Subsequently most of the 5,926 Beaufighters were used in ground attack, coastal strike and torpedo or rocket firing in all theatres of war, but many were Mk VI night fighters with AI.VII or VIII in a thimble radome. They equipped the USAAF night- fighter squadrons in the Mediterranean theatre.

**British Aerospace Sea Harrier** Today supported by a conglomerate called BAE Systems, the Sea Harrier was from the outset designed as a carrier-based multi-role fighter. Powered by a Rolls-Royce Pegasus Mk 104 or 106 turbofan, of 21,750 lb thrust, with four vectoring nozzles enabling the single engine to provide lift, thrust or powerful braking, the Sea Harrier FRS.1 (FRS = fighter, reconnaissance, strike) first flew on 20 August 1978. Fitted with a GEC/Marconi Blue Fox radar, this initial version could carry up to 8,000 lb (normal maximum, 5,000 lb) of a wide range of external stores, including Sidewinder missiles, Sea Eagle anti-ship missiles and two 30 mm Aden gun pods. A further twenty-three, designated Mk 51, were supplied to the Indian Navy. The mid-life update of the Royal Navy aircraft exchanged the radar for the larger, more powerful and more versatile Blue Vixen, with a flat-plate antenna, and among other things enabled four AIM-120A Amraam missiles to be carried. Designated Sea Harrier FA.2 (fighter, attack), a total of eighteen new builds were authorized, plus thirty-three conversions from FRS.1. Amazingly, these aircraft are to be withdrawn in 2005–6, leaving the Royal Navy with no seagoing air-defence capability apart from that from ships' own armament.

**D.H. 1** Designed by Captain Geoffrey de Havilland for the Aircraft Manufacturing Company, the pusher D.H. 1 fighter was often flown at night by Home Defence units, but was not built in quantity. Its more important successor, the D.H. 2, seems to have been used almost entirely by day.

**D.H. 4** Possessed of outstandingly high performance, the D.H. 4 day bomber was a most successful aircraft made in factories all over Britain, and planned to be built in vast quantities in the Unites States (where almost 5,000 were actually completed by the Armistice). Many were used in various forms of night interception, Zeppelin patrol and other non-standard duties. Night-fighter versions often had twin fixed Vickers firing forward and twin Lewises aimed by the observer, while two aircraft were fitted with the awesome 37 mm (1½-pdr) cannon designed and built by Coventry Ordnance Works (COW) for use against Zeppelins. The big gun was mounted at an angle of about 75° between the cockpits, with the breech in the bottom of the rear cockpit, loaded with rounds by the observer, and the muzzle near the trailing edge of the aluminium-covered centre-section. Here, surely, was the original *Schräge Musik* installation! The pilot flew under the airship, aimed via a tubular optical sight inclined parallel with the gun through the centre section, and told the gunner by signs when to fire. Unfortunately no Zeppelin got in the way before the Armistice.

**D.H. Mosquito** If one had to name the greatest night fighter of all time there are many who would answer 'the Mosquito', even though night fighters represented only a minority of the 7,781 of these beautiful wooden aircraft. Developed by de Havilland Aircraft in 1940 in the teeth of official opposition – having been refused the slightest support in the first two years since the company's original proposal in 1938 – the D.H. 98 Mosquito was planned as a bomber so fast it would need no defensive armament. The officials tried to get de Havilland to drop the idea, suggesting instead that the company should make wings for the Manchester or Halifax heavies, but eventually reluctantly ordered three prototypes, the first of which flew on 25 November 1940. The only use anyone could find for such an aircraft was reconnaissance, but once the prototype was flying – and, after feathering one engine, overtaking full-throttle Hurricanes – the seeds were sown for one of the greatest war-winning aircraft of all time. The second mark was a night fighter, with the extended nacelles that were standard after early flight trials, a flat bullet-proof windscreen, side door to the cockpit, four 20 mm Hispanos in the belly, with belt feed, four 0.303 in Brownings in the nose and AI Mk IV or V. For months de Havilland had to fight to avoid fitting a turret to the fighter, various turrets with four 0.303 in, two or four 0.5 in and two or four 20 mm guns being considered before it was agreed the best scheme was all fixed guns firing forward. Powered by 1,460 hp Rolls-Royce Merlin 21 engines, the Mosquito II became operational with 23 and 157 Squadrons in May 1942, and scored a probable on the night of 28/29th of that month. Over the next three years Mosquito night fighters shot down some 600 *Luftwaffe* manned aircraft and 600 flying bombs over or near Britain, as well as a further 700+ over the continent, one squadron alone (RCAF No. 418, on night intruder missions without use of radar) scoring 172½, plus numerous ground targets. After the 466 Mk II fighters, slowed by their matt black paint and external radar aerials, came the NF.XII with the first British centimetric radar, AI Mk VIII. This, though a vast improvement over the Mk IV or V of the Mosquito II, resulted in a bulged 'thimble nose' without the four Brownings. On the other hand the improved radar killed the Turbinlite searchlight, which had been flown in a Mk II. With centimetric radar, usable at all altitudes, the Mosquito was a lethal weapon by night against every type of hostile aircraft. The first XII was delivered to 85 Squadron in February 1943. Next came the NF.XIII with AI Mk VIII and underwing tanks, the modification of many night fighters as special ECM and spoofing/jamming aircraft with 100

Group, and the NF.XIX with a Universal Nose, also called the 'bullnose', able to take either AI.VIII or the American SCR-720 or 729 (called in Britain AI.X, later AI.10) which served the USAAF as well as the RAF. About a hundred Mk IIs were rebuilt with the US radar as Mk XVII. The final radar-equipped fighters were all fitted with two-stage Merlin engines driving paddle-blade propellers, giving greater performance above 15,000 feet (reaching over 400 mph around 30,000 feet). The NF.30 was basically a Mk XIX with Merlin 72s; the post-war NF.36 had AI.10 and the highly rated Merlin 113/114; nearly all the final mark, NF.38 with AI.IX, were sold to Yugoslavia. There were many other fighter Mosquitos, including high-altitude marks (one with extended, pointed wings) and another with a 57 mm 6-pdr gun, but they were not explicitly night fighters.

**D.H. Vampire NF.10** While the post-war British procurement machine fumbled, Egypt asked de Havilland for a night-fighter conversion of the Vampire. Only because arms exports to that country were later banned did the Vampire NF. 10 reach the RAF, the virtual fitment of the front end of a Mosquito NF. 38 onto a Vampire having gone very smoothly indeed. Powered by a 3,350 lb Goblin turbojet, the NF. 10 reached 550 mph and was actually marginally faster than most single-seat versions. Pilot and navigator sat side-by-side, without ejection seats; getting out involved opening the flattish canopy roof and squeezing through. Equipment included AI.10 and four 20 mm guns.

**D.H. Sea Hornet** None of the beautiful RAF Hornets were night fighters, but the carrier-based versions for the Royal Navy included seventy-eight of a much-modified NF.21 version, with ASH nose thimble, four 20 mm guns and a cockpit behind the wing for the navigator/radar operator. Large flame-damping exhausts were even more necessary than they had been on late (XIX, 30, 36 and 38) Mosquitos; without them the pilot was blinded at high power at night, quite apart from betraying his position. The Sea Hornet NF. 21 was the standard Fleet Air Arm night fighter from 1949 to 1954.

**D.H. Venom** A natural successor to the Vampire, the Venom had the 5,000 lb Ghost turbojet and a thinner wing. The first night fighter version was the N.F.2, with AI Mk 10, four 20 mm guns and the same seats and canopy as the Vampire NF.10. After delivering sixty, which entered service with 23 Squadron in 1953, de Havilland built 129 NF.3s with Westinghouse APS-57 radar, powered ailerons, redesigned tail and clear-view upward-hinged canopy.

**D.H. Sea Venom** All the Royal Navy's carrier-based Sea Venoms were night fighters. The 256 delivered began with the F(AW).20, rather like a navalized Venom NF. 2, following with the Mk 21 (and Mk 53 for Australia) with more powerful Ghost, Westinghouse APQ-43 radar, powered ailerons, new tail and new canopy – and, in the final batch, Martin-Baker ejection seats – and the F(AW).22 with 5,300 lb Ghost 105s and Firestreak missiles.

**Fairey Fulmar** Only just capable of exceeding 200 knots, with its Merlin flat out, the Fulmar two-seat carrier-based fighter carried night-flying equipment but had no AI radar. Its occasional night interceptions (mostly in the Mediterranean before 1943) were accomplished chiefly by luck.

**Fairey Firefly** Much more formidable than the Fulmar, the two-seat Firefly was initially powered by the 1,990 hp Griffon XII and entered service in October 1943. The first specialized NF. version was the Mk II, produced in small numbers with four 20 mm cannon and AI.10 in two faired wing nacelles near the roots. Other features included a long rear fuselage, to preserve centre-of-gravity position, and flame-damped exhausts. During 1944 many Mk I aircraft were converted as night fighters by the addition of more compact American AN/APS-6 radar in a pod under the fuselage. After the Second World War the much improved Mk 4 entered production, with greater power and wing radiators. The FR. 4 again had two wing pods, but this time on the folding outer wings; ASH radar was on the right and fuel on the left. The last NF version was the NF.5, with power-folding wings, but most of the 352 Mk 5 Fireflies were anti-submarine machines.

**Gloster biplanes** As in the case of other pre-war RAF fighters, the Gladiator and Gauntlet were equipped for night flying, but had no aids to night interception.

**Gloster Javelin** Designed to Specification F.4/48, several of whose requirements were ignored or never met (such as takeoff 'within ten seconds, and if possible within five'), the Gloster G.A.5 prototypes (initially two were ordered, changed to four, then three and finally six) were lumpy delta-wing aircraft, with a tailplane on top of the enormous fin and a broad fuselage housing the Armstrong Siddeley Sapphire engines. From the first flight on 26 November 1951 there were many problems, some resulting in loss of the aircraft, but by May 1956 the Javelin FAW.1 equipped 46 Squadron, and subsequently a total of 302 Javelins were made by Gloster and 133 by Armstrong Whitworth. Hardly any two were alike, the engines later becoming the uprated 200-series and then acquiring primitive afterburners giving 12,300-lb thrust. Early marks had AI.17 radar, followed by the Westinghouse APQ-43 (called AI.22), and while early marks had four 30 mm Aden guns in the wings, later versions carried four Firestreak missiles, and added a gigantic non-retractable flight-refuelling probe.

**Gloster Meteor** The first jet fighter developed outside Germany, but overtaken to first flight by the American Bell P-59A Airacomet, the Meteor first flew on 5 March 1943. Early marks had no radar, but after the outbreak of war in Korea the British government decided that perhaps it ought to do something about a jet night fighter to replace the Mosquito. The result was that, Gloster being busy with the Javelin, Armstrong Whitworth was asked to cobble together a night fighter, using the Meteor T.7 trainer as a basis. What followed were 547 aircraft of marks NF.11 to NF.14, with pilot and navigator in tandem and the four 20 mm guns moved to outboard of the engines. The NF.11 was a crude aircraft, in keeping with what the Treasury thought the RAF should have, and fitted with the old wartime AI Mk X radar. The other three marks had AI.21 (the imported Westinghouse APS-57), and the final NF.14 was a much less inadequate aircraft, serving at Tengah until August 1961!

**Hawker biplanes** The comments on Gloster biplanes applied to all Hawker fighters from the Woodcock onwards, the Fleet Air Arm Nimrod (carrier-based derivative of the Fury) even having special cockpit lighting.

**Hawker Hunter** Two Hunter F.6 day fighters, WW594 and XF378, were fitted with a lengthened nose for AI.23 radar and provision for two Firestreak missiles. It was found that they were the fastest Hunters ever built.

**Hawker Hurricane** The primitive Hurricane I, with fabric-covered wing and fixed-pitch Watts wooden propeller, hardly ever flew at night. The Mk II introduced the 1,280 hp Merlin 20, which with a v-p propeller raised speed to above 340 mph, and with the IIA series 2 provision was made for increasing the armament from eight to twelve 0.303 in Brownings. The IIA srs 2 was much used as a night fighter during the night Blitz of 1940–1. Though having no radar, these machines, painted black and with large anti-glare shields in lieu of exhaust flame-dampers, achieve many successes. To a considerable degree this was due to the skill and bitter determination of the exceptional men who flew them. Not until late 1941 were Hurricane night fighters fitted with AI.IV radar, with complete success. Later Hurricanes were used in trials of Project Sunflower Seed, in which high-velocity rockets were fired from tubes arranged at an inclination of about 80°. Again Britain was on the verge of an effective upward-firing system, but these trials were concerned only with the defence of B-17 Fortress formations!

**Hawker/Armstrong Whitworth Sea Hawk** The straight-wing Sea Hawk naval fighter powered by a 5,000 lb Nene turbojet, was normally a day fighter, but the final production version was the Mk 101 night fighter for the German *Marineflieger*. This had the same tall vertical tail as the German Mk 100 day fighter but also carried AI radar in a neat pod under the right wing.

**Hawker Siddeley Sea Vixen** Originally designed by de Havilland to meet a mixture of Air Ministry and Admiralty specifications of 1946–9, this fine aircraft was built in prototype form as the D.H. 110 and, after several years of delay and indecision, finally put into service with Royal Navy 892 Squadron in July 1959 as the Sea Vixen F(AW).1. Powered by 11,250 lb Rolls-Royce Avons, the Mk 1 Vixen seated the radar observer behind and to the right of the pilot, at a lower level inside the central nacelle ahead of the engines and inlet ducts. The AI.18 radar was by the British company GEC, and normal armament comprised two or four Firestreak missiles and two 14-round flick-out packs of FFARs; considerable additional interception or attack loads could be carried under the wings. In 1964 the Mk 1 began to be replaced by the F(AW).2 with enlarged tail booms housing additional fuel and equipment, and with the fire-control system modified to be compatible with the Red Top collision-course missile. Many earlier aircraft were rebuilt as Mk 2 Vixens, total production being 148.

**Royal Aircraft Factory B.E. 2c** The most common of all British combat aircraft in the first two years of the First World War, the B.E. (Blériot Experimental) series were too inherently stable to be any good as dogfighters, but in night defence they were more useful. Most 2c versions had a 90 hp RAF 1a engine, reached about 72 mph flat out, and in anti-Zeppelin night patrol duty carried assorted armament which included Ranken darts, two 20 lb bombs with HE filling and two 16 lb incendiaries. Some aircraft were fitted with ten Le Prieur rockets. Later, in 1916, some Home Defence squadrons received the B.E.12b, with 200 hp Hispano engine and capable of about 115 mph. This still suffered from excessive stability and ill-conceived armament.

**Royal Aircraft Factory F.E. 2b** Though a vast improvement on the B.E. family, the F.E. (Fighter Experimental) 2b was terribly slow, and even with the most powerful of its three kinds of engine, the 160 hp Beardmore, it could only just reach 90 mph and was unable to climb higher than 11,000 feet. A pusher, the F.E. (or 'Fee') had the observer in the nose of the nacelle, with the pilot behind on a higher level. Armament often comprised one or two Lewis guns aimed by the observer ahead or rearwards over the upper wing. Some, especially single-seaters, had one or two Lewises fixed to fire ahead, while Home Defence F.E. 2b versions sometimes carried one or two 0.45 in Maxim heavy machine-guns. At least one had a searchlight mounted in the bow cockpit, with a Lewis fixed on each side, to fire at targets the searchlight illuminated. At least the F.E. was docile, the pilot had a fine view and it was suitable for night flying.

**Sopwith Pup** Officially called Sopwith Type 9901, this beautiful little fighting scout was built for the RNAS in 1916. Powered by an 80 hp Le Rhône rotary, the Pup reached 111 mph, and usually had a fixed Vickers gun with Sopwith-Kauper interrupter gear. It was also probably the first type to carry the Le Prieur rocket. Many were used by Home Defence squadrons, these examples having the non-standard 100 hp Monosoupape engine.

**Sopwith Camel** Most successful of all fighters in the First World War, the hump-backed Camel was usually powered by the 130 hp Clerget rotary, with which it reached 115–120 mph. Many of these tricky but brilliant aircraft were used by RFC Home Defence squadrons by night, painted black or dark olive green and often with plain red/blue roundels with no white ring. About three-quarters had the 110 hp Le Rhône engine, possibly because this gave less visible exhaust by night. For night use the armament was also often modified. One of the best features of the basic Camel was its powerful armament of two synchronized Vickers guns, but at night the flash from the muzzles, directly in front of the pilot's eyes, was blinding. Some Camel night fighters were therefore fitted instead with twin Lewis guns above the centre section of the upper wing, the cockpit usually being repositioned about eighteen inches further back to facilitate use of these weapons. A few N.F. aircraft kept their Vickers guns and added an anti-flash screen.

**Sopwith Dolphin** In early 1918 at least one example of this back-staggered fighter (300 hp Hispano) was a night fighter. Half-hoop crash pylons were added above the upper wings.

**Supermarine P.B.31E Night Hawk** The greatest of Pemberton-Billing's creations, this edifice is difficult to take seriously, but in fact it was designed in 1916 in deadly earnest to lie in wait at around 20,000 feet ready to pounce on a Zeppelin. Despite having a mere 200 hp from two Anzani radial engines, it had four wings of 60 feet span, two pilots and a minimum of four other crew to man the Davis 1½-pdr cannon, two Lewis machine-guns, and a searchlight with its own electric generating set.

## UNITED STATES

**Boeing (originally McDonnell Douglas) F-15 Eagle** Probably the best all-round interceptor in the world in 1976, the F-15 is generally smaller than the Phantom, but has greater wing area and, with two 23,800-lb Pratt & Whitney F100 afterburning turbofans, far greater power.

Hughes Aircraft supplied the APG-63 multi-mode radar, one of the first truly modern radars, which, in addition to being of the pulse-Doppler type, is software-controlled. Following technical failure of the new 25 mm gun being developed for it, the F-15A entered Tactical Air Command service with an M-61 of standard type in the right wing root. It can carry four AIM-7F Sparrow missiles neatly attached to the lower corner edges of the broad box-like fuselage, as well as four AIM-9L Sidewinders. Up to 12,000 lb of other stores can be carried under the wings, and the already considerable fuel capacity can be greatly augmented by adding Fast packs (Fuel And Sensor Tactical) on each side, each holding about 5,000 lb of fuel and making virtually no difference to performance at subsonic or supersonic speed. Originally the F-15 was a totally uncompromised air-superiority fighter, designed to defeat the Soviet MiG-25. Since 1972 the emphasis has been strongly on multi-role capability, with a wide range of added options in surface attack, defence suppression, ECM and other missions. Including 236 upgraded F-15E attack versions, 1,120 F-15s were made for the USAF, plus 245 for Saudi Arabia, Israel and Japan and (2003–08) 40 for South Korea.

**Boeing (originally McDonnell Douglas/Northrop) F/A-18 Hornet** No aircraft had a more convoluted birth than this growing family of primarily carrier-based multirole fighters. It all began with the Northrop Cobra of 1968, which was developed into the YF-17 to compete against the F-16 as the USAF lightweight fighter. Northrop developed the basic F-17 design into the Navy Air Combat Fighter, which eventually was, in effect, hijacked by McDonnell Douglas and developed into the F/A-18 Hornet, the unique designation meaning dual fighter and attack capability. Compared with the YF-17 it had a wider fuselage, more powerful 16,900 lb General Electric F404 afterburning turbofan engines, and Hughes APG-65 multimode radar matched to Sparrow missiles. The F/A-18A and two seat F/A-18B were followed by corresponding F/A-18C and D Night Attack versions, with upgraded avionics including APG-73 radar, pilot's night-vision system, AAR-50 thermal-imaging navigation, forward-looking infra-red and new instruments and displays. These four versions sustained production of 1,479 aircraft, including 431 for Saudi Arabia, Canada and Australia, despite the fact that these countries have no aircraft carriers! From the original Hornet was developed the F/A-18E and two-seat F/A-18F Super Hornet, with a significantly larger airframe, 22,000 lb F414 engines and greatly enhanced capability. The first USN and USMC squadrons went into action over Iraq in 2003, and total Navy/Marines procurement is expected to be between 548 and 785.

**Convair (General Dynamics) F-102 Delta Dagger** First supersonic all-weather interceptor in the world, the F-102 was designed by Convair as an air vehicle to fit round the MX-1179 (MG-10) fire-control system by Hughes Aircraft. This system included a powerful AI radar, an autopilot linked with the radar output and with the aircraft powered flight controls, and the Falcon guided missile. The aircraft itself was a 60° tailless delta with a thin wing, powered by an afterburning Pratt & Whitney J57-23 two-shaft turbojet rated at 17,200 lb. Despite the size of the aircraft, this gave a peak-level Mach number of about 1.25. As first issued to Air Defense Command in 1956, the F-102A carried batteries of FFARs in the missile-bay doors, but these were soon removed to leave standard armament as three radar-homing Falcons and three infra-red homing Falcons. The MG-10 fire control was later augmented by adding an infra-red seeker ahead of the sharply raked vee windscreen. By the end of 1957 a total of 875 had been delivered, plus sixty-three subsonic TF-102 trainers. During the late 1960s the 'Deuce' was withdrawn from USAF service and many were transferred to Greece and Turkey, a few others being converted as remotely piloted drones.

**Convair (General Dynamics) F-106 Delta** Dart Developed from the F-102, the F-106 was completely redesigned to accommodate the Hughes MA-1 system, linked with the SAGE air-defence environment for semi- or wholly automatic interceptions. The air vehicle was powered by an afterburning Pratt & Whitney J75-17 two-shaft turbojet rated at 24,500 lb, giving a peak Mach number of 2.3 (about 1,525 mph). Normal armament comprised two AIR-2A or -2B Genie nuclear rockets and four AIM-4E or -4G Falcon missiles. In 1973, after having been the standard Air Defense Command interceptor for fourteen years, these aircraft were fitted with a 20 mm M-61 gun and a new sight for close-in dogfighting. Production amounted to 277, plus sixty-three tandem-seat F-106B trainers. Front-line ANG service continued until 1988.

**Curtiss PN-1** In 1921 Curtiss delivered to the US Army Air Service a single example of the PN-1 (pursuit, night, type I). It was a conventional biplane powered by the six-cylinder version of the Liberty, rated at 230 hp.

**Curtiss P-36 and P-40** Curtiss built the principal fighter (pursuit) biplanes of the US Army in the 1920s, and also delivered many important fighters to the Navy and Marine Corps, most of them with rudimentary night equipment. The radial-engined (Cyclone or Twin Wasp) monoplane of 1935 went into production as the US Army P-36 and Hawk 75A for export. Five *Groupes de Chasse* of the French *Armée de l'Air* were fully equipped with the Curtiss – called H75C1 – by 10 May 1940, trained in day and night operation. Compared with earlier equipment they were judged marvellous fighters, initially having two fuselage guns and two in the wing (all 7.7 mm Brownings), and later having two additional wing guns. They gained 311 confirmed victories over the *Luftwaffe*, including more than thirty by night. Subsequent P-40 versions had the liquid-cooled Allison or Packard Merlin, being named Tomahawk or Kittyhawk and used chiefly as ground-attack machines. Some units, including Free French, Soviet and Commonwealth squadrons, occasionally used the later P-40 variants as night fighters.

**Douglas DB-7** This outstanding high-performance twin-engined aircraft was designed by Ed Heinemann as an attack bomber. Many were used by the *Armée de l'Air* before the collapse, and 147 destined for France were diverted to the RAF. Powered by 1,200 hp Twin Wasp engines, they were to have been named Ranger and converted into night fighters. During the autumn of 1940 the conversions went ahead at the giant depot at Burtonwood, near Warrington, the end-product being called not Ranger but Havoc. This was the first time Britain had let herself go with a night fighter, and the aircraft were formidable, being handicapped only by the unfamiliarity of RAF pilots with modern aircraft and their incompatibility with short grass fields. Most early conversions had four 0.303 in Brownings in the nose, or in a ventral fairing, as specified by the French; they also had long flame-damped exhaust pipes extending back below the wing. The internal bomb bay was retained, with capacity for up to 2,400 lb. By November 1940 different mark numbers began to appear. The original night fighter was designated Havoc I. This had an all-gun nose containing eight Brownings, either in one battery or as a group of four augmented by the original French quartet below. Some had six Brownings firing obliquely upward. As AI.IV or V became available it was fitted as standard. These aircraft entered service with 85 Squadron in December 1940 but did not at once become operational. Another group were modified as night intruders, being successively called Moonfighter, Havoc IV and finally Havoc I (Intruder). These were again matt black with flame-damped exhausts but retained the nav/bomb aimer in a transparent nose for long-range night intrusion (today called interdiction) using bombs as well as guns. All Havocs retained the rear gunner, with a manually aimed Vickers K, who had rudimentary flying controls for emergency use should the pilot be incapacitated. A third group were modified in September–December 1941 for hunter/killer operations with the Helmore Turbinlite. Large generators fed the nose searchlight, which was flanked by duplex transmitter aerials for AI Mk V. As described in the text, these aircraft did not normally engage combat but illuminated the target for others. Each carried special formation-keeping lights, invisible from the front, to help Hurricanes or other fighters to stay in visual contact. Yet another experimental version was the Havoc III, later called Havoc I (Pandora), equipped with the Long Aerial Mine, as described in the text. By 1941 the much more powerful DB-7A was arriving on RAF or ex-French contracts, with 1,600 hp Wright R-2600 engines and a broader vertical tail. The main fighter version of these fine machines was the Havoc II, with a completely new nose designed and built by Martin-Baker at Denham carrying twelve Brownings with large ammunition tanks. AI Mk IV or V was fitted, and the all-round efficiency of this aircraft was so great that one might have expected more from it, especially had it been boldly used over Europe as was the later Mosquito. Many Boston bombers were also modified as night-intruder aircraft with a belly gun pack. In the US Army these developments were watched with interest, and in September 1941 the first MIT AI set was fitted into an A-20 bomber which had been converted into a fighter by adding a large gun pack, with four 20 mm M-2 cannon, under the bomb bay. Redesignated XP-70, this was the forerunner of a large group of night fighters and intruders operated by the Army in the Pacific. By late 1942 most P-70s were being used as trainers for P-61 crews. The A-20C became the P-70A and the A-20G the P-70B, the latter usually having four 20 mm guns in the nose instead of the six 0.5 in of the P-70A.

**Douglas XA-26 Invader** A later Heinemann design, the efficient Invader was originally planned in three versions, one a night fighter with AI radar, four 20 mm guns in the nose and four 0.5 in guns in the turret (normally locked to fire ahead). This variant was not proceeded with.

**Douglas F3D Skyknight** Yet another Heinemann night fighter, the F3D was the world's first carrier-based jet night fighter, entering service in 1950. Though only having unswept surfaces and two 3,400 lb thrust Westinghouse J34 engines, the Skyknight was popular and effective, the biggest problem being the unserviceability of the AI radar with its hundreds of vacuum tubes (thermionic valves). Usual set was the APQ-35, which filled the entire nose ahead of the pilot and radar observer seated side by side. In the lower nose there were four 20 mm M-2 cannon, and various tanks or bombs of Heinemann's new streamlined shape could be carried under the folding wings. The twenty-eight F3D-1s were followed by 237 F3D-2s, which served throughout the Korean War, destroying more Communist aircraft than any other Navy or Marine Corps type. After Korea many served as trials aircraft, the F3D-1M being the first to launch the Sparrow 1 air-to-air missile. The 2M was operational with Sparrow, the -2Q was an ECM carrier, the -2T and -2T2 were trainers and the -2B had special armament. In 1962 those left in service were redesignated F-10A and B, EF-10B, MF-10B and TF-10B.

**Douglas F4D Skyray** Heinemann designed this bat-winged interceptor along lines suggested by the German Alexander Lippisch, with an ogival delta wing and no horizontal tail. Delivered to the US Navy in April 1956, after having suffered crippling delays through the failure of Westinghouse to produce the engine, the production F4D-1 was powered by a 16,000 lb Pratt & Whitney J57-8 with afterburner. Usual radar was the Westinghouse APQ-50 (Aero 13). Armament was four 20 mm guns, plus various external stores, and survivors of the 419 delivered were redesignated F-6A in 1962. In its day this transonic fighter set world records for speed and climb, and two years in succession it won the premier trophy for all US-based interceptor squadrons (on each occasion equipping the only Navy unit taking part).

**General Dynamics F-111** The US Navy was originally scheduled to replace almost all its fighter squadrons with the GD/Grumman F-111B, fitted with the very advanced Hughes AWG-9 system and armed primarily with the most powerful air-to-air missile ever developed, the Hughes AIM-54 Phoenix. When this version of the F-111 was abandoned the weapons were transferred to the Grumman F-14.

**General Dynamics F-16** Designed as a demonstrator of advanced fighter technology in the 1972 Lightweight Fighter (LWF) competition of the US Air Force, the F-16 was hastily promoted in 1974 as a candidate for the re-equipment of four European air forces (Belgium, Netherlands, Denmark and Norway). Renamed Air Combat Fighter (ACF), 650 were planned for eventual use by the USAF, and after a prolonged evaluation of basic aircraft performance and financial and industrial-offset deals, the F-16 was announced winner of the European purchase in June 1975. Powered by the same 23,800 lb Pratt & Whitney F100 afterburning turbofan as the F-15, the F-16 is an outstanding dogfighter, with extremely high excess power for violent sustained manoeuvres. Armament includes an M-61 gun and an unprecedented variety of other weapons. An advanced Westinghouse pulse-Doppler radar is fitted in the nose for long-range search and lock-on by day or night. Many later F-16s have the General Electric F110 engine.

**Grumman F4F Wildcat** Though used in many Second World War theatres in huge numbers, there was no explicit NF version of this excellent little carrier-based fighter. Several interceptions were, however, flown at night by both the US and Royal Navies.

**Grumman F6F Hellcat** Powered by the 2,000 hp Pratt & Whitney R-2800 Double Wasp, the tough and formidable Hellcat carrier-based fighter-bomber did as much as any single type to win the Pacific war in 1943–5. In early 1943 the first F6F-3E appeared, with AN/APS-4 radar scanner in the standard pod carried near the tip of the folding right wing. Other modifications included dim red cockpit lighting, deletion of the curved outer Plexiglas windscreen ahead of the flat bullet-proof panel and rearrangement of the instrument panel to accommodate the radar scope with viewing hood (for day use in cloudy weather). Production soon switched to the F6F-3N, with the definitive AI set, the APS-6. More than 200 were delivered to the US Navy Pacific squadrons, many aircraft being based on USS *Enterprise*. Performance was not greatly impaired by the large radar pod, and the Hellcat proved the best single-seat night fighter used by the Allies in the Second World War. After further changes, which often included substitution of four 20 mm cannon for the usual F6F armament of six 0.5 in guns, the F6F-5 became the most numerous of all versions and of these about 1,190 were delivered as F6F-5N night fighters. In 1944 about eighty were supplied to the Royal Navy as the Hellcat NF. II, but though 891 and 892 Squadrons converted they did not see action.

**Grumman F7F Tigercat** Powered by two 2,100 hp Double Wasp engines, this impressive fighter was probably the most advanced carrier-based design to go into production in the Second World War, with great armament, range and climb, and a speed of around 430 mph. The first version had four 20 mm cannon in the wing roots and four 0.5 in guns in the nose, and could carry 2,000 lb bombs or a torpedo. Ostensibly the single-seat F7F-1 was a day fighter and ground-attack aircraft. One was modified into the first of the 66 F7F-2N night fighters with nose guns replaced by APS-6 radar monitored by the observer in a second cockpit above the wing. All were delivered to combat units during the Second World War. In March 1945 Grumman began delivery of the 250 F7F-3 versions, which included many long-nosed -3N night fighters with SCR-720 radar and a second seat. The final production model was the faster and stronger -4N with APS-6 in the nose and cleared for carrier operations. Two of the earlier -2N sub-type were evaluated by the Royal Navy in 1945.

**Grumman F8F Bearcat** A beautiful little dogfighter, this was the smallest aircraft Grumman could design around a Double Wasp engine to fly the required Navy missions, and had the Second World War continued it would have been the most important Allied carrier-based fighter. The prototype flew on 21 August 1944 and deliveries of the original day version to US Navy squadrons began on 1 December of the same year. Huge orders were cancelled after VJ-Day, but the Navy did receive thirty-six F8F-1N and twelve F8F-2N night fighters, both armed with four 20 mm cannon and capable of about 430 mph. The APS-6 pod was carried on the right wing. Some of these aircraft fought in Korea, and a few even survived to serve the *Armée de l'Air* in Vietnam and, subsequently (1956), the Vietnamese Air Force.

**Grumman F-11 Tiger** Capable of supersonic speed in level flight on the 11,000 lb afterburning thrust of its Wright J65 (Sapphire) turbojet, the F-11 (originally F9F-9, then F11F-1) Tiger was small, neat and a delight to fly. The 201 production aircraft delivered in 1957–8 carried nose radar and four 20 mm guns. One Tiger achieved the distinction of damaging itself by colliding from behind with shells fired by its own guns about a minute earlier.

**Grumman F-14 Tomcat** In 1976 the F-14A was perhaps the most formidable and versatile combat aircraft in service with any Western country. Originally powered by two 20,900 lb Pratt & Whitney TF30-412A afterburning turbofans, the swing-wing Tomcat carries pilot and observer in tandem, Hughes AWG-9 radar fire-control, six AIM-54A Phoenix missiles for long-range interception, four AIM-7 Sparrows for medium-range work and AIM-9 Sidewinders and a 20 mm M-61 gun for close-range combat. By the end of 1975 about 180 had been delivered to the US Navy and Marine Corps, and production of eighty for Iran was in hand. Later versions suffered budgetary problems, but by 1994 a total of 557 F-14As had been delivered, plus thirty-seven F-14Ds with 27,000 lb General Electric F110-400 engines. Almost all surviving F-14As were retrofitted with this engine to become F-14Bs.

**Lockheed P-38 Lightning** This long-range twin-engined fighter, typically fitted with 1,425 hp Allison V-1710 turbocharged engines and with the tail carried on twin booms, seemed a natural as the basis for a night fighter, but the US Army Air Force did nothing in this direction until the summer of 1945, when the P-38M appeared. This was originally a field modification by the Pacific Air Forces, and seventy-five were converted. Painted black, the M had APS-6 radar in a pod hung under the nose, receiver aerials under the wings and an observer in an added rear cockpit seated higher than the pilot with a forward view. Lockheed also built a much larger fighter, the XP-58, with night fighting as its primary role, but only the prototype flew.

**Lockheed F-94 Starfire** Derived by direct conversion of the P-80 Shooting Star, this was the first non-German jet night fighter. The prototype was a converted Shooting Star, and development was rapid. The first of 110 F-94A Starfires was delivered to the US Air Force in June 1950. Powered by a 6,000 lb Allison J33-33 with primitive afterburner, the F-94A had pilot and observer in tandem, Hughes E-1 radar above four 0.5 in guns and tip tanks underslung. Minor improvements, the most obvious being fitment of larger tip tanks centred on the wings, resulted in the F-94B, of which 357 were delivered, many of them serving in Korea. The final version was the F-94C, with an 8,750 lb Pratt & Whitney J48-5 (Rolls-Royce Tay with afterburner), thinner wing, swept tailplane, Hughes E-5 fire-control in a symmetrical nose surrounded by a ring of twenty-four Mighty Mouse FFARs and with twenty-four more of these rockets in pods on the wings. The C entered service in late 1953, the last of 387 being delivered in 1954.

**Lockheed F-104 Starfighter** Powered by a 15,800 lb General Electric J79 afterburning turbojet, the early versions of this radical Mach 2 fighter were sparsely equipped and used as day interceptors, equipped with ASG-14 radar, an M-61 gun and Sidewinder missiles. Night operations would have been marginally possible from a first-class airfield. The very widely used F-104G was usually fully equipped for multiple roles by day or night, with Nasarr R21G radar, though none ever served as a night fighter and the Canadian CF-104 was optimized for air-to-ground use. The only F-104 really intended for night fighting was the F-104S, built by Aeritalia (Fiat), described under Italy.

**Lockheed Martin F-22A Raptor** As the first fighter (the F-117 being a bomber) designed in the full knowledge of stealth technology, it is hardly surprising that the F-22A was in 2003 calculated as having a unit cost in full production of US$184 million per aircraft, or more than the 22,000 Spitfires! Powered by two Pratt & Whitney F119 augmented turbofans of 35,000 lb thrust each, with rectangular nozzles vectoring up/down through ±20°, the F-22A has a Northrop Grumman APG-77 actively scanned array radar, and many other avionics items (many of which could not be used if stealth capability was to be preserved), and three internal bays for various missiles and free-fall weapons.

**Lockheed Martin F-35** Winner in October 2001 of a flyoff competition in a programme called the Joint Strike Fighter, the F-35 is now in production in three versions. All have related airframes and, at least in the first four batches, the same Pratt & Whitney F135 augmented turbofan engine of some 40,000 lb thrust. The baseline F-35A needs a long paved runway and is to replace the A-10 and F-16; procurement for the USAF is currently 1,763. The F-35B has an almost identical wing, but a redesigned fuselage in which some tankage is replaced by a Rolls-Royce LiftFan (a registered name) driven from the main engine, which itself has a vectoring nozzle, so that maximum-weight Stovl (short take-off, vertical landing) capability is achieved. Customers for 759 start with the US Marines, RAF and RN, to replace the F/A-18 and all Harrier versions. The F-35C has no lifting fan, but a much larger wing and tail, and provision for catapult launch and arrested landing. The US Navy requires 480 of this version. Several thousand more will be built for a rapidly growing list of customers, the first nine of which are production-sharing partners. From the fifth production batch customers will have the option of selecting the more powerful General Electric F136 engine, which is a bolt-on alternative.

**LTV F-8 Crusader** The Vought Crusader, powered by a Pratt & Whitney J57 afterburning turbojet of from 16,200 to 18,000-lb thrust, was for twenty years one of the best of all fighters and a truly outstanding design for carrier operation. One of its unusual features was a variable-incidence wing, which enabled the fuselage to land level, on a short landing gear and with good pilot view. Early versions were day fighters, the prototype flying in March 1955 and first delivery taking place in 1956. The F-8B had a small AI radar but was still basically a day fighter, and the F-8C had more power. But the F-8D was a night and all-weather fighter, with Magnavox APQ-94 (later APQ-125 in the F-8J rebuild) radar and a Vought push-button autopilot. The F-8E retained this capability and added underwing ordnance for attack missions. Of 1,261 Crusaders built, about 450 were remanufactured in 1967–70 to extend their life and capability. A further forty-two with an advanced high-lift system were supplied as F-8E(FN) to the *Aéronavale*, with some French equipment, including the Matra R 530 missile. All fighter versions retained four 20 mm guns and Sidewinders.

**McDonnell F2H Banshee** First flown on 11 January 1947, the Banshee, with two 3,150 lb Westinghouse J34 turbojets, was ideal for development as a night fighter, with low wing loading, excellent view and docile handling. In 1951 the US Navy received fourteen F2H-2N night-fighter versions, followed by the much heavier F2H-3 (F-2C) with extra tankage, Westinghouse APQ-41 radar and four 20 mm Mk 12 guns moved aft. The final batch, making total production 888, was the F-2D (F2H-4) with 3,600 lb J34 engines and Hughes radar. The F2H-2 was the only carrier-based jet night fighter in the Korean war, the Skyknight usually operating from shore bases. Two squadrons of F-2Cs served aboard HMCS *Bonaventure* as the only Canadian naval night fighters.

**McDonnell F3H Demon** The early years of this advanced fighter were sheer disaster, its Westinghouse J40 engine being abandoned in 1954 and the aircraft being redesigned with the Allison J71, rated at 14,250 lb thrust with afterburner. Eventually McDonnell built 519 of the new versions, the F3H-2 strike fighter being followed by 79 F3H-2M missile carriers with four

AIM-7C Sparrow missiles and 146 F3H-2N night fighters with limited all-weather capability and four AIM-9C Sidewinders. In 1962 these big transonic machines were redesignated F-3B, MF-3B and F-3C.

**McDonnell F-101 Voodoo** Designed as a penetration and long-range escort for Strategic Air Command, the Voodoo eventually went into production for Tactical Air Command as a fighter-bomber, entering service in 1957. With two Pratt & Whitney J57 engines it had the unprecedented thrust for a fighter of 30,000 lb, and in 1957 set a world speed record of 1,208 mph. For Air Defense Command McDonnell then built 480 F-101B night and all-weather fighters with pilot and observer in tandem, Hughes MG-13 radar, three Hughes Falcons and two nuclear-head Douglas Genies, but without the four 20 mm guns of earlier A and C versions. Together with some dual TF-101Bs, these aircraft equipped nine ADC squadrons in 1957–64 and were later used until 1990 by the Air National Guard and Canadian Armed Forces, the latter calling the type CF-101B.

**McDonnell Douglas F-4 Phantom** The greatest fighter of the modern era was designed as an attack fighter for the US Navy, was modified into a missile-armed all-weather fighter and finally flew as a prototype on 27 May 1958. Powered by two 16,150 lb General Electric J79-2 turbojets, it was very big, with over 2,000 US gallons of internal fuel, and had flap blowing, powerful Westinghouse APQ-72 radar and an armament of four Sparrow III missiles semi-submerged on the underside, plus two more (or four Sidewinders) on wing pylons. First delivery to Squadron VF-101 took place in December 1960. So outstanding was the all-round performance of the Phantom that, following comparative evaluations against all the best US Air Force aircraft, it was ordered in March 1962 for the Air Force. This remarkable achievement was followed by huge orders not only for the USAF but also for Britain (in modified form with R-R Spey turbofan engines and British equipment), Japan (built by a Japanese consortium led by Mitsubishi), Germany (with substantial German manufacturing content), Iran, Israel, Australia, Spain, Greece, Turkey, Korea and other countries. Except for reconnaissance versions all Phantoms have a very large and powerful Westinghouse radar, either of the AWG-10/11/12 pulse-Doppler type or the small APQ-120, as described in the text. To improve combat manoeuvrability and reduce stall/spin accidents, the E and F versions have large leading-edge slats on the wing, and the E also has an M-61 gun mounted on the lower centreline. All have extremely advanced avionics, the combat versions being equipped for blind navigation, collision-course interception and accurate attack on ground targets by various methods. Including 140 made by Mitsubishi, the last being completed in 1981, 5,197 F-4s were built.

**North American F-82 Twin Mustang** Derived from the outstanding P-51 Mustang day fighter-bomber, the Twin Mustang was planned as a long-range escort to accompany the B-29 Superfortress. Powered by handed (turning in opposite directions) Allison V-1710-143/145 engines, each rated at 2,300 hp with water injection, the basic aircraft comprised two modified and lengthened Mustang fuselages mounted on a common wing and joined by a rectangular centre section and rectangular tailplane. Two prototypes were modified in 1946 as night fighters with an AI pod under the centre wing. The radars used were the SCR-720 and APS-4, the occupant of the right cockpit being the radar observer. Later in 1946 orders were placed for 100

F-82Fs with APS-4 and fifty F-82Gs with SCR-720, normal armament comprising six 0.5 in guns in the centre section and with five wing stations for tanks or weapons. The Twin Mustang was a formidable aircraft with great range and speed, and it replaced the Black Widow in Air Defense Command and also served throughout the Korean War. The first enemy aircraft to be destroyed by Allied Forces in that conflict fell to an F-82F of the 68th F(AW) Squadron.

**North American F-86 Sabre** Unquestionably the leading fighter aircraft of 1948–55, the F-86 was originally a simple day fighter. Though fitted with a radar-ranging gunsight, it had no other interception aids. All-weather and night development began with a proposal by North American Aviation in March 1949, which struck immediate USAF interest. In October 1949 a contract was placed for two YF-86D and 122 F-86D night and all-weather interceptors, and eventually 2,504 of this version were built, outnumbering all other F-86 variants. The aircraft was totally redesigned and the commonality with the day fighter was estimated to be only twenty-five per cent. Powered by an afterburning version of the General Electric J47, either the -17 or -33 rated at 7,650 lb, the F-86D (the 'Dogship') carried an APG-37 radar in the nose, a lead-collision computer and retractable box of twenty-four FFAR rockets. The prototype flew on 22 December 1949, and at the peak of its career through the 1950s the F-86D equipped twenty wings of Air Defense Command and was supplied by the Mutual Defense Assistance Program to eleven Allied nations. In 1956–7 the USAF modernized 981 with new avionics to tie in with the SAGE system, and the wing was given a new leading edge and tips, resulting in the F-86L, which continued in service until 1960 with the Air National Guard. From the D was derived the simpler F-86K for NATO countries, still with the APG-37 radar but with traditional provision for chasing targets from behind and then shooting them down with four 20 mm cannon instead of the rockets. The prototype K flew on 15 July 1954; NAA built 120, and 221 were delivered by a European group led by Fiat, to the reborn *Luftwaffe*, the *Armée de l'Air*, the *Regia Aeronautica*, Norway, Netherlands and Turkey.

**Northrop P-61 Black Widow** Probably the first aircraft in the world designed from the start as a night fighter that saw service in quantity, the P-61 came out large, cumbersome and very complicated, and could have proved ineffectual. In fact it was saved by the sheer power of its two Pratt & Whitney R-2800 Double Wasp engines, which, depending on sub-type, urged it on with 4,000 to 5,600 hp. The basic aircraft had a broad laminar-flow wing, with high-lift flaps and spoilers, and a tail carried on twin booms. In the large and lumpy central nacelle were a crew of three, SCR-720 nose radar, four 20 mm cannon in the belly and four 0.5 in guns in an electrically driven top turret. The Army Air Corps ordered two prototypes on 11 January 1941 and a test batch of thirteen YP-61 in March, followed by 150 for the inventory in September 1941 (all before the US entered the war). A further 410 were ordered in February 1942. First flight took place on 21 May 1942 and squadron deliveries began in late 1943. Painted all glossy black (hence the name), the P-61A soon showed itself to be formidable in its early night missions in the Pacific, though severe buffet from the turret caused this to be omitted from the thirty-eighth aircraft (usually reducing the crew to two). First recipients were the 18th Fighter Group, scoring their first kill on 7 July 1944. By the end of 1944 the P-61 had been issued to nearly all Army Air Force N.F. groups in the Far East and Europe. The 450 B models could carry the heavy underwing load of four 300 US gal tanks or four 1,600 lb bombs, the final 250 having the turret restored. The final forty-one, delivered mostly after the end of Second World War, had 2,800 hp engines and speed raised from 365 to 430 mph.

**Northrop F-89 Scorpion** It was natural that Northrop should propose a jet successor to the Black Widow, and a contract for two prototypes was signed in December 1946. The first, flying in August 1948, revealed the F-89 to be considerably bigger than the corresponding Navy aircraft, the F3D. The two 5,200 lb Allison J35 engines were slung under the belly of the slim body, which was centrally mounted on the huge but thin wing. To fit inside the wing the main wheels were thin but of very large diameter, and the nose-down, tail-high appearance resulted in the name Scorpion. The first production version, the F-89A, was delivered in natural metal finish, unlike the black prototypes. Fitted with Hughes E-1 radar, the pilot and radar observer seated in tandem practised the traditional stern-chase attack before opening fire with the six 20 mm guns in the forward fuselage. The B and C had slightly more powerful engines but the main production version, the F-89D, had the dramatically different Hughes E-6 collision-course fire control system, with computer and autopilot linked for semi-automatic interception from any direction. At the exact moment the computer would launch the 104 FFAR rockets from large wing-tip pods, which would 'blanket an area of sky larger than a football field'. Total D production was 682, and this type was followed by 156 F-89Hs, to bring total production to 1,050. The H retained the same rather ancient engines but had the E-9 fire-control matched with six Falcon guided missiles carried around tip pods that still housed a total of forty-two FFARs. Two nuclear Genie rockets were later added, the associated Hughes fire-control being the MG-12. In 1956 about 300 F-89D were rebuilt to H standard but were redesignated F-89J. They served until 1959.

**Northrop F-5G Tiger II** Though the F-5 family were generally simple day aircraft, the F-5E did have a new Emerson X-band radar which conferred some all-weather interception capability. Air-to-air weapons were close-range only: two 20 mm M-39 cannon and Sidewinder missiles.

**Republic F-105 Thunderchief** Powered by a 26,500 lb Pratt & Whitney J75 afterburning turbojet, the mighty 'Thud' was one of the most effective of all US tactical aircraft in 1958–75, serving with especial distinction throughout the campaign in SE Asia. Though used primarily for surface attack, all versions carried a 20 mm M-61 gun with no fewer than 1,029 rounds, as well as AIM-9C Sidewinder missiles. With Nasarr monopulse radar and an advanced (FC-5 or ASG-19 Thunderstick) fire/flight control system, the F-105D was no mean fighter by day or night, though it seldom had the chance to prove it.

**Vought F4U Corsair** So long did this distinctive inverted gull-wing fighter serve, it is hard to believe the US Navy ordered prototypes on 30 June 1938. Powered by a 2,000 hp Pratt & Whitney Double Wasp (one of the first of three such engines to fly) the first flight came on 29 May 1940, and later that year the Corsair became the first US combat aircraft to exceed 400 mph. In 1943, when hundreds were in service from carriers and shore bases throughout the Pacific, twelve were modified as F4U-2 night fighters with a small AI radar under the right wing. In October 1943 one of these semi-experimental single-seaters achieved the first US Navy radar interception, destroying a Japanese reconnaissance aircraft with its six 0.5 in guns. By

1944 the F4U-4E was in use with the APS-4 radar and the F4U-4N with APS-6, competing keenly with Hellcat units. After the Second World War the production line was re-started with the F4U-5, fitted with a later Double Wasp engine, all-metal skinning and advanced equipment, and capable of a speed of about 462 mph. Of this final batch (which brought production to 12,571 by December 1952) 315 were -5N night fighters, many of which served in Korea. Most of the night-fighter Corsairs had four 20 mm instead of six 0.5 in guns.

**Vought F7U-3 Cutlass** Powered by two 4,600 lb Westinghouse J46-8A turbojets, this curious fighter had no tail, the two fins and rudders being mounted on the slightly swept wing. Fitted with radar ranging only, the -3 and -3M were armed with four 20 mm guns or two early Sparrow missiles, and served as day or night interceptors with the US Navy in 1954–8.

## USSR AND RUSSIA

**MiG-15** All 11,073 production MiG-15 fighters were for day use, unlike several prototypes. The latter began with the SP-1, first flown on 23 April 1949, which featured several items of new equipment including a *Toriy* (thorium) radar above the nose. On 22 August 1950 testing began of the SP-5, with twin-aerial *Izumrud* (emerald) radar. Radar was also fitted to several of the two-seat UTI versions.

**MiG-17** Derived from the -15, the -17 was a much refined aircraft with no flight limitations. A total of 7,999 MiG-17s were built in the USSR. No fewer than sixteen versions were equipped with radar, several of which went into production. The first was the gun-armed MiG-17P, which retained the original VK-1 engine rated at 5,952 lb thrust. The afterburning VK-1F engine of 7,452 lb thrust powered the MiG-17PF, as well as the MiG-17PFU which exchanged two of the three NR-23 guns for four K-5 underwing missiles, which flew along a coded beam from the RP-1U *Izumrud* radar.

**MiG-19** Distinguished by its beautiful wings swept at 57½° and slim, closely spaced RD-9B engines of 7,165 lb afterburning thrust each, the MiG-19 was in its day the supreme dogfighter, and Western observers have never understood why only 2,069 (of fifteen versions) were made in the USSR. Larger numbers were made of the J-6 versions in China, but all these were day fighters. In contrast, the MiG SM-7 prototypes led to the MiG-19P with only two NR-23 guns and *Izumrud* radar. Next came the SM-7/M, leading to a run of about 260 MiG-19PM interceptors armed with four of the primitive RS-2U (K-5M) beam-riding missiles, guided by RP-2U *Izumrud* radar. The MiG OKB went on to test various SM-12 prototypes with radar in a conical centrebody in the nose, which completely changed the aircraft's appearance.

**Experimental MiG interceptors** In the 1950s the MiG OKB built and tested a succession of large radar-equipped interceptors. Most were fitted with a single very powerful afterburning turbojet. The I-3, I-3P and I-3U were stillborn prototypes powered by the Klimov VK-3 of 18,607 lb thrust. They led to the refined I-7U, powered by a Lyul'ka AL-7F engine, with afterburning thrust of 20,304 lb. This was converted into the I-75, with the *Uragan* (hurricane) 5B radar fire control and two large Biesnovat K-8 missiles. It reached Mach 1.93, but lost to the Sukhoi Su-9, which, though a more primitive weapon system, was already in production. The Ye-150 introduced a completely new family of aircraft with an R-15-300 engine of 22,377 lb thrust similar to that chosen for the MiG-25. Because of its light weight the Ye-150 reached Mach 2.72, 1,796 mph. This led to a succession of Ye-152 prototypes, powered by the R-15B-300 of 22,509 lb thrust or (Ye-152A) two R-11F-300, as fitted to early MiG-21s, rated at 12,654 lb each. The latter aircraft made a public flyby in 1961 carrying mockup K-9 missiles. Real K-9s were fitted, in this case on the tips of the kinked-delta wing, to the Ye-152A. With a maximum speed of Mach 2.85 (1,883 mph) the 152A set records which were reported to the FAI as achieved by 'the Ye-166'. The latter was a fictitious designation, which was actually painted on the Ye-152P interceptor of 1962, displayed in a public park after its wingtip K-80 missiles and their launchers had been removed.

**MiG-21** The number of versions of this beautiful little supersonic delta fighter almost defy counting. Most were day fighters with limited capability, but in 1961 the prototype MiG-21PF revealed its new enlarged nose fitted with R1L radar in the conical centrebody in the inlet. Powered by a 13,120 lb R-11 afterburning turbojet, this night and all-weather fighter reached Mach 2 and was variously armed with one or two 30 mm guns and FFARs or K-13 missiles. Later versions had flap blowing to reduce landing speed, and provision for boost rockets to shorten take-off run. In 1965 the MiG-21PFM introduced many refinements, including the R2L radar, though even this was still only a short-range (up to eight miles) set without sufficient clutter-suppression for use below an altitude of 3,300 feet. The MiG-21PFMA was a multi-role variant able to carry both the GP-9 gun-pack, with the outstanding 23 mm twin-barrel gun, and two or four K-13s or the radar-homing or infra-red homing K-13A missiles. Since 1968 further sub-types entered service, identified by numerous refinements in equipment, including enhanced ECM and avionics. Production of the MiG-21 in the USSR totalled 10,158 from three factories, augmented by 194 from Czechoslovakia. India's HAL built 657, and China added a further 2,400+, leading to mass-production of 'Chinese copies' and derivatives.

**MiG-23** From 1964 the MiG OKB carefully studied prototypes with either (23-01) special lifting turbojets mounted in the centre of the fuselage or (23-11) variable-sweep 'swing wings' with high-lift slats and flaps. It decided the latter was the better answer, and the original 23-11/1 was soon followed by the 23-11S (S for series), which went into production as the MiG-23S (S this time meaning *Sapfir*, sapphire, radar). Dating from 1977 the first major production version was the MiG-23M, powered by the Khachaturov R-29-300 afterburning turbojet with a maximum rating of 27,560 lb. A GSh-23L gun and its magazine were mounted on a quickly replaceable tray. Later aircraft had the *Sapfir*-23D radar matched to the R-23R missile. Other missiles, carried on pylons under the fuselage and fixed inboard wing, including R-23T, R-3 (K-13) and pairs of the R-60. Various ground-attack weapons were another alternative, but the next production version, the MiG-23ML, was an uncompromised fighter for 8.5 g manoeuvres and an R-35 engine rated at 28,660 lb in full afterburner. Later versions included the MiG-23P upgraded interceptor and MiG-23MLD frontal (tactical) fighter. The main production plant was Moscow's *Znamya Truda* (flag of toil), which delivered 4,278, and a similar number were made in other plants, which also made the MiG-27 ground-attack versions.

**MiG-25** In 1959 Artyom Mikoyan returned from the Paris airshow deeply concerned at the development of the Mach-2 B-58 and Vigilante, followed by the Mach-3 XB-70 and Lockheed Oxcart programme (which led to the YF-12A and SR-71). He almost casually said to lead designer Selitskiy, 'How about an interceptor along the lines of the Vigilante, but without high-lift devices, to have two R-15B engines and do 3,000 km/h?' Coming from him this was authority to proceed, and the result was a family of Ye-155 projects, some suffixed R for reconnaissance and others P for interceptor. The first R, the Ye-155R-1, was flown on 6 March 1964. The Ye-155P-1 followed on 9 September 1964. Factory 21 at Gorkiy (today Nizhni-Novgorod) began producing the MiG-25R as early as December 1965 – by which time prototypes had been displayed in public, causing shock in the West, which named them 'Foxbat', and triggering an avalanche of new US fighters. Production MiG-25P interceptors followed from 1970, powered by the same R-15B-300 engines of 22,510 lb thrust and fitted with RP-25 *Smerch*-AI radar and twenty-eight distinct items of weapon-system or navigation electronics. Four wing pylons were provided for R-40D and R-40TD missiles with ranges up to thirty-eight miles. A total of nine interceptor versions was included in the total of 1,189 of all versions.

**MiG-29** Since the start of the jet age the underlying policy in Russian fighter design has been for design teams to work with the Central Aero and Hydrodynamics Institute to achieve an ideal shape. The third-generation shape led to the MiG-29 and Su-27. Both have broad high-mounted wings tapered on the leading edge, widely spaced twin engines fed by ducts under the wings, and a large swept tail with a fin outboard of each engine. The first MiG-29 began flight testing on 6 October 1977. It was predictably outstanding, powered by Klimov RD-33 turbofans of 18,300 lb afterburning thrust. The brilliant GSh-30/1 gun is standard, the radar in initial versions was the N019, or RP-29, and up to 6,614 lb of stores could be hung on seven pylons. The author was astonished to be briefed on this aircraft in 1988, when it was known in the West only as a shape. According to Western sources the MiG-29's radar has been 'copied by spies from the APG-65 of the F/A-18'. The on-the-record briefing showed that, far from being a copy, the Soviet radar was dramatically superior. But the pilot did not even need to use it, because he had an infra-red search/tracker, and a helmet-mounted sight. Without emitting any external signal he could guarantee a first-round strike when using the gun. When the *Luftwaffe* took over MiG-29s pilots were told to play it down, though one admitted surprise at being able to launch missiles at unprecedented off-boresight angles. After the collapse of the USSR, production funding disappeared, leaving some 600 delivered, with 800 incomplete at three factories. Subsequently production has been concentrated at one plant, *Sokol*, at Nizhni Novgorod (previously called Gorkiy), where a further 640 have been completed for export customers in thirty-one countries. Production is well under way in India, and either India's HAL or *Sokol* may produce the MiG-29K for the Indian Navy.

**MiG-31** Superficially looking like a MiG-25, this impressive all-weather interceptor has range and endurance capabilities matched to the vast size of the former USSR. Powered by two Aviadvigatel D-30F6 turbofans, each with a maximum afterburning thrust of 41,843 lb, this immense aircraft has a maximum weight of 101,852 lb and can reach Mach 2.82 (1,864 mph). It has a GSh-6/23M six-barrel gun, and can carry various fits of up to four R-33 missiles (range up to seventy-eight miles) and/or larger numbers of the R-33, R-40 or R-60 families. The radar is the powerful electronically scanned *Zaslon* SBI-16, and as described in the text these aircraft were uniquely designed to defend the world's longest frontier.

**Su-9 and -11** Pavel Sukhoi's widely used Su-7B has never been used as a night fighter, but the generally similar Su-9 and -11 (NATO: 'Fishpot') were designed for night and all-weather interception. Superficially resembling the smaller MiG-21, these aircraft had delta wings (unlike the -7B) and seldom carried internal guns. Early versions of the -9 had the K-5M missile on four underwing racks, while the more advanced Su-11 was packed with avionics and ECM and had a normal armament of two large R-8M missiles under the outer wings, one homing on radar from the large AI scanner in the nosecone in the aircraft inlet and the other being steered by infra-red. Together these two types were in 1976 calculated to equip one-quarter of Soviet interceptor forces.

**Su-15** A direct descendent of the Su-9/Su-11 family, this sleek aircraft differs in being twin-engined. The T-58D-1 first prototype was flown by Vladimir Ilyushin (son of the OKB leader) on 30 May 1962. In the principal production version, the Su-15TM, the engine was the R-13-300, as in some late MiG-21s, and the radar the *Taifun*-M. The normal weapon fit comprised two missiles of the R-98 family and two of the small R-60 for close combat, and most aircraft were retrofitted with two UPK-23-250 external gun packs.

**Su-27** Designed to the same aerodynamic shape as the MiG-29, but on a larger scale, this aircraft got off to a bad start when it was found that much redesign was necessary. Following prolonged research, a new configuration was flown as the T10-7 on 20 April 1981. In the opinion of several Western observers, including all who have flown the production aircraft, the resulting Su-27 set a new world standard in flight control and agility. Powered by two Al-31F engines of 27,557 lb thrust, the Su-27 has given rise to a prolific family that includes various tandem-seat versions, carrier-based fighters and a long-range bomber with tandem-wheel landing gears to permit take-off weights up to 97,774 lb. By 1997 deliveries included an estimated 600 single-seat and 140 two-seat fighters for the former USSR republics, plus about 350 exports to eighteen countries. The latter include China and India, which are both completing tooling for production of later versions under licence.

**Sukhoi LFS** Russia's next-generation fighter, the Light Frontal Aeroplane, will weigh about twenty tonnes. Two Lyul'ka AL-41F engines will give a thrust/weight ratio of 2!

**Tu-128** The only jet fighter produced by the mighty Tupolev bureau, the Tu-128 was derived in the late 1950s from the Tu-98 and Tu-105 (Tu-22). Such a large interceptor was needed to defend the vast USSR airspace against such aircraft as the B-70 and carrier-based Vigilante, and Hound Dog cruise missiles. First flown on 18 March 1961, the Tu-28-80 was developed into the production Tu-128A with two AL-7F engines, enormous RP-5M *Smerch*-M (whirlwind) radar, and underwing pylons for four large missiles, two R-4PM and two R-4TM.

**Yak-25** By 1951 the Council of Ministers had decided that night and all-weather interceptors needed to carry a radar operator, and furthermore that the first generation of two-seaters (such as the MiG I-320 and La-200) were inadequate. On 10 August 1951 a requirement was issued which resulted in the start of testing of the Yak-120 on 19 June 1952. Features included two 4,410-lb AM-5 engines in slim nacelles hung under an untapered wing swept back at 45° mounted in the mid position on a tubular fuselage with a large radar in the nose and tandem ejection seats. Two massive N-37L guns were mounted underneath, between the nosewheel and the main twin-wheel unit of the bicycle landing gear. From this was derived the Yak-25, produced from January 1954 at Factory 292 at Saratov. The Yak-25 soon gave way to the Yak-25M, with the new RP-6 *Sokol* (falcon) radar. The 5,732 lb RD-5A engines gave a maximum speed of 682 mph or Mach 0.93. Production of this version, called 'Flashlight' by NATO, was 406.

**Yak-28P** From the Yak-25 were developed an astonishing fifty-seven types of later twin-jet, for many roles. One sub-family were night/all-weather interceptors. Via a group of missile-armed Yak-27Ks, the Yak-28P evolved with Tumanskii R-11AF2-300 engines rated at 13,492 lb in afterburner. The radar was RP-11 *Oryol*-D (eagle), and main armament two or four missiles of the R-8M1 (infra-red) and R-8M2 (radar) types. These respectively weighed 659 and 644 lb, the radar version having a range of twenty-two miles. Level speed with two (not four) missiles at medium altitudes was Mach 1.73 (1,143 mph), a figure slightly increased by later production with a more pointed radome. Production, at Novosibirsk, totalled 443. The NATO name was 'Firebar'.

**Yak-41M** First flown as a conventional runway aircraft on 9 March 1987, the jet-lift Yak-41 family were fully equipped for night and all-weather operations, the radar being the Fazotron S-41M *Zhuk* (beetle). Armament would have included a mix of air-to-air missiles (various species of R-27, R-60, R-73 and R-77), and a GSh-301 gun was scabbed on under the fuselage. In the course of testing, many FAI records were set, and following the usual procedure the aircraft was reported with a fictitious designation, 'Yak-141'. After the collapse of the USSR the money ran out, but Yakovlev did receive payment for collaborating with Lockheed Martin in the design of the X-35B (predecessor of the F-35B), which closely followed the Yak-43 configuration.

# BIBLIOGRAPHY

*Air Defence of Britain 1914–1918*, Christopher Cole and E.F. Cheesman
*Air War at Night*, Robert Jackson
*Air Defence of Great Britain*, John R. Bushby
*Night Fighter*, Jimmy Rawnsley and Robert Wright
*Cover of Darkness*, Roderick Chisholm
*Night Intruder*, Jeremy Howard-Williams
*Instruments of Darkness*, Alfred Price
*Battle over the Reich*, Alfred Price
*Airborne Radar*, George W. Stimson (the best textbook)
*Avionics*, Bill Gunston
*Radar, a Wartime Miracle*, Colin Latham
*Confounding the Reich, Operational History of Radar*, Martin Bowman
*The Secret War*, Brian Johnson

There are many books dealing with specific types of aircraft, such as the Beaufighter, Mosquito and Ju 88 (and a few dozen on the F-4 Phantom II). To the author's very limited knowledge, there are also over 180 books in the English language dealing with aerial fighting, hardly any of which have much to say about fighting at night.

# ACKNOWLEDGEMENTS

The author would like to thank Philip Jarrett for having supplied most of the illustrations from his enormous archive. Thanks are also due to the Russian Aviation Research Trust, and to Paul Jackson, editor of *Jane's All the World's Aircraft*. Some of the line drawings were done by the author, but those that look professional were done by Arthur Bowbeer, former head artist at *Flight International*.

# INDEX

Figures in bold refer to illustrations